A   E

MARTIN ELLIOTT-WHITE

MIKE WALTON

PEARSON
Longman

Harlow, England • London • New York • Boston • San Francisco • Toronto
Sydney • Tokyo • Singapore • Hong Kong • Seoul • Taipei • New Delhi
Cape Town • Madrid • Mexico City • Amsterdam • Munich • Paris • Milan

Pearson Education Limited
Edinburgh Gate
Harlow
Essex CM20 2JE
England

and Associated Companies throughout the world

Visit us on the World Wide Web at:
www.pearsoned.co.uk

ISBN 978-0-582-36871-2

British Library Cataloguing-in-Publication Data

A catalogue record for this book is available from the British Library.

ARP Impression 98

Set by 35 in 9.5/12pt Garamond Light

Printed and bound in Great Britain by Clays Ltd, Bungay, Suffolk

Summary Contents

Contents

CHAPTER 1   Introducing Research — 1

CHAPTER 2   Methodology and Research Design — 13

CHAPTER 9 *Summarising Data – Descriptive Statistics and the Graphical Presentation of Data* 163

CHAPTER 10 *Bivariate and Multivariate Analysis* 187

List of Figures

List of Tables

Preface

Research is about enquiry, about discovery, about revealing something that was previously unknown or testing the validity of existing knowledge. Good research adds to our body of knowledge. Research is therefore a creative process, and the researcher is engaged in producing something original. The sense of achievement and satisfaction which that brings can be considerable. To produce good research, however, requires more than just being comfortable with the use of methods of data collection and analysis; it requires good research design.

We had three main objectives in writing this book:

1. To produce a practical guide to the use of research methods. We have aimed to strike a balance between quantitative and qualitative approaches. On the quantitative side we look at survey research design, at quantitative secondary data analysis, and at univariate and bivariate data analysis. As for qualitative approaches, we deal with observations and unstructured interviewing, for example, as well as the analysis of qualitative data through content and semiological analysis.

2. To enable students to become reflective practitioners by evaluating their own and other people's research. We believe that there is no such thing as a good or bad research method, rather there are appropriate and inappropriate research methods depending on the research objectives. We therefore focus on the evaluation of research methods using the key concepts of reliability, validity and representativeness.

3. To develop students' awareness of existing research in the field of leisure and tourism. Throughout the book examples will be given of how leisure and tourism researchers have used research methods in their own work. This will enable the reader to appreciate the potential of different approaches in leisure and tourism research, and will also generate ideas for their own research projects.

This book has its origins in our work with undergraduate and postgraduate students. All three authors have considerable experience of teaching research methods and supervising dissertations. The book is aimed primarily at undergraduate and HND-level students of leisure and tourism, although some of the material may well be of interest to the postgraduate student, in particular some of the more advanced statistical work covered in Chapters 10 and 11.

There are twelve chapters in the book. Chapter 1 introduces different styles of research, and distinguishes between quantitative and qualitative research. An understanding of the two main research traditions of positivism and phenomenology is seen as an important prerequisite to designing research and engaging in the research process. Chapter 2 emphasises the importance of theory and its link with methodology. Both deductive and inductive research designs are assessed and illustrated using selected research projects from the leisure and tourism literature. Chapter 3 examines the key stages in research design, which are evaluated in terms of reliability and validity. In addition, Chapter 3 alerts the reader to ethical issues in the research design. Chapter 4 deals with secondary data and highlights some of the major sources of leisure and tourism data from both the public and private sectors at the national and international level. It also looks at the potential for using secondary data in leisure and tourism research as well as briefly discussing the use of the Internet for this type of research. In Chapters 5 and 8 we turn to the use of qualitative data. Chapter 5 examines the growing importance of qualitative research in leisure and tourism. Ethnographic research is evaluated emphasising the many different ways qualitative data can be collected. Such techniques include unstructured interviewing at the individual level and the use of focus groups. Special mention is made of life histories and the use of personal diaries as data collection methods. Chapter 8 deals with the analysis of qualitative data using content and semiological analysis. Worked examples of both approaches are provided, and the potential for computer-assisted qualitative data analysis is briefly discussed. Chapters 6 and 7 focus on survey research design and sampling. The techniques associated with survey research are probably the most frequently used in leisure and tourism research. While these chapters cover the essential elements associated with the survey method, researchers are urged to consider the potential of alternative means of data collection before embarking on yet another survey. Survey research is methodologically demanding and the fundamental requirements are examined at some length. The issue of sampling strategy is not exclusive to survey work and Chapter 7 is just as relevant to the sections on content and semiological analysis. Without a grounding in sampling and survey methodology it would be difficult for students to evaluate published work, let alone define and justify their own research design. Chapters 9, 10 and 11 together form the quantitative data analysis section of the book. Chapter 9 is concerned with univariate data analysis and begins by looking at the use of tables and graphs to summarise data before moving on to a consideration of descriptive statistics and, in particular, measures of location, measures of dispersion and the notion of skewness. Chapters 10 and 11 deal with bivariate and multivariate analysis, and inferential statistics. Research questions are seldom simple and usually demand the analysis of two or more variables simultaneously. Chapter 10 is written specifically with survey data in mind and the principle means of analysing such data are outlined. However, there will be times when students utilise data from other sources or in time series and consequently the range of techniques is extended to cover multiple regression and time-series analysis. Chapter 11 explores the potential for inferential statistics within the data analysis process. This chapter needs to be read with Chapter 7 in mind. Sampling strategy is a key determinant of the form of data analysis and nowhere is this more apparent than in the use of inferential statistics. These three chapters also constitute a mini course in the use of the Statistical Package for the Social Sciences (SPSS). The reader is shown how to set up an SPSS data file and is then taken through the steps in using SPSS to undertake the various statistical tests as they are introduced. Chapter 12 covers the writing of a research report and, as well as looking at the structure of a research report, also deals with the correct use of textual referencing and the construction of an accurate list of references.

Most chapters end with activities to test your understanding of the chapter material. The nature of the activities will vary. As already stated, Chapters 9–11 deal with quantitative data analysis. We have, therefore, included as appendices a sample data file from research undertaken by one of the authors of this book along with a copy of the questionnaire used. This will enable the reader to set up their own data file and tackle the questions that go with these three chapters. Selected answers to the activities can be found at the end of the book.

At the end of each chapter you will also find a list of references. Given the scope of this book, it has not always been possible to deal with topics in depth. Where this has been the case, we have directed the reader towards additional sources that will develop your understanding of the material. These sources are fully referenced in the reference section at the end of each chapter.

This is the first edition of this book and, while we might be somewhat optimistic in thinking about a second edition, we would very much like to hear from users of the book – evaluation applies just as much here as it does to the research methods we discuss! Critical comments and suggestions will, we think, be gratefully received. As good academics, we have attempted to always acknowledge our sources. Any errors are, of course, the fault of one of the two other authors.

Mick Finn
Martin Elliott-White
Mike Walton

Acknowledgements

Sincere thanks go to Richard Voase, our colleague at the University of Lincolnshire and Humberside, whose semiotic analysis of a tourism advertisement appears in Chapter 8, and to Sian Harris of Hull University whose step-by-step guide to textual analysis also forms part of Chapter 8. We would also like to thank Stuart Rigby from the English Tourist Board who filled in some of the gaps in Chapter 4. Our thanks go to Margaret A. Hall for her permission to allow us to reproduce part of her poem 'Withernsea in Verse' in Chapter 5. Our thanks also go the following organisations for permission to reproduce material in the text – Lowe Lintas, Holiday Cottages Group, John Wiley & Sons Ltd and Elsevier Science Ltd. We are also grateful to the anonymous reviewers of our proposal and draft chapters for their positive and helpful comments throughout, and to Sue for her comments on work in progress. Finally, a big thank you to our editor at Pearson Education, Ian Little, for his patience, encouragement and good humour throughout.

SPSS for Windows

The material in this book relating to the use of SPSS for Windows is based on version 8.0. Since completing the book versions 9.0 and 10.0 have become available. These operate in virtually identical ways to the previous version but there are a few changes to the names of the menu items etc. To avoid any confusion the changes that are relevant to the material covered in this book are included here for readers who have access to versions 9.0 and 10.0.

1. The **Statistics** menu in version 8.0 is called the **Analyze** menu in versions 9.0 and 10.0.

2. The **Summarize** option in version 8.0 is divided into **Reports** and **Descriptive Statistics** in versions 9.0 and 10.0.

3. The **Frequencies** and **Explore** options are generated from the **Descriptive Statistics** drop-down menu.

4. The method for defining variables (see Figure 9.1) has changed in version 10.0. When you open an SPSS spreadsheet you will find two options in the bottom left-hand corner, **Data View** and **Variable View**. **Variable View** is used to define your variables. This involves the same headings and steps as set out in Figure 9.1, but they are already on the screen for you in **Variable View**. Once the variables have been defined, data entry is carried out by switching to **Data View.**

Chapter 1

Introducing Research

Learning Outcomes

At the end of this chapter you will be able to:

- conceptualise the research process
- distinguish between pure and applied research
- summarise the strengths and weaknesses of research styles
- distinguish between positivism and phenomenology
- describe the characteristics of quantitative and qualitative research
- combine qualitative and quantitative methods

Introduction

Students on HND and undergraduate courses in leisure and tourism are increasingly required to undertake their own research. This may take the form of a 'live' project with a leisure or tourism organisation, where students work in partnership with industry on an agreed project, or an extended research project where students work on their own under supervision. Such a task is usually the culmination of two year's work for an undergraduate and contributes to the student's final award. As preparation for their research project, students may have engaged in fieldwork that has provided an opportunity to develop and extend their research skills in data collection and analysis. In addition, a carefully structured programme of research methods is usually provided for students as an essential foundation for individual research work. We believe that research skills are best presented to the student as an integral part of the academic programme.

To help develop good practice in research methods, the academic literature of leisure and tourism has been extensively used as it contains numerous examples from which the student can learn. Although many of the research skills discussed in this book are generic to a more general social science approach, issues, problems and controversies raised in the leisure and tourism literature will be given special prominence. From a detailed analysis of research examples, methodological and design issues will be highlighted to help the student develop a more critical approach to published research and improve their own research practice.

Research skills are not developed in isolation. To research effectively the student needs to develop a range of personal skills to design, implement, analyse, interpret and write up research findings. These skills include communication, organisational, computer and presentation skills. Although transferable skills are not specifically addressed in this book, it is important that they are developed over the course of the academic programme before the student engages on independent research. This book has been written to help the student understand what the research process is about, what decisions have to be made in research design, and how data are collected, analysed and interpreted.

What is research?

Before engaging in the research process, it is useful at this point to think more about what research is. Authors of texts on research methods spend little time on conceptualising the idea of research, and they do not necessarily agree on what it comprises and what it aims to achieve. An examination of business and management texts (many of which are used in the teaching of leisure and tourism research methods courses) tend to emphasise the logic and objectivity of research. For example, Zikmund (1991: 6) defines business research as 'the systematic and objective process of gathering, recording and analysing data for aid in making business decisions'.

He suggests that the researcher must be objective i.e. the role of the researcher is one of detachment from the research process. Sekaran (1992: 4) defines research as 'a systematic and organised effort to investigate a specific problem that needs a solution'.

This is elaborated upon by saying that the processes of research inquiry have to be carried out diligently, critically, objectively and logically with the desired end to 'discover new facts that will help us to deal with the problem situation' (Sekaran 1992: 4).

What is contentious here is the claim to be 'objective' in the research process. Many researchers in leisure and tourism would argue that objective research is not possible and it is more important to be explicit about the values of the researcher. Much will depend on the philosophical orientation of the researcher and the kind of knowledge produced. Other researchers may take a critical stance to research and bring with them their own agenda. For example, some feminists use the concept of patriarchy to try to understand a world in which men dominate and oppress women for their own benefit. Yet even with this one term 'patriarchy' it can have different meanings depending on the value system of the researcher. Some researchers see it as simply male power over women, while others see it as a system which legitimates the dominant position of men.

In many of the definitions of research there is also an implicit assumption that research will discover something new or make an óriginal contribution to the development of knowledge. For the student, this makes research daunting and, to many, unattainable.

Preece (1994: 18) offers a much broader conceptualisation of research. He maintains that research is conducted within a system of knowledge and that research should be probing or testing that system with the aim of increasing knowledge:

> *The increase in knowledge may be something entirely new and original or, more commonly, it may consist of checking, testing, expanding and refining ideas which are themselves still provisional. In particular, research should continually question the nature of knowledge itself, what it is and how it is known.*

It is only at postgraduate level that a dissertation might be expected to make an original contribution to the growth of knowledge. At the undergraduate level, the student is more likely to be testing out ideas, perhaps even refining ideas. This should give the student more confidence to take on a more substantial piece of research under supervision.

This confidence to undertake research should supplement other qualities that help make a good researcher. Apart from intellectual skills like the ability to analyse, apply knowledge, synthesise and evaluate, a good researcher should be strongly motivated. Student motivation comes from a variety of sources. For many it is the opportunity to concentrate on a topic of their choice and not be pre-determined by curriculum demands. Important in that choice of topic is the notion of an interesting and manageable area of research. Motivation on its own is not enough; the researcher needs organisational skills to manage the research and communication skills to put thoughts down effectively in a written form. If the research takes place over an extended period of time, then perseverance and the will to succeed become key factors in the successful completion of the research.

From the student's point of view, tourism and leisure research should increase knowledge of the subject. Before an issue or problem is researched a review and synthesis of existing relevant literature is undertaken. Following this the student will engage the research process. It is at this point that decisions have to be made. Which style of research to use? How will the research design be structured? How will the data be collected? What type of data is appropriate? How will I analyse the data? These are not easy decisions to make. This book will provide guidance on how to answer these questions using examples drawn from tourism and leisure research.

Types of research

Many texts on research methods make the distinction between two different types of research: pure and applied research. For many researchers the distinction is not clear-cut. Pure research for Kumar (1996: 8) is 'concerned with the development, examination, verification and refinement of research methods, procedures, techniques and tools that form the body of research methodology'.

If this definition is accepted then students are unlikely to undertake research in its purest form. For other researchers pure research is about expanding the limits of knowledge by adding to theory. If the research were being conducted to improve understanding of an issue without an immediate application to leisure or tourism, then it would be referred to as pure research.

On the other hand, applied research is conducted to analyse and find a solution to a problem that has direct relevance to the recreation and travel industry, for example. A form of applied research is research undertaken for consultancy reasons, where the researcher acts as an advisor or consultant for the organisation. It is unlikely that students will be acting as consultants for the industry, although they may be undertaking a project in collaboration with an organisation as part of their assessment.

To illustrate the problem of distinguishing between pure and applied research, consider the two fictitious student research projects in Figure 1.1. The focus for both pieces of research is the high street travel agent. It is clear from the second example that applied research may also have relevance to the refinement of pure research. The situation is more difficult when research in a consultancy context is carried out. In many cases such research may not be published in the public domain. Yet for the student embarking on research, such consultancy may be inspirational and help develop ideas that can be explored on a smaller scale. A good example of published research is the work carried out by Ross (1997) on the views of black audiences on how black people are represented on the television. Her research was undertaken for BBC TV Equal Opportunities in 1995, and her views are highly critical of BBC TV programmes portraying black people. The research showed that black

Figure 1.1
Student research
proposals – two
examples.

Example 1 Pure Research
Over the last ten years there appears to have been a growth in middle class British holiday-makers travelling to long haul destinations. It appears that cultural motives are replacing recreational motives for this service class. The student is interested in the extent to which travel agents are reflecting a changing demand by a growing service class or whether they are structuring (determining) this demand to maintain their competitive advantage. There is a clear research question here, and the results of the research will be of academic interest and will help to further the debate on the emergence of the post-tourist or a new form of mass tourist (Urry 1990). Here is an example of pure research in which the consumption of holidays is analysed to shed light on the postmodern condition of contemporary society and the emergence of a new service class. The theoretical debate will have little relevance for the travel industry, although the results of the empirical research may help identify new tourist destinations and new market segments.

Example 2 Applied Research
Travel agents are likely to be interested in improving their customer care. In an environment of increasing competition between high street travel agents and with independent travel agents, such knowledge would be valuable. A student researching the encounter between the customer and the travel agency counter staff is likely to produce results that could be utilised by the manager of the travel agency. This would be an example of applied research, as the travel agent will benefit by identifying how and why a successful holiday booking is secured. The research would also have academic value in terms of improving our understanding of social interaction and communications between the customer and the quality management of the organisation.

audiences were dissatisfied with the stereotypical characterisations of black people, as most people responsible for the TV programmes are white and there was a strong belief among the participants in the research that they had no idea of how black people live. Here is a piece of research that has implications way beyond the portrayal of black people on TV. There are issues of racist assumptions of what black people are like, cultural authenticity, black role models and media power relations. Research into black cultural identities and representation (pure research) will benefit from the publication of the results from this national project as well as the BBC (applied research).

Research styles

There are essentially three main styles of research in the social sciences that researchers in leisure and tourism can draw upon. They include the:

- survey method
- experimental method
- ethnographic method

The survey requires a sample of respondents to reply to a number of questions that have been previously determined as relevant to the research. By using the same questions for the selected sample of respondents, individuals in the sample may be compared. Data may be collected through an interviewer-administered questionnaire or a self-completion questionnaire. Surveys have the chief advantage of collecting a lot of information in a relatively short period of time. The survey can be used deductively by testing hypotheses, or inductively by looking for patterns in the data. It is the most common type of research style used by researchers in leisure and tourism, and students undertaking their own research favour it.

Experimental research is less common in leisure and tourism research. Gunn (1994: 5) refers to airlines that run experiments on special price-destination packages, and advertisers who use experiments to assess the content and presentation of advertisements. The experiment involves testing variables under controlled circumstances to measure the effect of one variable on another. In the experimental research design, the independent variable is manipulated to find out its impact on the dependent variable. This is achieved by setting up an experimental group and a control group, and treating one group differently from the other. With a well-designed experiment, all other variables that could affect the outcome of the research are controlled for and eliminated, to make it easier to connect a cause (independent variable) with an effect (dependent variable). This type of pure experimental research is difficult to carry out in tourism and leisure research.

A variation on the pure experiment is the quasi-experiment or field experiment. Researching leisure and tourism involves actual events and subjects in real life who cannot be randomly allocated or systematically allocated to experimental and control groups. Although it might be possible to identify control and experimental groups in the field, the researcher has no control over allocation to the groups. Nevertheless the researcher in the field experiment will try to match as closely as possible the two groups to analyse the effect of the experimental treatment on the behaviour of the two groups.

Ethnographic research involves a method of investigation where a culture is observed in its natural setting. Ethnographers study the complexity of social interaction as expressed in daily life. Focus is on the meanings the participants themselves attribute to these interactions (Marshall and Rossman 1999: 2). The emphasis on naturalism is one of the main advantages of the method. It is also time-consuming, and this is one of its drawbacks.

Although tourism and leisure researchers rarely use the experimental style of research, it is important to appreciate its strengths. The main aim of the experiment is to demonstrate a causal effect by an independent variable on a dependent variable, by controlling all relevant sources of variance. The survey may also aim to carry out a causal analysis by collecting data on a range of respondents, and attempt to control for extraneous sources of variance by statistical techniques. This is an important difference between these two styles of research. Whereas the ethnographic style of research studies the totality of the culture in greater depth, to gain an understanding of the point of view of participants in the research.

Research traditions

The student researcher should be aware that there are better and worse ways of doing research but, what might come as a surprise, is that there is little agreement on what precisely is good research. This can be illustrated by examining two research traditions that begin with very different assumptions about how to research a leisure or tourism topic. Each research tradition has its own methodological approach. The nature of the issue or problem, and the philosophical stance of the researcher will govern the choice of approach. In simple terms, two different traditions can be identified (see Figure 1.2).

These two different perspectives should encourage the researcher to reflect on the aims and methods of the research to be undertaken. Should the research focus on cause and effect to develop and explain human behaviour, or should research concentrate on the way people socially construct reality and seek to understand and interpret human behaviour?

The researcher now enters the dark murky waters of ontology, the form and nature of reality and epistemology i.e. what counts as knowledge? Answering the above question means that the researcher has to consider what does or does not count as reality and knowledge. On one side of the debate is the *positivist* who argues that we should be able to explain

Figure 1.2
Two research
traditions.

Research tradition 1

This perspective argues that we as people react to our environment, and that the aim of the research should be to explain and predict behaviour. This can only be achieved if our behaviour is directly observable and measurable, utilising the methods of natural science. The idea is that the researcher detaches himself/herself from what is being researched and attempts to explain behaviour in order to predict future behaviour. The ultimate aim is to produce laws of human behaviour (known as 'covering' laws). Human behaviour is explained in terms of cause and effect. It is argued that the methods of the natural sciences produce the most reliable results.

Research tradition 2

Rather than being conditioned by the environment in which we live, some argue that we are able to make our own judgements that affect our behaviour. Our consciousness would then become the focus of the research process. This perspective concentrates on the meanings we give to the environment i.e. subjectivity. Our main interest here is on our understanding and interpretation of behaviour. It is an interpretative approach with a concern for the inner world of the subjects to understand why they act as they do.

phenomena in terms of what causes the behaviour we observe. Cause and effect underpins the positivist methodology, whereas the *phenomenologist* focuses on social processes and how individuals shape and give meaning to the social world. Understanding and interpreting these meanings underpins phenomenological methodology. These two different approaches to research or research traditions have their own set of rules and standards to ensure that valid and reliable knowledge is produced. This general agreement over methods and procedures is referred to as a 'paradigm'.

The student researcher needs to be aware that publications in leisure and tourism journals are examples of research that have been accepted by the research community. Published articles are commonly reviewed by three academics who themselves publish in that academic community. Not only does the research community play a major part in defining the methods and procedures, but they also act as gatekeepers to reduce the incidence of bad research. Academics who submit their work to a journal voluntarily accept a common language and set of criteria for evaluating their work. When published, an academic's research is then open to wider critical scrutiny. Whereas textbooks in leisure and tourism concentrate on the main findings of research, and synthesise them into a digestible form for students, journals usually give a greater emphasis to methodology. This allows other researchers to examine the findings in order to challenge or confirm them.

Henderson (1990) explores the different approaches to research in the field of leisure. She argues that the paradigm of positivism has dominated leisure research, but is now being challenged by an interpretive paradigm where the emphasis is on the richness of meaning. The notion of an interpretive paradigm corresponds to the approach known as phenomenology. Henderson argues that the two paradigms should not be mixed. She lists the characteristics of each one.

Positivist

- Assumes an external world determining behaviour
- Strives for explanation, prediction and control by dividing into parts and isolating them
- Mechanistic processes for explaining social behaviour
- Researcher is objective and value-free
- Truth has to be confirmed with empirical evidence

Phenomenologist

- Social reality is multiple, divergent and interrelated
- Analysis from the actor's own perspective
- Human behaviour is how people define their own world
- Reality is the meaning attributed to experience and is not the same for everyone

It is not just in the field of leisure research that a positivist paradigm has dominated. The same is true also of research in tourism. Walle (1997: 524) recognises this when discussing quantitative versus qualitative tourism research:

> *Much tourism scholarship, working within such a cross-disciplinary context, reflects this bias in favour of rigorous, quantitative, and scientific methods.*

This rigorous scientific method typifies the approach of the positivist. It is in the field of social anthropology that research using phenomenological or naturalistic approaches has challenged the supremacy of the positivist and the scientific method. For the researcher engaging in tourism or leisure research there is a key choice to be made. It is a choice between paradigms. It is a choice based on one's view of the world.

A researcher needs to ask himself/herself some fundamental questions:

1. Can behaviour be measured and the results regarded as facts?
2. Can the measurement be carried out objectively without the distortion of the value judgement of the researcher?
3. Should concern be only with what is observable?
4. Is human action a response to the external system?

If the answers to these questions are 'yes', then the researcher will be following a positivist approach to explaining human behaviour in tourism and leisure research.

But a different set of questions need also to be considered:

1. Is reality socially constructed by the interactions of individuals?
2. Should investigation focus on what is meaningful to individuals in the social world?
3. Should the conscious experience of human life be studied?
4. Is human action a response to interaction with others and the perceptions and experiences of others?

If the answers to these questions are 'yes', then the researcher has a different view of what constitutes knowledge and a different focus for research in leisure and tourism. For a fuller discussion of philosophical issues in social research, the reader is referred to Williams and May (1996) Chapter 6.

It is not the intention here to delve into the realms of philosophy, and it is certainly not the view of the authors to advocate a course in philosophy before the commencement of a course on research methods. What is important is that researchers should be aware of how different philosophical perspectives inform on the research process. All too often students begin with a preference for a style of research and how they propose to carry out the investigation, without some consideration of how one's philosophical stance can impact on how the research is carried out.

Table 1.1
Quantitative
and qualitative
approaches to
research

	Quantitative	*Qualitative*
Design characteristics	Pre-ordinate design	Emergent design
Data	Measurement using numbers	Meaning using words
Setting	Impersonal, controlled, manipulative	Natural, interactive, personal
Relationship with theory	Confirming theory	Developing theory
Process and procedure	Rational	Intuitive

Source: Based on Henderson 1990: 177

Quantitative or qualitative research?

At one level it is very easy to distinguish between quantitative and qualitative research. Punch (1998: 4) refers to quantitative research as empirical research where the data are in the form of numbers, and qualitative research where the data are not in the form of numbers. This can be extended to refer to approaches to research. Here, rather than emphasising differences between quantitative and qualitative approaches, it is better to view the characteristics of each as defined in relation to each other (Henderson 1990). These two different approaches are summarised in Table 1.1.

At this point it is worth examining the ideas of Walle in more detail and see how they compare to those of Henderson. Walle (1997: 527) argues that there are two distinct trends in research styles. One is the rigorous scientific method (which represents the quantitative approach) and the other is less rigorous and employs more flexible tools of investigation (the qualitative approach). Walle sees this as a fundamental debate between science and art. He uses the term 'etic' to represent the rigorous research of the scientific, quantitative method, and 'emic' to qualitative research that views cultures and people in their own terms. Tourism researchers, in his view, can be etic/scientists and deal with verifiable 'facts' using rigorous scientific methods, whereas emic/humanistic researchers can examine 'reality' in all its complexity because they are free to ask questions a quantitative researcher cannot easily pursue. It is about trade-offs. The quantitative researcher can reach large numbers of people by oversimplifying reality, whereas the qualitative researcher deals with the complexity of reality but with more limited numbers.

Combining methods

There does seem to be a strong association in the minds of students undertaking research that quantitative research is associated with the hypothetico-deductive method of theory testing, and qualitative data with seeking patterns in the data to inductively generate theory. Evidence from leisure and tourism research would tend to support these, as there is a relationship between the purpose of the research and the method of data collection. But this is not set in tablets of stone. Methods using quantitative data can be used to generate hypotheses and develop theory, and qualitative research can be used to test hypotheses. The student must not see one approach to research as superior to the other. Some research questions may demand qualitative data, others quantitative or a combination of the two.

What emerges from our previous discussion on these two approaches is that quantitative and qualitative methods have their strengths and weaknesses. It is highly likely that a researcher using quantitative methods will mix quantitative methods by using a questionnaire survey and published statistics. The same would be true of a qualitative researcher, mixing observation with in-depth interviewing. So why not mix the two approaches? An argument could be put forward to support combining the two approaches. The two approaches could be combined so as to maximise the strengths and minimise the weaknesses of each method. The assumption here is that quantitative and qualitative methods are complementary rather competing approaches. To explore further this idea of combining methods, the reader is referred to the work of Bryman (1988). Bryman explores a range of different ways of combining qualitative and quantitative methods. Examples from leisure and tourism research are explored in more detail in Chapter 3. Here we can mention just a few:

1. Either quantitative research helps facilitate qualitative research, or qualitative research helps facilitate quantitative research. For example, a piece of qualitative research could be used to establish the research questions to be addressed by quantitative research.

2. Quantitative research can explore large-scale macro structures whereas qualitative research can focus on small-scale micro aspects of the project. This might also allow a broader range of issues to be addressed by the research.

3. At different points in the study quantitative methods might be more appropriate than qualitative methods, or vice versa.

different

Whether the two approaches have equal weighting in the research as in 2 and 3 above, or where one approach is more dominant as in 1 above, combination of approaches can improve the validity of the research. Where qualitative and quantitative methods are used in combination in the same study, findings of one investigation can be checked against the findings from the other type. This is what is meant by 'triangulation'.

There is a further point to consider when combining methods. A distinction should be made between mixed methods and multiple methods (Philip 1998). Mixed methods are where two or more methods are used to address the research question at the same time in the research process. In an interview situation you may wish to collect quantitative data on the age, job, household size of the respondent, and qualitative data on their experiences on holiday. Multiple methods are used to examine different perspectives on the same research question. To examine the impact of festival in a holiday resort you may conduct a questionnaire survey to generate quantitative data, but also observe revellers during the festival to obtain qualitative data. Philip (1998: 273) concludes that:

> . . . *researchers should think beyond the myopic quantitative-qualitative divide when it comes to devising a suitable methodology for their research, and select methods – quantitative, qualitative or a combination of the two – that best satisfy the needs of specific research projects.*

Henderson (1990: 181) also argues that it is possible to combine qualitative and quantitative methods in both the positivist and phenomenological paradigms. She quotes the research of Glyptis (1985) in her study of attitudes towards women and sports participation, and Samdahl's (1988) study of the meaning of leisure. Henderson concludes, 'the value of multiple methods is that they lead to multiple realities' (page 181).

For a more in-depth analysis of the value of the multiple method, attention is drawn to Hartmann's (1988) research that focuses on young American and Canadian tourists during a European excursion. Hartmann is critical of single research methods and the over-emphasis on quantitative research in the fields of leisure and tourism. The thrust of his paper in the *Annals of Tourism Research* is that field methods in combination with a questionnaire (quantitative) survey are complementary and offer counterchecks (triangulation). Hartmann's research combined both quantitative and qualitative methods of data collection.

The young tourists from North America were interviewed three times using structured questionnaires generating quantitative data. Information was gained on the interviewee's travel behaviour in Europe, their patterns of behaviour in Munich and before staying in Munich. Although the broader (macro level) picture of the young North Americans' travel behaviour was discovered through the interviews, there was no information on their day-to-day activities (micro level) in the city of Munich. Hartmann employed participant and non-participant observation for this next stage in the research. The diversity of tourist activities emerged from the non-participant observation, and the meaning and purpose of the activities were discovered by the participant observation methods. We will examine these qualitative methods in more detail in Chapter 5.

Combining methods seems to be a strategy that will enhance the research findings. Multiple methods appear to be preferable to single research methodology. From the previous discussion, positivists and phenomenologists are not opposed to combining data collection methods within the same paradigm. Moreover, a pragmatic researcher can see the value of using two different methods to act as counterchecks to strengthen the validity of the results. But what if different methods produce inconsistent results? Dann, Nash and Pearce (1988: 20) warn against uncritically accepting that consistent results will always emerge from strategies that combine methods: 'One needs to know which is the method of choice in certain circumstances, which procedures will complement that method, and which are beyond the pale'.

Summary

This chapter has introduced the notion of the research process using examples taken from tourism and leisure studies. Undertaking research for the student should not be seen as series of stages that can be learned and applied to a chosen topic. Research is not that simple. There are important key decisions that have to be taken before the research process is set in motion. The research may have direct relevance to the leisure or tourism industries (applied research) or it may be exploring a theoretical argument seeking empirical evidence to test out assumptions in the model (pure research). Three styles of research were also introduced, survey, experimental and ethnographic. The aim here was to describe each research style briefly emphasising their strengths and weaknesses.

Equally important is the notion of different research traditions. Two contrasting traditions have been presented in this chapter, *positivism* and *phenomenology*. Research that seeks to explain human behaviour through cause and effect (positivism) differs from research that aims to understand and interpret human actions through the individual's own perspective (phenomenology). These two research traditions should be viewed as two different 'paradigms' as each makes different assumptions about the real world.

Two different approaches to data collection are quantitative and qualitative. Whereas a quantitative approach is usually structured, collects numerical data and tests theories, qualitative research explores meaning through words and text, is more flexible and develops theory. This should not be seen as a clear-cut distinction as it implies that a quantitative approach is invariably used by a positivist, and a qualitative approach by a phenomenologist. The methods of data collection do not exclusively belong to one research tradition or paradigm. Although a positivist may use a quantitative approach and collect data using the survey method, this does not mean that the phenomenologist does not employ

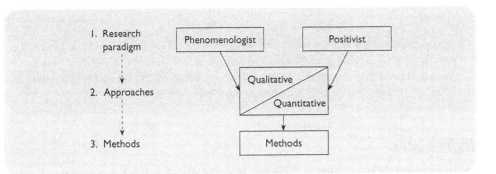

Figure 1.3
Model of choice in tourism and leisure research.

survey methods to collect data. The relationship between research tradition/paradigm, approaches and methods is summarised in Figure 1.3.

Rather than using just one method to collect data, students are encouraged to consider combining methods. This can be done to maximise the strengths and minimise the weaknesses of each combination of methods. Multiple methods do, however, need a rationale and should not just be combined to create more data.

Student Activities

Activity 1

There is much for the student to 'take in' and reflect upon in this opening chapter. It is suggested that the following questions form the basis of a discussion:

1. How does a small-scale research project differ from an extended essay?
2. How important is it for the researcher to approach a tourism or leisure topic with no pre-conceived ideas of the outcome of the research?
3. Is value-free, neutral research possible?
4. What are the main defining features of 'good' research?
5. Up until recently, research in leisure and tourism has been dominated by positivist research – why do you think this is so?
6. Is there a role for the field experiment in leisure and tourism research?
7. Why is the survey the most common research style used by students in undergraduate research projects?

In addition, students are strongly advised to undertake the following tasks.

Activity 2

Search the leisure and tourism journals and find examples of:

- an essentially quantitative approach to research
- an essentially qualitative approach to research
- research that combines the two approaches.

Be able to justify your choices.

▷

Activity 3

Choose a tourism or leisure topic and write a research proposal from the point of view of a positivist and a phenomenologist. Include a description of how you are going to approach the topic and which methods of data collection you will be using, and why? Be able to say why the two research proposals are different.

References

● Bryman, A. (1988) *Quantity and Quality in Social Research*, London: Routledge.
● Dann, G., Nash, D. and Pearce, P. (1988) 'Methodology in tourism research', *Annals of Tourism Research*, Vol. 15, pp. 1–28.
● Glyptis, S. (1985) 'Women as a target group: the views of the staff of Action Sport – West Midlands', *Leisure Studies*, Vol. 4, pp. 347–62.
● Gunn, C. A. (1994) 'A perspective on the purpose and nature of tourism research methods', in Brent Ritchie, J. R. and Goeldner, C. R. (eds) *Travel, Tourism, and Hospitality Research: A Handbook for Managers and Researchers*, New York: John Wiley and Sons, pp. 3–9.
● Hartmann, R. (1988) 'Combining field methods in tourism research', *Annals of Tourism Research*, Vol. 15 (1), pp. 88–105.
● Henderson, K. (1990) 'Reality comes through a prism: method choices in leisure research', *Society and Leisure*, Vol. 13 (1), pp. 169–88.
● Kumar, R. (1996) *Research Methodology: A Step-By-Step Guide for Beginners*, London: Sage Publications.
● Marshall, C. and Rossman, G. B. (1999) *Designing Qualitative Research*, Third Edition, London: Sage Publications.
● Philip, L. J. (1998) 'Combining quantitative and qualitative approaches to social research in human geography – an impossible mixture?', *Environment and Planning A*, Vol. 30, pp. 261–76.
● Preece, R. (1994) *Starting Research*, London: Pinter Publishers.
● Punch, K. F. (1998) *Introduction to Social Research: Quantitative and Qualitative Approaches*, London: Sage Publications.
● Ross, K. (1997) 'Viewing (p)leasure, viewer pain: black audiences and British television', *Leisure Studies*, Vol. 16, pp. 233–48.
● Samdahl, D. (1988) 'A symbolic interactionist model of leisure: theory and empirical support', *Leisure Sciences*, Vol. 10 (1), pp. 27–39.
● Sekaran, U. (1992) *Research Methods for Business: A Skill Building Approach*, Second Edition, New York: John Wiley and Sons.
● Urry, J. (1990) *The Tourist Gaze: Leisure and Travel in Contemporary Societies*, London: Sage Publications.
● Walle, A. H. (1997) 'Quantitative versus qualitative tourism research', *Annals of Tourism Research*, Vol. 21 (3), pp. 524–36.
● Williams, M. and May, T. (1996) *Introduction to the Philosophy of Social Research*, London: UCL.
● Zikmund, W. G. (1991) *Business Research Methods*, Third Edition, Orlando: The Dryden Press.

Chapter 2

Methodology and Research Design

Learning Outcomes

At the end of the chapter you will be able to:

- link theory to research methodology
- design a hypothetico-deductive approach to research
- derive hypotheses from conceptual models
- operationalise concepts into variables
- design an inductive approach to research
- analyse the strengths and weaknesses of deductive and inductive research

The importance of theory

For many students the role of theory in leisure and tourism research is the most problematic. For these students collecting and analysing data is manageable, but they argue that the data 'speaks for itself'. This is a false stance, as there will probably have been assumptions or pre-suppositions about the issue or topic that would have influenced the data interpretation. What is missing is a guiding framework for analysing and interpreting the data. Theory is used as a guiding framework to help explain and understand the research findings, and indicate the types of conditions under which the research has taken place. Theories are conceptual frameworks to help make sense of the research findings. For the student it is important to appreciate that theory and empirical evidence are linked through the research process.

There are many different types of theories. Grand theories attempt to explain macro changes in society, and may be fairly abstract. They include theories of deindustrialisation, globalisation, Fordism and post-Fordism. Each of these grand theories has relevance to the study of tourism. Deindustrialisation is the relative decline in industrial employment, counter-balanced by a growth in service industries like tourism. Globalisation is the increasing interconnectedness of different parts of the globe through economic, environmental, political and cultural change. As a result of deindustrialisation and the impact of globalisation, many former industrial cities have sought economic regeneration strategies through re-imaging and tourism. Fordism represents a system of economic organisation based on mass consumption, characterised by the growth of domestic holidays in Britain during the 1950s and mass international tourism to Spain and the near continent in the 1960s and 1970s. Post-Fordism refers to a period in the 1980s and 1990s when there has been an increased preference for non-mass forms of production and consumption. There have been changes in tourism trends with cultural and heritage tourism, for example, becoming more popular.

It is unlikely that a student researcher would attempt to seek evidence to verify or reject these theoretical constructs. Rather they are more likely to determine the context of the research or form the broad framework to influence the questions the researcher wants to answer. The examples given above refer to the importance of historical change, and how academics are coming to terms with changing global, national, regional and local environments.

Postmodernity has been mentioned earlier to distinguish between pure and applied research. Space does not permit a detailed exposition on postmodern culture. The student is referred to the seminal work of Urry (1990). Urry refers to postmodernity as a new 'cultural paradigm' (Urry 1990: 83). He quotes from Lash who defines postmodern as 'a regime of signification whose fundamental structuring trait is "de-differentiation" ' (Lash 1990: 11).

What this means is that with postmodernism there is a breakdown of the distinction between high and low culture, and a breakdown of the barriers between genres and styles. Distinction between fantasy and reality are blurred, and in the postmodern culture, style is more important than content. When these cultural changes of postmodernity are combined with economic change of post-Fordism, key areas of tourism research emerge.

From the grand theories, ideas that are more narrowly defined can be researched. Grand theories can give birth to middle-range theories that are less speculative and can be empirically researched. Urry (1995: 151) examines the significance of changing patterns of consumption with examples from tourism. Research questions include:

- Is mass tourism on the decline? (consumer choice/type of holiday)
- Are repeat visits to destinations declining? If yes, what are the implications for the resort? (volatility of consumer choice/destination development)
- Is there a match between the lifestyle of the tourist and the type of holiday? (market segmentation/destination choice)
- How are destinations responding to changes in fashion? (new products/shorter life-span)
- Are alternative types of tourism increasing in popularity? If yes, then why? (individualised consumption/type of holiday)
- Are leisure and shopping becoming difficult to distinguish between? (aestheticised consumption/functional consumption)

Emphasis has been given to the link between theory and research. Research needs theory as a framework for analysis and interpretation, and theory needs research to constantly review/modify/challenge theoretical details. We have argued earlier that the student researcher is not expected to add significantly to theory at undergraduate or higher national diploma levels, but you may uncover evidence that questions some aspect of the theoretical construct. To understand how theory is related to research evidence we need to explore two different methodological approaches, one of which tests theories, the other generates theory.

Deduction: concepts, variables and hypotheses

But what approach to theory should be taken? In simple terms, two different approaches can be identified which link theory, method and evidence. Theorising can take place before the research enquiry, and a *deductive* approach taken, or theorising can take place after the research, employing an *inductive* approach. The theory testing approach (deductive) is usually associated with quantitative data, whereas the theory construction approach (inductive) is more commonly associated with qualitative data. This is not to say that qualitative data cannot be used with a deductive approach and quantitative data with an inductive approach.

With the deductive approach, the researcher begins with the theory and collects empirical evidence to analyse with a view to either accepting or refuting the theory. Theorising comes before the research enquiry. Before the research process associated with the deductive approach is examined in more detail, some basic terms need defining. Silverman (1998: 103) defines the basic research terms in the following way:

1. *Theory*: a set of concepts used to define and/or explain some phenomenon
2. *Model*: an overall framework for examining reality
3. *Concept*: an idea deriving from a given model
4. *Variable*: unit of analysis that represents features that are changeable (Pizam 1994)

This can be illustrated by looking at a well-known model used in tourism research. The model referred to is the Tourist Area Life Cycle (TALC) devised by Butler (1980). Most students of tourism are familiar with the model as it charts the fortunes of a tourist destination over time. For further information on TALC readers should consult the work of Cooper (1992 and 1994). A model such as this is a framework for studying how destinations change over time. It identifies the basic elements of change as stages from exploration to stagnation followed by decline or rejuvenation. The model is based on the product life cycle used in sales marketing. Essentially it is a functional model where a destination's success, as measured by visitor numbers, is a function of time. There are key concepts associated with the TALC model. For example, in general terms, it models the interaction between demand for and supply of the tourism product. Patterns of demand generated by different types of visitors are incorporated as well as changing patterns of facilities supplied at the destination. Concepts such as 'tourism product', 'visitor type' and 'tourist facilities' are linked to explain how and why destinations appear to inevitably move towards a decline stage if intervention is not forthcoming. Here we are theorising about the interaction between different types of visitors and the nature of the destination.

The deductive approach begins with theorising and the identification of key concepts derived from the theory. These concepts have to be defined more specifically before hypotheses can be set up to test. Take one of the concepts referred to above, 'tourist type'. Here the student is confronted with a range of typologies of tourists. They include the classifications of Cohen (1972), Plog (1973) and Smith (1977).

Taking Cohen's typology as an example, as the destination grows the type of tourist changes from the drifter, explorer to the individual mass tourist and the organised mass tourist. The concept of 'tourist type' has been divided into four sub-groups. These sub-groups have to be defined in a way that allows them to be measured. Concepts that have been operationalised and defined become variables, so that they can be analysed. Let us take one of the sub-groups, 'organised mass tourist' and create variables to define it. Firstly, what are the key dimensions of the concept?

Organised mass tourist:

- Tourist who buys a package holiday
- Tourist who eats similar food on holiday as at home
- Tourist who has little contact with the local culture or people

These dimensions can now be turned into variables:

Variable 1: tourist who buys a package holiday through a travel agent or directly through the tour operator

Variable 2: tourist who eats the main evening meal at restaurants serving food that is normally eaten at home for over 80 per cent of evening meals

Variable 3: tourist whose daily routine involves mixing socially with people of the same nationality for 90 per cent of the time

Apart from the first variable, the other two variables are not completely satisfactory. It may be that each dimension of the concept requires more than one variable to measure it satisfactorily. Clearly, the inclusion of a proportion of the time for the activity/behaviour is also arbitrary.

In their excellent book on the *Geography of Tourism and Recreation*, Hall and Page (1999) examine different approaches to recreational motivation. The authors quote the research of Kabanoff (1982) who lists 11 factors representing leisure needs. Kabanoff's table quoted in Hall and Page (1999: 28) illustrates how concepts are operationalised for testing. Each concept has been split into two more specific dimensions. Just to take two examples. The concept 'autonomy' is measured in two ways: the ability to 'organise own projects and activities', and 'do things you find personally meaningful'. 'Esteem' is measured by gaining 'respect or admiration from others', and showing 'others what you are capable of'. Variables will be created for each of these dimensions by devising a scale for inclusion on a questionnaire. For example, an excursionist could be asked on a questionnaire:

Indicate how strongly you agree or disagree with these statements:

I organise my own projects and activities	SA A NA/D D SD
I do things that I find personally meaningful	SA A NA/D D SD

where: SA = strongly agree; A = agree; NA/D = neither agree or disagree; D = disagree; SD = strongly disagree.

The process of deduction can be seen in more detail in Figure 2.1.

The flowchart begins with the theory, and from that theory, a number of concepts are identified which form the basis of the research. The concepts identified are then set out as a series of hypotheses, which will be tested by collecting data. The hypothesis is the key element in this deductive approach. In simple terms a hypothesis is a proposition that is presented in a testable form. It is a statement that predicts the relationship between two or more variables (Pizam 1994). Before the hypotheses can be tested the concepts are operationalised into variables/indicators that can be measured in quantitative terms. Data are then collected, analysed and the hypotheses are either accepted or rejected. If accepted, then the theory is assumed to be corroborated by the empirical evidence as a valid explanation. These are known as 'covering law explanations' because the variables that are explained are covered by the assertions about those phenomena in the theory. These 'covering law explanations' where relationships have been established between variables not only explain past events but can also be used to predict future observations. The sequence of stages in the research process can be summarised as:

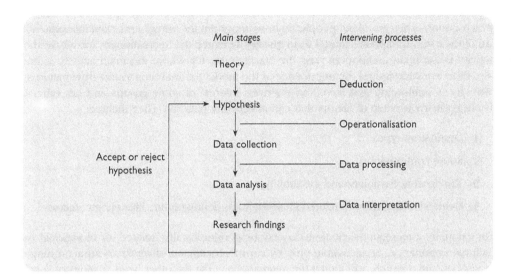

Figure 2.1
The structure of the hypothesis testing approach to research.

1. Theory

2. Identify concepts to be researched

3. Set up hypotheses

4. Operationalise concepts into indicators/variables

5. Collect empirical data

6. Test hypotheses with collected data

7. Covering law explanation

8. Predict future observations

Concepts and models from leisure and tourism

Leisure and tourism still lack a strong theoretical and conceptual base. This is not to say that there have been no theoretical developments, there have. But many of these 'models' were developed 20 years ago and borrowed from other disciplines and applied to leisure and tourism. In many respects there has been an uncritical acceptance of these 'models', as many of them have not been subject to rigorous empirical testing (Pearce 1995). Those models that have been incorporated into the tourism and leisure literature and which form the foundations of the academic discipline can, potentially, form the framework for research. There are many types of models that fall into this category:

1. Tourist travel models

2. Origin and destination models

3. Evolutionary or 'stage' models

4. Consumer behaviour models

It is not the intention here to give a comprehensive account of all models in leisure and tourism, but to use several examples to illustrate how the models can be used in a deductive approach to theory testing.

For 'tourist travel' models, Pearce (1995: 3) quotes the example of Campbell's 1967 model which distinguishes groups of people on how important the 'travel' and 'stay' components are of their trip. Campbell's model distinguishes between the 'recreationist', for whom the activity is the main component, and the 'vacationist', for whom the main activity is the trip. Pearce acknowledges the importance of the model for analysing tourist flow patterns, but why is sightseeing and travelling the main interest of some groups and not others? There is clearly a range of factors that can affect flow patterns. They include:

1. Destination types

2. Route configuration

3. Transport accessibility and availability

4. Demand characteristics related to household, demographic, lifestyle etc. factors

For example, a recreational destination may be geographically isolated, or of regional or national importance, or accessible only by car or of sufficient diversity to attract a range of visitors, and, as such, will attract the 'recreationist'. On the other hand, a series of small heritage centres, accessible by private and public transport on main roads set in an attractive rural countryside may attract the 'vacationist'. Using the deductive model, a hypothesis can be set up to test (see Table 2.1).

Shaw and Williams (1994) quote the research of MacNulty (1985) who explored the relationship between socio-economic groups and the motivation to travel. Based on values and lifestyles (VALS typology), MacNulty found a relationship between needs-driven individuals and their working class status. There was also a relationship between outer-

Table 2.1
An example of hypothesis testing

1. Theory	Campbell's model of recreational and vacational travel
2. Identify concepts to be researched	Patterns of travel and household type
3. Set up hypotheses	(a) For households with young children the main element of the trip is the activity at the destination (=recreationist) (b) For retired couples the main element of the trip is the journey (=vacationist)
4. Operationalise concepts into variables	(a) Households with dependent children and one destination for day trip (b) Households with two people 60 years or older and more than one destination for day trip
5. Collect empirical data	Design a simple sample survey at a recreational destination using a questionnaire
6. Test hypotheses with collected data	Analyse data with cross-tabulations and significance levels
7. Covering law explanation and predict future observations	If hypotheses accepted at the appropriate level of significance, then further support for theory where household type is a key variable affecting travel patterns

and inner-directed individuals and professional and managerial groups (middle class). In this case, a lifestyle and values hierarchy formed the basis of research that examined the relationship between social class and consumer types. This model has been used to examine the changes in consumer types and access to tourism from 1800 to the present day, and has been used to predict future changes (Shaw and Williams 1994: 48).

When it comes to models of consumer behaviour, there is a choice of models from which hypotheses can be developed. Cooper *et al.* (1998) list some of the more well-known models. For example, the models of Schmoll and Mathieson and Wall are discussed. The Schmoll (1977) model argues that there are four stages in the travel decision-making process: travel stimuli, personal and social determinants, external variables and the characteristics and features of the service destination. The Mathieson and Wall (1982) model refers to four inter-related factors that affect travel-buying behaviour. They are the tourist profile, travel awareness, destination characteristics and resources and trip features. Cooper *et al.* (1998) discuss the assumptions of the models. Essentially, they focus on the behaviour of a 'rational' individual, who actively seeks information with access to full information, which eventually narrows the choice down to a few alternatives. Using the deductive methodology the relative importance of these consumer behaviour models can be assessed. They are a rich source of hypotheses.

This process of deduction clearly links theory with research, arguing that if hypotheses about an aspect of tourism and leisure, which are derived from theory, hold true, then they must be substantiated by the data collected in the research process. As Table 2.1 shows, theories must be expressed in a form that can be tested, or, more precisely, is capable of being refuted. This is referred to as 'falsification'.

The hypothetico-deductive method or approach to research is linked to the philosophical tradition of positivism. This philosophical approach, as has been described earlier, is based on two main assumptions:

1. The social world exists externally and should be measured using objective methods.
2. Knowledge is only significant if based on observations of this external reality.

Induction and grounded theory

In his book *The Kingdom by the Sea*, Paul Theroux (1983) describes a typical English coast towards the end of his journey around the coastline of Britain. It is not an actual British seaside resort that he describes, but a collage of observations derived from his circular coastline adventure. Here are a few extracts:

> *There was always a Funfair and it was never fun, and the video machines were always busier than the pin-ball machines or the one-armed bandits . . . Beyond it was a caravan park called Golden Sands. The best hotel was the Grand, the poorest the Marine, and there was a guest house called Bellavista . . . The pier had been condemned. It was threatened with demolition. A society had been formed to save it, but it would be blown up just the same. There was now a car park where the Romans had landed . . . The museum was shut that day, the swimming pool was closed for repairs . . . The art-deco cinema was now a bingo hall . . .*

(Theroux 1983: 349–51)

It is not the detail of his description of a typical English seaside resort that is important here, but how he arrived at his view of a typical stretch of British coast. His journey around Britain gave him the opportunity to observe a large number of English resorts from Worthing to Blackpool. From these observations he identified features and characteristics that seemed to occur frequently in most resorts he visited. So his description of a 'typical' coastal resort is grounded in his own observations. His approach was inductive. The characteristics he describes could be generalised into a model to represent English seaside resorts in the declining stage of the Butler (1980) tourist area life cycle. The book does not begin with expectations about what to expect in England's seaside resorts. There are no hypotheses to test. It is from his detailed observations that a picture of English resorts emerges.

In contrast to the deductive approach, induction involves researching a particular aspect of tourism and leisure and attempting to derive theories from the data produced. The research precedes the theorising. This is a theory-building approach to research, or, more simply, theory is the outcome of induction. The rationale behind this approach is that explanations must be grounded in observations and experience to be of value. This approach to research developed out of a criticism of positivism arguing that positivism was an inappropriate method of researching social science phenomena in disciplines like leisure and tourism.

This can be illustrated by referring to the work of Kohn (1997) who studied tourism on a Scottish island. She adopts an inductive approach, and from her detailed text she attempts to develop theory, grounded in her descriptions.

Her theoretical grounding is based on Jafari's model (1987) where an individual tourist passes through a number of different phases:

Stage 1: everyday working life – referred to as the 'springboard'

Stage 2: non-ordinary phase – tourist is emancipated physically and psychologically – suspended in a period of non-ordinary flotation where there are new rules of a tourist culture, temporarily

Stage 3: return to ordinary life – after the holiday is over

Kohn argues that this model is useful for understanding the individual tourist experience, but needs adapting for a tourist who takes many holidays at the same destination. The island still retains its magical qualities to bring the visitor back each year – the non-ordinary, but the behaviour of the visitors changes from anonymity to one of friendship with the locals. Their behaviour is adapted to meet the requirements of the receiving community. The incomer may begin to feel that he or she belongs to that place – it has many of the characteristics of the 'ordinary' springboard. Here is an example where research in a specific cultural context has produced evidence that has modified existing theory. Jafari's model requires modification to fit the specific example studied by Kohn.

The inductive approach is associated with a philosophical tradition that argues that the world is socially constructed and is given meaning by people i.e. an interpretative approach or a method used by phenomenologists. The researcher should be clear about what should pass as knowledge about the world of leisure and tourism – philosophical assumptions must be considered.

Same topic: different approach?

In conducting leisure and tourism research, it is possible that the research topic can be tackled from two different approaches depending on the aims and objectives of the research. The same topic could be researched inductively or deductively. This can be illustrated with an example borrowed from an associated discipline and applied to a tourism or leisure context. Here the focus will be on stress management.

For the would-be researcher the symptoms of stress could have been observed among the staff in a local leisure centre or in a high street travel agent, and from further enquiries it is clear that stress had developed into a major problem affecting the productivity of the workforce. Management is becoming concerned and is thinking of making a decision to intervene. Here we have the beginnings of a research project.

The next phase would entail a literature search to explore the theoretical frameworks that will help in narrowing down the research idea into a series of research questions. A useful starting point would be to use the definition of Lazarus (1971) quoted in Powell and Enright (1990: 3). This definition focuses on the demands placed upon a person's physiological, social and psychological systems and the response of those systems. In addition, how a person reacts to stress depends on how the person perceives the events that make demands on the system.

The definition assumes that a person is not stressed when their physiological, social and psychological systems are in equilibrium. To understand a person's feeling of stress, a researcher would need to identify and evaluate what the demands are which have resulted in stress and evaluate the response of that person's systems and how he/she perceives the threatening events. Powell and Enright argue that the demands on an individual are the result of the interaction between external and internal factors. The external forces refer to the external environment in which the individual lives and this would include events that may make unnecessary demands on an individual and cause stress, or the lack of social support outside the workplace or the work environment itself. The internal factors refer to the individual traits, attitudes and temperament that may make him or her more or less susceptible to stress. This interaction may be perceived differently by individuals and the researcher could explore this dimension.

On the other hand, the focus could be on the coping strategies used by individuals to respond to stress. Powell and Enright refer to adaptive and maladaptive responses to stress and whether there are negative long-term effects if the coping strategy is unsuccessful.

To draw some of the threads together in this example of stress in organisations, a deductive approach to researching the effect of the work environment on employees' levels of stress would set up hypotheses. For example, a hypothesis may be:

The greater the workload the higher the level of stress.

Here the proposition or hypothesis is linking two concepts, 'the quantity of work' and 'the level of stress'. Each of these concepts is then operationalised into variables. The number of work-related tasks completed in one day could measure 'quantity of work'. Levels of stress could be operationalised by the number of days absent from work due to stress-related illness. In addition, the researcher may want to explore a possible causal relationship between the two variables. In this case 'the number of work-related tasks completed in one day' would be the independent variable, and 'number of days absent from work due to stress-related illness' would be the dependent variable. The independent variable is hypothesised to affect the outcome. The dependent variable is presumed to be the effect of the independent variable. Data would be collected using a simple questionnaire. The quantitative data would then be analysed and the hypothesis either accepted or rejected.

As an alternative to the deductive approach, the researcher would adopt an inductive approach and concentrate on how the employees perceive stress and how they deal with it. Data would be collected by a variety of methods including observation and interviewing. Essentially, but not exclusively, qualitative data would be collected, analysed and interpreted. Theory would help guide the main areas of concern from the observations and interviews. This approach would be useful if the aim of the research was to examine the meanings ascribed to stress from the point of view of the employee, and how employees cope with stress.

The problem of stress is not confined to the leisure and tourism industries, but is more widespread in the service sector. From the point of view of the student researcher it would be to useful to identify and analyse any factors, either singly or in combination, that are peculiar to leisure and tourism organisations and are likely to generate stress. How distinctive are organisations and enterprises in leisure and tourism?

Theory and method in tourism and leisure research

This section draws mainly on tourism research although most of the points also apply to the field of leisure studies as well. Here the work of Dann, Nash and Pearce (1988) is of paramount importance. They begin by separating out the key notions of methodology (set of ground rules necessary to the logic of the social inquiry), techniques of investigation (interviewing, observation) and theory ('. . . body of logically interconnected propositions which provides an interpretative basis for understanding phenomena'). Dann *et al.* (1988: 4) argue that in tourism research there has been 'an unfortunate tendency to gloss over questions of theory and method, and a concomitant failure to acknowledge their interrelationship'. They argue that tourism research falls into one of three categories. Either the research is theoretical without empirical evidence, or empiricism without theory or descriptive studies that are impressionistic and anecdotal. This is a potentially damaging criticism of tourism research up to 1988 when the article was printed in the *Annals of Tourism Research*. There appears to have been little progress in reversing this critique, until *Tourism Management* (Vol. 20 (1)) published in February 1999.

Students embarking on research should follow the advice offered by Dann *et al.* (1988). In particular, the section on methodological sophistication is well worth studying. They examine the problems of conceptualisation, operationalisation, measurement, data collection and data analysis in the research process (pages 14–19). The recent volume of *Tourism Management* (1999) is about innovations in tourism and management research and conceptualisation, and is very welcome. The student activities at the end of this chapter are based on one of the articles in the journal that examines the relationship between theory and practice.

Summary

Rather than initially engage in a questionnaire survey or make several appointments to conduct interviews, the student is strongly advised to seek out a guiding framework at the conceptual or theoretical level. This will help make sense of the data whether it is through the testing of hypotheses derived from theory or the search for patterns grounded in theory. Research questions can emerge when the grander, more abstract theories are broken down into more manageable concepts. If the deductive approach is employed in the research, then issues of conceptualisation, operationalising concepts and measuring variables have to be addressed. This quantitative approach has dominated research in tourism and leisure until recently when it has been challenged by a more inductive, qualitative approach.

The student is encouraged to examine their chosen research topic from both a deductive and inductive methodology. Ultimately the decision to research the topic will depend on what, in the view of the student, constitutes leisure or tourism knowledge.

Student Activities

The focus for this section is on the article called 'Ecotourism: towards congruence between theory and practice' written by Ross and Wall (1999) in the journal *Tourism Management*. Ross and Wall highlight the gap between ecotourism theory and practice by examining how ecotourism is defined and what is achieved through ecotourism. In addition, ecosystem interrelationships and effective management are examined.

Activity 1

Identify the main elements that comprise a definition of ecotourism. Make sure that you understand the relationship between ecotourism and sustainability as found in Figure 1 on page 124 in the article.

Activity 2

The article contains good examples of how concepts that make up ecotourism are broken down into indicators. See Tables 1 (page 125), 2 (page 127) and 3 (page 128) for examples of indicators that are operationalising objectives of ecotourism, relationships between people and protected areas, and benefits to local people, respectively. Choose one of these tables and assess the problems of measuring the specified indicators.

Activity 3

Choose your own case study of ecotourism (see Fennell 1999) and assess the success of the development using Table 5 (page 130) as your guide. Did your case study measure success through indicators derived from theory?

> *Indicators informed by theory, and validated by stakeholders, can facilitate assessment of the status of ecotourism at a given site, and aid in identifying existing strengths, weaknesses and opportunities to be explored.*
>
> (Ross and Wall 1999: 131)

References

- Butler, R. (1980) 'The concept of a tourist area cycle of evolution: implications for management of resources', *Canadian Geographer*, Vol. xxiv (1), pp. 5–12.
- Campbell, C. K. (1967) 'An approach to research in recreational geography', in *B.C. Occasional Papers No. 7*, Department of Geography, University of British Columbia: Vancouver.
- Cohen, E. (1972) 'Towards a sociology of international tourism', *Social Research*, Vol. 39, pp. 164–82.
- Cooper, C. (1992) 'The life cycle concept and strategic planning for coastal resorts', *Built Environment*, Vol. 18 (1), pp. 57–66.
- —— (1994) 'The destination life cycle: an update', in Seaton, A. V. (ed.) *Tourism: the State of the Art*, New York: John Wiley and Sons, pp. 340–6.
- Cooper, C., Fletcher, J., Gilbert, D. and Wanhill, S. edited by Shepherd, R. (1998), Second Edition, *Tourism: Principles and Practice*, Harlow: Addison Wesley Longman.

● Dann, G., Nash, D. and Pearce, P. (1988) 'Methodology in tourism research', *Annals of Tourism Research*, Vol. 15, pp. 1–28.
● Fennell, D. A. (1999) *Ecotourism: An Introduction*, London: Routledge.
● Hall, C. M. and Page, S. J. (1999) *The Geography of Tourism and Recreation: Environment, Place and Space*, London: Routledge.
● Jafari, J. (1987) 'Tourism models: the sociocultural aspects, *Tourism Management*, pp. 151–9.
● Kabanoff, B. (1982) 'Occupational and sex differences in leisure needs and leisure satisfaction', *Journal of Occupational Behaviour*, Vol. 3, pp. 233–45.
● Kohn, T. (1997) 'Island involvement and the evolving tourist', in Abram, S., Waldren, J. and Macleod, D. V. L. (eds) *Tourists and Tourism: Identifying with People and Places*, Oxford: Berg, pp. 13–28.
● Lash, S. (1990) *Sociology of Postmodernism*, London: Routledge.
● Lazarus, R. S. (1971) 'The concept of stress and disease', in *Society, Stress and Disease Vol. 1*, London: Oxford University Press, pp. 1–21.
● MacNulty, W. K. (1985) 'U.K. social change through a wide-angle lens', *Futures*, August, pp. 18–25.
● Mathieson, A. and Wall, G. (1982) *Tourism: Economic, Physical and Social Impacts*, London: Longman.
● Pearce, D. (1995) *Tourism Today: A Geographical Analysis*, Harlow: Addison Wesley Longman.
● Pizam, A. (1994) 'Planning a tourism research investigation', in Brent Ritchie, J. R. and Goeldner, C. R. (eds) *Travel, Tourism and Hospitality Research: A Handbook for Managers and Researchers*, New York: John Wiley and Sons.
● Plog, S. (1973) 'Why destination areas rise and fall in popularity', *Cornell HRA Quarterly*, November, pp. 13–16.
● Powell, T. J. and Enright, S. J. (1990) *Anxiety and Stress Management*, London: Routledge.
● Ross, S. and Wall, G. (1999) 'Ecotourism: towards congruence between theory and practice', *Tourism Management*, Vol. 20 (1), pp. 123–32.
● Schmoll, G. A. (1977) *Tourism Promotion*, London: Tourism International Press.
● Shaw, G. and Williams, A. M. (1994) *Critical Issues in Tourism: A Geographical Perspective*, Oxford: Blackwell.
● Silverman, D. (1998) 'Research and social theory', in Seale, C. (ed.) *Researching Society and Culture*, London: Sage Publications.
● Smith, V. L. (1977) *Hosts and Guests: The Anthropology of Tourism*, Oxford: Blackwell.
● Theroux, P. (1983) *The Kingdom by the Sea*, London: Penguin.
● Urry, J. (1990) *The Tourist Gaze: Leisure and Travel in Contemporary Societies*, London: Sage Publications.
● —— (1995) *Consuming Places*, London: Routledge.

Evaluating Research

Two different research styles

Before examining examples of research from leisure and tourism in detail, let us begin by referring to two pieces of research recently published in two edited volumes. Hall and Lew (1998) have edited a series of case studies illustrating current approaches to the geography of sustainable tourism, whereas Abram, Waldren and Macleod (1997) have edited a volume on the nature of the tourist experience. One chapter from each book will be used to illustrate two different approaches to research. Hull's essentially quantitative approach is published in Hall and Lew (1998) and Kohn's qualitative approach in Abram *et al.* (1997).

Let us begin with Hull's (1998) research on 'Market segmentation and ecotourism development on the Lower North Shore of Quebec, Canada'. This part of Quebec is remote but has witnessed an increasing number of tourist arrivals. With the decline in fishing local people have shown a greater interest in developing tourism in the area, and at the same time protecting cultural and natural resources. Local residents wish to target the niche market of ecotourists – more responsible travellers who are likely to be sympathetic to conservation initiatives. Ecotourism can be defined as responsible travel to natural areas that conserves the environment and improves the welfare of local people. Thus, ecotourists have the potential to contribute to the local economy without degrading or altering the environment. Thus, the sustainability of tourism on the Lower North Shore of Quebec will depend on how well local planners identify and target the ecotourist market.

In the summer of 1995 a survey of departing visitors was conducted at two ferry terminals on the Lower North Shore. Over a ten-week period during the high tourist season, 538 questionnaires were collected. The survey aimed to find out what type of tourist came to the area, why they came, how satisfied they were with the tourist experience and their patterns of expenditure. One of the main concerns was to analyse tourist demand. Based on previous research the survey attempted to establish a correlation between what the visitor does at a destination and their socio-economic status. In addition, visitor attitudes, perceptions and motivations at a destination were asked in the survey to determine whether they are influenced by factors like age, education, income and family situation.

As Henderson (1990: 178) points out, a quantitative approach like this relies on a research design and a set of procedures worked out in advance of the data collection. Surveys using questionnaires are designed and piloted before the main survey. This study relies on the treatment of statistical data derived from the questionnaire where variables are controlled for to seek out relationships and patterns in the data. For example, to determine whether education determines perceptions, attitudes or motivations, other factors like age have to be controlled for. Referring back to the positivist/phenomenological debate earlier, here is a piece of research where the behaviour of tourists has been measured and quantified. Research questions were devised before the data collection process, and the results analysed to confirm or reject those ideas. Although this may oversimplify reality by concentrating on pre-conceived ideas that determined the content of the questionnaire, it is seen as a rigorous data-gathering process. This quantitative approach using a questionnaire survey is in the positivist tradition.

In contrast to this is Kohn's research on tourist identities on a Scottish island. Kohn's research is based on her D.Phil. unpublished thesis (1988), and derives from the work of social anthropologists. In fact, Kohn refers to her research as an example of the 'anthropology of tourism' (page 13). Her research was conducted on a small island in the Inner Hebrides of Scotland. She examined the role of tourism as 'one modern element in the larger process of shifting identities, whereby incomers may become islanders' (page 15). It is clear from her opening sentence that she is interested in tourism as a process. In the introduction to her study she points out some of the limitations of current research in tourism. They include:

1. Definitions of 'tourists' have tended to be inflexible and based around structural typologies.

2. Research on socio-cultural change has focused on how the receiving community has changed with the corrosion of the traditional way of life.

3. Tourist places are shaped and changed for the benefit of the tourist.

4. The assumptions that 'hosts' and 'guests' are discrete and different from each other.

In a sense she is criticising previous research conducted in a positivist tradition i.e. predetermined categories of tourists and impact studies where tourists and residents are defined differently. Kohn's research questions the definition of a tourist, and argues that conceptions of what is a 'tourist' change over time. Her focus is more on the experiences of the tourist as seen through the eyes of the islanders. Rather than being just another impact study, she is more interested in the way the identities of tourists change as perceived by the receiving community, and how this shapes their conception of place. She aims to 'unpack' the dualistic distinction between 'host' and 'guest', arguing that there is more fluidity within these identity categories.

This particular topic lends itself to a qualitative approach in the phenomenological tradition as it is concerned with conceptions of 'identity' and 'place', at the level of the individual tourist. This is not a positivist impact survey where the categories of 'tourist', 'host', 'incomer' and 'islander' are pre-defined, nor where hypotheses are developed to test out the impact of tourism on a community. Research is at the level of the individual tourist, but more importantly, it is about how the islanders define the tourists. Kohn spent three years conducting her fieldwork on the Scottish island (1984–7). It was only during this time that she could observe and interpret the processes whereby incomers may become islanders.

Kohn describes the landscape of the island, its people and its economy, and how life on the island changes when the visitors arrive in the summer months. What singles this study out as a qualitative piece of phenomenological research is that the mass of visitors are distinguished and categorised by the resident population. These categories emerge in the course of the research. The main categories are:

1. 'Day-trippers' – arrive on an excursion by ferry, spend three hours on the island and then return to the mainland by ferry.

2. 'Yachties' – arrive in their own boat, for a variable length of time, instantly recognised, snide remarks from locals, class prejudice, little spending on island.

3. 'Tourist' – all other holiday-makers, explorers and independent travellers, learned about it from friends, many of whom return to the island.

4. 'Summer swallows' – live on the island in summer in homes that they have bought, and live on the island as they imagine it should be lived in.

There seems to be a collapse of incomer and islander identities for these groups, many of whom were originally tourists. Valuable as these four categories are, the situation is more complex than this, Kohn calls them 'ambiguous categories'. In some contexts all four categories are referred to as 'tourists', for example if they are crowded into a shop. Everyday encounters and experiences are used as key reference points to contextualise the incomer.

5. 'Glasgow cousins' – island-born people who came to holiday on the island as they live and work in the Central Lowlands of Scotland, many of these retire back into the community.

What is clear is that a number of tourists had returned to the island year after year and eventually set up a permanent home there. Some married into the community. Kohn, firstly, attempts to explain why tourists returned year after year. Her evidence suggests that it has something to do with the island's 'magic', that people are 'bewitched' by the place. In addition, she points out that Gaelic is not a boundary between islanders and incomers as it is elsewhere in Scotland.

Kohn is very critical of other island studies where the role of newcomers to the islands has been ignored. They have been seen as 'marginal' to island community life. Her study argues that, given the right context, tourists need not be marginal, and that their identities and interests can change. Kohn's three-year study has yielded a vast range of qualitative data about how an island community perceives incomers and how many of them return to the island year after year and eventually become islanders themselves. Her research challenges the notion of fixed categories of tourists, the declining number of repeat visits to a location and the marginal position of tourists on island communities. Thick description dominates her text as she builds up a picture of life on the island from the point of view of the islanders.

It is clear from the detailed discussion of these two pieces of research that Hull's survey research was essentially quantitative, with data collected through a survey, whereas Kohn's ethnographic research collected mainly qualitative data. This tends to give the impression that the researcher either collects quantitative or qualitative data. It is true that the positivist researcher will tend to analyse quantitative data and the phenomenologist interprets qualitative data. But how do we assess whether these are good examples of research?

Reliability and validity

Our concern here is whether a piece of research will stand up to outside scrutiny. From a methodological point of view research is assessed using terms like 'reliability' and 'validity'. Of the two, reliability is the easiest to describe. Reliability is about consistency of the results obtained from a measuring instrument in a piece of research. If the measuring instrument is a questionnaire, then the questions included should obtain the same answer from a person each time it is asked. Chapter 6 covers questionnaire design and highlights various ways by which a question can bias the results by either being ambiguous or by the way the interviewer asks it. A reliable question will be a simple, clearly worded question that will yield the same results on different occasions. Earlier we examined the problems of operationalising concepts into variables. Each variable representing the concept should be as specific as possible to enhance reliability. Unfortunately, measuring devices like questionnaires are not always included in a published piece of research, making it difficult to assess reliability.

Ethnography has a particular problem with reliability. It is the researcher himself/ herself that is the collector of data. Human observers are notoriously unreliable. Whereas the experimental and survey styles of research place great emphasis on reliability, it is accepted as more of a problem in ethnography. To what extent would different observers produce the same data on the same research project? Ethnographers tackle the problem of reliability by reflecting on their own involvement in the research and assessing their own impact. The use of more than one observer would also help with this problem.

In general terms, validity is whether a measuring instrument measures what it is supposed to measure. But there are various components to the idea of validity. At this point we can make the distinction between 'internal' validity and 'external' validity. Internal validity refers to whether the hypothesised cause produces the given effect in the piece of research. In the experimental style of research, if the controls have been effectively set up and all extraneous variables have been eliminated then the internal validity of the research is likely to be high. This cannot be said for the survey style of research, where the only controls are statistical when the data are being analysed. Internal validity is much lower with this style of research.

External validity refers to the extent to which the results of the research can be generalised. This is also referred to as the 'representativeness' of the research's results. Here we can identify two aspects of external validity, 'population' and 'ecological'. Population validity is about whether the research can be generalised to other groups of people outside the sample researched. Ecological validity is about generalisation to other settings. To illustrate the difference between these two forms of external validity, comparison can be made between the sample survey and the small-scale ethnographic project. If sampling has been carried out using probability methods then one of the strengths of the survey is that the results of the research can be generalised to the population from which the sample was drawn. The survey's strength is the degree to which results from a small sample can be generalised to a larger number of people (population validity), whereas with an ethnographic project, with the emphasis on researching a whole natural setting, it may be possible to generalise the findings to a similar natural setting.

In our discussion of reliability, we referred to deriving variables from concepts, and how these variables should be reliable. In addition, these variables, or indicators of the concepts, should also be valid. This is referred to as measurement validity. It is quite possible for a concept to be operationalised into a variable that is reliable but not valid i.e. a good measure of the concept(The student researcher should be aware that there are ways of improving the validity of the operationalised concepts. They include:

- approaching people who are employed in leisure and tourism industries for their professional advice
- consulting with previous published research
- using more than one method of data collection to triangulate the results
- sound understanding of the theory underpinning the research)

Gill and Johnson (1997: 128) emphasise the point that if the strengths and weaknesses of research are to be evaluated then the strategies need to be compared and contrasted in terms of criteria derived from the validity and reliability of the findings.

Sample evaluations

Research quoted in edited volumes can give some indication of the methodology adopted and allow the reader to make some critical judgements on how good the research is. A richer source of research where methodology is given more prominence is the journals. The student researcher is encouraged to explore the full range of journals to seek inspiration for topics to research and to carry out a literature search. Examples of good leisure and tourism journals include:

Annals of Tourism Research

International Journal of Tourism Research

Journal of Applied Recreation Research

Journal of Hospitality and Leisure Marketing

Journal of Hospitality and Tourism Research

Journal of Leisure Research

Journal of Sports Tourism

Journal of Sustainable Tourism

Journal of Tourism Studies

Journal of Travel and Tourism Marketing

Journal of Travel Research

Journal of Vacation Marketing

Leisure Studies

Society and Leisure

Tourism Geographies

Tourism Management

Tourism Recreational Research

Travel and Tourism Analyst

World Leisure and Recreation Association Journal

Let us now focus on an example to evaluate in more detail. An example of the survey style of research has been chosen to illustrate some of its strengths and weaknesses. The topic chosen is the effect of race on tourism choice. Philipp, who conducted the research, investigated race and tourism choice arguing that racial prejudice and discrimination may account for differences in travel preferences. The full title of the research is 'Race and tourism choice: a legacy of discrimination?' and was published in the *Annals of Tourism Research* (Vol. 21 (3)) in 1994. You are strongly advised to read the journal article through thoroughly before proceeding.

Here are some key points and issues raised by the research:

1. The research is based in the United States and focuses on blacks and their tourism preferences. It is claimed that this is an under-researched topic. The author justifies his topic in these terms. For students in the UK, a question that needs consideration is whether the research will have implications for blacks outside the United States. How strong is the population validity of the research?

2. There is an impressive literature review on race and tourism behaviour, which concludes that previous research has examined racial differences in leisure participation and explained black and white differences by income and cultural differences (referred to as 'marginality' and 'ethnicity'). This implies that black people's leisure activities reflect their low economic position in US society or that their activities are determined by their black culture; whereas Philipp argues that prejudice and discrimination affect leisure/tourist behaviour. You will notice that the literature review concentrates on leisure rather than tourism activity. Yet the research is about tourism rather than leisure. Is there a difference between leisure and tourism preferences?

3. There are problems in sampling a minority group in any location. To research differences in tourism preferences between blacks and whites, an approximate equal proportion of both was required – but blacks make up only 32 per cent of the population, thus black areas were over-sampled. Will this affect the 'representativeness' of blacks in the sample? Those blacks living in more mixed black/white areas will be under-represented – maybe these will be a different class of blacks?

4. Random sampling was used to select the research groups and this allows inferences to be made to a larger population. This increases the population validity of the research. But the response rate was disappointingly low at 53 per cent. Consequently, there may be a bias in the sample selected if those who refused were a distinctive group missed from the survey i.e. the poorest blacks. We are assured that interviewer bias was minimised but we have no details of the race, class and gender of the interviewers, and reasons for the low response rate.

5. The survey employed a deductive methodology as the questions in the sample survey were determined by the four basic tourism preference dichotomies developed by McIntosh and Goeldner (1990). Here is an example of where Philipp's research has benefited from previous work, and the model of basic preferences will help increase the validity of the results obtained.

6. The model recognises eight concepts representing travel preferences, dependence, autonomy, activity, relaxation, order, disorder, familiarity and novelty. Each one was operationalised by two statements, using the Likert scale (see Chapter 6). The process of operationalising the eight concepts has been achieved, but a more important question is whether each variable created on the Likert scale is reliable and valid. Socio-economic data was also collected on each respondent. An interesting point to consider is whether the survey was about household tourism preferences or individual tourism preferences? An adult member of the household was interviewed, but will there be different tourism preferences within the household?

7. This is a highly reliable form of research with a simple attitudinal survey based on statements, which the respondent is asked to agree or disagree with. The structured and controlled nature of the survey increases the reliability of the results. The model employed in the research lends itself to a quantitative analysis. Yet on closer examination, can terms like 'dependence' and 'autonomy' be reduced down to two statements each? These terms are multi-dimensional and may be not fully conveyed in the two statements. It may have been better to explore the meanings behind these terms in more detail through exploratory/qualitative interviews, before devising the Likert scales. It is possible to question the measurement validity of the statements representing each preference.

8. The quantitative analysis is thorough, with a focus on the differences between blacks and whites that are statistically significant i.e. the probability of the results occurring by chance is less than 5 per cent or 1 in 20 (see Chapter 11 for a discussion of statistical significance). The chi-square statistical test, which compares observed frequencies with expected frequencies, draws attention to six travel preference indicators, differences in which were statistically significant. Philipp concentrates on these significant results in his analysis and conclusions.

9. In the sample there were differences between blacks and whites in terms of education and household size. These were controlled for in the analysis to eliminate their influence on the results. This is an attempt to increase the internal validity of the causal analysis.

10. The results show that blacks are more likely to travel as part of a large group, in more known areas, avoid streets they do not know, be occupied with activities, and eat at well-known restaurants.

11. The author maintains that the previous explanations of racial difference do not explain all these findings. There is an inference from the data that hostility of the 'outside' world through prejudice and discrimination is a more powerful explanation of tourist behaviour than previous explanations centred on socio-economic status and cultural norms. But the data is not proof of this – we do not know why blacks and whites behave differently. For example, one explanation not considered is the degree of sophistication of the traveller. Whites may be more 'seasoned' travellers reflecting their socio-economic status and the importance of tourism to that status.

12. There is an acknowledgement that the study is 'suggestive', based as it is on one urban area. The extent to which this can be generalised to other cities is debatable and does require a more comprehensive study. In the UK there are important inter-racial differences between ethnic groups classified as 'blacks'. Do those whose parents originated from Asia have the same preferences as those whose parents are from the Caribbean? Even if these groups are born in Britain there may be cultural differences between them.

13. The key to this debate is whether these differences, which are clearly associated with class, education and disposable income, also reflect prejudice and discrimination. This could be explored using more in-depth interviewing with smaller groups of blacks and whites to penetrate the meanings associated with their touristic behaviour. To allow the different groups to 'set their own agenda' through their own experiences would give more insight into the reasons for their tourist behaviour i.e. whether it is by choice or constrained by prejudice and discrimination.

This evaluation of Philipp's research is meant to highlight the strengths and weaknesses of the survey style of research. Using stratified random sampling, Philipp has attempted to increase the external validity of the research and to justify the use of inferential statistics to analyse the results. Travel preference categories have been operationalised in a clear, logical way employing a tried and tested attitudinal scale. There has been an attempt to control for variables that would affect the main purpose of the research, that is to highlight differences between blacks and whites. The use of an established model of travel preferences builds upon previous research. Conclusions are suggestive and not definitive, opening the way for more research on the issue.

Any weaknesses in the research reflect inherent problems in the survey as a method of causal analysis. Selecting a sample from a minority group is problematic, particularly if their geographical distribution may result in a biased sample. Operationalising concepts that can have multiple meanings present the survey researcher with a real problem of measurement validity. Unlike the experimental style of research in its purest form, internal validity is more of a problem with the survey. There could have been other factors that affected the results that the researcher has not controlled for. Decisions on which factors are likely to affect the results have to be made before the questionnaire is designed, and key variables could have been omitted. One of the main problems confronted by the researcher is how to interpret statistically significant results. One of the variables that was statistically significant when whites and blacks were compared was 'When I travel I like to be part of a large group'. Evidence from the research shows that blacks do like to travel as part of a large group, whereas whites do not. Philipp suggests that this can be interpreted as blacks seeking safety in large numbers as a reaction to (racial) hostility from the 'outside world'. There is no evidence that this is the correct interpretation, it could be explained by other factors like blacks going on holiday with the extended family and relations. Philipp's interpretation may be right, but the point is, this cannot be inferred from the analysis of the data as presented.

Philipp's research can be contrasted with that of Davidson (1996) who researched the holiday and work experiences of women with children published in *Leisure Studies* (Vol. 15, pp. 89–103). Your attention is drawn to the following key characteristics of the research design and research process:

1. Davidson introduces this piece of research as an example of 'phenomenology'. The focus for the inquiry is the meaning of holiday experiences for women with young children. She argues that this population group often faces significant leisure constraints, a theme she decides to pursue. Davidson (1996: 90) describes her approach as 'constructionist' and 'seeks to understand individual and intersubjective meanings and motives'. This piece of research will explore the experiences of a group of women with young children from their perspective, relating their experiences in their own words. There are no hypotheses to test. This is not a deductive methodological approach. The research will be carried out inductively, which may lead to emergent theory.

2. The researched population is defined as women who have at least one child below school age. Sampling from this population has not been done randomly, but rather the sub-group has been purposefully selected from volunteers. In addition, snowball sampling has been used where one respondent selected provides more names for potential inclusion in the sample. There was no attempt to collect statistical information in this research and make inferences from the sample to the population using probability theory. Random sampling was not deemed appropriate (see Chapter 7 for a fuller discussion of sampling).

3. Twenty-four semi-structured interviews were conducted to allow the women to express 'their perceived reality' (page 90). The idea behind the sample selection was to select volunteers from a broad range of socio-economic situations. There is no doubt that

the sample was varied and included women with or without a partner, in paid work or not working, and with more than one child under school age. What is also clear is that the household had access to paid employment increasing the ability to take a holiday. It is also interesting to note that the volunteers taking part in the survey belonged to one or other of the organised groups for mothers and children in a rural and service centre in Australia. But can these results be generalised to a wider population?

4. Interviewing of the respondents took place at the women's home, in a setting where the interviewees would be most relaxed. The interviews were described as 'informal' and allowed the women to talk about their holidays in their own way and in their own terms. In terms of the research process, data collection and analysis took place concurrently. Analysis involved the identification of categories and themes from the interview data.

5. A review of the literature on the holiday experiences of women by Davidson reveals a dearth of research, particularly how women's experiences are different from men's. Davidson decides to focus on two aspects of the holiday experience for women. Firstly, the idea that the holiday is a period of less pressure and relative rest, and secondly, how the holiday is the place to maintain and develop relationships. Qualitative research like this does need a focus, but a focus not presented in the form of hypotheses to test.

6. These two themes are explored in more detail using quotations from the women. Actual names of the interviewees are not revealed as detailed verbatim extracts are used to support the analysis. Davidson draws some general ideas together on how women define periods of reduced pressure as holidays. Relationships were also significant in the way the women assessed the success of their holidays. Examples included relationships with the children, partner and friends.

7. Implications of the research are discussed in detail. There is an acknowledgement that the sampling process could have included a greater variety of cases and that other themes could have been pursued. The author argues that the case studies have helped increase an understanding of women's lives and leisure, by demonstrating that 'work' is an accepted part of the holiday experience. In particular, she questions the usefulness of the work/leisure dichotomy to understand women's experiences on holiday. For example, 'relaxation' is not about doing nothing but being in a state of no anxiety with a change in attitude to work while on holiday. It is interesting to reflect on these experiences and the social expectation promoted by the media, that holidays are periods of rest and relaxation. Women's holidays are also constrained by other factors like no one to provide relief for them, guilt if the woman does something for herself and the commitment to mothering. Davidson concludes that there is no clear demarcation between leisure and work and that women with children require greater support on holiday.

More common in leisure and tourism today is research using a combination of methods. The two examples shown in Figures 3.1 and 3.2 have been chosen to illustrate how different methods of data collection can be combined. For each example the aims, methods and results are described, followed by an evaluation of the research methodology.

There are several points worth emphasising that emerge from Squire's (1994) research:

● The research is essentially in the phenomenological research tradition employing qualitative methods

● She has borrowed a conceptual framework (circuits of culture) from cultural studies and applied it to tourism

Figure 3.1
Example 1:
combining a
range of
quantitative and
qualitative
methods.

This study focuses on Hill Top Farm in the Lake District, the home of Beatrix Potter and Peter Rabbit and friends. Here Squire chooses to explore the meanings of a tourist place like Hill Top Farm as interpreted by visitors. Of general concern is the relationship between tourism, culture and society. From a theoretical perspective, Squire examines tourism as a form of cultural communication and employs Johnson's (1986) theory of the circuits of culture as a framework. The 'circuits of culture' model examines the relationship between production and consumption and how meanings are transformed between the two. Squire applies a model devised for another purpose i.e. trends in cultural studies research, to tourism. The producers are the individuals and agencies facilitating the tourist experience (at Hill Top Farm) and the consumers are the visitors to Hill Top Farm. From Johnson's model, the cultural texts mediate the experience between production and consumption. The attractions at Hill Top Farm represent the tourist text by which visitors make sense of their experience. Interpretation of these tourist texts differs according to a range of factors like age, ethnicity and (what Squire concentrates on) gender. The point is made that it is women more than men who help to define and perpetuate the stories of Beatrix Potter.

Squire's research employs a range of qualitative and quantitative techniques to relate theory to empirical contexts. Although there is a theoretical framework, the research has not set up hypotheses to test, and cannot in any way be described as positivist. The use of a questionnaire interview with 626 visitors with closed and open questions emphasises that the research was more about visitors expressing their experience in their own words (open questions), rather than a profile of visitors (closed questions). The additional data collecting techniques make it clear that this is an inductive piece of research using an interpretist approach where the experiences of the visitors are not constrained by pre-defined structure. Focus group discussions with members of the Beatrix Potter Society and participant observation were used by the author to collect qualitative data. Analysis of the qualitative data yielded insights into childhood and family life. Examples include the intergenerational sharing of experiences, parent-child bond, memories of childhood, communicating family values, reading to children, maternal warmth and closeness and nostalgia. Results of the research are presented in a variety of ways. Interpretations are grounded in previous research e.g. the work of Williams (1987), and the circuits of culture model. Results from the questionnaire interview are presented in two ways. Percentages of responses to the closed questions are used as well as verbal quotes from the focus groups.

Squire devotes the second half of her research article on shopping and souvenir buying at Hill Top Farm. These activities are considered as part of the Beatrix Potter experience and at the 'nexus between production and consumption' (page 203). Rather than researching souvenirs as commodities, Squire sees this as selling cultural values. Shopping is seen as a means of 'marking symbolically and/or remembering the visit'. Squire spends time examining Japanese tourists at Hill Top Farm and questions the extent to which the Potter heritage centre has been commercialised and new meanings created.

The author concludes that the Hill Top Farm heritage centre illustrates the relationship between gender and tourists' experiences. Tourism is seen here as a powerful form of cultural communication where men and women (especially women in this example) reshape places and tourist experiences derived from childhood and family life.

Source: Squire (1994)

- The model is not used to generate hypotheses but to make sense of the visitors' experiences
- Semi-structured interviews, participant observation and focus groups were used to collect qualitative data
- Questionnaires were used to get quantitative information on the types of visitor
- The gendered nature of the research

It is interesting to compare this research with that of Kohn. Both researchers have carried out qualitative research employing a range of data collecting techniques. Both are interested in the experiences of the visitors/tourists. But there are key differences in the design of the research.

Figure 3.2
Example 2:
structured and
semi-structured
interviews linked.

This piece of research is about the experiences and benefits gained by visitors to the Rhondda Heritage Park in South Wales. Essentially, it is a case study of visitors' experiences in a newly established industrial heritage park. What makes the research different is that the authors 'ground' their investigation 'in the realities tourists themselves describe'. They use an inductive approach initially to determine the structure of an interview schedule. Rather than rely on previous models of tourism experience, they create their own from semi-structured interviews. Their aim is to inform on already developed hierarchical models of experience.

These hierarchical models are reviewed in the research article. They comprise a benefits-based, means-end, expectancy-value, typological and insider-outsider frameworks. These models or frameworks have not yet been applied to the experience of industrial heritage centres. The authors decided to select one of the models to inform their research design. A goal-orientated conceptual framework was thought to be the most appropriate, although reference to other frameworks would be made when analysing the results. The research design consists of a sample survey using a structured interview schedule. Semi-structured interviewing, previously carried out, determined the types of questions asked to visitors. In total 403 visitors were interviewed with a high response rate (although the actual figure is not given). From the survey, the authors identify a visitor profile of the park. A key part of the research was the investigation into the dimensions of the visitor experience. This was achieved with a Likert scale using statements derived from the previous interviewing. The eight opinion statements on the dimensions of experiences were 'both feelings and cognitive manipulations, and centred on learning goals'.

Opinions on benefits were also obtained using the Likert scale using five statements derived from the previous interviewing. Although the results of the survey are not really important here, the authors claim that visitor experiences and benefits are largely independent of the socio-demographic profile of the visitors. The authors conclude that the benefit chain of causality is applicable to the understanding of industrial heritage visitation. In addition the same tourism product can be experienced in different ways. Other models, that were reviewed earlier, are also commented upon in the light of the results obtained. A more sophisticated cluster analysis was used to identify the main visitor segments. Five groups were identified, and, although generalised, could provide the basis for product development and promotion. It is suggested in the conclusion that this type of survey, which investigates experiences and benefits, could be combined with a SWOT analysis to benefit the managers of such attractions.

Source: Prentice, R. C., Witt, S. and Hamer, C. (1998)

The research summarised in Figure 3.2 is an interesting variation on the survey style of research as used by Philipp earlier. Prentice *et al.* use semi-structured interviews to determine the structured interview schedule in the main survey. An inductive approach used to determine a deductive approach. A questionnaire using a Likert scale was used to determine opinions of the visitor experience. This contrasts with the research of Squire (1994) where more qualitative methods were used.

Decrop (1999: 158) quotes the work of Lincoln and Guba (1985) for identifying four criteria by which both qualitative and quantitative research can be assessed:

1. *Credibility*: How truthful are the research findings?

2. *Transferability*: Can the results be applied to other settings or populations?

3. *Dependability*: Can the results be replicated? Are the results consistent?

4. *Confirmability*: Are the results the product of the researcher's own biases and prejudices? How neutral are the research findings?

Decrop (1999) argues that triangulation is a good way of enhancing the trustworthiness of the research findings and the credibility of the researcher. Triangulation can take the form of using a variety of data sources, more than one method to study the problem, using more than one researcher to interpret the data and using multiple perspectives to interpret a single data set. As a researcher in tourism and leisure you are asked to consider seriously the four criteria of Lincoln and Guba (1985) and to use the strategy of triangulation to enhance your research design.

Ethical considerations in research

Banister *et al.* (1994: 173) emphasise the importance of considering ethical questions at all stages of the research for all types of researchers:

> *Ethical concerns must be part of the fundamental design of any research project, and ideally any proposed research (including even undergraduate, A level and GCSE practical work) should be talked through with an ethics committee and/or colleagues, to ensure that the research does not, as a minimum, contravene the published ethical principles.*

Whether you are undertaking a questionnaire survey or engaging in ethnographic interviewing, the participants in the research must give their consent to take part. But that consent must be *informed* consent. As a researcher you need to be open and honest about:

- your role in the research
- the aims of the research
- how the participants were selected
- what the research involves for the participants
- time it will take to complete
- what happens to the results of the research.

With this information about the research, participants are more fully informed and are able to give informed consent as to whether they participate or not. This can be communicated to participants either through a letter (questionnaire survey), individual chat (qualitative interviewing) or a group discussion (focused groups). Even when consent has been given to take part in the research, participants do have the right to withdraw at any time. It is also good practice to provide participants with a contact number where you as the researcher can be reached if there are any queries or problems. Mason (1996: 57) argues that gaining informed consent is 'actually quite a complex and difficult business . . .'.

The researcher has the responsibility of protecting participants in the research from harm. Harm does not just include physical harm, but discomfort and embarrassment as well. If there are any potential threats to participants' mental health or psychological well-being then this must be seriously considered during the design of the research.

Figure 3.3
Informed consent:
key questions.

1. Whose consent do you ask?
2. How can you be sure that the consent is actually informed consent?
3. Does this consent mean that the participant answers all questions asked?
4. Does this give you the researcher the right to use the data as he/she sees fit?
5. Does the researcher have the right to interpret and analyse the data as he/she sees fit?
6. Does the researcher have the right to publish the data?

Can the researcher adequately inform participants in the research on all these aspects?

Source: Mason (1996)

— *Part 2.*

Two ethical issues in research that need to be addressed are confidentiality and anonymity. Confidentiality is about protecting the individual from potential harm when research results are made public. Survey researchers commonly assure respondents that their replies will be treated in the strictest confidence. This means that personal details of the respondent are kept secret and are not released by the researcher. In addition, results will only be published in aggregate form so that individual responses cannot be identified. This is good practice and helps generate trust between the researcher and the researched. For a researcher undertaking participant observation then it might be possible for individuals in the research to be identified. Here anonymity is vitally important. This can be achieved by changing the names of the researched and by changing information that might lead to individuals being recognised. This is particularly important when the results of the research are published.

But there are situations when informed consent is not possible. They include participant and non-participant observation carried out covertly. Hartmann (1988: 101) used non-participant observation and participant observation in his study of young North Americans in Munich. He acknowledges that there are ethical problems with participant observation where an observer joined a small group of young Americans or Canadians pretending to be on his/her own. It is argued that the nature of the participant observation with a group of transient tourists is different from that found in community studies where effects are more permanent. The implication is that there is less of a problem in studies of recreational travel and tourism, further justifying the method. But he does highlight a key ethical issue. When the tourists shift from public to private experiences, how far should the researcher as a participant observer report these findings? Perhaps the best advice in this situation is that observations should be confined to situations and localities that are public, and terminate observations when those being researched seek privacy.

For a more detailed discussion of ethics in research the reader is advised to consult Homan (1991). In addition, Marshall and Rossman (1999: 90–101) discuss the main ethical guidelines in qualitative research using examples drawn from current social research. The British Psychological Society (1993) and the British Sociological Association (1993) produce a full code of ethics.

Summary

This chapter has concentrated on examining in detail current pieces of research in leisure and tourism with the aim of identifying examples of good practice. No research is perfect. We have learned that research styles have strengths and weaknesses and one research style may be more appropriate for a research subject than another. This does not mean that the chosen research method is better, just that it is better suited to the researcher's philosophical position and will be more effective in meeting the aims of the research. Hull's questionnaire survey work in Canada has been contrasted with Kohn's participant observation on a Scottish island. Surveys and ethnographic studies can be compared in terms of their reliability, validity and their ability to generalise. Using these criteria the strengths and weaknesses of the two research styles can be compared (see Table 3.1).

To help you understand the importance of research methodology Philipp's (1994) research has been deconstructed and compared with that of Davidson (1996). The remaining research articles have been chosen to illustrate how leisure and tourism researchers have combined methods. Many students take the cynical view that the means justifies the end when research is conducted that contributes to their final award. Whether the university or college has an ethics committee or not, supervisors should be aware and sensitive to ethical considerations when students are undertaking research in the name of the academic institution.

Table 3.1
Survey and
ethnographic
research
compared

	Survey research	*Ethnographic research*
Reliability	Much emphasis on the reliability of the data – a strength for this method of research	Less emphasis on reliability, although can be improved through using more than one researcher, triangulation and reflecting on the research process
Validity	Although it lacks the tight controls of the experimental design, it places much emphasis on internal validity (cause and effect) through statistical analysis	Main strength of this research is the understanding gained of the research setting that is natural rather than artificial as in the laboratory or the interview
Representativeness (generalisability)	Data collected from random samples can be generalised to the population using inferential statistics. High emphasis on external validity	Less commitment to generalisation, although research can be generalised to other settings

Student Activities

Activity 1

Examine the ethical issues which should be considered in designing research on:

1. a survey of the role played by sex tourism in motivating single young people to visit Thailand
2. a participant observation study of the negative impacts of tourism at a resort destination
3. a study of management styles at a leisure centre
4. a survey of young children's recreation activities during holiday periods

Activity 2

Carry out your own evaluation of published research from one of the journals quoted in this chapter. Four good examples are:

- Carr, N. (1999) 'A study of gender differences: young tourist behaviour in a UK coastal resort', *Tourism Management*, Vol. 20 (2), pp. 223–8
- Santos, J. (1998) 'The role of tour operators' promotional material in the formation of destination image and consumer expectations: The case of the People's Republic of China', *Journal of Vacation Marketing*, Vol. 4 (3), pp. 282–97
- Ryan, C. (1995) 'Learning about tourists from conversations: the over-55s in Majorca', *Tourism Management*, Vol. 16 (3), pp. 207–15
- Smith, V. and Hughes, H. (1999) 'Disadvantaged families and the meaning of the holiday', *International Journal of Tourism Research*, Vol. 1 (2), pp. 123–33

Consider issues of reliability, validity and whether the research can be generalised.

References

- Abram, S., Waldren, J. and Macleod, D. V. L. (1997) *Tourists and Tourism: Identifying with People and Places*, Oxford: Berg.
- Banister, P., Burman, E., Parker, I., Taylor, M. and Tindall, C. (1994) *Qualitative Methods in Psychology: A Research Guide*, Buckingham: Open University Press.
- British Psychological Society (1993) 'Revised ethical principles for conducting research with human participants', *The Psychologist*, Vol. 6, pp. 33–5.
- British Sociological Association (1993) *Statement of Ethical Practice*, Durham: British Sociological Association.
- Davidson, P. (1996) 'The holiday and work experiences of women with young children', *Leisure Studies*, Vol. 15, pp. 89–103.
- Decrop, A. (1999) 'Triangulation in qualitative research', *Tourism Management*, Vol. 20 (1), pp. 157–61.
- Gill, J. and Johnson, P. (1997) *Research Methods for Managers*, Second Edition, London: Paul Chapman Publishing.
- Hall, C. M. and Lew, A. A. (1998), *Sustainable Tourism: A Geographical Perspective*, Harlow: Addison Wesley Longman.
- Hartmann, R. (1988) 'Combining field methods in tourism research', *Annals of Tourism Research*, Vol. 15 (1), pp. 88–105.
- Henderson, K. A. (1990) 'Reality comes through a prism: method choices in leisure research', *Society and Leisure*, Vol. 13 (1), pp. 169–88.
- Homan, R. (1991) *The Ethics of Social Research*, Harlow: Longman.
- Hull, J. (1998) 'Market segmentation and ecotourism development on the Lower North Shore of Quebec', in Hall, C. M. and Lew, A. A. (eds) *Sustainable Tourism: A Geographical Perspective*, Harlow: Addison Wesley Longman, pp. 146–58.
- Johnson, R. (1986) 'The story so far: and further transformations?', in Punter, D. (ed.) *Introduction to Contemporary Cultural Studies*, London: Longman.
- Kohn, T. (1988) 'Seasonality and identity in a changing Hebridean community', unpublished D.Phil. thesis, University of Oxford.
- Lincoln, Y. S. and Guba, E. (1985) *Naturalistic Inquiry*, Beverly Hills: Sage Publications.
- Marshall, C. and Rossman, G. B. (1999) *Designing Qualitative Research*, Third Edition, London: Sage Publications.
- Mason, J. (1996) *Qualitative Researching*, London: Sage Publications.
- McIntosh, R. W. and Goeldner, C. R. (1990) *Tourism: Principles, Practices and Philosophies*, New York: John Wiley and Sons.
- Philipp, S. (1994) 'Race and tourism choice: a legacy of discrimination?', *Annals of Tourism Research*, Vol. 21 (3), pp. 479–88.
- Prentice, R. C., Witt, S. and Hamer, C. (1998) 'Tourism as experience: the case of heritage parks', *Annals of Tourism Research*, Vol. 25 (1), pp. 1–24.
- Squire, S. J. (1994) 'Gender and tourist experiences: assessing women's shared meanings for Beatrix Potter', *Leisure Studies*, Vol. 13, pp. 195–209.
- Williams, P. (1987) 'Constituting class and gender: a social history of the home, 1700–1901', in Thrift, N. and Williams, P. (eds) *Class and Space: The Making of Urban Society*, London: Routledge and Kegan Paul.

Chapter 4

Secondary Data Analysis in Leisure and Tourism Research

Learning Outcomes

At the end of this chapter you will be able to:

- appreciate the differences between primary and secondary data
- understand the difference between secondary data collection and secondary data analysis
- identify some of the major sources of leisure and tourism data
- acknowledge the potential of the Internet as a data source
- assess the advantages and limitations of conducting secondary data analysis
- provide an evaluation of secondary data analysis

Introduction

The chapter commences with a definition of secondary data analysis, and the distinction is drawn between primary and secondary data. The potential of secondary data analysis in leisure and tourism research is then considered before we move on to look at some of the main sources of secondary data for leisure and tourism. This includes data provided at the international, national and regional level by governments, government agencies and by private sector research organisations. Specific mention is made of the Internet as a source of secondary data, but students are also warned about the limitations of using this as a key source. The chapter concludes by looking at some of the specific problems involved when undertaking secondary data analysis along with a more general evaluation of the method.

What is secondary data analysis?

The phrase refers to the analysis of information collected for a purpose other than that of the researcher – in this sense the researcher becomes the secondary user of the data. We can contrast this with primary data, which is original data generated by new research using techniques such as surveys, interviews or observations. Most research will, of course, include an element of secondary data collection to discover what work has already been carried out on a particular subject. This is a necessary first step in any research design, and forms an important part of the literature review stage. This is an important point – you should always consult secondary sources of information before you start collecting primary data as you may well find that the information you need is already there. A great deal of time, effort and money can therefore be saved if you are aware of available data, and where to look for it. So, secondary data collection should always come before primary data collection!

The word 'analysis' in the title is, however, the key one. When carrying out this type of research, you are not just collecting information and reproducing it in similar or identical form; you are, instead, re-working the data to address your own research objectives. Hakim (1982: 1) defines secondary data analysis as 'any further analysis of an existing dataset which presents interpretations, conclusions, or knowledge additional to, or different from, those presented in the first report on the inquiry as a whole and its main results'. This method usually refers to the analysis of quantitative data (in particular government/official statistics) generated usually by surveys or a process of registration, although time-budget data can also be used. The term secondary analysis can, however, also be applied to the analysis of diaries, letters, reports, television and radio broadcasts etc. The research associated with these sources of qualitative information is more usually referred to as content analysis, and this is dealt with in detail in Chapter 8. At this stage it is important to appreciate, therefore, that secondary data analysis can be carried out on both quantitative and qualitative data. Indeed, Dale, Arber and Procter (1988: 2):

> take the position that, with many research problems, an adequate understanding can only be gained through the use of qualitative methods together with the more structured approach of the survey . . . Secondary analysis can provide a means by which the benefits of the survey, particularly its ability to provide a national-level dimension, may be combined with other methods to bridge the traditional dichotomy of qualitative and quantitative research.

You should certainly not consider secondary data analysis as somehow inferior to other methods, although you do need to be confident that the primary data collection methods were appropriate. Just because you are working with existing data does not make your research less interesting, less important or less impressive than the work of someone collecting primary data. It is your research idea and research design that is original and creative and, as we have tried to stress throughout this book, it is not a question of good or bad research methods but of appropriate research methods. Given a particular set of research objectives, secondary data analysis may well be the most appropriate method, indeed it may well be the only possible research method.

The potential of secondary data analysis in leisure and tourism research

In this section some suggestions are made for possible research projects using secondary data analysis in order to increase your awareness of the potential of this approach. Two detailed examples, one from the field of tourism research and the other from leisure research, are provided later in this chapter in Figures 4.1 and 4.2 respectively.

● We can use secondary data analysis to examine trends over time. For example, you may wish to examine visitor numbers at UK seaside resorts since the Second World

War and compare trends with those for inland 'heritage' regions. Using this data we could also predict future trends by using some of the statistical forecasting techniques discussed elsewhere in this book. Similarly, the leisure researcher might wish to look at trends in participation in particular sports to examine whether there has been a shift from team sports to individual pursuits. Alternatively, the leisure researcher might test the notion that participation in leisure activities increased dramatically in England and Wales over the period 1977–96.

● We can use secondary data analysis to undertake before and after studies looking at the impacts of a particular piece of legislation, or of a new policy, or of a specific event. For example, what has been the impact of the departure tax on flights from the UK? What impact did the Compulsory Competitive Tendering legislation have on sports participation rates in local authority leisure facilities? What impact did a particular terrorist outrage have on tourism in that area?

● We can explore relationships through the use of secondary data analysis. For example, is there a relationship between social class and patterns of tourist activity? Alternatively, you could test the hypotheses that the type and intensity of leisure activity vary according to gender, age and socio-economic grouping.

● We can 'map' areas of the UK using secondary data. For example, you could look at areas of 'honey pot' tourism activity; or membership lists could be used to map membership patterns as part of a marketing campaign for a health and fitness studio.

● Using census data, the manager of a leisure facility could undertake a catchment area study, and also investigate penetration rates to see what proportion of target market segments is being attracted to the facility.

● A feasibility study for a new leisure facility could be undertaken by combining census data with participation rate data from a national survey.

● We can make international comparisons through secondary data analysis. For example, you could compare levels and trends in second-break tourism in England with those in Germany.

● We can look at the use of time-budget research to explore how people classify and use their leisure time, and therefore track changes in the use of time over a certain period.

The actual techniques used in secondary data analysis are similar to those used in primary data analysis, and are discussed elsewhere in this book (see Chapters 9, 10 and 11). For a more detailed discussion of the issues and techniques involved see Hakim (1982) and, in particular, Dale *et al.* (1988), although developments in computer technology and software design mean that many of the practical points made in these two texts are out of date.

Secondary data for leisure and tourism

We live in the information age. Information never goes away, it just gets added to, and at an exponential rate. The amount of information out there, if only we knew where it all was and had the time and money to access it all, is frighteningly large. You cannot possibly become familiar with all available sources of information – we doubt if anyone is in that dubiously privileged position! Your task as a leisure and tourism researcher is, instead, to familiarise yourself with the most important and accessible sources of data. Most of the available data is quantitative in nature i.e. details of tourist numbers, tourist nights, tourist expenditure and leisure participation rates. Sources of such data include international bodies, central and local government, non-governmental organisations and commercial organisations. These are discussed below. This is not, however, meant to be a definitive list as such a task is beyond the scope of this book. Indeed, any such guide will, to a certain extent, be out of date before it is published; such is the nature of the information revolution. What follows are examples of the major and regular data sources available with a brief description of the sort of information contained within them.

International tourism data

International bodies put together data from central government organisations and national statistical services. Arguably the two most important sources for tourism are the World Tourism Organization and Eurostat.

The World Tourism Organization (WTO)

Based in Madrid, the WTO's main publication is the *Yearbook of Tourism Statistics*. Data is provided by region (e.g. Central America) and by country, and includes arrivals at frontiers or in accommodation establishments, mode of transport, accommodation capacity (i.e. rooms and bed-spaces) and tourism receipts and expenditure. The data is provided over a period of several years, and so trends can be observed. The data is also available by the country of origin of the visitor.

Eurostat

Eurostat is The Statistical Office of the European Communities and produces data not just on European Union countries but also on members of the European Economic Area. Its publication *Tourism in Europe* includes both supply-side data and data on tourism demand. On the supply side the data covers tourist accommodation, restaurants, cafes and bars, travel agencies and other tourist-related activities. The data on tourism demand looks at holiday patterns and the main tourism generating countries, and at inbound tourism. Country reports are then provided for all European Union and European Free Trade Association member states. Each country report has three main sections:

1. General Situation and Key Indicators: Development and Impact of Tourism
2. Tourism Supply
3. Tourism Demand

Much of the data is not only provided at the national level but is also broken down by region within countries. This data from Eurostat began in 1980 so trends can now be observed.

The nearest thing that exists to a European Tourism Survey is the continuous survey of European Outbound Travel (European Tourism Monitor). This involves a sample of approximately 400,000 and provides data on volume and value as well as travel characteristics. It is a commercial initiative funded by subscriptions from public and private sector clients.

UK government statistics on tourism

Government, at both national and local level, provides a range of tourism statistics. Statistics collected by the state and its agencies are usually referred to as 'official statistics'. Some examples from the tourism sector are set out in Table 4.1 and are discussed below.

Table 4.1 Sources of national statistical data on tourism

Survey	Began	Organisation responsible	Sample size	Examples of topics covered	Level of analysis
Population Census	1801	Office for National Statistics	N/A	Household composition, housing, education, employment, migration, country of birth	National, regional, county, enumeration district and standard areas e.g. local authority boundaries
International Passenger Survey	1964	Office for National Statistics	200,000	International arrivals and departures, destination, length of stay, expenditure, purpose of visit, mode of transport, age and gender	Seasonally adjusted data. For visitors to UK – country, regional, county and city data is provided as well as by Tourist Board area. Results published annually, quarterly, monthly
British National Travel Survey	1960*	British Tourist Authority	3,000 approx.	A survey of British holiday-makers – frequency and duration of holidays, destinations, and expenditure	National and regional level data with comparative findings from previous years
UK Tourism Survey	1989	British Tourist Authority	83,000	Trips by UK residents in the UK lasting one night or more. Number of trips, destination, purpose, expenditure, leisure activities engaged in	National and regional data with comparative data from previous years
British Conference Market Survey	1993	British Tourist Authority	224 venues	Volume of activity, type of conference, revenue, conference size and length	Great Britain and regional level data

*Note: The British National Travel Survey was conducted in 1951 and 1955. It has, however, run every year since 1960

The first item in Table 4.1 is perhaps a surprising source, and that is the Population Census. While the Census is clearly not primarily a source of leisure and tourism data it can be used in leisure and tourism research as we shall see below. The Census began in 1801 and occurs every ten years in Britain, although there was no census in 1941, and there was an additional census in 1966. Participation in the Census is compulsory and so the response rate is virtually 100 per cent. It is, therefore, the most comprehensive and reliable data source available to the researcher. Because census data is made available at the level of the enumeration district of between 250 and 500 people, it has the particular advantage of providing detailed information on small or geographically dispersed groups. Data from the enumeration districts can be aggregated to produce statistics for standard areas such as local authority boundaries or for areas defined by the researcher such as the catchment area for a retail park.

Census data is also widely used by marketers as part of geodemographic market segmentation systems such as A Classification Of Residential Neighbourhoods (ACORN) and, increasingly, as part of lifestyle segmentation systems. This is achieved through the ability to link enumeration district data to postcodes and other data sets. Details of the use of census data in marketing can be found in most standard marketing textbooks.

Two examples of the use of census data in tourism research can be found in the work of Whyman (1972) and Butler (1985). Whyman utilises the data from the summer census of 1841 to develop a picture of early Victorian holiday taking in Margate. He not only estimates the total number of visitors to Margate on census night but also provides an analysis by age, gender and social class. He concludes that 'Margate had become by 1841 one of the holiday resorts of an extensive and diverse middle class' (p. 28). In addition, he looks at the geographical origins of visitors and their distribution within Margate. In doing so, he highlights an important feature of Victorian holiday-making in that hotels were primarily used as a temporary form of accommodation while alternatives were sought in lodging houses, spare rooms and elsewhere.

Butler traces the development of tourism in the Scottish Highlands from the early eighteenth century to the beginning of the twentieth century. He identifies five periods within this time span, and highlights the social, economic and technological forces that shaped them. In doing so, he makes brief reference to the census data of 1921 as this was carried out in June, and thus included tourists staying in holiday areas. As a result, he concludes that in the Scottish Highlands, 'the development of the tourist industry in the early decades of the twentieth century had not proceeded on a large scale' (p. 387).

More direct sources of tourism data include The International Passenger Survey, carried out at main air and sea ports; The British National Travel Survey, a survey of British holiday-makers; and The UK Tourism Survey (UKTS), a continuous survey involving face-to-face interviews conducted monthly. The UKTS looks at trips undertaken by UK residents in the UK lasting one night or more in the previous two months, thus tackling the problem of respondent recall.

The British Tourist Authority (BTA) undertakes a range of regular research programmes such as surveys of overseas visitors to Britain in general and to London in particular, visits to tourist attractions and the conference market. The BTA produces a *Digest of Tourist Statistics*, which provides a wealth of data on tourism to, within and from the UK. In addition, their annual *Regional Tourism Facts* provides data for each of the English tourism regions covering topics such as expenditure, accommodation, transport and the demographic profile of visitors. Arguably the most comprehensive and up-to-date UK tourism statistics are provided by the BTA and the English Tourist Board (ETB) in their *Tourism Intelligence Quarterly*. This looks at trends in the global tourism industry and their implications for UK tourism, as well as the economic impact of tourism in the UK. Data is also provided on

UK outbound tourism and mode of travel. Together, the BTA and the ETB also produce *Insights*, which includes statistics on UK tourism along with specific research reports, market profiles, articles and case studies. *Insights* also includes a valuable guide to available tourism research findings and recent tourism publications. The BTA also produces a series of country market guides aimed at companies interested in marketing British tourism products overseas. Individual country data is provided such as the number of visits to the UK from the country in question, total spending, length of stay, purpose of visit, region of stay, mode of travel to the UK and the age and gender of visitors.

In response to demand from the tourism industry and from tourism researchers, the BTA is making more statistical data on inbound and domestic tourism available for free on the Internet via the STAR UK website (http://www.staruk.org.uk). This is the official website of the tourism research liaison group of the United Kingdom. The group comprises representatives from the national tourist boards of Britain, England, Scotland, Wales and Northern Ireland plus the Department for Culture, Media and Sport.

So far we have been looking at the national picture, although much of the data collected is analysed at the regional level. At the local level, most local authorities in the UK have tourism departments or sections; many of them linked to economic regeneration. They will produce data on tourism activity in their area including tourist numbers, visitor attraction data and accommodation use data.

Other government departments without a direct interest in tourism, and national agencies such as The Countryside Agency will also, from time to time, generate data that will be of interest to the tourism researcher. As is the case with most of the organisations discussed in this chapter, The Countryside Agency, for example, is making more of its data available on the Internet – see, for example, their 'Research Notes' section on their website. The use of the Internet as a source of secondary data is discussed later in this chapter.

There is also a range of central government statistical returns and publications that are of relevance. These are catalogued in the *Guide to Official Statistics* produced by the Office for National Statistics about every five years. At the time of writing the most recent edition was 1996. The *Guide* enables you to locate statistics produced by government and other official organisations, it does not include any data itself. *The Annual Abstract of Statistics* produced by the Office for National Statistics is a compendium of statistics from numerous sources that provides information on aspects of economic and social life. The section on 'transport and communications' is of direct relevance providing, for example, figures over a ten-year period of arrivals and departures by sea and air. *Social Trends*, on the other hand, is more of a journalistic account than a statistical volume. It is produced annually by the Office for National Statistics, and it provides a detailed study of UK society utilising data from a variety of sources with an accompanying commentary. The two sections on 'transport' and 'lifestyles' will be of particular value. In 1998 the lifestyles section looked at areas such as holiday taking, time use, participation in a range of home-based and out-of-home leisure activities, readership habits, attendance at cultural events, sports participation and much more.

Commercial sources of tourism data

Given the economic importance of tourism globally, commercial provision of tourism data is more important, and more extensive, than in many other areas of research. Companies require, and generate, data on areas such as market trends, tourist satisfaction, employment and expenditure on tourism. However, given the commercial nature of this data, it is often either deemed to be commercially confidential or is extremely expensive to access.

Reports from commercial research organisations can cost thousands of pounds, thus putting it beyond the budgets of many university libraries.

Commercial sources of tourism data fall into two broad categories – data that can be purchased from commercial research organisations (see Table 4.2), and data generated by tourism companies themselves as part of their normal operating procedures. Both are discussed below.

Euromonitor specialise in international consumer market analysis, and part of their portfolio includes travel and tourism. Their reports, which are outlined in Table 4.2, are based on a combination of primary and secondary data. Travel and Tourism Intelligence (TTI) is the former travel and tourism division of the Economist Intelligence Unit. TTI produces four regular subscription publications – *Travel and Tourism Analyst, TTI Country Reports* (a subscription to which includes *Country Updates*, a quarterly newsletter that updates the data in *Country Reports*), *Travel Industry Monitor* and *TTI City Reports* – all of which are based on published and unpublished statistical data supported by original research. In addition to these regular publications TTI produces specially commissioned research reports on particular sectors of the tourism industry or aspects of the travel business. Recent topics have included The European Travel Agency Industry, Prospects for Tourism in South America, Regional Airlines in Europe, and EMU, the Euro and the Travel Industry.

As well as the commercial research companies, tourism organisations generate a mountain of information as part of their normal operating procedures. This includes things like visitor numbers, occupancy rates, employment records, satisfaction survey data and brochure pick-up and conversion rates. This can be a valuable source of information for the tourism researcher, providing they can get access to it. However, you are likely to come up against the issue of commercial confidentiality. This problem can be tackled in a number of ways. When approaching organisations you can stress the limited circulation of your research. It is likely, for example, that a student research project will stay within the confines of the college or university, and will need to go no further. You can also offer to 'disguise' the organisation by changing its name and location so that it cannot be identified in your research. Depending on the nature of your research, you might also restrict yourself to requesting historical data so that the more recent, and thus commercially sensitive data, are not required.

One source of information on commercial organisations that is readily available is the company annual report. These provide a wealth of information, particularly financial statistics, and most of the major leisure and tourism companies will be happy to send you a copy. The financial pages of the broadsheet newspapers are similarly rich in financial data.

You should, however, prepare yourself to be disappointed with approaches to commercial organisations for data of this nature. This has important implications for the planning of your research, particularly if your project is solely or heavily dependent on secondary data analysis. You need to check at a very early stage in the research process whether this information will be made available to you. If you leave approaching organisations to late in the day you run the very real risk, if they are not prepared to release information, of not being able to complete your project. Projects that rely on data from commercial organisations should not therefore be contemplated unless you are sure that the necessary information will be forthcoming (see Figure 4.1).

International leisure data

There have been, to the best of our knowledge, no surveys of global leisure participation. Many of the economically developed countries around the world do, however, conduct their own leisure participation surveys, and it is expected that more countries will

Table 4.2 Commercial sources of tourism data

Organisation	Product	Frequency	Examples of topics covered
Euromonitor	(1) Emerging market reports (2) Market direction reports (3) International market intelligence reports	Periodic	(1) Eastern Europe, Latin America and South East Asia covering tourism trends, demographics, infrastructure, attractions, growth areas and five-year forecasts (2) The leading industrialised countries – market trends, emerging product sectors, companies and their strategies, market shares, advertising and promotion and the future (3) Global perspective – tourism trends, retailing and tour operating, accommodation and strategic corporate profiles
Travel and Tourism Intelligence	Travel & Tourism Analyst	Bi-monthly	Transport (e.g. No-Frills Airlines In Europe), outbound markets (e.g. New Zealand Outbound), market segments (e.g. The Youth and Student Travel Market), accommodation/financial/leisure industries (e.g. Hotel Investment in the South Pacific) and occasional studies (e.g. Tourism and the Internet)
	TTI Country Reports	Quarterly	Detailed profiles of five destination countries – trends in arrivals, expenditure, accommodation supply, occupancy rates, transport, length of stay, purpose of visit, tourism policy and management, tourism funding and promotion and future prospects
	Travel Industry Monitor	Monthly	Market trends, destination information, market segments, company performance, new technology, policy and legislation
	TTI City Reports	Quarterly	Detailed profiles of five urban tourism destinations – visitor trends, infrastructure development and tourism management
MINTEL	Leisure Intelligence	60 reports per annum	e.g. Self-catering holidays, tourism and the over 45s, crossing the Channel, city breaks. Standard format – market factors, market size and trends, market segmentation, supply structure, advertising and promotion, distribution, findings from consumer attitudes and needs research, assessment of future trends

Figure 4.1
Secondary
data analysis: a
tourism example.

Seaton and Palmer (1997) start from the position that our present understanding of visiting friends and relatives (VFR) tourism is limited, and that there has been little useful comparative or longitudinal data generated on the topic. The objective of their research was to examine four key issues – expenditure, the timing and duration of VFR trips, destinations and social class, age and life cycle factors. These four areas were identified as being crucial for an assessment of the importance of VFR tourism from a marketing point of view.

To do this they used data from the United Kingdom Tourism Survey (UKTS) gathered over the period 1989–93. The UKTS was introduced in 1989 and so by 1993 the authors had five years of data that had been generated without any changes to the methodology, thus allowing them to conduct a reliable longitudinal study.

Results

If we take expenditure first, it has long been assumed that VFR tourism is smaller in value terms than other forms of tourism, and an initial look at the UKTS data from 1989–93 appears to support that view. However, as Seaton and Palmer point out, VFR tourism by its very nature will not include package trip costs and will have much lower accommodation costs than other forms of tourism as VFR tourists are likely to be staying with their friends and relatives. Total expenditure data may be masking important detail. The authors therefore disaggregated expenditure data into categories, and re-worked the data to exclude package trip costs and accommodation expenditure. This revealed VFR tourists to be spending more proportionately than other tourists on travel, eating and drinking and shopping, and on a per nightly basis to be actually spending more than other tourists on certain expenditure categories. In other words, their analysis revealed that we need to re-think our views of the economic importance of VFR tourists.

Their analysis of the timing and duration of VFR trips revealed that they constituted a much higher proportion of short breaks (1–3 days) than all UK trips, ranging from 81 to 83% in the five-year study period. They also found that VFR tourism was spread remarkably evenly throughout the year with the only noticeable peak occurring in December. They suggest, therefore, that 'VFR tourism serves a major function for tourism planners of "seasonal compensation" to the temporal flow patterns found in tourism more generally' (p. 348).

In looking at the destinations chosen by VFR tourists, Seaton and Palmer found a pattern that was opposite to that of recreational tourism as most VFR tourism takes place in towns and cities for the obvious reason that the high density populations of such areas mean that more friends and relatives are likely to live in such areas. This, they argue, has implications for city marketers who have tended to concentrate their efforts on attracting business tourism, and have not given sufficient attention to the VFR market.

Finally, we come to the demographic characteristics of VFR tourists. The social class profile developed by Seaton and Palmer is a complex one but shows that between 1989 and 1993 the higher social class groupings (ABs and C1s) dominated the VFR market in terms of trips, nights spent and expenditure. As a result the authors speculate that VFR tourism can be viewed as yet another form of discretionary travel for these groups. When one looks at the DE social class category, however, we find that this group has a larger average length of stay than other VFR tourists, and are more likely to engage in VFR tourism than other kinds of tourism. Seaton and Palmer suggest that, rather than being a discretionary form of activity, for this group VFR may be a cheaper, substitute form of holiday.

Looking at age and life cycle factors, Seaton and Palmer found that groups in the 15–35 age group were responsible for over half of all VFR trips and expenditure, and nearly half of all VFR nights. In terms of life cycle, the picture was dominated by young singles or couples with children under 15.

This has, of necessity, been a brief account of this research, but it does demonstrate how by conducting a longitudinal study and by re-working aspects of the data, Seaton and Palmer have developed our understanding of the nature and importance of the VFR market.

Source: Seaton and Palmer (1997)

follow suit as leisure becomes an important aspect of economic activity. A comparison of data from these surveys allows us to develop a tentative picture of global leisure participation. There are, however, a number of factors that make direct comparisons impossible such as different sample sizes, different 'reference periods' for participation, different categorisations for concepts such as age and the different frequencies with which the surveys are held. As Cushman, Veal and Zuzanek (1996: viii) point out:

> *The prospect of being able to compare survey results from different countries is a distant one; differences in survey methodology and in definitions and attitudes arising from cultural diversity make the results of existing surveys virtually impossible to compare. Therefore, it is not possible to state with any confidence that, for example, one country is more active than another in sport or in the arts.*

Results from numerous national studies have, however, been pulled together in the volume edited by Cushman *et al.* (1996) that looks at leisure participation in Australia, Canada, France, Germany, Great Britain, Hong King, Israel, Japan, New Zealand, Poland, Spain and the United States of America. This volume provides a useful glance at international leisure patterns, and the authors intend to produce future volumes covering additional countries.

UK government statistics on leisure

In this section we discuss some of the main sources of leisure data available at the national level (see Table 4.3).

The General Household Survey (GHS), which is now published under the title of 'Living in Britain', is the main source of sport and leisure participation data. Recently, the future of the GHS has been called into question as a result of government spending reviews, and the GHS was in fact suspended in 1997/98. At the time of writing, however, work on the GHS is underway for the 1998/99 survey. The plans are that it will not run in 1999/2000 but will run for five years after that, at the end of which the future of the GHS is uncertain. Since 1988 the fieldwork for the GHS has been carried out on a financial year rather than calendar year basis. So for the most recent survey (1996) interviews were conducted between April 1996 and March 1997.

Leisure is not one of the five core topics of the GHS, and so sport and leisure questions have only been included every three years on average since 1973, appearing in 1973, 1977, 1980, 1983, 1986, 1987, 1990, 1993 and 1996. The leisure section asks people to state their participation in sport and leisure activities in the previous four weeks and in the previous 12 months, as well as the frequency of their participation. The results are then reported as percentages. The problem of seasonality is overcome as the interviewing takes place throughout the year as the GHS is a continuous survey, and many of the results are reported by quarter. The GHS does not provide data on the total number of people participating in the various activities, but on the people participating in the four-week period prior to interview. In 1996 the GHS included new questions looking at the use of leisure facilities, at club membership, at competitive involvement and at levels of tuition.

A restriction of the GHS is that it only covers people aged 16 and over. We get no feel, therefore, for the levels of youth sport and leisure participation, but in some sports, skateboarding for example, youngsters may constitute a large percentage of the total number of participants. The data is, however, presented by age, gender and social class thus making it possible to explore the divisions that exist in participation. While the GHS is valuable in providing the 'big picture', the sample size prohibits useful analysis at the local level.

Changes in the methodology were introduced in 1987. Up to 1986 the leisure section utilised an open-ended question that required respondents to recall all the leisure activities which they had engaged in during the four weeks before the interview. In 1987 a pre-coded format was introduced thus prompting respondents with a list of activities. The

Table 4.3 Sources of national statistical data on leisure

Survey	Began	Organisation responsible	Sample size	Examples of topics covered	Level of analysis
General Household Survey (Living In Britain)	1971	Office for National Statistics	10,000 households 18,000 adults	Participation in sport and leisure activities in previous 4 weeks and 12 months. Frequency of participation	Data presented by age, gender and social class. Comparative data from previous years also provided
National Readership Survey	1956	National Readership Surveys Ltd	40,000	Readership of newspapers and magazines, and ownership/usership of other types of media	Data for Great Britain also analysed at regional and county level. Demographic data also provided
Family Expenditure Survey	1957	Office for National Statistics	6,500	Household expenditure on a range of goods and services including leisure services and leisure goods. Household income	Age, social class, family size. Results reported down to regional level
UK Day Visits Survey	1996	Social & Community Planning Research	7,500	Extent and value of leisure day visits in Great Britain	Data provided for England, Scotland and Wales classified by three types of destination – towns/cities, countryside and seaside/coast

result of this change to the data collection methods was some startling increases in sports participation rates e.g. cycling up by 440 per cent between 1986 and 1987. In other words, the old methodology had consistently under-recorded participation. The upshot of this change was that it made it difficult to make comparisons with earlier data. Long-term trend analysis using GHS data is, at the moment, problematic as 1987 must be viewed as a new base year from which to begin examining trends over time unless a new approach to analysing the data is developed (see, for example, Gratton and Tice 1994). Finally, and this is a weakness with much quantitative data, the GHS data gives you no feel for the reasons behind participation, and thus the meaning(s) that participation in sport and leisure activities has for individuals.

As the GHS is such an important resource for leisure researchers, it is worthwhile spending a little time considering the inherent weaknesses and limitations for the researcher undertaking secondary data analysis using the GHS. Gratton (1996) lists five weaknesses inherent in the GHS data:

1. The inability to locate sports participation within wider leisure lifestyles as the GHS is strong on the former but weak on the latter.

2. The continuing use of basic socio-economic and demographic variables as the basis of analysis means that the GHS is falling behind other approaches where psychographic segmentation is proving to be a more fruitful area of analysis.

3. The absence of expenditure data.

4. The absence of time data. While frequency of participation is recorded, the absence of time data means that a restricted picture of the intensity of participation is provided.

5. There is no supply-side information. Participation rates are only a measure of expressed demand; they give no feel for the level of latent or potential demand that might be satisfied by the provision of additional facilities. It is impossible to develop comprehensive models of demand using only data for expressed demand.

Other surveys that may be of interest to the leisure researcher include The National Readership Survey; The Family Expenditure Survey, which contains expenditure data on, for example, alcoholic drink, leisure goods and leisure services; and The UK Day Visits Survey, which replaced the National Surveys of Countryside Recreation, and which, at the time of writing, was last undertaken in 1996 on behalf of a consortium of national agencies including the Scottish Tourist Board, British Waterways and the Countryside Commission (now The Countryside Agency, and from whom the full report is available). It is planned to repeat The UK Day Visits Survey every two years.

At the local authority level two important annual statistical publications are provided by The Chartered Institute of Public Finance and Accountancy (CIPFA). Their *Leisure and Recreation Statistics Estimates* provide data on local authority expenditure on leisure facilities along with income generation data from those facilities. CIPFA's *Charges for Leisure Services* details the prices charged by local authorities for their various leisure facilities.

Finally in this section, you should be aware that government agencies can be useful sources of data on sport and leisure. For example, the Sports Council periodically publishes a *Digest of Sports Statistics for the UK*, which includes data on trends in sport club membership and on facilities for over 150 sports. The national Sports Councils for Wales, Scotland and Northern Ireland also undertake periodic surveys of sports participation in their area. National agencies such as the Sports Council (along with the various governing bodies of sport), the Arts Council and The Countryside Agency are obvious first points of contact for data. The Countryside Agency, for example, conduct regular surveys of our National Trails looking at both their condition and use. The data generated covers visitor numbers and patterns, the age, gender, employment status and socio-economic grouping of trail users, attitudes, accommodation used, transport taken and expenditure. As a standard methodology is used, comparisons between National Trails are possible.

Commercial sources of leisure data

Euromonitor, which has already been discussed above in the context of tourism, also produce a range of reports that would be of interest to the leisure researcher. Topics have included an analysis of the international markets for leisure goods such as television and video, alcoholic and soft drinks, clothing, caravans and camping equipment, gardening, consumer catering and consumer lifestyles. In addition they produce a range of CD-ROM databases. For example, World Consumer Markets 1997/98 provides market data for 56 countries on 248 product sectors including leisure goods such as magazines, cameras, compact discs, toys and games.

The Henley Centre is an international consumer consultancy that produces a quarterly journal entitled *Consumer and Leisure Futures*. The 11 categories that they provide data for are reading, listening, screen-related activities, photography, family activities, DIY and gardening, gambling, entertainment, eating and drinking out, sport and holidays. They include five-year forecasts of consumer spending as well as trend data from the previous six years. Of particular interest is their regular quarterly *Time Use Survey*, which explores all aspects of household time use, and so looks at trends in free time and how that time is being used. This has a sample of 4,000 and has been conducted continuously since 1985. Another regular section is Futurescan, which details the top 15 trends in the global consumer and leisure sector. Detailed sector analyses have covered areas such as holidays, football, golf, the cinema, eating out, gambling and DIY.

MINTEL Marketing Intelligence is part of the Mintel International Group, an independent consumer-market analysis company. MINTEL produce a range of research reports (see Table 4.2), available in hard copy and electronically, of which *Leisure Intelligence* – covering the three broad areas of leisure pursuits, travel and catering – is of most direct relevance. As with all the sources detailed in this chapter, there is overlap between the leisure and tourism sectors, and so many of the MINTEL reports will be of value to the tourism researcher. Recent leisure reports have included betting shops, golf, leisure centres and swimming pools, pub visiting and wedding venues.

Key Note is a market research organisation that produces regular market reports. The sectors covered that will be of particular interest to the leisure and tourism researcher are 'leisure' and 'lifestyle'. Recent reports in their leisure series include *Betting and Gaming*, *Camping and Caravanning*, *Cinemas and Theatres*, *Health Clubs and Leisure Centres* and *The Film Industry*. In the lifestyle series, recent reports include *The Under-16s Market*, *The Grey Market in the UK* and *The Youth Market in the UK*. These reports follow a standard format and include data on market size, competitor analysis, company profiles and sector forecasts.

Using the Internet as a source of secondary data

The Internet is a network of computer networks linking millions of computers around the world. The World Wide Web (WWW) is part of the Internet network with web pages

Gratton and Tice (1994) undertook secondary data analysis utilising the data from the General Household Survey (GHS). The GHS looks at participation in individual sports and, as Gratton and Tice acknowledge, conventional analysis of GHS data has been useful in identifying the most popular sports, and in showing how participation rates are linked to gender, age and socio-economic status. They argue, however, that we know less about trends in sports participation from this conventional analysis. The aim of their research was, therefore, to develop a number of indicators that would enable them to provide a clearer measure of the nature of sports participation, and then to show how participation had altered in the period 1977–87.

The need to develop appropriate indicators arose from what Gratton and Tice saw as limitations with the existing GHS data. First of all, they argue that it is inappropriate to include camping/caravanning in the outdoor sports activity section as these activities could not be viewed as sports. Secondly, they argue that it is also inappropriate to include snooker/billiards/pool and darts in the indoor sports activity section as one of the thrusts of public policy has been to encourage participation in healthy and active sport, and none of these activities fit that profile. In addition, investment in sport has been about encouraging excellence in the international arena and, again, this argument cannot be applied to such activities. Thirdly, and most importantly, Gratton and Tice argue that the figures are being distorted by the inclusion of snooker and darts. For many years these had been the second and third most popular indoor sports activities as measured by the GHS, but over the period 1977–86 participation in snooker had grown significantly while participation in darts had declined to a similar extent. Any analysis of that period would, therefore, be masked to a certain extent by changes in these two activities. When they came to do their analysis they found that participation in indoor sports had increased by nearly 58% over the period 1977–86 whereas conventional GHS analysis (i.e. including snooker and darts) showed an increase of only 29%.

Gratton and Tice ultimately developed 14 participation groups (previously GHS data had been analysed under just four groups), which excluded snooker/billiards/pool, darts, and camping and caravanning. It is also important to appreciate how they treated the activity of 'walking' as this provides a useful example of how re-defining categories and re-working the data in secondary analysis can uncover previously 'hidden' facts. The inclusion of walking as an outdoor sports activity in the GHS has long been a subject of debate as one could never be sure whether the respondent was referring to a 20-mile hike in the countryside or a stroll to the newsagents. Walking has, however, always been the most popular category, and does distort the findings. Gratton and Tice therefore developed categories that included and excluded walking in order to produce a clearer picture of what was going on.

We need not concern ourselves here with a detailed consideration of their 14 categories or with the results, which were subsequently analysed by age, gender and retirement. Their main conclusions were, however, that:

- Participation in indoor sport grew at a much faster rate than outdoor sport during the period 1977–87.
- Frequency of participation also grew over that period.
- The average age of participants increased for all 14 of their groups.
- The percentage of retired participants increased in all 14 groups and in most cases by a huge amount.
- Female participation rates increased in all groups over the period 1977–87 except for those engaged in outdoor sports only.

The work of Gratton and Tice provides a useful example of the use of secondary data analysis in leisure research. In particular, it highlights how a clearer picture can emerge by utilising a more appropriate definition of the concept under investigation (in this case, sports participation) and by using a greater number of indicators to measure the concept.

Source: Gratton and Tice (1994)

organised into websites. The address of a website is known as a Universal Resource Locator (URL) – see Chapter 12 for details of how to reference a website in your list of references or bibliography. The URL tells you a number of things. Take, for example, the following address – http://www.lincoln.ac.uk:

- 'http' is the type of file, and stands for 'hyper text transfer protocol'.

- 'www' stands for the World Wide Web. The majority of sites are part of this network.

- 'ac' is short for academic. In other words, a site with 'ac' in its address will belong to a college or university. Other common abbreviations are 'com' (company) and 'gov' (government).

- 'uk' tells you the country the site is located in. In this case it is obviously the United Kingdom.

- 'lincoln' – when you take this into consideration you will have probably by now figured out that the address above is the URL for the university where the authors of this book work.

Web pages are connected to other web pages via links, which are usually words, photographs or buttons. You can always tell where links are on the screen as your cursor will change to a hand when it moves over the link.

The amount of information available on the Internet is growing at a phenomenal rate, and there is no doubt that it is becoming a very important resource for researchers as more and more organisations make information available in this way. According to Cringely (1998), in 1989 there were just 130,000 host computers connected to the Internet. This figure had risen to 6,600,000 in 1995, and was an incredible 29,600,000 in 1998. Cringely also estimates that the volume of Internet traffic is doubling every 100 days! Many of the sources discussed earlier in this chapter are now accessible via the Internet. Some of this information is free, but in many cases you will have to pay an advance subscription before you can access the data or pay by credit card at the time of use. It is beyond the scope of this book to provide a listing of web pages that would be of use to the leisure and tourism researcher – such a listing would in any case be out of date as soon as it was produced, such is the speed of change in this area. There is, however, a list of the addresses of organisations discussed in this chapter at the end of the chapter along with the organisation's URL. Students are encouraged to visit these sites to see what is available.

We will restrict ourselves instead to a few words of warning and some tips for using the Internet. First of all, surfing the Internet can waste a great deal of time. The paradox is that the more sources of information that exist, the harder it becomes to find the information you are after. You need, therefore, to develop search strategies that minimise the amount of wasted time and effort. The most obvious point, but one that is often overlooked, is that, as with any information search, you need to know what it is you are looking for before you start. If you approach the Internet with a view to seeing what is there, you have just taken on a job for life. Tyner (1998) estimates that the World Wide Web contains in excess of 320 million pages and that it is growing at an exponential rate, doubling in size every four months! 'Not surfing, drowning' might be a more accurate description of many people's experience of searching for information on the Internet.

Rule number one for any search strategy must therefore be to have as clear an idea as possible about your information requirements before commencing your search. You should adopt, to use an often-quoted analogy, a rifle approach to the Internet rather than a shotgun approach. To help locate information on the Internet you will need to make use of search engines. You should check out the various 'search engines' to see how each of them operates and what each of them does. Most will have a 'help' or 'search tips' facility to guide you. The use of search engines is one of two basic approaches to surfing the Net. Search engines allow you to enter keywords so that documents matching the keywords are retrieved from the database. Tyner (1998) argues that 'In most cases, search engines are best used to locate a specific piece of information, such as a known document, an image, or a computer program, rather than a general subject'. Examples of popular search engines include:

- Alta Vista (http://altavista.digital.com)
- Excite (http://www.excite.com)
- Infoseek (http://guide.infoseek.com)

Be warned, however, most search engines index every word in a document. This greatly increases the chance of your search producing vast amounts of irrelevant material due to words occurring in what are, for you, inappropriate contexts. When writing this chapter, a search in Alta Vista for British Airways produced 32,177 matches! Looking at the contents of all those pages is clearly an impossible task, thus making the point that a more sophisticated search strategy was required with more specific search objectives. To help with this, search engines make use of what is known as Boolean logic in their searching. The basic Boolean operators are 'and', 'or' and 'not'. If, for example, you instructed the search engine to search for 'leisure and unemployment', it would retrieve documents that contain reference to both 'leisure' and 'unemployment'. If you search by 'leisure or unemployment' it would retrieve documents that contain reference to either 'leisure' or to 'unemployment'. If, however, you search by 'leisure not unemployment', then it will retrieve documents that contain reference to 'leisure' but not to 'unemployment'.

Search engines go about their work in different ways, and also display their results in different formats. Some offer additional operators to the three basic Boolean operators described above. Some offer the facility to search different parts of documents rather than simply defaulting to search the whole text. It is a case of sampling the various search engines, learning how they operate and seeing which one works best for you.

The other standard approach to searching the Internet is through the use of 'subject guides'. Tyner (1998) defines subject guides as 'hierarchically organized indexes of subject categories that allow the Internet searcher to browse through lists of websites by subject in search of relevant information'. Many of these subject guides include a search engine for use with their database. While subject guide databases tend to be smaller, they are more likely to produce relevant results, although searching in Magellan for 'tourism and the environment' produced 65,238 results ranked by relevance! As is the case with search engines, subject guides work in different ways and so it is a case of trying them out and deciding which you find most useful and user-friendly. Examples of subject guides include:

- Galaxy (http://www.einet.net)
- Magellan (http://www.mckinley.com)
- Yahoo (http://www.yahoo.com)

You are advised to use subject guides if you are looking for information on a general subject rather than searching for a specific piece of information. Most subjects now have specialist subject guides available on the Web – see, for example, Sportsonline (www.sportsonline.co.uk) for information on British sport. In addition, some websites function as collections or clearing houses of specialist subject guides. Tyner lists three examples:

- Argus Clearinghouse (http://www.clearinghouse.net)
- The Mining Company (http://www.miningco.com)
- WWW Virtual Library (http://www.vlib.org)

As you use search engines and subject guides you will naturally find pages that you will want to record for future use. In addition, many of the leisure and tourism journals now have regular features that look at Internet sites and provide a brief description of what they provide. Once you have visited these sites you may wish to store these for future use. To do this you should use the 'bookmark' or 'favourite' facility, which are quick ways of retrieving websites. For ease of reference you can organise stored addresses into folders of different subjects.

Our last tip for search strategies is to stay focused on what you are doing. The Internet is a big place and is full of dead-ends and distractions! The website discussed here (Tyner 1998) is a valuable resource for students. It is an online Workshop, which is periodically updated, and which provides guidance on the use of the Internet. It contains links to a number of search engines, subject guides and clearinghouses. In addition, there are a number of books that provide a more detailed guide to the Internet and to other sources of leisure and tourism data than we are able to provide here – see, for example, Scarrott (1999).

A final word of warning in this section, however. We have observed a virulent condition among students that has come to be known as Web Rot. The symptoms of Web Rot are as follows:

- a belief that if the information you are searching for is not on the Internet it does not exist or is not worth looking for
- a resulting inability to tear oneself away from the computer screen and look in the library
- an unquestioning belief in the information provided by an organisation's home page.

In other words, reliance on the Internet can make you lazy. Having said that it is a vast store of information, and that it is growing at a phenomenal rate, it is not a definitive source and, for the foreseeable future, much valuable secondary data will still only be found in books, printed reports, academic journals and on CD-ROM etc. Because the Internet is not regulated and because it is relatively easy to publish information on the Internet, the quality of the information can be poor and of dubious accuracy. You should therefore treat information found on the Internet in the same critical way that we hope you would treat all information. It is common for students when researching the marketing activities of a tourism company, for example, to go in the first instance to that company's website. You must appreciate, however, that the site itself is part of the organisation's marketing activities, and so the information made available and the 'spin' that is put on it will not be 'neutral'. The limitations of using secondary data that are discussed in detail below apply just as much to information on the Internet as anywhere else.

The advantages of secondary data analysis

Hakim (1982: 16) argues that 'One advantage of secondary analysis is that it forces the researcher to think more closely about the theoretical aims and substantive issues of the study rather than the practical and methodological problems of collecting new data'. Hakim also suggests that another advantage of secondary data analysis is that it shifts the focus from individual data subjects to a broader analysis of social conditions and change. Secondary data analysis also allows you to merge data from various sources in order to provide larger and more useable data sets, taking care of course to ensure that the data are compatible e.g. consistent definitions are used (see discussion below). Different individual data sets can also be used to test the same hypothesis thus establishing reliability if the same results are achieved.

Secondary data analysis also appeals for many practical reasons, not the least of which is the fact that it requires less time and effort to collect the data, making it much cheaper than most primary data collection. Freed from the time and effort involved in financing and obtaining primary data, the secondary data analyst can devote more of both to analysis and interpretation. The fact that a great deal of the material discussed in this chapter is readily available in the reference section of libraries means that the data is free of charge; added to which you are also getting for nothing the accumulated expertise of highly regarded research organisations. Secondary data analysis also offers a more flexible approach in that, subject to any deadlines, it can usually be carried out as and when it suits the researcher, and over long time periods. Having said that, secondary data analysis is also useful if quick results are needed and there is insufficient time to plan and conduct primary research.

Another attraction is that much of the data covers long time periods, thus allowing you to examine trends over time. Time can thus be used as a variable in the research. The Population Census is the obvious example here but data from continuous or regular surveys also allow us to conduct research of this nature as many of the important leisure and tourism surveys began in the 1960s and 1970s. The generation of time-series data, be it longitudinal or cross-sectional, is by definition a costly and time-consuming exercise taking it beyond the resources of most researchers. The researcher looking to examine trends over time is thus forced into considering secondary data analysis, although she/he could also consider primary research, with the results being compared with those from a previous similar survey. This process gives the results a time dimension. It is a perfectly legitimate research technique to repeat questions from previous surveys (suitably acknowledged, of course) as a means of assessing the reliability of findings, and of tracking changes over time.

A less obvious advantage is offered by Dale *et al.* (1988: 54) who suggest that serendipity can play a valuable role in secondary data analysis. As they point out, 'Secondary analysis of existing data can provide an opportunity to establish relationships that were entirely unforeseen at the time of data collection'.

Using secondary sources also means that you do not require access to data subjects and, as discussed elsewhere in this book, this can be a significant problem with other research methods. Secondary data analysis can also be used as a means of comparison against information collected by other methods, and it also allows researchers from different disciplines to bring fresh perspectives to a topic. Finally, as McNeill (1990: 103) reminds us, official statistics 'may be the only source of data on the topic in question'.

Problems and issues in undertaking secondary data analysis

Most of the problems associated with using leisure and tourism data, indeed with using any form of secondary data, arise from the fact that they have been collected for a particular purpose, usually an administrative one, and may not therefore be 'neutral' or in a form that the researcher would ideally like them to be. Government departments, tourism companies and tourism organisations have a vested interest in showing the economic importance of tourism, for example, whereas environmental pressure groups may be more concerned with highlighting the negative impacts associated with tourism development. Both 'sides' are likely to use different data in support of their argument or to interpret the same data in different ways. This is not to suggest some sort of conspiracy theory is at work, or to suggest that there are indeed lies, damned lies and statistics. Rather it is to alert you to the fact that in many cases, and for a number of different reasons, statistics are 'massaged', and that there are, therefore, potential problems in interpreting and using secondary data sources. More specific issues concerning the use of secondary data are discussed below under three broad headings:

- Problems of definition and reference periods
- Collection methods
- The form and reporting of secondary data

Problems of definition and reference periods

A fundamental and common problem is that of definition. This is not the place to get into debates about the definition of tourism, such debates are well covered in all the standard tourism texts – see, for example, Cooper *et al.* (1998) or Holloway (1998). While academics may agree, and there may be international agreements, different organisations may still be using different definitions of tourism or related concepts. Comparisons between data sets thus become fraught with difficulties. For example, the International Passenger Survey defines a 'visit' as a stay of 0–365 nights, whereas the United Kingdom Tourism Survey defines a 'visit' as a stay of 1–60 days.

Differences in definition and recording/reporting practices can lead to data that is apparently contradictory. For example, Lickorish (1997) points out that WTO figures for American visitors to Europe in 1990 show in excess of 15 million, whereas the European Travel Commission (ETC), utilising US government departure figures, has the total at under 7 million. The difference occurs because the ETC records individuals visiting Europe from America whereas the WTO counts border crossings by Americans. In other words, an individual American tourist visiting several European countries on the same trip will be counted more than once.

Most definitions of tourism require a person to be away from their normal place of residence for at least one night. For example, the WTO and the United Nations Statistical Commission define tourism as 'The activities of persons travelling to and staying in places outside their usual environment for not more than one consecutive year for leisure, business and other purposes' (quoted in Cooper *et al.* 1998: 8). In other words, people going on a day's shopping trip from Britain to the hypermarkets of Europe, for example, are not classified as tourists. They will be termed 'day-trippers' or something similar. The impact of day trips is clearly a crucial one in assessing overall levels of activity however. As Edwards (1991: 64) points out:

> *many of the really big country to country flows are dominated by day trips. Two thirds of all US trips to Canada and an even bigger share of Canadian visits to the USA are day trips. Their share is also very high for many country to country flows within Europe.*

The problem is that many of these day trips will be undertaken by people living in one country and working in another. Some countries include such movements in their tourism data, which will clearly distort the figures as just one worker may well be making over 200 such crossings each year! The economic impact of day trips is also variable. Where cheaper shopping is involved, the economic impact may be considerable. It is, however, easy to think of a day trip that will involve zero expenditure in the destination country.

The problem of different 'reference periods' can arise when attempting to compare leisure data sets. This is evident in Cushman *et al.* (1996), who show that national leisure participation surveys use vastly different time periods within which participation is recorded. These range from a couple of days to a year. Clearly, the greater the reference period the higher the participation rates will appear. Having a one-year reference period has the advantage of tackling seasonality, but the disadvantage of requiring accurate recall over a long period of time. Some surveys, such as the GHS in Great Britain, include short time periods (four weeks) and lengthy ones (12 months) within which participation is recorded.

The issue of changing definitions is important in leisure and tourism research, and a relatively minor change can radically alter how we view things. If we take the UKTS as an example, one of the topics that this survey measures is the extent of visiting friends and relatives (VFR) tourism. However, in measuring this, the UKTS defines a VFR tourist as someone who gives this as the main motive for their trip (VFR motive trip). People who stay with friends and relatives but who do not give this as their main motive are recorded separately (VFR accommodation trip). Research by Seaton and Palmer (1997 – see Figure 4.1) shows that the level of VFR activity by accommodation is twice as large as actual recorded VFR activity. They argue that, for a number of reasons, this distinction between VFR by motive and VFR by accommodation is unsatisfactory and that:

> *A case could be made for arguing that accommodation VFRs should be counted as VFRs like any other. The effect of so doing, as the UKTS data shows, would be a massive increase in the importance of VFR tourism and a proportionate reduction in the importance of all other tourism categories.*   (Seaton and Palmer 1997: 353)

Collection methods

Leaving aside these very real problems of definition, and the associated one of how to consider day-trippers, there are also a series of logistical problems concerned with the collection of tourism data, which casts further doubt on their accuracy. For example, given the difficulties of recording cross-border traffic flows on busy routes, many countries record only accommodation arrivals, but here too we have problems as it is often only hotel information that is recorded. In other words, people visiting friends and relatives, people staying in second homes, holiday cottages or timeshare accommodation, and people camping or staying in bed and breakfast accommodation may not find their way into the tourism figures. For some countries, given the nature of their accommodation supply, this can create a far from accurate picture of tourism activity.

Tourism statistics are thus collected in a variety of ways around the globe. In some countries it is a legal requirement for accommodation businesses to collect data, in other countries statistics are generated by border crossings either through a process of registration or by a sample survey. As Latham (1998: 46) reminds us, 'Methodologies range from the highly scientific and sophisticated to the clumsy and naïve'. Given these problems of definition and differences in data collection methods, Latham concludes that the secondary data analyst cannot be sure of the accuracy of the figures, but can have confidence about the direction and size of any changes that are apparent.

The data collection methods may then change over time, again making comparisons difficult, if not impossible. Let us take a leisure example from the GHS, and compare participation in leisure activities between 1973 and 1977. In 1973, 38 per cent of respondents listed gardening as one of their leisure activities. In 1977, this figure had risen to 57 per cent. This remarkable increase could be explained by aggressive marketing or by some other phenomenon. A more likely explanation is that in 1977 the interviewers prompted the respondents by mentioning certain leisure activities, one of which was gardening. A similar pattern was in fact found for the other 'prompted' activities. In other words, the method of data collection had, in part, accounted for the changes in the findings.

The form and reporting of secondary data

Another problem is that much of the tourism information may only be available at the national level, whereas the researcher may require data at the regional or local level. Following on from this, the aggregation of data may lead to an important loss of detail. We often talk about the North/South divide in the UK, but this fails to acknowledge that there are areas of considerable affluence in the North of England as well as areas of significant deprivation in the South of England. We need, also, to be careful in our use of geographical definitions. We may, for example, be researching tourism in Eastern Europe, but there is no agreement on the countries that constitute Eastern Europe.

As mentioned earlier, the data may often be unavailable in the form you would like it to be, and so may only approximate to what is required. Harvey and MacDonald (1993: 90) refer to this problem as arising from the 'rigidity of the data'. For example, data may only be made available in tabular form in which case you can only carry out your secondary analysis within the framework of the table, which may or may not be restricting. If it is restricting, then one solution, assuming you have the time and the data is available, is to consult the original data in the appropriate data archive. The largest source of electronic data in the UK is The Data Archive located at the University of Essex. This holds in excess of 7,000 data sets, and includes not only UK data but also access to foreign data. Users of the Data Archive can be supplied with data in a variety of formats such as cartridge, floppy disk, CD-ROM, and via the academic computer networks of JANET and SuperJANET. Access to the data is charged for but the scale of charges varies according to the funding source of the applicant. The best way of finding out about the information held in the Data Archive is via the Internet and the archive's online catalogue and topic index known as Bibliographic Information Retrieval Online (BIRON). This catalogue provides abstracts of the studies held. At the time of writing, 137 studies were listed in the 'leisure, recreation and tourism' topic section of BIRON including National Park visitor surveys, accommodation surveys, sports facility surveys and day visitor surveys. The Internet address for BIRON can be found at the end of this chapter.

Another problem with conducting secondary data analysis is that there can be considerable delay between the research being conducted and the statistics being made available. Mention has already been made of the GHS, but data from this annual survey is often not published until at least 12 months after the year to which the data refers. For the manager having to respond quickly to rapidly changing market conditions, as so often occur in the leisure and tourism environment, such a delay is unacceptable.

Finally, the ways in which statistics are reported are also of interest; indeed embarrassing data may never see the light of day or may be hidden away in the corners of reports. If you look at recent editions of *Social Trends*, for example, and the press reporting of their publication, then you could easily get the impression that we are all getting richer, having more leisure time and taking more holidays. While this may well be true for some sections of society, it most certainly is not for others.

Evaluating secondary data

The quality of tourism data is variable, and you should appreciate from what has been said so far that there is a potential problem of validity with much of the data you are likely to use. This has led Ryan (1995: 128) to conclude that 'tourism and economic statistics are actually notorious for being subject to quite significant levels of error'. Similarly, Edwards (1991: 67) argues that when considering tourism statistics, 'even when full allowance is made for differences in definition and coverage, a significant proportion of tourist data do not measure very accurately what they are aiming to measure, whether frontier arrivals, accommodation arrivals, nights spent, receipts or expenditures'. Edwards attributes this situation to three main factors – unsatisfactory data collection methods, poor sample design or small samples producing unacceptably high levels of sampling error and a failure to follow agreed data collection procedures.

A similar criticism can be levelled at the leisure statistics. We have seen that the key source of leisure participation data is the GHS but, as this information is generated from an interview survey, it suffers from the same potential problem of all such surveys i.e. the accuracy of the data. How confident can we be that the answers people give to questions about their leisure lifestyles are actually a true reflection of their leisure participation rates? If you ask someone which leisure activities they participated in during the previous four weeks, and the frequency of that participation, there are a number of reasons why their answer may be inaccurate. They may have trouble remembering that far back. They may wish to impress the interviewer. They may give an answer that they think pleases the interviewer. They may give, erroneously, what they think is the right answer. They may not want to reveal the right answer (perhaps because someone else is present!) The only way we could be 100 per cent confident about the accuracy of people's leisure participation rates is to follow them for a month, which is clearly impractical, or perhaps to use a diary method of data collection, although this too suffers from many of the drawbacks just mentioned. There is always therefore a potential problem of validity with such data.

Reliability, as we have already seen, can also be an issue. Data generated from official surveys comes from rigorously adhered to methods and is thus a reliable source. The professionalism of organisations such as the Office for National Statistics is well known, and so we can have confidence in the reliability of the data they generate. In addition, the sample sizes of their surveys are large, and so the level of statistical error is small. Referring to the GHS, Veal (1992: 70) argues that:

> *the fact that there has been little dramatic variation in the findings of the various surveys over the years is reassuring . . . , erratic and unexplainable fluctuations in reported levels of participation would have led to suspicions that the surveys are unreliable, but this has not happened.*

We cannot be so confident about the reliability of other sources. For example, the UK tourism industry contains a large number of small businesses. Running a small business is not easy, and those involved have more urgent concerns than providing data for government or whoever. The reliability of data from such sources is therefore questionable.

This last point is important as it reminds us that not all official statistics are generated from social surveys, many are collected by a process of registration i.e. form filling. Slattery (1986), however, points out that this process too can suffer from problems of reliability and validity. Unreliable data can arise if forms are not completed, or are not completed properly, or if they are collated and analysed incorrectly. A problem of validity occurs with the registration process if, for example, a lack of clarity with the form means that respondents are not actually answering the questions being put. Indeed, many of the issues discussed earlier, the problem of definition, for example, apply just as much to data generated by registration as to that obtained by social surveys.

For a more detailed discussion of the issues raised in this section, readers are referred to the paper by Edwards (1991). Although this paper was written before the WTO's 1991 International Conference on Travel and Tourism Statistics that clarified many of the issues of definition and measurement, it remains a valuable and comprehensive discussion. Indeed, as the WTO itself acknowledges, many problems still remain. In the introduction to their *Yearbook of Tourism Statistics* they discuss the progress made concerning the compatibility of their data and point out that 'much work remains to be done in this area and therefore, a number of tables serve only as a source of data which might require further adjustment before being used for any meaningful studies' (World Tourism Organization 1995: viii). For a discussion of the history of tourism statistics and recent initiatives to harmonise their collection along with a consideration of the issues involved in developing reliable tourism data, see Lickorish (1997).

Summary

This chapter has drawn the distinction between primary and secondary data, and has focused on the analysis of secondary data using examples of published research. Major sources of quantitative leisure and tourism data have been discussed, and students of leisure and tourism are strongly advised to follow up these sources in order to see what is available. Secondary data analysis has been evaluated throughout this chapter, and the advantages, issues and problems have been discussed in some detail. The leisure and tourism researcher should be aware of these potential pitfalls and be prepared to work within these constraints. In particular she/he should not rely on just one data source or on just one indicator, but instead should look, for example, at tourist flows from both the country of origin and the country of destination, and should support that analysis with data on other aspects such as nights spent and receipts/expenditure. Only then is an accurate picture likely to emerge. As Harvey and MacDonald (1993: 85) write:

> published statistics, then, should be seen not as 'facts' but as evidence for the social researcher. In the end, published statistics are data like any other data and they cannot be detached from the theoretical context within which they were generated. It is important to read statistics, and the commentaries on them, as critically as any other forms of evidence.

This is not to say that this sort of data is unusable. Far from it, much valuable research can and has been undertaken using secondary data analysis. You should, however, treat your secondary data sources as just one more piece of the jigsaw that you, the researcher, are trying to complete.

Student Activities

Activity 1

1. Test the notion that participation in leisure activities increased dramatically in England and Wales over the period 1977–96.

2. Investigate the hypothesis that the type and intensity of leisure activity varies according to gender, age and socio-economic grouping.

Activity 2

1. Test the hypothesis that between 1975 and 1995 visitors to inland 'heritage' attractions increased at the expense of seaside areas.

2. Investigate the hypothesis that between 1975 and 1995 there was a growing North/South divide in the UK in terms of tourism numbers.

Useful Addresses

This section provides an alphabetical listing of the organisations discussed in this chapter along with their address, telephone number and website.

Arts Council of England
14 Great Peter Street
London SW1P 3NQ
Tel: 0171 973 6458
Website: http://www.artscouncil.org.uk

British Tourist Authority/English Tourist Board
Thames Tower
Black's Road
Hammersmith
London W6 9EL
Tel: 0181 846 9000
Website: http://www.bta.org.uk

The Countryside Agency
John Dower House
Crescent Place
Cheltenham GL50 3RA
Tel: 01242 521381
Website: http://www.countryside.gov.uk

The Data Archive
University of Essex
Wivenhoe Park
Colchester CO4 3SQ
Tel: 01206 872001
Website: http://dawww.essex.ac.uk

English Sports Council
16 Upper Woburn Place
London WC1H 0QP
Tel: 0171 273 1500
Website: http://www.english.sports.gov.uk

Euromonitor
60–61 Britton Street
London EC1M 5NA
Tel: 0171 251 8024
Website: http://www.euromonitor.com

EUROSTAT
Statistical Office of the European Communities
Jean Monnet Building
Rue Alcide De Gasperi
L-2920 Luxembourg
Tel: (+352) 4301–34567
Website: http://europa.eu.int/

The Henley Centre
9 Bridewell Place
London EC4V 6AY
Tel: 0171 955 1812
Website: http://www.henleycentre.com

Key Note Ltd
Field House
72 Oldfield Road
Hampton TW12 2HQ
Tel: 0181 481 8750
Website: http://www.keynote.co.uk/

Mintel International Group Ltd
18–19 Long Lane
London EC1A 9HE
Tel: 0171 606 4533
Website: http://www.mintel.co.uk

Office for National Statistics
1 Drummond Gate
London SW1V 2QQ
Tel: 0171 533 5444
Website: http://www.ons.gov.uk

Travel & Tourism Intelligence
48 Bedford Square
London WC1B 3DP
Tel: 0171 814 3800
Website: http://www.t-ti.com/index.htm

The World Tourism Organization
Capitán Haya, 42
28020 Madrid
Spain
Tel: (34) 91 567 81 00/20
Website: http://www.world-tourism.org/wtich.htm

References

- Butler, R. W. (1985) 'Evolution of tourism in the Scottish Highlands', *Annals of Tourism Research*, Vol. 12 (3), pp. 371–91.
- Cooper, C., Fletcher, J., Gilbert, D., Shepherd, R. and Wanhill, S. (1998) *Tourism Principles & Practice*, Second Edition, Harlow: Addison Wesley Longman.
- Cringely, R. X. (1998) 'The Glory of the Geeks', Oregon Public Broadcasting, Channel 4, 3 October 1998.
- Cushman, G., Veal, A. J. and Zuzanek, J. (eds) (1996) *World Leisure Participation: Free Time in the Global Village*, Wallingford: CAB International.
- Dale, A., Arber, S. and Procter, M. (1988) *Doing Secondary Analysis*, London: Unwin Hyman.
- Edwards, A. (1991) 'The reliability of tourism statistics', *EIU Travel & Tourism Analyst*, No. 1, pp. 62–75.

● Gratton, C. (1996) 'Great Britain', in Cushman, G., Veal, A. J. and Zuzanek, J. (eds) *World Leisure Participation: Free Time in the Global Village*, Wallingford: CAB International, pp. 113–30.

● Gratton, C. and Tice, A. (1994) 'Trends in sports participation in Britain: 1977–1987', *Leisure Studies*, Vol. 13 (1), pp. 49–66.

● Hakim, C. (1982) *Secondary Analysis in Social Research: A Guide to Data Sources and Methods with Examples*, London: Allen & Unwin.

● Harvey, L. and MacDonald, M. (1993) *Doing Sociology*, Basingstoke: The Macmillan Press Ltd.

● Holloway, J. C. (1998) *The Business of Tourism*, Fifth Edition, Harlow: Addison Wesley Longman.

● Latham, J. (1998) 'Patterns of international tourism', *Progress in Tourism and Hospitality Research*, Vol. 4, pp. 45–52.

● Lickorish, L. J. (1997) 'Travel statistics – the slow move forward', *Tourism Management*, Vol. 18 (8), pp. 491–7.

● McNeill, P. (1990) *Research Methods*, Second Edition, London: Routledge.

● Ryan, C. (1995) *Researching Tourist Satisfaction*, London: Routledge.

● Scarrott, M. (ed.) (1999) *Sport, Leisure & Tourism Information Sources, A Guide for Researchers*, Oxford: Butterworth-Heinemann.

● Seaton, A. V. and Palmer, C. (1997) 'Understanding VFR tourism behaviour: the first five years of the United Kingdom tourism survey', *Tourism Management*, Vol. 18 (6), pp. 345–55.

● Slattery, M. (1986) *Official Statistics*, London: Tavistock Publications.

● Tyner, R. (1998) Sink or swim: Internet search tools & techniques [online], available from: http://www.ouc.bc.ca/libr/connect96/search.htm [last accessed 27 April 2000].

● Veal, A. J. (1992) *Research Methods for Leisure and Tourism*, Harlow: Longman.

● Whyman, J. (1972) 'Visitors to Margate in the 1841 census returns', *Local Population Studies*, No. 8, pp. 19–38.

● World Tourism Organization (1995) *Yearbook of Tourism Statistics*, Forty-Seventh Edition, Madrid: WTO.

Chapter 5

Qualitative Methods

Learning Outcomes

At the end of this chapter you will be able to:

- demonstrate the importance of ethnographic work to leisure and tourism research
- define and carry out ethnographic research
- make an informed choice on how to collect qualitative data
- assess the strengths and weaknesses of ethnographic research using qualitative methods
- distinguish between different types of interviewing, including focus groups
- undertake life history research
- assess the value of personal diaries as a method of data collection
- use a case study strategy to research

Ethnography

We have argued earlier that phenomenological approaches used by ethnographers employing qualitative techniques differ fundamentally from positivist approaches used by researchers using survey and experimental methods generating quantitative data. The emphasis from the phenomenological or interpretative point of view is on theory 'grounded' in data (seeking generalisations from the particular), whereas a positivist is more likely to be testing hypotheses with data. Although this is normally the case, it must be made clear that ethnographers sometimes do test hypotheses.

An ethnographer is less likely to be narrow and restrictive in his/her approach to research. The hypothetico-deductive method used by positivists is a rigid procedure, whereas the ethnographer will use a more flexible approach to the research process and focus on emergent themes or even alter the course of the research during the research process. For the ethnographer the perspectives and interpretations of those being researched become the key to understanding human behaviour. The ethnographer does not consider research to be an objective process because the main interest is the subjectivity of human behaviour. Individuals actively shape situations and events and are not passive responders to external stimuli. The context of the research assumes great importance as ethnographers carry out their research in naturalistic settings, and aim to give a holistic view of individuals in their setting to enhance understanding. Context and behaviour are interlinked.

The word 'ethnography' means a description of peoples or their cultures. Social anthropologists have used it in social science research for a long period of time. It was originally used to study small, isolated tribes before they became 'contaminated' by contact with the 'civilised' world. From these early beginnings, the research strategy used by anthropologists was widened to study more contemporary cultures like communities, gangs, the police, factory workers etc., and has been used by researchers in leisure and tourism, as will be explained later.

Unlike the experimental style of research, which imposes artificial controls over the research setting, ethnographic research studies people in their natural setting. Understanding the meanings and cultural practices of the people from within becomes the focus of study. Ethnographers interpret everyday events in which they become involved. The values and structures of a society are seen as having an internal structure of their own. As an outsider, the researcher enters the group under study and is confronted with a strange and possibly incomprehensible world. The ethnographer enters this world and a process of learning takes place. The outsider becomes an insider and begins the process of understanding the culture of the group, a culture that is self-explanatory to the group members but problematic to the researcher. For the ethnographer this world is socially constructed and he/she has entered the group to understand how members of the group make sense of their own world. But involvement and entering into relationships with the people being researched can disturb the natural setting. This prompts the ethnographer to reflect on the research process and assess the degree to which the natural setting has been disturbed.

An excellent example of the reflective ethnographer is Bruner's (1995) discussion of his dual role as a researcher and as a tour guide to Indonesia for affluent American tourists. As an ethnographer his aim was to study how tourists experienced the tourist sites in Indonesia. But he encountered a fundamental problem. As tour guide it was his job to structure the experience for the American tourists. He realised that:

> *My talk mediated their experience and, in a sense, I found myself studying myself . . . I constructed for the tourists the meaning of the sites and then I studied that meaning as if I had discovered it.* (Bruner 1995: 231)

Bruner's (1995) account of his experiences deserves to be read in full.

The case for qualitative methods

For many, ethnography is viewed as a reaction to a positivist approach to research. Indeed, much of the debate about ethnography and qualitative methods in general in leisure and tourism confirms this (see, for example, Hemingway 1995). Ethnography attempts to understand the complexity of people's lives in a way that the survey or the experiment cannot. For example, Scott and Godbey (1990: 189) argue that 'A number of investigators in recent years have criticised the state of leisure research for its over-reliance on survey methods that yield strictly quantitative data'.

Putting the case for qualitative methods, they emphasise that '. . . qualitative methods provide valuable insight into the social and contextual circumstances surrounding leisure involvement'.

Figure 5.1
Ideas for
qualitative
research.

Cohen (1988) analyses how academics from disciplines outside of tourism have contributed to research developments. He argues that Boorstin's (1964) concept of the 'pseudo-event' and the modern tourist's quest for the security of the familiar, contrasts with MacCannell's (1976) idea that tourists search for 'authenticity'. Cohen emphasises that concepts like 'authenticity' and 'staged authenticity' are not 'given', they change and evolve. He points out: 'Instead of asking whether the tourist's experience *is* authentic, one can now ask what is the connotation and denotation of authenticity in the tourist's own eyes...' Cohen also describes the work of Turner (1973) and his three stages approach of separation, liminality and reintegration. All three academics described by Cohen have contributed to our understanding of the tourist experience, and he concludes his paper by comparing the three authors: 'The three traditions thus stand in an intriguing, and often ironic contrapuntal relationship. They relate to touristic phenomena on different levels and from varying perspectives which induce them to widely different interpretations of the same empirical data'.

Source: Cohen (1988)

Scott and Godbey's paper (1990: 194–9) discusses how qualitative research can be used to study leisure behaviour:

1. Leisure as experience – where leisure is viewed in subjective terms as a state of mind, experience or feeling, and not as a fixed measurement.

2. Leisure behaviour as a formative process – the form and meaning of leisure involvement changes over time as new situations and circumstances are confronted.

3. Leisure behaviour as a group phenomenon – the individual can be analysed in the context of a group as leisure involvement is embedded in social interaction.

Scott and Godbey (1990: 201) conclude that 'The biggest reason for the continuing emergence of qualitative methods in leisure studies, however, is a more fundamental one – the appropriateness of such methods to the understanding of the subject matter'.

Two years earlier Cohen (1988) outlined three main traditions in what he called the qualitative sociology of tourism. Like Scott and Godbey, Cohen argues that qualitative methods have been neglected in tourism and says that sociologists of tourism have given qualitative methodology '... scarce, if any, explicit consideration' (page 30).

For the would-be researcher the three emergent traditions of Boorstin, MacCannell and Turner, cited in Cohen (1988), are well worth closer attention.

For the serious researcher in leisure and tourism there is much inspiration in these pleas for more qualitative research. Ideas abound, as demonstrated in the Cohen (1988) article. Conceptual developments as detailed in Figure 5.1 will help give qualitative methodology a more theoretical orientation. There is clearly more to qualitative approaches than 'thick description'.

Characteristics of ethnographic research

The main characteristics of the ethnographic style of research are:

1. The researcher usually spends a considerable amount of time among the people he or she is researching, in order to understand the culture of the people. As an ethnographer, the researcher will share the lives of the people he or she is studying and observe them from a position of detachment. Time is needed for the ethnographer to gain access to the research setting and to be accepted by the people being researched.

2. The ethnographer regards routine and normal aspects of life worthy of consideration. The mundane and ordinary parts of life are seen as just as important as major events or incidents out of the ordinary.

3. How the people being researched see their own world is more important to the researcher. What meanings those being researched attach to their reality and how they perceive the situation themselves are more important. The ethnographer does not come into the research setting with pre-conceived notions of what to expect.

4. The ethnographer is also interested in all aspects of the culture being studied, and avoids isolating individual aspects of the culture. Rather than focus on individual parts, the ethnographer takes a holistic view stressing processes, relationships, connections and the interdependency of the component parts.

5. Inevitably, the final research report will contain much description. But it is not just description. There will be an attempt to interpret the data to give the reader an understanding of what processes have shaped the culture, and how relationships have formed etc. This will usually be done by reference to a conceptual framework derived from theory.

We can summarise these five characteristics as time-consuming, importance of the everyday, gaining an insight into the perspectives of those being researched, holistic and interpretation through theory.

The ethnographic researcher should also be aware that ethnographic methods have weaknesses relating to lack of representativeness and the ability to replicate the study. These points have been dealt with earlier. Here it is worth alerting the enthusiastic ethnographic researcher to the problem of gaining access to the group under study. For example, if our researcher wants to interview key personnel in a leisure or tourism organisation, then there are problems of gaining access. You are strongly recommended to read the article by Thomas called 'Interviewing important people in big companies' in the *Journal of Contemporary Ethnography*, April 1993. Thomas reflects on the barriers to access and data on what top business executives do, and offers advice on how these can be surmounted, emphasising the importance of preparation of both the researcher and the people being researched.

Gill and Johnson (1997) recognise a number of problems that arise in management research using ethnographic methods. They include:

- gaining access to boardroom meetings
- interpreting formal and informal events
- learning the culture
- stress of maintaining objectivity and empathising with the 'actors'
- generalising from small samples.

For more information on the activities of senior managers or 'elites' using ethnographic methods, see Gill and Johnson (1997: 105–8).

Methods of data collection

Ethnographers can choose from a variety of approaches to collect data. Nevertheless, the nature and purpose of the research, and the time and resources available will all affect how the research is carried out. Once the constraints on how the research is to be carried out have been recognised, the ethnographer has to decide what role he or she is going to adopt to collect the relevant data.

For the researcher there is a simple method of classifying the various roles of the ethnographer. The researcher's role can be either a full participant or an observing spectator, and is dependent on whether the subjects of the research are aware of the researcher's role (overt) or not (covert).

Participant observation involves participating fully in the lives of those being studied to share their experiences. Here the researcher can get very close to the focus of the research and penetrate the complexity of the society or culture. This form of in-depth probe may uncover hidden meanings and aid a deeper understanding of external behaviour. The researcher usually has to adopt 'an almost passive demeanour, absorbing information through observation and conversation in a non-directive manner' (O'Connell Davidson and Layder 1994: 168). If the role is one only of observation, then the lack of interaction with the subjects can raise problems. As a researcher just observing events, there is the danger that interpretations of events will reflect the researcher's own value judgements and not that of the culture being studied. Yet standing back from the research situation mitigates against 'going native', where the researcher is unable to take a dispassionate view of events, and may fail to gain any real understanding of nuances of everyday interaction. As an observer the researcher is less likely to 'contaminate' or change behaviour in the research setting. On the other hand the full participant observer, by involving himself/herself in events, may unwittingly influence events in the field.

But should the ethnographer conduct research where the role of the researcher is hidden (covert research), or should those being researched know and be aware of the presence of the researcher? Any community that is being researched may behave differently if they are aware that they are being observed. This reactivity between the subjects of the community and the researcher in a piece of covert research may therefore reduce the validity of the data. This lends support for participant observation carried out covertly as a method of data collection. Covert research is favoured by ethnographers as it allows them to use their role more effectively in the research process and, through manipulation, to focus more on the aims of the research. In addition, some research would not be possible if the community knew that research was being undertaken. To what extent the deception associated with covert participant observation is defensible has been aired earlier (see the discussion of ethical considerations in research in Chapter 3).

Participant observation is a technique of ethnographic research that is probably best suited to projects which emphasise interpretations of events, interaction between 'actors' and the importance attached to language and meanings. For the would-be participant observer there are some general, practical points which need to be borne in mind (see Table 5.1).

Recording of data is in itself a selective exercise and the researcher may have concerns over whether the notes are too general or that something important has not been recorded. This would cast doubt on the validity of the data. May (1997: 145) quotes the work of Bruyn (1966) who used six indices of 'subjective adequacy' to enhance the understanding of the researcher. They are:

- *Time*: as process is the focus of research then the more time spent with a group the greater the understanding

- *Place*: physical locations influence actions as they are the context for behaviour

- *Social circumstances*: relating to the group in a variety of roles or activities

- *Language*: the more familiar with language the greater the understanding

Table 5.1
Key issues in
participant
observation

Stages in the research	Key issues to consider
Access and entering the research setting	Covert or overt research?, entering public/private settings – implications?, conceal or reveal my intentions?, identify and 'brush-up' on interpersonal skills
Conduct during the research	Be positive, adopt a non-threatening approach, be polite, respectful, interested and empathise with those being researched
Recording data	Note-taking techniques: time-consuming with self-discipline, use more than one source of data
Leaving the research setting	Practical or theoretical reasons for finishing, ease out gently and keep actors informed after the research if possible

Table 5.2
Typology of
qualitative
organisational
research
strategies

Type	Degree of participation	Number of organisations and data collection techniques
1	Total participant	1–2 organisations, covert/overt, participant observation, some interviewing and document examination
2	Semi-participant	1–2 organisations, overt/covert, observer, interviewing and document examination
3	Interview-based	1–5 organisations, overt, interviews, some observation and document examination
4	Multi-site	6+ organisations, overt, interviews and observations, some document examination

- *Intimacy*: the greater the personal involvement the greater the understanding
- *Social consensus*: how the meanings in the culture being researched are used and shared among the group

If the focus of the research is centred around understanding organisations in leisure and tourism, then Bryman (1989: 152) provides a typology of qualitative organisational research that combine the degree of participation, number of organisations and techniques of data collection.

Table 5.2 illustrates the point that the degree of involvement varies across the four types based on the number of organisations that form part of the research.

Examples from leisure and tourism research

Sandiford and Ap (1998) provide the best recent overview of the application of ethnography to tourism. They emphasise that ethnography can assist in putting a tourism planning model like that of Getz (1986) into practice. Ethnographic insights can help understand and interpret planning issues and community attitudes (Sandiford and Ap 1998: 10). The two authors identify various ways ethnographic research can help in the planning process. They include:

- tourists' perspectives
- assess social and cultural impacts on host populations
- full descriptions to help understand and interpret current and past tourist phenomena
- help interpret data from other sources like a survey.

Sandiford and Ap (1998) illustrate the usefulness of ethnographic research by drawing on a range of examples. In particular, they refer to the work of Adams (1992) who researched the impacts of tourist trekking on a Sherpa community in Nepal.

Although it is unlikely that a student undertaking research as part of a degree or BTEC course will opt for an extended period studying a remote community, ethnographic work can offer important insights into issues geographically nearer and more accessible. Robinson and Marlor (1995) carried out a small-scale study that aimed to find out the level and type of information given to the prospective tourist by tour operators and travel agents. Their research focused on tourism and violence and how these risks are communicated. The data collection method used in the research was participant observation and was conducted covertly. The researcher posed as a potential customer wanting to buy a holiday in either Florida, Turkey or Egypt (countries where foreign tourists have been attacked recently).

Fifty travel agents were sampled from northeast England. Where this study differs from the more traditional ethnographic community/village studies is that a pre-determined framework was used to compare responses from the different travel agents. The framework or set of 'benchmarks' was derived from a pilot study of five travel agents. These benchmarks were deemed necessary as points of reference in the holiday booking process when advice was most likely to be offered. In many respects Robinson and Marlor conducted a sample survey, but the data collected were qualitative and not obtained by a questionnaire or interview. The results of the research were based on the interaction between the researcher and the booking clerks in a naturalistic setting (the travel agency). The pre-determined benchmarks made it possible to compare results across the 50 travel agents.

Figure 5.2 shows an example of ethnographic research. Another good example that is well worth a more detailed analysis is the research by Glancy (1986) which examined the social-psychological context of recreational sport-group participation.

Interviewing

Choosing to collect data using an interview needs to be thought out carefully as there are different types of interviews depending on the aims of the research. We can identify three main types of interviews defined by their degree of structure:

1. *Structured interview*: This type of interview is associated with the survey style of research where a standard interview schedule is designed to answer a series of specific questions on a face-to-face basis. This interview structure will produce quantitative data for analysis.

2. *Semi-structured interview*: Interviews of this nature will have specified questions but will allow more probing to seek clarification and elaboration. They would have more latitude than the structured interview.

Figure 5.2

An example of
ethnographic
research.

Another example examines sport tourism as a celebration of a sub-culture. This is the research of Green and Chalip (1998). In their research, recreation is viewed as an important component of the tourist experience, but Green and Chalip argue that sport tourism has rarely been researched on its own. A distinction is made between attendance at sports events and participation in sports activities. The two authors focus on a participative sports event – the Key West Women's Flag Football Tournament – to study the relationship between the players and the event. Participant observation was used in this exploratory study which took a 'qualitative, grounded theory approach'. Each author researched the tournament from a different perspective. One author concentrated on an insider's account, observing and interviewing players and officials, while the other author focused on an outsider's account, observing and interviewing participants. The aim was to obtain two perspectives, one from an active participant and the other a detached view from the outside. Fieldwork was carried out in an overt way as players and officials were informed of the research.

In addition to observation, interviewing and tournament documents were used to collect data. Interviews were open-ended and generated qualitative data supplementing the observational data and information from newsletters and programmes. This inductive, exploratory piece of research generated data that was analysed for the generation of grounded theory. Concepts and categories emerged from the data analysis that the two authors compared, discussed and refined. Their aim was to produce a reliable and valid description of the tournament experience and the 'social context from which it obtains its market'.

After a detailed description of the tournament, Chalip and Green provide an understanding of the sub-culture of women's flag football. This analysis is backed up by quotations from actual participants. Participants have attended the tournament for more than just playing the game together. Key categories that emerge from the data analysis include:

- players make a statement about themselves, unconstrained by conventions
- teams develop into social communities – importance of socialisation
- both lesbian and heterosexuals participate – effect on language, status and humour.

There is a clear link between the sub-culture of women's football and a player's sense of identity. The tournament provides an opportunity to celebrate being a football player. Everyday events like walking around and chatting to each other give players an opportunity to parade their identity and socialise. Teams at the tournament use the actual games differently. For some it is the image of being a football player that is the most important, whereas for others it is the level of skill demonstrated.

There does seem to be a message for event organisers as official social events, informal social life, and the game complement each other 'as a mosaic of sub-culture celebrations'.

The two authors refer to existing tourism research to understand and ground their data analysis in theory. Reference is made to:

- Iso-Ahola (1989): escaping everyday lives (opportunity to be a football player)
- Graburn (1989): partaking in non-ordinary experiences (travel to the tournament is a pilgrimage)
- Geertz (1972): concept of deep play (no material gain, celebration of the sub-culture).

Chalip and Green claim that there are lessons for sports event organisers based on this research:

- guidelines for intensifying the celebrations of the sub-culture
- use of formal (official) and informal spaces
- facilitation of informal and formal social interaction.

They conclude that what makes a tournament worth travelling for is that it gives the participants an opportunity 'to escape the conventionality of their daily lives by celebrating the sub-culture they uniquely share'.

Source: Green and Chalip (1998)

3. *Unstructured interview:* The name 'unstructured' is a misnomer as no interview can have a total lack of structure. This type of interview has also been called a 'semi-structured' interview (using the same name as the previous type), a 'depth' interview, a 'qualitative' interview or an 'exploratory' interview. This type of interview is the one associated with ethnographic research where the aim is to understand the perspective of the interviewee and the meanings that the interviewee attaches to situations and contexts important to him or her.

To undertake a successful ethnographic interview the researcher must establish a feeling of trust and rapport with the interviewee. The interviewer should be understanding, non-judgemental, sympathetic, able to empathise, knowledgeable of the situation and able to appreciate the interviewee's point of view. These are the personal attributes that make a good ethnographic interviewer.

One of the main problems with any interview is that it involves the establishment of an asymmetrical relationship between the interviewer and the interviewee. The interviewer controls the topics and comes to know the interviewee without having to engage in a reciprocal process of personal 'social striptease'. The ethnographic interviewer aims to minimise this conception of the social process by sharing experiences, giving personal details to solicit personal details from the interviewee, avoiding a special 'researcher' pose and aiming to be unobtrusive in as 'natural' a context as possible. An interview is seen as an open, democratic, informal, free-flowing, two-way process, involving an element of negotiation to gain co-operation with guarantees of protection of identity.

The advantages and disadvantages of the three types of interviews are summarised in Table 5.3.

Type of interview	Advantages	Disadvantages
Structured	Interviewees answer same questions, increasing the comparability of the responses	Very little flexibility and the standardised wording may inhibit responses
	Interviewer bias reduced	Pre-determined questions may not be relevant
	Data easily analysed using statistical techniques	
Semi-structured	Combines the flexibility of the unstructured interview with comparability of key questions	Bias may increase as interviewer selects questions to probe and may inhibit comparability of responses
Unstructured	Interviewer responds in a flexible way to the interviewee	Comparability is much reduced and data analysis is more difficult
	Interviewer's role is minimal allowing interviewee to express ideas in his/her own words	Data quality depends on listening and communicating skills of the interviewer

Table 5.3
Advantages and disadvantages of three types of interviews

Whereas some researchers use one of the above types of interview in their research, it is more common to find examples of research where a combination of two interviews is used. Couldry (1998) researched the social significance of visits to the Granada Studios, Manchester, UK, the home of the popular TV 'soap' *Coronation Street*. Over a three-week period he conducted 80 short, 20 minute interviews on the site of the Granada Studios Tour. During these site interviews visitors were 'encouraged to talk as freely as possible' (page 96). Questions were about reasons for visiting and their reaction to the tour. It would seem that Couldry used semi-structured interviews. In addition, he conducted ten longer interviews in visitors' homes. These unstructured interviews lasted up to three hours and aimed to 'elicit unconstrained talk about GST [Granada Studios Tour]' (page 96). Interviews used in combination with each other can enhance the research findings through method and data triangulation.

Life histories

Musson (1998: 10) describes the life history approach as a method that 'prioritises individual explanations and interpretations of actions and events, viewing them as lenses through which to access the meaning which human beings attribute to their experience'.

A life history or biography has been used extensively in ethnographic research. In essence life histories are collected through interviewing. Usually data are collected from a series of interviews in a largely unstructured fashion. Other forms of information like documents and photographs can supplement interviews such as this. It is accepted that each individual story is unique and this may be seen as a weakness to the method. But a collection of individual stories can help improve our understanding and knowledge of social and cultural processes in general (Davies 1999: 169). Representativeness is a key issue in this form of data collection. Care must be taken if generalisations to a wider population are being considered. Analysis of many life histories can identify themes and categories from individual lives that have a wider significance. Here issues of sampling and identification of the population are important. As Davies (1999: 170) argues 'theoretical induction, in which social and cultural processes observed in individual cases are argued to be relevant in other contexts'.

For many ethnographers it is the ability of life histories to challenge generalisations, rather than make generalisations that is more important. As Ladkin (1999: 37) points out, 'The collection of life and work history data is an established methodology for the social sciences, but has received little application in hospitality and tourism research'.

Her study of hotel general managers in the UK uses a work history analysis, which she distinguishes from a life history analysis. Her research was essentially a questionnaire sample survey gathering quantitative and qualitative data on the detailed career history of hotel managers (Ladkin 1999: 41). For the student of the life history, Ladkin summarises its growth as a social science methodology and analyses its attraction and weaknesses. The main points she makes about life histories are:

● the past, through remembered lives, helps understand the present
● rich intimate detail from a close encounter with the respondent
● greater understanding of social relationships
● exploration of social change
● exploration of issues or problems where little is known
● complements other sources of data. (Ladkin 1999: 38)

Yet there is no research using life histories in tourism and hospitality research identified by Ladkin in the article. In her review of qualitative research methods for the travel and tourism industry, Peterson (1994) makes no specific reference to life histories, only to focused group discussions and individual interviews. This should not discourage the student researcher to try out this method of qualitative research. There is a wide range of potential research topics that lend themselves to a recollection of lived memories. For example, in a study of seaside tourism, past experiences from the point of view of the tourist and the resident could be explored. Young student researchers can learn much about older people's childhood holidays in an era long gone. For the young academic whose holidays consist of a package holiday to the Costas of Spain, the attractions of Britain's seaside resorts seem remote. Local historians have used oral history techniques to build up a picture of the past, many are published and languish in local history libraries. For example, Hall (1989: 6) remembers, in verse, Withernsea on the Yorkshire coast (UK):

> *Do you remember Withernsea*
> *As once it used to be –*
> *The skating-rink-cum-Dance Hall,*
> *The bandstand by the sea?*
> *People on the promenade wall,*
> *Or strolling up and down –*
> *Residents and visitors*
> *To our little town,*
> *All dressed in their Sunday best,*
> *A promenade parade,*
> *As they listened to the music*
> *The Silver Band once played.*
> *The pierrots with their quips and songs*
> *Who gave so much delight –*
> *The notice – 'In the Floral Hall*
> *If it's wet tonight.'*
> *Dancing in the open air*
> *Beneath a harvest moon,*
> *And, as they played the last waltz,*
> *That* Goodnight Sweetheart *tune?*

Here is a rich source of documented evidence on the growth and development of leisure and tourism activities at the seaside. Life history interviews will open up this intimate and personal world to the researcher providing evidence for understanding social change along the coastline.

Students looking for themes to research using life histories can seek inspiration from a variety of sources. For example, on seaside holidays the beach was a popular destination for tourists and day-trippers. How do people remember the beach? Ryan (1997) examines the attraction of the beach as areas of fun, as organised spaces, as arenas for the gaze of gender and one of a carnival. Lencek and Bosker (1999) examine the historical evolution of the seaside and the beach in particular. They describe the spirituality, charm and romance of the beach as a social history. In both texts there are a range of conceptual frameworks that can be used by the student researcher to help in the interpretation of the qualitative data generated through the life histories.

An alternative approach to the life history interview to tap into people's memories has been developed and applied to tourism by Small (1999). Her method is called 'memory-work' and is derived from the work of Crawford *et al.* (1992) and Haug (1987). The strength of the method is that it is firmly set in a theoretical context, feminist social construction-ism, where method and theory are inexorably linked to study women's and girl's tourist

Figure 5.3
Memory-work.

> Small (1999: 28–30) argues that memory-work goes through three stages:
>
> Stage 1: The participating female group is asked to write a memory of a holiday experience at specified ages focusing on positive and negative holiday experiences. Written accounts must be between one and two pages long, in the third person using a pseudonym with all details no matter how trivial included and should be description and not interpretation.
>
> Stage 2: Memories are collectively analysed. The group meets and each woman reads out her account; these are discussed with the main themes summarised from the discussion.
>
> Stage 3: Theorisation of the collective analysis of the previous stage done by the researcher and fed back to the group.
>
> Source: Small (1999)

experiences. It has the hallmarks of an ethnographic approach to research, emphasising process, social relations, importance of everyday experiences, and subject and object of the research become one, with the researcher joining the researched (see Figure 5.3).

Student researchers interested in this approach to understanding past experiences in the fields of leisure and tourism are encouraged to read Small's (1999) account in more detail. She concludes that, 'Researchers interested in the gendered nature of tourism might consider memory-work as a research method in further studies of women as tourists, women as hosts, and women employed in the tourism industry' (Small 1999: 34). Innovation in method such as this is to be commended.

Focus groups

Peterson (1994: 487) argues that the role of qualitative methods used in general marketing are 'underutilised in travel and tourism marketing research'. One of the methods she refers to is focused group discussions. The idea behind focus groups is that a small group of people interacts with one another and a group leader to explore a topic in a relatively unstructured way. Group dynamics are used to generate ideas and pursue a topic in greater detail.

There are no definitive guidelines on the number in the focus group, although between six and 12 is the norm. The group leader will usually be the researcher who uses an unstructured topic list to stimulate discussion. The atmosphere needs to be relaxed with all members of the group participating. Discussions may last between one and two hours, and are tape-recorded, with the researcher making observation notes during the discussions. It is usual to balance the groups by age, sex and economic status, or group people by sex and age to create a permissive atmosphere.

Focus groups are used to supplement other methods or used as triangulation in multi-method research strategies. One of the main advantages of the method is that both the researcher and the participants gain insights and understanding of a particular social situation during the research process. Focus groups can test generalisations and theories developed by other methods, and generate questions that can be tested by other methods.

Essentially the main characteristics of focused group discussions are:

- discussion is a social event with a range of personalities and a skilled moderator sustaining participation
- exchange of opinions and experiences, with different and sometimes contradictory perspectives
- enjoyable and learning experience for all

- collective productions of ethnographic knowledge
- goal is not to produce a single meaning, but to share experiences from which multiple meanings can be made
- collaborative inquiry between researchers and participants (empowerment to participants).

Peterson (1994) identifies five criteria for successful focused group discussions:

- participants must be screened as to their relevance to the topic
- potentially biased people should be excluded
- moderator/researcher should be director and facilitator
- participants should be experiencing no physical discomfort
- analysis and interpretation of the sessions depends on the purpose of the study.

It should be noted that focused group discussions are increasingly being used by market research consultants and less so by undergraduate student researchers. This is not surprising as setting up focused groups needs co-operation, organisation, time and resources that few students have on an academic programme.

John Arden Research was commissioned by Ash Consulting Group, Transport for Leisure, Hadrian's Wall World Heritage Site Visitor Services Sub-group to undertake an in-depth consumer research survey to examine visitors' attitudes and motivations for visiting Hadrian's Wall. Although there is no published information about any issues or problems associated with the method, it is interesting to see how the results are presented. For example, it was reported that three of the five focus group discussions were particularly keen on the idea of a major new visitor centre. Selected quotations were used to justify that it should be placed well away from the Wall, and why it would be particularly attractive to visitors (Arden 1995: 26).

The results of the discussions are presented as lists of points derived from the focus groups. To be confident in these findings the reader must be sure that the research has been carried out professionally and effectively. Peterson (1994: 491) asks ten pertinent questions about focus groups as a method of qualitative research, all of which must be answered 'yes' if we are to have confidence in the results. Without this information it is not possible to assess the reliability or validity of the data.

For a more detailed consideration of the value of focus group research and its potential for leisure and tourism research, you are referred to Goss (1996) for an introduction to the method, and the work of Burgess (1996) and Holbrook (1996) as examples of its application.

Personal diaries

In their research note, Markwell and Basche (1998) have alerted researchers to the potential value of using personal diaries to collect data. They describe personal diaries as a means of collecting 'rich, contextualised narrative' (page 228) and see personal diaries as a qualitative methodology informed by a phenomenological framework. They list the advantages of using this method of data collection as:

- monitoring processes and change
- understanding human emotions
- information is gained from multiple situations and perspectives
- information is revealed from a developmental, longitudinal perspective
- participant perspective   (Markwell and Basche 1998: 229)

Diaries do appear to offer much more information on tourist behaviour, formal and informal, than other methods such as a questionnaire. But, as Thornton, Williams and Shaw (1997: 1852) point out:

> *Because diaries have been used for a wide variety of purposes they do not comprise a uniform field of study. Therefore, there is considerable variation in underlying methodologies, and important methodological and technical issues have not yet been settled satisfactorily.*

Issues around the use of diaries include:

- *Degree of structure*: Should the day be structured into time zones or completely unstructured?
- *Response rate*: How to improve response rates for a time-consuming activity (an extra burden for the holiday-maker)?
- *Consistent data quality*: Varies according to respondent enthusiasm and educational level?
- *Behaviour modification*: Undertake activities to give a favourable impression?

The above points are derived from Thornton *et al.* (1997: 1852) who make specific reference to 'time-space diaries', and contrast with Markwell and Basche's (1998) use of diaries to gain a more complete understanding of the tourist experience.

In their study of tourist behaviour in Cornwall, UK, Thornton *et al.* selected a random sample of tourists, stratified in terms of their destination type and accommodation, who were staying for at least one week in the area. Markwell and Basche (1998) refer to a 'second study' where 11 ecotour participants were asked to fill in a diary. Whereas Thornton *et al.*'s study was a more comprehensive sample survey in which 80 diaries were completed (helped by an incentive payment of a £5 book token), Markwell and Basche give no indication of how their 11 participants were chosen. Of greater importance is the way the diaries were used in the two studies. For the Cornish study, the diary divided the day up into two-hour time blocks and respondents were asked to record their activities and their locations from 9.00am to 9.00pm. No such structure was imposed on the 11 ecotourists whose entries ranged from one to four pages, and ranged from description to an analytical review.

The diary illustrates how a method of data collection can be used in either quantitative or qualitative research. Ethnographers and survey researchers have used it. It is a form of data collection employed by phenomenologists and positivists. Despite its versatility, it is an under-used method of data collection in leisure and tourism research. Published diaries as documentary evidence are another source of valuable data. This is particularly true if the research project aims to examine the tourist experience of the past. Much can be made of old postcards, posters, biographies, novels, legal and administrative documents, but the personal diary gives an edited version of reality as experienced at that time.

Examples of diaries that have survived Victorian and Edwardian times in Britain can be found in local history or university libraries. Many such diaries are published by local presses for local consumption. An example is the holiday diary of George Eaton of Norwich written in 1883. It gives a unique insight into the activities of a middle-class family spending a month's holiday in Whitby, Yorkshire, UK. An edited version of the manuscript by White has been published in a collection of local history articles on *Aspects of the Yorkshire Coast* (1999). This short extract illustrates how interested a traveller George Eaton was:

> *June 22nd Friday 1883 [A walk into the town of Whitby]*
> *The houses are not so picturesque as I expected to find them and the general dirtiness and smokiness give a forbidding instead of attractive look such as picturesque*

sea side places have. The children, many of them barefoot, are awfully dirty. As for the dangers of the place which we have heard so much – they are certainly real if care be not taken. The cliffs have a treacherous edge and are consequently dangerous above and below. The beach under the East cliff is especially dangerous as the sea comes close up to the cliff at high water and rises rapidly. The river is very deep at high water and there are plenty of places where children could slip into it. The pier has no railings. Sometimes I wonder any Whitby children get beyond childhood, but I suppose those that escape these pitfalls are skilful and bold in proportion to the dangers by which they are surrounded. (White 1999: 63)

This extract is George Eaton's first impression of Whitby where poverty was widespread in a Victorian fishing port. At this time Whitby was not primarily a seaside town but had a working harbour and a thriving fishing fleet.

Here we have a Victorian diary written by a middle-class man of private income giving a brief insight into a destination in the early stages of tourism development. Not only are diaries like this an edited version of reality, but their survival when others must have perished add to the selectiveness of the past lived experience. Together with other sources they can be used to build up a picture of the leisured class and early tourism in countries like Britain.

Case studies

This form of research consists of a detailed investigation, often with data collected over time, of one or more organisations or groups within organisations (Hartley 1994). The aim is to provide an analysis of the context and processes of whatever is being researched. The context is deliberately part of the design, and, due to the complexity and number of variables involved, other research designs like the survey are not appropriate.

Thus, the case study is not distinguishable from its context. A project or programme in an evaluation study would be suitable for case study research. For example, this could be the setting up of a new leisure centre, or the introduction of community participation in a sustainable tourism project.

The richness of the context means that the research cannot rely on a single data collection method. The case study is a method that usually combines quantitative and qualitative data:

- participant observation/observation
- interviews
- questionnaires/interviews/observations.

The use of a combination of methods will be used because of the complexity of phenomena and to triangulate to improve validity. From a theoretical point of view the emphasis is on understanding processes alongside their contexts. Interviews carried out in a case study approach aim to explore and probe in depth the particular circumstances of an organisation and to analyse organisational behaviour in a specific context.

Case studies can provide a richness and uniqueness in data. It may contain intricate detail of descriptions of events that may have little relevance outside the organisation being researched. Case studies tend generally to be inductive by exploring issues in depth and in context to generate or replicate theory. The aim is to understand the particular and unique features of the case but also to draw out analysis that has a wider applicability.

The strengths of the case study approach are:

- capacity to explore social processes as they unfold in organisations
- understand social processes in their organisational context
- exploring processes or behaviour that is little understood
- explore atypical processes
- exploring behaviour which is informal, secret or even illicit
- essential in cross-national research to understand the meanings attached to particular behaviours.

Whereas to most students a case study is a detailed description of a particular case to illustrate a particular theme, issue or problem like those quoted in many tourism and leisure texts (Cooper *et al.* 1998; Williams 1998; Hall and Page 1999 etc.), case study research is a research strategy. The seminal work is that of Yin (1994) and students who want more information on this approach to research are advised to consult his text *Case Study Research: Design and Methods.* Gummesson (1991) also considers the role and importance of case study research in a management context.

Summary

Ethnographic research using qualitative methods is growing in stature. Researchers in leisure and tourism are beginning to apply qualitative methods in the social sciences with increasing effectiveness in their own fields of study. This is more than just a reaction to quantitative methods and statistical analysis, it is a genuine concern to see issues and problems from a different perspective. Grounded in a phenomenological tradition, ethnographers are challenging many of the assumptions implicit in a more positivist approach. Unfortunately, such an approach has not infiltrated undergraduate research, and many student dissertations or independent research projects employ the questionnaire survey and the structured interview. This chapter has tried to reverse this trend by indicating that there are a variety of methods of qualitative data collection that can be effectively used by students. It is intended to dispel the notion, commonly voiced by students, that qualitative methods are time-consuming and highly subjective. Participant observation may not be an option for all students, but semi-structured and unstructured interviews are rewarding both as a method of data collection and as a social experience. Insights into social and cultural change can be gleaned from life history interviews. Personal diaries, whether contemporary or historical journals, can give greater understanding to events and experiences past and present. Qualitative methods are also appropriate when combined with quantitative methods as used in a case study strategy to contextualise process in an organisational framework. Although care must be exercised in adopting these research methods, the rewards make the effort well worthwhile.

Student Activities

Activity 1

To highlight the importance of personal skills in unstructured interviewing students can be divided up into pairs with an observer. One student will act as the interviewer, the other as the interviewee with the observer present. A theme is decided before the interview e.g. my most memorable holiday. The interview should last ▷

about 20 minutes. Each pair of students with the observer report back to the whole class on what issues/problems emerged from the interview. The observer begins with his/her analysis of the interview and should include:

- Location of the interview – effect?
- Questioning skills of the interviewer
- Silences/gaps in the interview – how were they dealt with?
- Did the interviewee's perspective emerge in the interview?
- Was it a structured or flexible interview?
- Body language of interviewer and interviewee
- Was 20 minutes too short or too long for the interview?

Try to identify the factors that may have inhibited the interview. Interviewer and interviewee should contribute to the discussion.

Activity 2

Find out from local history sources what range of resources are available that give insights into tourist and leisure patterns of the past. Make a critical assessment of the value of these written and pictorial sources. Use the Internet to locate local history publications. For example, the University of Hull, UK library has a bibliography that includes books, journals and articles on East Yorkshire seaside resorts. (See http://library.hull.ac.uk:81)

References

- Adams, V. (1992) 'Tourism and Sherpas, Nepal: reconstruction of reciprocity', *Annals of Tourism Research*, Vol. 19, pp. 534–54.
- Arden, J. (1995) *Hadrian's Wall Area Visitor Management Plan: Market Research Survey Report*, Manchester: John Arden Research.
- Boorstin, D. J. (1964) *A Guide to Pseudo-Events in America*, New York: Harper.
- Bruner, E. M. (1995) 'The ethnographer/tourist in Indonesia', in Lanfant, M-F., Allcock, J. B. and Bruner, E. M. (eds) *International Tourism: Identity and Change*, London: Sage Studies in International Sociology, pp. 224–41.
- Bruyn, S. T. (1966) *The Human Perspective in Sociology: The Methodology of Participant Observation*, Englewood Cliffs: Prentice-Hall.
- Bryman, A. (1989) *Research Methods and Organisational Studies*, Contemporary Social Research: 20, London: Routledge.
- Burgess, J. (1996) 'Focusing on fear: the use of focus groups in a project for the Countryside Forest Unit, Countryside Commission', *Area*, Vol. 28 (2), pp. 130–5.
- Cohen, E. (1988) 'Traditions in the qualitative sociology of tourism', *Annals of Tourism Research*, Vol. 15 (1), pp. 29–45.
- Cooper, C., Fletcher, J., Gilbert, D. and Wanhill, S. edited by Shepherd, G. (1998), Second Edition, *Tourism: Principles and Practice*, Second Edition, Harlow: Addison Wesley Longman.
- Couldry, N. (1998) 'The view from inside the "simulacrum": visitors' tales from the set of *Coronation Street*', *Leisure Studies*, Vol. 17, pp. 94–107.

● Crawford, J., Kippax, S., Onyx, J., Gault, U. and Benton, P. (1992) *Emotion and Gender: Constructing Meaning From Memory*, London: Sage Publications.

● Davies, C. A. (1999) *Reflexive Ethnography: A Guide to Researching Selves and Others*, London: Routledge.

● Geertz, C. (1972) 'Deep play: notes on the Balinese cockfight', *Daedalus*, Vol. 101, pp. 1–37.

● Getz, D. (1986) 'Models in tourism planning: towards integration of theory and practice', *Tourism Management*, Vol. 7, pp. 21–32.

● Gill, J. and Johnson, P. (1997) *Research Methods for Managers*, Second Edition, London: Paul Chapman Publishing.

● Glancy, M. (1986) 'Participant observation in the recreation setting', *Journal of Leisure Research*, Vol. 18 (2), pp. 59–80.

● Goss, J. D. (1996) 'Introduction to focus groups', *Area*, Vol. 28 (2), pp. 113–14.

● Graburn, N. H. H. (1989) 'Tourism: the sacred journey', in Smith, V. (ed.) *Hosts and Guests: The Anthropology of Tourism*, Philadelphia: University of Pennsylvania.

● Green, B. C. and Chalip, L. (1998) 'Sport tourism as the celebration of subculture', *Annals of Tourism Research*, Vol. 25 (2), pp. 275–91.

● Gummesson, E. (1991) *Qualitative Methods in Management Research*, Revised Edition, London: Sage Publications.

● Hall, C. M. and Page, S. J. (1999) *The Geography of Tourism and Recreation: Environment, Place and Space*, London: Routledge.

● Hall, M. A. (1989) *Withernsea in Verse*, Beverley: Highgate Publications Ltd.

● Hartley, J. F. (1994) 'Case studies in organisational research', in Cassell, C. and Symon, G. (eds) *Qualitative Methods in Organisational Research: A Practical Guide*, London: Sage Publications, pp. 208–29.

● Haug, F. (1987) *Female Sexualisation*, London: Verso.

● Hemingway, J. L. (1995) 'Leisure studies and interpretive inquiry', *Leisure Studies*, Vol. 14, pp. 32–47.

● Holbrook, B. (1996) 'Shopping around: focus group research in North London', *Area*, Vol. 28 (2), pp. 136–42.

● Iso-Ahola, S. E. (1989) 'Motivation for leisure', in Jackson, E. L. and Burton, T. L. (eds) *Understanding Leisure and Recreation: Shaping the Past, Charting the Future*, State College PA: Venture.

● Ladkin, A. (1999) 'Life and work history analysis: the value of this research method for hospitality and tourism', *Tourism Management*, Vol. 20 (1), pp. 37–45.

● Lenček, L. and Bosker, G. (1999) *The Beach: The History of Paradise on Earth*, London: Pimlico.

● MacCannell, D. (1976) *The Tourist: A New Theory of the Leisure Class*, London: Macmillan.

● Markwell, K. and Basche, C. (1998) 'Using personal diaries to collect data', *Annals of Tourism Research*, Vol. 25 (1), pp. 228–45.

● May, T. (1997) *Social Research: Issues, Methods and Process*, Second Edition, Buckingham: Open University.

● Musson, G. (1998) 'Life Histories', in Symon, G. and Cassell, C. (eds) *Qualitative Methods and Analysis in Organisational Research: A Practical Guide*, London: Sage Publications, pp. 10–27.

● O'Connell Davidson, J. and Layder, D. (1994) *Methods, Sex and Madness*, London: Routledge.

● Peterson, K. I. (1994) 'Qualitative research methods for the travel and tourism industry', in Brent Ritchie, J. R. and Goeldner, C. R. (eds) *Travel, Tourism, and Hospitality Research: A Handbook for Managers and Researchers*, New York: John Wiley and Sons, pp. 487–91.

● Robinson, M. and Marlor, R. (1995) 'Tourism and violence: communicating the risks', in Evans, N. and Robinson, M. (eds) *Issues in Travel and Tourism Vol 1*, Sunderland: Business Education Publishers Ltd.

● Ryan, C. (1997) 'Memories of the beach', in Ryan, C. (ed.) *The Tourist Experience: A New Introduction*, London: Cassell.

● Sandiford, P. J. and Ap, J. (1998) 'The role of ethnographic techniques in tourism planning', *Journal of Travel Research*, Vol. 37, pp. 3–11.

● Scott, D. and Godbey, G. C. (1990) 'Reorienting leisure research – the case for qualitative methods', *Society and Leisure*, Vol. 13 (1), pp. 189–205.

● Small, J. (1999) 'Memory-work: a method of researching women's tourist experiences', *Tourism Management*, Vol. 20 (1), pp. 25–35.

● Thomas, R. J. (1993) 'Interviewing important people in big companies', *Journal of Ethnography*, Vol. 22 (1), pp. 80–96.

● Thornton, P. R., Williams, A. M. and Shaw, G. (1997) 'Revisiting time-space diaries: an exploratory case study of tourist behaviour in Cornwall, England', *Environment and Planning A*, Vol. 29, pp. 1847–67.

● Turner, V. (1973) 'The center out there: pilgrim's goal', *History of Religions*, Vol. 12, pp. 191–230.

● White, A. (1999) 'Wish you were here! The holiday journal of George Eaton of Norwich', in Whitworth, A. (ed.) *Aspects of the Yorkshire Coast: Discovering Local History*, Barnsley: Wharncliffe Publishing.

● Williams, S. (1998) *Tourism Geography*, Routledge Contemporary Human Geography Series, London: Routledge.

● Yin, R. K. (1994) *Case Study Research: Design and Methods*, Applied Social Research Methods Series Vol. 5, London: Sage Publications.

Chapter 6

Social Surveys

Learning Outcomes

At the end of this chapter you will be able to:

- determine the appropriateness of the survey as a research design
- demonstrate the importance of questionnaire layout, structure and presentation
- design reliable and valid questions
- utilise a variety of question types and attitudinal scales
- draft a short questionnaire
- assess the strengths and weaknesses of the different approaches to survey research

Introduction

In our experience the survey method is one of the most frequently utilised designs in undergraduate dissertations in leisure and tourism. Furthermore, an examination of the various academic journals would reinforce the claim made by Smith (1995: 42) that 'surveys are, arguably, the most important source of information for tourism analysis, planning and decision-making'. However, the manner in which the survey is applied, in academic as well as undergraduate research, is often far removed from what most research methods texts would regard as best practice. Moreover, the survey is not always the most appropriate research instrument for satisfying research goals, as Chapter 3 indicates. Therefore, prior to embarking on a formal survey some consideration should be given to alternative data sources and research methods. Relevant information may already be available from secondary sources or other designs may be more appropriate.

The advice on survey design from existing research methods texts is enormous and it is not our intention to offer too much technical detail but to alert you to the key issues and refer you to more specialised sources where necessary. In this chapter the main approaches to surveys in tourism and leisure research will be outlined. In addition, the manner in which the survey has been utilised in published research and the practicalities of undertaking this style of research will be examined.

Survey research involves asking participants direct questions either as part of a face-to-face interview, by telephone interview or by post (self-administration). The normal survey tool is a series of printed questions in the form of a questionnaire or interview schedule of some sort. The purpose of the questionnaire is to obtain reliable and valid data on the subject being researched (see Chapter 3 to remind yourself of these terms). The most distinguishing feature of survey research is probably the size of the sample or the number of participants involved. Surveys are usually large scale, though it is impossible to give a precise range, as the size can range from less than 100 to over 250 million (in the case of the US Population Census). A key objective of survey research is to obtain data which is representative of the population. In other words, research based on surveys is usually used to generalise from the sample to a larger population. Consequently the issue of sampling is an important one (see Chapter 7).

The questionnaire is not the defining feature of survey work, but it is one component. Questionnaires and interviews are the prevalent methods of data collection in this research design but they are also used within experimental and case study designs. In his classic text on the survey method, Moser (1963: 1) argues that any definition of the survey would have to be 'so general as to defeat its purpose, since the term and the methods associated with it are applied to an extraordinary wide variety of investigations . . .'. The survey can be regarded as a structure, in which methods of data collection are employed. A survey involves:

- collection of data (invariably, but not exclusively, by self-administered questionnaire, structured or semi-structured interview)
- a given set of units (people or organisations)
- a snapshot at a single moment of time (may be repeated over a given time interval)
- systematically obtaining quantifiable data on pre-determined variables, which are then analysed. (Bryman 1989: 104)

Thus, the survey is normally a means of collecting quantitative evidence. The survey method incorporates considerations other than those associated with questionnaire design or

1. Appropriate conceptualisation and structuring of the research problem
2. Derivation of appropriate measures of the key concepts
3. Determination of the sampling strategy
4. Construction of the questionnaire/interview schedule
5. Pre-testing the survey instrument
6. Piloting the survey
7. Refining and modifying the instrument and implementation process
8. Administration of the questionnaire
9. Data coding and processing
10. Data analysis
11. Report writing.

Figure 6.1
Stages in survey research.

interview technique. Survey design and implementation entail the systematic application number of related techniques or stages (see Figure 6.1).

The design and execution of any survey must proceed in a systematic and logical manner. The pre-testing and piloting of a survey is just as important as designing questions. All too often students pay insufficient attention not only to the design of the questionnaire, but fail to pre-test and pilot it. Consequently, early mistakes are compounded and much of the data collected become either difficult to analyse or meaningless. As you will already realise such technical considerations are not wholly exclusive to the survey methodology. This chapter will focus on the construction and implementation of questionnaires and structured interviews.

The success or failure of a survey is essentially determined by the response rate, or the percentage of the total number of people surveyed who responded. It is clearly important that the number of respondents is maximised and the non-respondents minimised; ideally the respondents should outnumber the non-respondents. A high response rate is an important prerequisite for population validity in survey research. If the number of non-respondents is high then there is a chance that a certain 'type' of person has not replied thus giving a biased result. The design and implementation of a survey is an important determinant of the response rate.

Identifying the purpose: descriptive or analytical?

In Chapter 1 of this book different styles of research were outlined. Surveys have been used for descriptive, predictive, exploratory and explanatory research. It is common to identify two broad categories of survey method: descriptive and analytical (de Vaus 1986). The difference between these two categories may be blurred in practice but the distinction is important in that each raises different design issues.

Descriptive surveys are designed to identify the characteristics of a specified population either at a given moment in time, or over a period of time. The visitor survey (see Figure 6.2) is probably the most common example of this in the leisure and tourism area, though customer attitudes to services or employee attitudes to work are other examples. The key consideration in the descriptive survey is the representativeness of the data obtained. As a key objective is to be able to generalise from the survey findings to the specified population, the sampling method assumes importance (see Chapter 7).

The *analytical* survey, on the other hand, seeks explanations for observed variations in given phenomena. A visitor/user survey that seeks to account for different levels of satisfaction may be considered an example of this type of survey. In the introductory chapter the distinction was made between inductive and deductive research designs. Analytical surveys may be inductive or may be designed to test specific hypotheses. A key difference between descriptive and analytical surveys is that in the latter the independent, dependent and extraneous variables need to be identified before hand. Thus, in analytical surveys the literature search assumes much more importance as this provides the background information necessary for the identification of key variables. In the analytical survey, control for extraneous variables is achieved during the data analysis phase through the use of appropriate statistical techniques (see Chapters 10 and 11). Therefore it is particularly important that all pertinent variables are identified and operationalised in the research design. Without due consideration of these variables in the questionnaire or interview schedule, the internal validity of the survey will be threatened. Conceptualisation of the research problem prior to implementation is crucial in analytical surveys and this is facilitated by a thorough review of the literature. An example of an analytical survey on tourist satisfaction is shown in Figure 6.3.

Recreation in woodlands is a key concern of the Forestry Commission (FC) in the UK. The executive agency of the FC (Forest Enterprise) is responsible for the efficient and sustainable management of forests to deliver multiple benefits, including recreation. Although the UK Day Visits Survey provides some useful information on day trips to woodlands, it does not inform the Forestry Commission about:

● trips made while away from home

● trips which are not seen as having a leisure purpose

● which woodlands are visited.

Consequently, a number of visitor surveys have been carried out. Given the large number of potential forestry and woodland sites in the UK (i.e. a large population), a sample survey, rather than a complete enumeration, is used. A number of sites are chosen as sample points and potential respondents are approached in the Forest Car Parks. Respondents (individual or group) are selected on return to their vehicles and selected on a *next to pass* basis. The surveys are spread out over several weeks and administered in shifts of between 2 and 4 hours. The survey aims to interview 150 or more respondents at each site.

    The survey uses an interviewer administered questionnaire that is based on a standard set of questions, supplemented by questions specific to that forest. The standard set of questions allows comparisons to be made between forests and different years. Key information collected as standard includes:

● the number in the group

● day visitor or holiday-maker

● frequency of visit

● how first found out about the forest

● main purpose of visit

● home postcode.

The postcode is a useful piece of information which can be used not only to locate the respondent but also in geodemographic analysis of the user population (Elliott-White and Finn 1998). The results of these surveys have been summarised by Bellringer and Gillam (1997).

Source: Bellringer and Gillam (1997)

Figure 6.2
An example of a descriptive survey, the Forest Enterprise Survey Programme.

The importance of the literature review

Survey research involves much more than the design of questions. An essential prerequisite of survey design is to know what kind of information is needed, to describe the parameters of the population or to test hypotheses and analyse variance (see Chapters 7 and 10). Like any research design, a survey is designed to answer particular questions or to illuminate particular subject areas. Survey designs pre-suppose that the research questions have been pre-determined. This does not necessarily imply that they have been expressed as precise hypotheses, but rather that the boundaries of the field of investigation have been established. It is imperative that the research topic is thoroughly conceptualised and that existing literature is consulted. Design and implementation of the questionnaire should follow an appropriate review of the literature. This is particularly important if the research is seeking to test the validity of published findings, albeit in a different temporal and geographical context, or established theories. Published research will not only provide clues as to how the subject can be investigated, but should provide detailed methodologies where studies are to be replicated. Replication is an important means of verification or refutation of published material or established ideas and can form an important component of student dissertations and independent study.

Figure 6.3

An analytical
survey: tourist
satisfaction.

An example of an analytical survey can be found in the work of Weber (1997). This is particularly pertinent as the article is based on research conducted as part of a Bachelor of Business degree. The research uses the *expectancy disconfirmation model* to evaluate consumer satisfaction/dissatisfaction. Basically the model suggests that consumers are satisfied when they experience positive disconfirmation; that is when the actual perceived performance exceeds that expected. Likewise, dissatisfaction results from negative disconfirmation, or where actual perceived performance is lower than that expected. It is not our place to comment on the theoretical framework here, rather the research is presented as an example of the analytical survey. The theory suggests that both confirmations (perceptions match expectations) and disconfirmations determine levels of trip satisfaction.

The theory was tested using a self-administered questionnaire which was distributed to a *convenience* sample of 300 German tourists to Australia. The low response rate (23%) and the non-probability sample are acknowledged as weaknesses by the author. The questionnaire was developed following a review of the literature and incorporated 14 attributes (landscape, fauna, shopping, etc.), measuring expectations and perceptions. Expectations were measured on a five-point scale, where one indicated very low expectations and five very high expectations. Perceptions of these attributes were also measured on a five-point scale. Respondents were asked to evaluate their trip overall as a means of measuring satisfaction. The questionnaire was administered on arrival, when respondents were asked to complete the pre-trip section (dealing with expectations) and to complete the post-trip section (measuring perceptions and overall satisfaction) at the end of the holiday.

Multiple regression analysis was then employed to determine whether, and if so to what extent, independent variables can explain the variance in level of trip satisfaction. Fulfilment of overall trip expectations represent the dependent *variable whereas the confirmation/disconfirmation variables and selected demographics and travel characteristics . . . constituted the* independent *variables.*

(Weber 1997: 42)

The study concluded that 'the concept of confirmation/disconfirmations can indeed be applied to the assessment of travellers' satisfaction with a destination . . . it was found that it is disconfirmations rather than both disconfirmations and confirmations that impact significantly on trip satisfactions' (Weber 1997: 43). Thus, this article evaluated and refined a theoretical framework using evidence collected using the survey method.

Source: Weber (1997)

Techniques of data collection

There are a number of different ways of administering a survey, each has costs and benefits. There is no cut and dried solution to any single research problem since the purpose of the research, the participants and resources available will vary from project to project. The survey method uses either a formal, *structured* interview or a questionnaire. We tend to use the term questionnaire to describe the research instrument but questionnaires do not usually involve interviewers; respondents complete the questions on their own. In an interview, the interviewer asks the respondents the questions sequentially and following a pre-determined schedule; in effect the interviewer reads out the questions. Thus, a questionnaire can be used in several ways: oral questions with answers filled in by the interviewer (either face to face or by telephone), answers completed by the person being interviewed or sent by post and completed by the person and either returned by post or collected individually (postal questionnaire). Often the techniques can be combined. In tourism and leisure research, visitors may be interviewed on arrival about their expectations and on termination of the interview, handed a self-completion questionnaire to be completed at the end of their visit to ascertain experiences and levels of satisfaction. The resulting data files can be merged in Statistical Package for Social Sciences (SPSS) if each file contains the reference number for each questionnaire (see Chapter 9). A key aspect of the survey is that each respondent is presented with the same question in the same manner, so producing standardisation and control.

Face-to-face interviews

Face-to-face interviews are essentially structured conversations, or question and answer sessions. The conversation is structured by a schedule of questions which is administered by an interviewer to every respondent in the same way. The face-to-face interview, in its structured form, has one main advantage – the interviewer. The face-to-face contact between participant and researcher is one of the reasons for such surveys generating high response rates. The interviewer does not merely read questions from a schedule. The potential respondents have to be found, an interview has to be obtained and the respondent's answers recorded in an accurate manner. You should establish who is to be approached and how. This is partly related to your sampling strategy (see Chapter 7) but you should establish a set of procedures which are to be used throughout the survey. If your survey involves calling at the respondent's house you or the interviewer needs to know what to do if the respondent is out. Do you call again and if so when, or do you substitute someone else and if so how? Once you have found your respondent you have to persuade him/her to participate in your survey. Your opening statement and manner is quite important; you should identify yourself, be polite, confident, brief, re-assuring and ensuring confidentiality. If you are carrying out a house-to-house survey, consider pre-notifying your respondents as this may increase the response rate (Ryan 1995: 161) and would be considered ethical.

The implementation of the interview schedule is vitally important. The interview should be efficient and effective – your respondent's time is precious and should not be wasted. The interview should be structured and the questions should flow in a logical order; instructions need to be built into the schedule to remind the interviewer to skip sections or pose additional questions. When asking open questions the interviewer should record the answer as accurately as possible and seek clarification of ambiguous answers where appropriate. Ideally, the responses should be recorded on the interview schedule or the questionnaire. If resources are really tight you could consider using a separate matrix (that is a sheet divided into columns, representing questions, and rows, one for each respondent). When interviewing at a recreational or tourist site some consideration needs to be given to where the interviews will take place (see Chapter 7), to ensure that the situation is appropriate. Likewise, remember when you are interviewing on private property you will need to obtain the permission of the owner; this applies to shopping centres, visitor attractions, leisure centres and so on.

The interview can introduce many sources of bias into the research and thereby undermine the reliability of the research instrument. The respondent will make available only that information which they think will be of interest. This is known as the *interview effect* and is inevitable to some extent. When you employ others to interview for you a number of things can go wrong. Interviews may not be completed correctly, the wrong people may be interviewed, answers may be made up by the interviewer or recorded inaccurately. Hired-hands are unlikely to demonstrate the same commitment to the research as yourself!

Interviewer bias has long been recognised as a potential problem for this style of research. Firstly, the attitudes and opinions of the interviewer may affect the replies to certain questions. Secondly, it is possible for the interviewer to misrepresent the respondent or the interviewee to misunderstand the question. Thirdly, the ethnic origin, religion, age and social class of the interviewer or interviewee can introduce bias. Fourthly, the interviewer can influence replies to questions by changing the tone of voice or facial expression, by

- Practise the interview beforehand.
- Prepare a standard introduction explaining the purpose of the questionnaire and ensuring confidentiality. Make sure you have an identity card and a covering letter if appropriate.
- Make sure you have sufficient questionnaires, pens, etc.
- Dress appropriately.
- Inform the participant how long it will take – be pessimistic.
- Treat respondents with care.
- Do not appear judgemental about the responses – be careful about your body language too.
- Follow the schedule and instructions systematically and closely.
- You should not interview children without the permission of their parents.
- Always thank the respondents for participating.

promotion or putting answers into the respondent's mouth. However, many of these problems can be avoided if adequate training is given to the interviewer and by providing appropriate instructions on the interview schedule.

Finally, you should not put yourself in a difficult or dangerous situation. Do not be afraid of terminating the interview prematurely if the situation becomes threatening. In certain circumstances it may be preferable to interview in pairs.

Postal surveys

Distributing questionnaires by post is a kind of self-administered survey, since respondents complete the questionnaire on their own. The postal survey is relatively inexpensive, not very time-consuming and often a highly effective and quick means of reaching a specific sample. The self-completion questionnaire has the advantage that it may be completed in privacy, but the likelihood of misunderstandings and incomplete questionnaires is increased. Nonetheless, the techniques lack one important ingredient – that of the interviewer. Consequently, instructions are of paramount importance in postal surveys since there are no opportunities to clarify inconsistent responses.

Filling in a questionnaire is inevitably not as rewarding as the 'social exchange' which takes place between interviewer and interviewee. Therefore the incentive to respond to a postal survey is less than face-to-face interviews. This makes the organisation and layout of the questionnaire all the more important; questions should be clear, well spaced-out and the design should be simple. Instructions should be clear, unambiguous, bold and attractively displayed. Completing the questionnaire should be seen as a learning process. Initial questions should be simple but with a high interest value to encourage participation. The middle section should contain the more difficult questions. The last few questions should also have high interest value to encourage completion. Respondents should be encouraged to check through their responses and be thanked. It is now common practice to offer an incentive to encourage a response to this kind of survey. Whether this secures a higher response rate is debatable; certainly the results obtained by this author suggests the effects are highly variable. The example indicated in Figure 6.3 offered an incentive but only secured a response rate of 23 per cent!

In mailing a questionnaire it is useful to use good quality envelopes with a typed name and address, using first class postage and a stamped addressed envelope for the reply. If

Figure 6.5
Tips for postal
questionnaires.

- Make sure that the questionnaire has been pre-tested and piloted (see later in this chapter).
- Make sure the questionnaire is 'professionally' presented.
- Consider pre-notifying the participants.
- Construct an informative but brief covering letter – include a contact address or telephone number.
- Ensure that you include a post-paid envelope for the return.
- Prepare and implement a reminder as responses begin to wane.
- Consider sending a second reminder and questionnaire to boost the response rate.

people fail to respond then a follow-up letter may be productive, stressing the importance of the study and indicating disappointment, giving the impression that non-response is not normal. A further copy of the questionnaire and a stamped addressed envelope should be enclosed. You should monitor the response rate during the period of the survey by counting the number of responses per day. Responses peak in the first few days after the survey was posted and then begin to tail off. You should plan your follow-up to coincide with this tailing-off period. In a well-planned postal questionnaire an initial response rate can be about 40 per cent, with this rising to 60 per cent after an initial follow-up and 70 per cent after a second follow-up; with the law of diminishing returns setting in thereafter. At its best the response rate is usually between 70 and 80 per cent and frequently much lower; indeed response rates of between 30 and 40 per cent are common.

Postal questionnaires have a number of further disadvantages. You can never be sure that the right person filled in the questionnaire. Since many participants will examine the questionnaire before responding, answers will not be spontaneous and may not be independent. A person is unlikely to admit to not having voted at the last election when they have previously specified that voting is the duty of every responsible citizen! The format is clearly limiting – questions must be simple as there is no opportunity to probe further. However, it remains a useful research instrument in competent hands!

Telephone surveys

The telephone survey is an alternative survey method, albeit one with a bad reputation. Generally they have the advantages of being cheap, the physical appearance of the interviewer does not matter and the potential sample size is huge (since most people have access to a telephone). However, the response rate can be low and it is only suited to a small number of questions; certainly the interview should last no longer than 15 minutes! The texts by Lavrakos (1987) and Frey (1989) cover the subject of telephone surveys in some detail.

Designing the research instrument: the questionnaire

Earlier in this chapter a distinction was made between questionnaires and interview schedules. For the purpose of question design the principles are largely the same. Any survey must have a focus, or a central issue to which most items in the survey are related. This focus depends upon the purpose of your research, but it is important to avoid generating unnecessary and useless data. Each item must have a good reason for inclusion in a survey. The final questionnaire or interview schedule reflects the manner in which the research problem or focus has been operationalised. Survey questions are a means of measuring or obtaining information on the key concepts within the research. So the design of questions involves a staged process:

1. define the concept
2. break this concept down into a number of dimensions
3. develop indicators for each dimension
4. select one (or more) indicators for each dimension
5. design questions to collect information for each indicator
6. pre-test the questions in order to ensure that they are valid and reliable
7. the resultant questions form the variables in your data analysis

This process was illustrated in Chapter 2 and we need not spend much time on it here, other than to note that the questions should reflect the objectives of the research. Too often questionnaires fail because insufficient attention has been paid to the focus of the research; that is the review of the literature and the conceptualisation of the research were inadequate. In particular Ryan (1995) reminds us of the importance of analytical frameworks in attitudinal research. The meaning of questions should not be taken for granted. Even apparently unambiguous variables such as nationality can be problematic (Dann 1993). Questions should relate to your hypotheses, key indicators and should be arranged so that the questionnaire flows in a logical manner.

General issues associated with questionnaire design

Before considering the way in which questions can be worded and structured, it is important that we establish some general principles of questionnaire design. Remember that in a questionnaire you usually only get one opportunity to ask the questions. Any survey instrument, whether postal questionnaire or interview schedule, needs to be well laid out and presented. A professional questionnaire is more likely to be taken seriously and is not only easier for the respondent to complete (an important prerequisite of responding) but also makes data analysis more straightforward later on.

Questionnaires should be word-processed. This does not only give a more professional 'feel' but also means that alterations (as a result of pre-testing and piloting) can be easily made. The questions should be presented in the correct order, numbered and appropriately spaced. The questionnaire should not be too long (keep it as brief as possible) so as to avoid respondent fatigue. Always ask yourself whether the question is actually needed; it may seem interesting but is it necessary given the purpose of your research? Neither should you crowd the questions together but space them out; do not try to make the questionnaire look shorter by cramming questions together – the respondent will not be fooled!

Although most people will be happy to respond to a survey in tourism or leisure, it is important to guarantee confidentiality for the respondent. This will remove any doubt from the mind of the respondent and is vital when sensitive questions are to be asked; otherwise, at best, certain questions may be answered incompletely, and at worst the whole survey may be ruined! It is important that respondents are treated as you, the researcher, would wish to be treated – courteously and honestly.

The arrangement of questions or items in a questionnaire is also important. Generally sensitive items, such as personal details, should be placed at the end so that respondents can be led into them gently. In questionnaires it is important that the most interesting and least sensitive questions come first. Your initial objective at the beginning of a questionnaire is to get the respondent interested and to give the impression that the questionnaire is about what you said it was in the cover letter or introduction.

Question types

When constructing a questionnaire the flow and format of the questions is important. There are basically two types of question in questionnaires – open and closed questions. Closed questions have pre-coded answers, whereas in open questions respondents are encouraged to express themselves more freely:

> Please state below the main reason for your visit to this destination.
> ....
> ....

In closed questions, respondents are restricted to a series of pre-determined answers:

> What is the major reason for your visit to this destination? Please tick one category only.
> 1. Visit friends and relatives
> 2. Recreation
> 3. Business
> 4. Sightseeing
> 5. Health
> 6. Other (please specify) . . .

The advantages of closed questions are that they are easy to analyse and quick to answer. The disadvantage is that the respondent may be forced into an answer which only approximates to what they want to say. Open questions pose problems for the researcher later on. Do you record the answer verbatim or do you code it in some manner? If you record the answer verbatim then you will have to deal with them in a qualitative manner. Post-coding the response is probably the most common way of handling this data but this pre-supposes that appropriate categories can be developed. Usually, such categories are developed inductively by simply trawling through the questionnaires to identify commonalities (see Chapter 9).

Generally speaking, open questions are particularly useful in determining a respondent's feeling on a topic or for identifying the reasons why they hold particular points of view. Open questions are better at determining how strongly views are held and opinions on specific aspects. The following section deals with the construction of closed questions.

Question scaling

In many leisure and tourism surveys the measurement of attitudes or opinions is of some importance. Many attitude questions require answers on some sort of rating scale. The detailed issues associated with attitudinal and satisfaction surveys are adequately discussed in other texts (McDougall and Munro 1994; Ryan 1995), so we will restrict our discussion to general issues here. Different types of scale will yield different levels of data and consequently permit different kinds of data analysis.

At its simplest a scale may have two possible answers: YES/NO or AGREE/DISAGREE. However, it is more common to find a four- or five-point *Likert scale* in operation. A Likert scale requires respondents to indicate a degree of agreement or disagreement with a statement or set of statements concerning a particular object. Usually they employ a five-point scale of 'strongly agree', 'agree', 'undecided', 'disagree' and 'strongly disagree'.

To what extent do you agree or disagree that the resort is relaxing?

	Please circle
Strongly agree	1
Agree	2
Neither agree nor disagree	3
Disagree	4
Strongly disagree	5

The Likert scale is popular because it is easy to construct and administer.

Another form of scaling involves semantic differentials. This combines verbal and dia-grammatic techniques by inserting opposing adjectives at either end of the scale such as 'bad–good', 'strong–weak', 'hot–cold' and so on. Normally, respondents are asked to rate an object on a five- or seven-point scale. For example:

How do you rate the park and ride service? Please tick

	1	2	3	4	5	
clean						dirty
fast						slow
safe						unsafe

It is an easy scale for respondents to use and can be applied rapidly to a large number of items. However, it is important to ensure that the adjectives are meaningful and appro-priate. In order to avoid the halo effect the positive and negative adjectives should be altern-ated between the right- and left-hand sides of the scales.

Semantic differentials and Likert scales are the most commonly used techniques in leis-ure and tourism surveys. Five- or seven-point scales are probably the most frequently employed, easiest to understand and sufficient for most purposes. These tend to be fine enough to differentiate between responses and coarse enough to enable respondents to place themselves (Moser and Kalton 1989). The choice between an odd or even number of categories depends whether it is important that respondents are forced to decide the direction of their opinion; the mid-point of an odd number representing a neutral posi-tion. The interpretation of the neutral position is often confounded by respondents who use it when they have no opinion, rather than a neutral one. This could be overcome by introducing a separate category to record such occurrences (see Ryan and Garland 1999).

The main drawback of Likert scales and semantic differentials is that they do not have interval properties. As these scales yield data which is categorical rather than numerical, they impose restrictions on the type of data analysis that is possible. Although researchers have been prone to assume interval properties this should only be done when several Likert scales are combined to form an overall score.

When designing scaled questions you should consider the nature of your investigation and the scales used by previous pieces of research. If you are to compare your findings with those of others then your scales should be comparable (McDougall and Munro 1994).

General rules in question design

Question design is an important factor in determining the quality of the survey results. We can identify a number of important rules:

1. Avoid leading questions. Such questions assume that a respondent holds particu-lar views and fails to provide for the opposite view:

Are you in favour of improved access for disabled persons to the leisure pool? YES/NO

This would tend to encourage answers which are politically correct. This question could be re-phrased using a Likert scale as:

To what extent do you agree or disagree that access for the disabled to the leisure pool needs to be improved?

	Please circle
Strongly agree	1
Agree	2
Neither agree nor disagree	3
Disagree	4
Strongly disagree	5

Some thought should also be given to this issue when constructing scaled questions for example:

How would you describe the changes in the quality of service since your last visit?

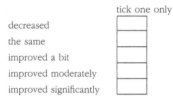

Here there is clearly an imbalance between positive and negative categories; there is only one negative category. When designing scaled questions you should endeavour to achieve a balanced set of categories.

Similarly, some consideration should be given to the overall tone of the questionnaire, particularly when soliciting opinions or levels of satisfaction. For example, a series of negative questions (like those below) should be avoided.

To what extent do you agree or disagree with the following statements; where 1 is strongly agree and 5 is strongly disagree.

	1	2	3	4	5
tourists disturb livestock					
tourists erode footpaths					
tourists spend little money in the area					

This may also produce *response set bias* which is when the respondent ticks the same category for every question, particularly when the form of questions and wording are similar (Ryan 1995: 153–7).

2. Avoid double questions, such as:

How often do you go to the cinema or theatre?

Such questions are really two questions in one. To attempt to reduce the number of questions in this way is counter-productive as two separate responses are required.

3. Avoid unfamiliar words or phrases. Terms such as 'modern youth' or 'sport' do not have common meaning to all respondents; thus a question containing such a word may be unreliable. You should avoid technical words or slang when addressing the public but technical terms may be used if you are interviewing professionals or specialists. Remember the adage: keep it simple stupid (KISS). Always consider a simpler or more everyday version of the words you are using (use a Thesaurus). For example, in the UK the word 'holiday' would be preferred to 'vacation'.

4. Vague and general questions should not be used. Phrases such as 'fairly' and 'kind of' have no precise meaning, as do words such as 'normally' or 'usually'. However a certain degree of vagueness is often necessary. For example when asking respondents how important some feature is the response categories could be left relatively vague: very important, somewhat important and not important. At other times vagueness is unnecessary. For example:

How often do you visit?

tick one

Often	
Sometimes	
Rarely	
Never	

Should be reworded as:

How often have you visited in the past 3 months?

tick one

Once	
Twice	
Three times or more	

5. Hypothetical questions are of little value – they are difficult to implement and potentially unreliable, for example:

If you were buying a holiday, what features would be most attractive?

Would you answer realistically or what you dream of? Another example of this would be the apparently simply question:

If the sauna improved, would you come again? YES/NO

The answer 'No' could be interpreted in a number of ways. The respondent may be from out of the area and therefore would be unlikely to return anyway, the respondent may not have experienced the sauna or the service in question may be deemed to be unimportant. In these circumstances you should include a further option such as 'don't know'.

6. Use filter questions where necessary. There may be instances where some of the questions are irrelevant to particular respondents. In which case you should include filters of some sort; or instruct the interviewer to skip questions where necessary. Say you were evaluating a shuttle bus service, you may need to filter out those who have and have not used it. Those who had used the service may be asked to comment on the nature of the service, while those who had not may be questioned on the reasons why. This can be accomplished by a simple set of instructions:

1. Did you use the shuttle bus service today? Yes/No
If 'no', please answer question 2. If 'yes' please go to question 3.

There may be times when such instructions are not possible. For example, when asking a respondent their opinions of particular facilities, you may need to know whether they have actually used it or whether they are able to comment. To illustrate:

How would you rate the following services? Where 1 is 'very poor', 2 is 'poor', 3 is 'neither good nor poor', 4 is 'good' and 5 is 'very good'.

	1	2	3	4	5
the sauna					
the swimming pool					
the bar					

In this case a simple filter question is not possible so you would add another category (0) for those who didn't use it or are unable to comment:

How would you rate the following services?
1 is very poor
2 is poor
3 is neither good nor poor
4 is good
5 is very good
If you cannot comment please tick (0)

	1	2	3	4	5	0
the sauna						
the swimming pool						
the bar						

Alternatively, where you have also asked a question about the frequency of use of the same set of services, you can cross-check use with opinion at the analysis stage.

7. The use of negatives in questions makes it difficult to understand the question at first hearing:

> To what extent do you agree or disagree with the following statement:
> Children who steal whilst on holiday should not be punished.

Likewise double negatives should be avoided:

> To what extent do you agree or disagree with the following statement:
> Children who do not steal whilst on holiday should not be punished

8. Long and over-elaborate questions may not yield accurate answers:

> Do you use a car regularly to get to your sports club? – by car I mean 3-wheeled cars, 4-wheeled cars and estate cars; by regularly I mean 4 days out of 5; by club I mean the one you go to most often to play most sport?

Such elaboration obscures rather than clarifies the question.

9. When asking questions on sensitive topics you should first consider whether you need the information. Questions on the use of illegal substances, exercise, sex, income and address can be regarded as falling in to this category. The use of broad categories can get round these in some instances; for example use the postcode rather than the address or broad ranges of income in a closed rather than open question. An alternative would be to ask the respondent to self-administer that part of the interview, or be asked to read their answer from a prompt card. Sensitive topics should always be left until the end of the questionnaire if possible. If the respondent becomes offended you should apologise but at least you will not have completely wasted your time. The asking of sensitive questions does raise ethical issues and you should be certain that such questions are necessary.

10. Questions which require the respondent to recall something that happened some time ago should be avoided if possible. The reason for this is that the nature of the response will be influenced by the respondent's ability to remember the past event, which will vary from respondent to respondent. In travel research the en route survey is frequently used to overcome this problem (Hurst 1994).

11. Be aware of those questions where the responses may not be mutually exclusive. For example:

Which of these best describes the main purpose of your trip today?

1. Going for a short walk (up to 2 hours)
2. Going for a long walk (over 2 hours)
3. Visiting the Wall
4. Visiting a World Heritage Site
5. Sitting and relaxing, enjoying the view
6. Passing through
7. Visiting tourist/historic attractions
8. Education to increase knowledge
9. Visiting friends and relatives
10. Enjoyment/Fun day out
11. Travelling round and sight-seeing
12. Attending an event
13. Other
(please state)

Although the question asks for the *main* purpose, respondents may consider a combination of the items in the list as appropriate, and tick more than one. In these situations you would have to think carefully about coding the questionnaire for data entry (see Chapter 9).

Demographic questions

Most surveys include demographic questions in order to classify the respondents by age, life-stage, socio-economic group, gender and so on. These questions are now quite standard and examples are provided below.

How old are you?

16–24 yrs   a
25–34 yrs   b
35–44 yrs   c
45–59 yrs   d
60+ yrs   e

What is the occupation of the main earner in your household?

Occupation:

Note Characteristics of Respondent:

Male   Female

The researcher needs to consider whether such questions are required given the research aims, as they may lengthen the questionnaire unnecessarily.

Survey instructions

Each questionnaire survey will need a set of instructions regardless of whether it is self-completion or interviewer administered. The first part of these should inform the participant about the purpose of the survey, how the results will be used, why individual responses are important and the degrees of anonymity and confidentiality with which the data will be treated, and if appropriate briefly mention how participants were selected. In a postal questionnaire these can be covered in a covering letter, while in a face-to-face interview they should be communicated orally.

In many instances a respondent will need to be guided through a questionnaire. Some questions may be inappropriate, so respondents or interviewers will need to be told to 'skip and go to' the next relevant question. In a long questionnaire the topic may change; in such instances the respondent should be informed; for example 'In this section you will be asked to provide details about the quality of your holiday accommodation'.

So interviews may necessitate the use of prompt cards. These are simply flip cards which suggest a range of answers. For example:

Which of these best describes the *main* purpose of your trip today?

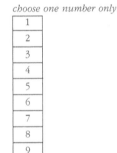

choose one number only

Going for a walk	1
Sitting and relaxing, enjoying the view	2
Just passing through	3
Visiting tourist/historic attractions	4
Education to increase knowledge	5
Visiting friends and relatives	6
Travelling round and sight-seeing	7
Attending an event or festival	8
Other	9

The absence of the interviewer causes particular problems for self-completion questionnaires. Consequently, the questionnaire must not only capture the interest of the respondent but should also contain clear instructions on how to complete it. It may be tedious but if you expect the respondent to tick one box then you should instruct them to do this. Without an interviewer, respondents may be reluctant to provide detailed answers to open questions. Consequently, these questionnaire designs are best restricted to closed questions. However, respondents often demonstrate an annoying tendency to ignore your instructions:

Which of the following do you consider to be the most important? *Please tick one only.*

This can still result in more than one selection which causes problems for data entry later on; you could either select one answer randomly or create more than one variable.

Pre-testing survey instruments

Whether you are conducting a postal survey or a series of face-to-face interviews, it is important that the instrument (questionnaire) is pre-tested to ensure that respondents understand the questions and provide appropriate responses. Pre-testing involves giving the questionnaire or interview schedule to a small group of people in order to test the measures or questions you intend to use; these individuals should be similar to your target population. Quite often this will involve trying some or all of the questions out on a small group of pre-test respondents. In this context you wish to determine how well the instructions and questions

)id the cover letter give the impression you intended? Are the instructions
ain questions and sections clear? Check that respondents have com-
e appropriate sections and so on. It was during pre-testing that errors
questionnaire designed to ascertain employment characteristics in
estion on wage rates was not clear – do you mean pre-tax, exclud-
ne or what? As a result it was possible to clarify the section con-
nstrument involves an interviewer-administered questionnaire, it
.ne interviewers are also pre-tested for efficiency, development of rap-
...ing of questions etc. The results of pre-testing can be annoying, but can make
..e difference between an instrument yielding data or not, or giving meaningful or useless data! Pre-testing involves more than simply asking your friends to complete some
questionnaires. You need to seek feedback on whether they understood the questions or,
whether some respondents interpreted the questions in a manner which was different
from that which was intended.

Piloting the survey

Pre-testing is different from piloting a survey. Pre-testing involves the instrument or the
questionnaire, whereas a pilot involves a small-scale (25 interviews or questionnaires is
usually sufficient) administration of the survey procedure as a whole. In this way the whole
procedure may be checked to determine whether or not things will run smoothly.
Generally, a pilot will not be necessary if the survey has been well designed, but how do
you know unless you pilot it first? The aim of the pilot survey is to test the reliability and
validity of the survey. The reliability of the survey rests to some degree on the quality of
the questionnaire. The internal reliability of the survey can be tested using the *split halves*
technique. The questionnaires from the pilot survey are randomly allocated to two groups.
The answers of the two groups are then compared. If similar results are obtained then this
suggests that the questions are reliable; reliability cannot, however, be confirmed. The validity of the survey instrument rests on whether it measures what it is intended to measure.
To some extent this depends upon how well the subject was conceptualised. A crucial issue
is whether the questions are understood consistently by all respondents; that is, that the
question can be assumed to have a single meaning. This is often not that straightforward
as different words/activities are interpreted differently in other cultures. Smith (1995: 56–7)
cites a survey conducted in Hong Kong where 60 per cent of the respondents stated a lik-
ing for outdoor sports. The research team considered outdoor sports to be golf, tennis,
skiing, fishing and hunting, but respondents considered horse and dog racing as outdoor
sports. Piloting and pre-testing are crucial elements in the survey process. Students tend to
forget this in their eagerness to complete the data collection and subsequently regret it!

A final word about response rates

The success of the survey is measured to a large degree by its response rate. Unfortunately
response rates can be very low, particularly for telephone and postal surveys. Response
rates of between 10 and 40 per cent are quite common for postal surveys. The advantages
of postal surveys are reduced by low response rates. Although postal surveys are relatively
cheap, the low response does increase the 'unit' cost; if only 20 per cent are returned the
cost per response is significantly higher than the cost per questionnaire! Non-responses
introduce errors into your research and consequently call into question the precision or
accuracy of your findings. Moreover, they undermine your confidence in the findings.
Precision and confidence are important concepts and are discussed in Chapter 7.

To some extent the problem of low response can be addressed by using a larger sample than originally intended. This may ensure that you obtain a relatively large number of responses but does not necessarily mean that the sample is more representative. Higher response rates can be obtained if the questionnaire is well designed, implemented professionally and sufficiently interesting. In a recent survey at a World Heritage site we obtained a 95 per cent response rate for an interviewer-administered survey and 56 per cent for a follow-up postal survey. Although we offered an incentive for respondents to follow-up the survey, the high response was possibly due to the rapport we built up during the interview. Ryan (1995: 159) evaluates some of the techniques used to improve response rates and so little more will be said here. However, the pre-notification of participants may improve the response rate, as may the message in the covering letter (Ryan 1995: 162).

Low response rates are a problem because sample surveys are supposed to be representative of a population. If response rates are low you have to ask whether the respondents differ significantly from non-respondents. In order to ascertain whether non-response is a problem consider the following:

- If you have some information on the demographic characteristics of non-respondents, you can compare them with respondents to see if they differ significantly. If non-respondents do not differ from respondents then you can be more confident that your results are representative of those demographic variables analysed.

- In the likely event that you do not have any information about non-respondents you could examine the characteristics of late respondents. This makes the assumption that late respondents are more like non-respondents, than respondents! If the analysis suggests that there are differences then your results are likely to be biased and therefore inaccurate.

- Contact non-respondents by telephone to obtain a sub-sample (for comparison with those who had already responded) and potentially boost the response.

The problem of non-response should be addressed at the design stage. You should do everything in your power ensure that the participant will be sufficiently interested to respond. Moreover, you should seek to boost the response rate through reminders, follow-ups and perhaps a telephone survey. To argue that you had insufficient time or resources is to admit to poor or flawed research design. Always allow sufficient time and realise that it may take longer than you initially expected (see Figure 6.6).

Designing the questionnaire:	Could take days
Pre-testing questionnaire:	Allow one day at least
Obtaining a sampling frame:	Could take several days to assemble
Sampling:	Could take some time to assemble a data-file containing the names and addresses
Piloting:	7–10 days?
Pre-notification of the sample:	Minimum seven working days to allow responses
First mailing of questionnaire:	Allow time for stuffing envelopes, etc.
First reminder:	:Monitor responses but send out seven working days after first mailing
Second reminder with questionnaire:	Possibly send ten working days after first mailing, depending on response rate
Telephoning non-respondents:	Allow several days

Figure 6.6
Planning a postal survey.

Response rates can be increased by rewarding respondents (prize draw, gift voucher), but this does not guarantee a high response. Explain the purpose of the survey and respect their time; inform them of how long it will take (time it and be pessimistic – five minutes may seem more like ten to them). Respect the right of respondents to refuse, treat them with respect (they are giving you something after all), keep your questionnaire short, logical and simple. Remember when using postal questionnaires that multi-stage approaches may yield greater responses than single mailings. The use of official letterheads on covering letters gives an indication of professionalism and credibility. Ensure that you include a post-paid envelope for the reply; stamps are more expensive than pre-paid envelopes. Always say 'thank you' at the end.

Some analytical issues

Surveys are very useful from a 'descriptive' point of view, in that they can produce information on common or distinguishing patterns within the defined population, but are of limited 'explanatory' value. Although findings may be representative of a population, they should not be extended to other populations at different times or places. Furthermore, the problem of the *ecological fallacy* makes inferences about individuals within the sampled population dangerous. The ecological fallacy is the 'spurious inference of individual characteristics from group level characteristic' (Sayer 1992: 102). For example, a survey may reveal that British tourists are more likely to express dissatisfaction than others. This is a tendency and should not be taken to imply that individual British tourists are dissatisfied; further analysis would be required. The ecological fallacy is most likely to be committed when the 'unit of analysis' is geographical. For example, if a survey of Spanish resorts revealed a strong association between levels of crime and the percentage of British tourists vacationing there, it would be incorrect to conclude that British tourists are more likely to commit crimes than others; it may be that such individuals are most likely to be victims of crime!

Analytical uncertainty is typical of the survey for a variety of other reasons which are outlined in chapter 4. However, mention needs to be made of the common method variance problem. This 'refers to the tendency in many studies to derive measures of different concepts from a single source, such as a self administered questionnaire, and then to examine relationships amongst measures' (Bryman 1989: 129).

In other words, respondents may attempt to be consistent (by checking later responses against earlier ones) or because the design of the questionnaire may encourage such consistency. This may be a problem in research into tourist satisfaction (see Ryan 1995) where respondents are asked a series of questions about expectations (How important are the following to a good holiday?) followed by some question on how satisfied they are with those elements. Although there are various responses to this problem, merely considering the format, wording and location of questions on the questionnaire may not be sufficient to overcome the problem (see Bryman 1989: 130).

Summary

Survey methods are a means of obtaining 'self-report' information from participants. Such information may be 'factual', about behaviour or about opinions. Confidentiality should always be guaranteed. The format and layout of the research instrument (questionnaire) must make it easy for the participant to respond; questionnaires and schedules should always be pre-tested. Face-to-face interviews are usually to be preferred to postal questionnaires; the former producing higher response rates than the latter as a rule. Response rates in face-to-face interviews can be enhanced by determining strategies for dealing with some sources of non-response before hand. For example, if the person is not at home or unavailable after two or three visits, or the address could not be located, it may pay to have a replacement.

This chapter has dealt with some of the elements of the survey method. Sampling strategies, data coding and data analysis are covered elsewhere in this book. We have explored the key issues associated with the survey research instrument, the questionnaire. The information contained in this and associated chapters of this book should be sufficient to enable you to carry out an effective survey.

Student Activities

Activity 1

1. Make sure that you can distinguish between descriptive and analytical surveys.
2. From the previous chapters remind yourself of what independent, dependent and extraneous variables are and say why it is important to collect information on all three in an analytical survey.

Activity 2

1. On the face of it telephone surveys seem to offer considerable potential. What are the pros and cons of this format?
2. Draw up a list of advantages and disadvantages of face-to-face interviews and postal surveys.

Activity 3: A poorly designed questionnaire

The survey below is an example of a survey of customers of a leisure centre designed by a student. The questionnaire is to be administered by a number of interviewers (fellow students) within the given set of neighbourhoods. Identify and correct the errors.

Leisure Survey

To the interviewers
Call at houses at random and obtain an interview with the woman in the household. Introduce yourself. Tell them that we are a bunch of students from the local University doing a study on the local leisure centre.

What is your age?   Less than 20 . . . . . . 20–30 . . . . . . 30–40 . . . . 40–50 . . . . . . over 50 . . . . . .
What is your marital status?   Married . . . . . . Single . . . . . . Widowed . . . . . .
How many dependent children do you have? . . . .
How long have you lived in this area? . . . .
Do you possess any of the following: Home gym
                                         Sky TV
                                         Computer
                                         Video recorder

Do you go to the local leisure centre at all?
How often do you go?
Have you always gone there?
Do you have a car?
Do you do any physical exercise?

▷

If yes, do you enjoy it or do you not enjoy it?   Yes/No/Don't Know
When you go to the leisure centre what is on your mind?   Is it?:

> I've got to go
> I'll meet Mrs X and have a chat
> It'll be a break from my housework
> It's off-peak

Do you associate the public leisure centre with a class concept?

Which social class would you say you were?   Lower Class
                                                    Working Class
                                                    Middle Class
                                                    Upper Class

Do you go to the leisure centre because it is nearby and convenient or because it offers a wide range of things to do when you are bored?

Do you regard the leisure centre as

   clean and efficient?   Yes/No
   expensive and dirty?   Yes/No

Do you think that the staff are friendly, warm and personal?
Are you known to the management of the leisure centre?

Do you think that you could steal from other customers if you wished to?   Yes/No
Do you think it would be easy to steal?   Yes/No

If NO, why not?
Thanks for your time. Do you know if anybody is in next door?

Activity 4

You have been approached by the manager of an Indoor Sports Centre to carry out a user survey of the facilities. The Centre specialises in snooker, five-a-side football and indoor cricket. The manager is interested in the following:

- customer opinions on the facilities (the manager is somewhat vague about this but mentions cleanliness, staff, particular facilities, whether the customers think the Centre has improved)
- the opinion of snooker players about the quality of the facilities relative to the other places where they play
- the demographic characteristics of the snooker players and where they come from
- information which will help in the promotion of the Centre.

He has a list of members and their addresses. You need to:

1. Decide on an appropriate method of data collection.

2. Draft a questionnaire for the manager to comment on.

References

- Bellringer, A. J. and Gillam, S. R. (1997) *Forest Visitor Surveys*, Edinburgh: Forestry Commission.
- Bryman, A. (1989) *Research Methods and Organization Studies*, London: Unwin Hyman.

- Dann, G. M. S. (1993) 'Limitations in the use of "nationality" and country of residence variables', in Pearce, D. G. and Butler, R. W. (eds) *Tourism Research: Critiques and Challenges*, London: Routledge, pp. 88–112.
- de Vaus, D. A. (1986) *Surveys in Social Research*, London: Allen & Unwin.
- Elliott-White, M. P. and Finn, M. (1998) 'Growing in sophistication', *Journal of Travel & Tourism Marketing*, Vol. 7 (1), pp. 65–84.
- Frey, J. (1989) *Survey Research by Telephone*, London: Sage Publications.
- Hurst, F. (1994) 'En route surveys' in Brent Ritchie, J. R. and Goeldner, C. R. (eds) *Travel, Tourism and Hospitality Research: A Handbook for Managers*, New York: John Wiley and Sons, pp. 453–71.
- Lavrakos, P. (1987) *Telephone Survey Methods*, London: Sage Publications.
- McDougall, G. H. G. and Munro, H. (1994) 'Scaling and attitude measurement in travel and tourism research', in Brent Ritchie, J. R. and Goeldner, C. R. (eds) *Travel, Tourism and Hospitality Research: A Handbook for Managers*, New York: John Wiley and Sons, pp. 115–29.
- Moser, C. A. and Kalton, G. (1989) *Survey Methods in Social Investigation*, Aldershot: Gower.
- Ryan, C. (1995) *Researching Tourist Satisfaction: Issues, Concepts and Problems*, London: Routledge.
- Ryan, C. and Garland, R. (1999) 'The use of a specific non-response option on Likert-type scales', *Tourism Management*, Vol. 20 (1), pp. 107–14.
- Sayer, A. (1992) *Method in Social Science: A Realist Approach*, Second Edition, London: Routledge.
- Smith, S. L. J. (1995) *Tourism Analysis: A Handbook*, Harlow: Longman.
- Weber, K. (1997) 'The assessment of tourist satisfaction using the expectancy disconfirmation theory: a study of the German travel market in Australia', *Pacific Tourism Review*, Vol. 1, pp. 35–45.

Chapter 7

Sampling Techniques

Learning Outcomes

At the end of this chapter you will be able to:

- formulate appropriate sampling strategies
- distinguish between probability and non-probability samples
- use a variety of sampling techniques
- calculate the optimum sample size for probability samples
- anticipate the effects of non-sampling errors and account for them within sampling strategy

Introduction

The purpose of this chapter is to introduce a range of methods by which you can select people or things from which you plan to obtain data. Sampling techniques are closely associated with quantitative methods such as the survey and the experiment. However, as the chapters on qualitative methodology indicate (Chapters 5 and 8), sampling issues arise in content analysis and ethnography to some extent. Therefore, it is important that you are acquainted with the nature and demands of these different methodologies before considering sampling techniques in detail. Different methodologies will feed through to structure particular sampling strategies.

Generally speaking, it is normally neither feasible nor effective to try to include every person or potential item in a survey or research study. Consequently, most survey research will involve sampling of some kind. Sampling is simply a process of selecting participants for a piece of research. It is the means by which we obtain a *sample*, or a portion of the *survey population* – the latter referring to all known cases. Thus, a sample is a sub-set of the population selected for inclusion in the research. Therefore the sample is smaller than the population from which it is drawn. The principal objective in sampling is to obtain a representative selection of the sampling units within the population. Some consideration should also be given to the reliability of the data obtained. If the sample is representative and free from bias, then the results obtained would not be dissimilar to other potential data sets obtained from the simultaneous sampling of the same population. In other words, the results of data obtained from a sample should be repeatable or reliable.

Early on in the design stage some thought should be given to defining the target population and thereby the sampling unit. Who is your survey to be directed at? Populations in question are not necessarily people or respondents in a survey. Sampling units could be organisations, businesses, geographical areas, households or individuals. When sampling individuals you may be interested in particular segments of that population – youth, pensioners, students and so on. While the sample may be a small proportion of the population, technically the sample is selected from a *sampling frame*. The sampling frame is a listing of all known cases in a population. So a sample of holiday-makers with a given travel agent could be selected from a listing of the names of all their customers; such a listing of the population would constitute a sampling frame. In those cases where the population is known and listed as a sampling frame, then sampling is a relatively simple task. A sample of members of a squash club can be easily obtained from a membership list or database. Theoretically, the sampling frame should list every member of the population, but in reality this is rarely the case. In the United Kingdom, the electoral register should list everyone who is eligible to vote in a political election and as such is a good sampling frame for individuals over the age of 18 years. However, the register is not always up to date as it depends upon voters registering, it is only updated periodically (usually when an election is imminent) and there are inevitably lags in registrations and de-registrations associated with population change. So, sampling frames may be an incomplete listing of the population and may contain information that is incorrect (such as name and address errors). Although sampling frames are seldom complete, so long as they are reasonably complete and do not contain any systematic bias then they are usually appropriate for our task. Potential sampling frames are listed in Figure 7.1.

Households are potentially problematic units for sampling purposes – for many surveys they are actually clusters of individuals rather than individual sampling units in their own right; you will need to devise a procedure for ensuring that the right member of the cluster is approached. Figure 7.1 only lists some potential sampling frames and it should be noted that these are not the same as sample sources. Sampling frames are only available where there is a finite population; that is where the population can be easily defined. Sample sources would include shopping streets, visitor attractions, museums, sporting and

Figure 7.1
Potential sampling frames in leisure and tourism in the UK.

Electoral register	Individuals over 18
Telephone directories	Households
†Royal Mail	Households
†Market research companies	Households/postcodes/census areas
*Businesses (inc. travel agents)	Customers
*Organisations/clubs/trade associations	Members e.g. ABTA, Tourism Society, etc.
Magazines/newsletters/mailbases	Subscribers
*Credit rating companies (e.g. Dun and Bradstreet)	Private sector businesses
Local authorities/†business link	Employers/training providers
Business/trade directories	Businesses
Yellow Pages	Clubs, organisations, businesses
*Tourism offices	Inquiries, reservations, visitors'
*Hotels/accommodation sector	registration records/reservations

† Financial costs
*Access and confidentiality issues need to be negotiated

hallmark events and so on. Sample sources are those points in time/space where a potential population is available – individuals present will not be listed in a form which would constitute a sampling frame. Sampling at source tends to be dependent on availability and is commonly associated with non-probability sampling as discussed below. In these instances when the population is somewhat vague (milling around) and a complete sampling frame is unavailable, then sampling becomes more challenging.

So, the first questions to ask when seeking to compile a sample are:

- Is the population known and clearly defined (the population being defined by the research aims)?
- Can the population be listed as a sampling frame?

If the answers are 'yes' to both these questions then sampling can proceed simply and systematically, using probability sampling. If the answers are negative or uncertain, then sampling is more complex, and will be based on non-probability techniques outlined later. The problem is that in many situations in tourism research a sampling frame cannot be established and there is a simple reliance on sampling sources. Consider the methodology employed by Hull (1998) in Figure 7.2.

The purpose of taking a sample is to generalise to the survey population. In other words, the characteristics of the sample will be used as estimates of the parameters of the population. In the case of Figure 7.2 the parameters were referred to as the visitor profile. If a survey sought to measure the leisure attitudes of full-time students at a university, then a sample of students would be taken, and the views of that sample would be used to generalise to the whole population (all students at that university). The principles of sampling are best exemplified in opinion polls, where a sample of political constituencies and people within those constituencies is taken as representative of the whole voting public.

Figure 7.2
Sampling
ecotourists in
Quebec, Canada.

In his study of ecotourism on the Lower North Shore of Quebec, Canada, Hull (1998) is faced with a problem typical of many tourism studies; destinations have very little information concerning the nature of their visitors and consequently it is virtually impossible to construct a sampling frame of all visitors. Consequently, alternative sampling methods have to be employed. Hull describes his methodology thus:

> In the summer of 1995, a survey of departing visitors was conducted on the Lower North Shore at Kegaska and Blanc-Sablon ferry terminals. These terminals were selected because they target the two major travel circuits available to visitors.... Previous tourism studies in the region indicated that ferries servicing the region were the major means of transport for tourists (Jones 1993). Over a ten-week period during the high tourist season, 538 questionnaires were collected. This sample size represents an estimated 6% of total visitor arrivals in 1995.   (Hull 1998: 148–9)

The purpose of his research is to describe visitor profiles so that local planners may identify and target particular market segments. Given the problem he faced it is important not to be too critical but we should note that his sample was restricted to those travelling in a ten-week period and departing by the ferry terminals. These terminals were the main means of departure. However, this means that those travelling by other methods and outside the high season are excluded from the analysis. These two omissions may introduce some bias into the results, particularly if those outside the sampling remit were significantly different from those who were sampled. Furthermore, we have no information on how the tourists at the point of departure were sampled. The problems faced by Hull are typical of much research in tourism, but without further information it is difficult to evaluate his research findings. His sampling strategy is reasonable given the situation but the reliability of the visitor profile cannot be established even though he interviewed 6% of the survey population.

Source: Hull (1998)

A key outcome of most questionnaire surveys is the ability to generalise to the population – to say something meaningful about the situation in general rather than just restricted to the sample. So, referring back to Chapter 3, reliability and representativeness are two key and interrelated evaluative criteria when sampling.

In this chapter we are concerned with good practice in sampling which means, choosing an appropriate sampling method and minimising errors. We have already seen in the example in Figure 7.2 how the implementation of sampling in the field is often far removed from the ideal. The practicalities of the research situation often necessitate a more pragmatic approach than that expected in sampling theory. Having said that, it is important to understand the principles upon which sampling is based as too much published research in tourism in particular, is characterised by cavalier sampling methodology. Before embarking on data collection it is important to have considered your sampling strategy.

Sampling strategies

There are two key questions which have to be addressed in any sample survey:

1. How should the sample be obtained?
2. How large should the sample be?

The answers to these questions will be based on a consideration of sampling theory, the nature of population, the purpose of the research and the resources available to complete the survey. The first question can be broken down still further into a range of sub-questions. Firstly, who or what should be sampled? This should be determined by the definition of sampling units, which in turn delimits the eligibility criteria. Secondly, when should the sampling take place? Some consideration should be given to the time of year, the time of day and the duration of the sampling process. It is useful to have some prior knowledge of the phenomenon to be sampled. Certain categories of visitor may arrive at a visitor attraction at particular times of day or year and this may bias the results. Such weekly, diurnal and season variations need to be accounted for by the sampling strategy. When sampling visitors to tourist attractions, it would be best to spread the sampling over different days of the week and different times of the year. In a recent survey of a World Heritage Site, one of the authors carried out interviews on each day of the week for several weeks, during different calendar months; interviewing started in the morning before the site opened and continued until closing time. Thirdly, where should the survey be administered? In the example given in Figure 7.2 the survey was administered at particular exit points. In certain surveys, the point of survey is determined by the definition of the population; surveys will be sent to postal addresses. Where the sampling strategy involves a number of on-site surveys (such as visitor attractions or cultural events) some consideration should be given to where the interviewers will be located. At most venues there will be pre-defined points of entry and exit which provide suitable points for obtaining a fair sample. At informal venues or recreational sites there may be a series of 'natural' entry and exit points which could serve the same purpose. When there are a number of interviewers, they should be issued with precise instructions about where to stand. Finally, how should the participants be selected? This partially relates to a point made earlier about defining the sampling units and the problems of clustering. At visitor attractions, interviewees are seldom alone and it is difficult to obtain the responses of a single individual within the group. Some effort should be made to ensure that the data obtained is from a single and appropriate sampling unit (i.e. individual). A full answer to this question is more complicated and depends upon the definition, and hence the nature, of the population. There are basically two generic types of sampling:

● In a *probability sample* every item in the sampling frame has an equal chance of being included in the sample. In other words, a probability sample is a technique which ensures a random sample; which by implication is likely to be free of potential bias. Furthermore, probability samples allow the precision of the results to be quantified and the level of confidence associated with them to be stated. Precision means how accurate the results are, and refers to the degree of error in the sample estimates. Confidence is the degree to which you can feel confident that a sample estimate approximates to the value in the population. However, the availability of an accurate sampling frame is a prerequisite for this type of sampling. Where a sampling frame does not exist, this kind of sampling is not usually possible and non-probability sampling is used.

● There are several different types of *non-probability sampling* but all have one thing in common – not all elements have an equal chance of being selected. Such samples are not random and the degree of sampling error cannot be determined. Non-probability samples are common when individuals are interviewed at source, as in visitor attractions, sporting events and so on.

Probability sampling is theoretically the preferred technique for reasons associated with precision and confidence outlined previously. Another reason for preferring this style of sampling is that many of the statistical and data analysis procedures detailed later make the assumption that the data was obtained by this method; and strictly speaking such analytical techniques should not be used with non-probability sample data. Moreover, the aforementioned relationship between sample size and sampling error is only practically applicable to probability samples.

Types of probability sample

Simple random sampling is the classic form of probability sampling, in that all other forms are variations on its procedures. The work of Lawson *et al.* (1998) makes use of this procedure and their methodology is summarised in Figure 7.3.

Simple random sampling is defined as drawing units from the working population such that every unit has the same chance of selection. This method requires statistical independence of the units being sampled; that is the drawing of each item must not depend on the drawing of any other item (as in tossing a coin where each toss is independent of every other toss). In order to ensure independence, some type of mechanical means of sampling should be used – such as *random numbers*. Random number tables are generated by computer and are usually available in statistical tables (see Table 7.1 and Appendix 1).

Random sampling consists of a number of stages:

1. Each item in the sampling frame is given a number or code. If there are 100 units in the frame, then they are numbered from 1 to 100.

2. If a sample of 20 items is needed then 20 random numbers are selected from the above table (or by SPSS). In a case where there are only 100 items in the sampling frame, only numbers between 0 and 100 are selected. Using the above table, starting at the top left-hand corner, using the first three digits and going down the table, the following numbers are extracted: 54, 62, 78, 14, etc. These numbers correspond to the code or reference number of each case to be included in the sample.

3. If the same number comes up twice it is ignored the second time round. This is known as sampling with replacement. If the sample was taken without replacement then the sample would not be a probability sample in that the other units not drawn have

Surveys of residents tend to lend themselves to some form of probability sampling because sampling frames are usually available in some form. Lawson *et al.* (1998) were interested in residents' attitudes to tourism in ten destinations in New Zealand. The destinations were not selected randomly but on the basis of the variety of tourism conditions that exist in the country. Within these destinations random sampling was used:

> A mailing list was constructed by randomly selecting names from the telephone directories of the chosen towns. Since it was the intention of the researchers to retain the names and addresses of the respondents to administer a second questionnaire in 1996/7 it was necessary to obtain prior agreement to participate in the survey to meet both university codes of ethical practice and New Zealand privacy regulations. 4044 New Zealand residents were pre-notified about the research by means of a letter asking them to partake. They also received a post-paid reply card to encourage response. The number was selected in order to ensure a final sample size of over 1000 after allowing for mailing list inaccuracies and non-response... Of the 1246 people who agreed to participate 1056 (85%) returned completed questionnaires.
> (Lawson *et al.* 1998: 249)

The methodology section of this article is detailed and worthy of greater consideration than will be given here. A number of further points are made in the article about the representativeness of the sample and this is further evidence of good practice. The procedure used was not pure random sampling and indicates that any methodology needs to balance a number of issues, rather than focusing sampling alone. The role of ethics in the decision-making process is interesting and not often commented on in research. Although the initial sample was randomised, the final sample (*n* = 1246) only comprised those who had agreed to participate. However, the benefit of this approach is that a high response rate is obtained and those who refused to participate probably wouldn't have replied anyway. Any errors in the final sample will be due to non-sampling errors (see below).

Source: Lawson *et al.* (1998)

Figure 7.3
Random sampling of residents.

68327	00067	17487	49149	25894	23639	86557	04139	10756	76285
55888	82253	67464	91628	88764	43598	45481	00331	15900	97699
84910	44827	31173	44247	56573	91759	79931	26644	27048	53704
35654	53638	00563	57230	07395	10813	99194	81592	96834	21374
46381	60071	20835	43110	31842	02855	73446	24456	24268	85291
11212	06034	77313	66896	47902	63483	09924	83635	30013	61791
49703	07226	73337	49223	73312	09534	64005	79267	76590	26066
05482	30340	24606	99042	16536	14267	84084	16198	94852	44305
92947	65090	47455	90675	89921	13036	92867	04786	76776	18675
51806	61445	32437	01129	03644	70024	07629	55805	85616	59569
16383	30577	91319	67998	72423	81307	75192	80443	09651	30068
30893	85406	42369	71836	74479	68273	78133	34506	68711	58725
59790	11682	63156	10443	99033	76460	36814	36917	37232	66218
06271	74980	46094	21881	43525	16516	26393	89082	24343	57546

Table 7.1
Table of random numbers

more chance of being selected. For example, if you started with 100 marbles and drew one, the probability of selection on the first draw would be 1/100th, on the second 1/99th and so on; the probability of selection increasing as each is withdrawn.

Experience has shown that picking numbers out of your head or drawing slips from a bowl are non-random methods of sampling!

Figure 7.4

When is random
sampling not
random sampling?

The discussion of random sampling as discussed above should indicate that it involves much more than simply 'stopping people in the street at random'. To approach visitors at an event on a haphazard basis is *not* random sampling – not everyone has an equal chance of being selected (this is physically impossible as the number of interviewers is inevitably small) and interviewer bias may be apparent in the selection process (aggressive or angry looking spectators are unlikely to be interviewed). This confusion between the correct use of the term *random* and the common usage does unfortunately spill over into otherwise informative pieces of published work.

In his study of user satisfaction in urban tourism, Bramwell describes his methodology as:

Separate questionnaires were used for visitors and residents, with these being administered face to face at seven city centre locations during June and July 1996 over a spread of days of the week and times of day. Random samples of 390 visitors and 191 residents were interviewed at these locations. Because of the city's major investment in sport tourism the survey period was selected to include two large sport events: the VI World Masters Swimming Championships and three matches in the European Football Championships. This facilitated separate analysis of views on tourism products among a sample of visitors whose main reason for coming to Sheffield was to attend a sport event.... 101 visitors in this sample were visiting for a sporting event... (Bramwell 1998: 39)

Now the article has much to commend it and is informative to say the least, but there is insufficient methodological detail here. One can assume given the manner in which the questionnaire was administered that there was no sampling frame and that visitors were approached on an *ad hoc* basis. This is not a form of probability sampling and is therefore not random. It would be more accurate to describe this as a non-probability sample of 390 visitors. This error is also compounded by another. Bramwell then treats his data as though it had been obtained using a probability sample – inferential statistics are used to analyse the data (see Chapter 11). Bramwell is not alone in these errors but his work illustrates the methodological problems associated with leisure and tourism as research subjects.

Source: Bramwell (1998)

In random sampling the cases have to be numbered and placed in order. When this is not the case *systematic sampling* may be preferable because the sampling frame is too large. This is one of the most direct and least expensive sampling methods and the procedure is quite simple:

1. Use the table of random numbers to determine a starting point.

2. Determine the sample size and divide the total number of units in the sampling frame by the sample size, to give the interval of progression **n**.

3. Take every **n**th unit after the randomly chosen starting unit equal or less than **n**. For example, say we have 20 dwellings on a block of which we wish to sample 5 of them. This works out to be every fourth one. We would choose randomly a number between 1 and 4 and there on choose every fourth dwelling unit. If '3' came up as our starting unit, this would be:

2 **3** 4 5 6 **7** 8 9 10 **11** 12 13 14 **15** 16 17 18 **19** 20

If the working population units are thoroughly mixed and shuffled, systematic sampling would be equivalent to simple random sampling. The danger is in hitting a cycle: unusual properties associated with similar numbered units. For instance, imagine a housing development with seven houses to each side of every block. With a random start of 2 and a selection interval of 7, corner lots would be under sampled. Unfortunately, many events such as unemployment and marriage are also cyclical. Also, many lists have built-in cycles (such as hotel rooms). Sometimes, in order to decrease the likelihood of hitting a periodic cycle, a researcher unfamiliar with a particular sampling frame will divide it into equal parts and take different random starts and selection intervals in each half.

Figure 7.5
Random sampling
in SPSS for
Windows.

Some sampling frames may be available in computer readable format. Where such data exists and can be read into SPSS, then a simple random sample may be generated. Electoral registers and mailing lists can be made available in this form and organisational and business databases can also be used in this manner. To extract a random sample from a sampling frame:

1. **Open** the sampling frame as a **data** file in SPSS.
2. Select the **Select Cases** option in the **Data** menu.
3. Check the **Random Sample of Cases** item and then click on the **Sample** button.
4. Within the dialog box you have a choice of either extracting a proportion of the data file or a given number of cases.
5. When you have made your choice click on **Continue**.
6. The cases are now filtered (a temporary dichotomous variable is added to the data file (filter_$)).
7. To print a list of the sample cases, select **Summarise** from the **Statistics** menu, followed by **List Cases**.
8. Select those details (**variables**) which you require to identify the cases. Click on **OK**.
9. The sample is placed in the SPSS output window.

Stratified sampling pre-supposes existing knowledge of the working population in order to separate the units into separate types of analytical importance. Say, for example, that social class was likely to be a key variable in your analysis, you could use your knowledge of the population (obtained from a population census for example) to determine the correct proportions of participants from each social class. If the new service class comprised 25 per cent of the population you would structure your sample to ensure that 25 per cent of the participants were from this class. A stratified sample involves two stages:

1. The working population is divided into homogeneous sub-parts (strata), such as women and men, or large cities and small cities.
2. Random samples are taken from each sub-part.

For instance, if one were interested in sampling urban tourists in order to test for the effect of city size, it would be foolish to treat New York's 11 million population equivalently to Podunk, Iowa's 200. Thus, cities could be stratified according to some criteria such as population of more than 1 million, 500,001 to 1 million, 100,001 to 500,000, and so on. Within each stratum, one would then proceed to take simple random samples of urban tourists. Intuitively one would correctly expect a better estimate from a stratified than a simple random sample since the built-in sampling heterogeneity ensures against a lop-sided or homogeneous simple random sample. However, ensuring that the sample is representative on a single variable does not ensure that it is representative on other key demographic criteria. Indeed, as the number of key variables increases the utility of stratified sampling diminishes in favour of simple random sampling. The objective in stratified sampling is to achieve a reliable sample based on prior knowledge of the population and the basis for stratification should be systematic or grounded in theory. Given that data analysis of survey data is likely to draw upon a number of key independent variables, then simple or stratified sampling is likely to be preferred. If the sample size is sufficiently large (see later), then there is likely to be a representative cross-section of each sub-group anyway.

A random sample may produce a sample which is geographically too dispersed. A sample of British holiday-makers based on a national sampling frame would produce a survey which would be expensive to administer on a face-to-face basis. Where face-to-face interviewing of a geographically dispersed population is to be undertaken, then some form of cluster sampling would be appropriate. In *cluster sampling* you sample from units selected because of close spatial proximity, such as small geographic areas (i.e. counties), and then you sample all, or a sub-sample, of the units within those designated spatial areas. Whenever the sampling frame for a large population does not separately list all the elements, but only clusters with counts of elements for each cluster (e.g. counties), cluster sampling is most appropriate. Because different clusters are often unequal in numbers, stratified cluster sampling is often utilised where clusters are ordered by size (strata), and then clusters from each stratum are sampled. This is particularly appropriate when there are a few clusters with extremely large populations. For instance, if a country has two counties with over a million population and the rest are under 100,000 population, it would make more sense sampling separately from two strata based on cluster size rather than chance losing the two largest counties through random selection from all clusters.

In actual practice, sampling experts recommend that cluster sampling be used in *multistage sampling designs*. For instance, imagine a listing of all counties in the USA; these could further more be stratified according to size of population. Within each list stratified clusters (counties) might be sampled at stage one (technically called primary sampling units or p.s.u's). In the second stage, clusters (say, city blocks) within those clusters might be sampled (secondary sampling units). Within these secondary sampling units a simple random sample of dwelling units might be drawn at a third stage. Of course, many social elements form natural clusters, in which case the utility of cluster sampling is most obvious, for instance, army platoon, school classrooms or industrial/organisational department. Cluster sampling is perhaps the most skilled sampling art and demands extremely skilled sampling experts in order to get reliable sampling estimates.

Multistage sampling designs are increasingly being used as sampling experts become more sophisticated. Usually these designs combine various types of sampling methods in order to take advantage of the positive features of each. So, multistage cluster sampling involves a number of stages. Say that you wished to sample attitudes towards tourists in UK cities, you could:

1. Draw up a sampling frame of appropriate cities.
2. Randomly (using simple, systematic or stratified sampling) select an appropriate number of cities.
3. In each chosen city, randomly select an appropriate number of electoral wards (geographical units from which politicians are elected).
4. In each selected ward, randomly select an appropriate number of voters from the electoral register.

Types of non-probability sampling

Probability samples require a sampling frame which reflects the target population as accurately as possible. There may be instances where a sampling frame is not available. Questionnaire surveys of residents or businesses will usually be able to use a form of probability sampling as sampling frames are either readily available or can be easily constructed from other sources. The construction of a sampling frame and sample selection can be time consuming but the extra effort is likely to produce more reliable and representative data, and enable more rigorous analysis. The work of Bramwell (Figure 7.4) is illustrative of this situation to some extent. Certainly he could not have constructed a sampling frame of visitors *a priori* but he could have used a form of probability sampling for residents. Figure 7.6 sketches the methodology of Dimmock (1999) which is based on a form of non-probability sampling, but is this adequately justified?

Figure 7.6
Justifying non-
probability
sampling.

Dimmock (1999) carried out some potentially informative work on the relationship between management style and competitive strategy. The operationalisation of management style is particularly interesting and the questionnaire, which is included in the article, is worthy of further evaluation. The sampling
technique is described as *convenience sampling*, which is a form of non-probability sampling:

> Small to medium size businesses comprise many of the region's tourism operators (Anon, 1996)
> and a *directory of tourism operators* within the region (Anon (a) 1997) identified categories of
> tourism operators as Activities, Hotels and Clubs, Accommodation, Tours and Packages,
> Conference Centres and Attractions. Two of the largest categories are Accommodation and
> Attractions.   (Dimmock 1999: 326)

Now, probability sampling is clearly feasible given the existence of a directory of tourism operators. So
why wasn't it used? The justification is rather weak:

> To incorporate the diversity in employee size ownership structure, location, type of customer,
> product and price range from the two categories, one result of this selection method is that
> randomness is difficult to obtain. The approach is known as convenience sampling (Zikmund 1991)
> and Brewster and Hunter (1989) maintain that it is possibly the most widely used sampling strat-
> egy. They suggest that if the technique is employed for exploratory purposes, with appropriate
> controls, results can be quite valid within certain limits.
>   The exploratory nature of this work, coupled with the research design that includes pri-
> marily qualitative approaches, added with limitations of time, cost and length meant that restric-
> tions had to be imposed. This motivated design of a sample limited to business managers employing
> less than 100 staff and sample size was reduced to twelve firms. Of the two categories being
> investigated in the region, accommodation contains a much larger population size than attrac-
> tions. For this reason eight firms offering accommodation services were investigated, while the
> remaining four operate tourism attractions.   (Dimmock 1999: 327)

Randomness is easy to obtain using probability samples. A simple random sample would ensure that
the diversity is likely to be encapsulated in the final selection. If certain variables were regarded as central to the discussion, then stratified sampling should have been used. Given the effort which went into
the questionnaire design it is a shame that the sampling is so weak. The final sample size is only 12
firms – is this sufficient to facilitate satisfactory analysis? Fortunately, the article does not rest on a
questionnaire survey of this sample alone.

Source: Dimmock (1999)

Most texts on the subject of surveys or sampling recommend that non-probability
sampling should be used only as a last resort. Research findings with non-probability
sampling are often difficult to evaluate in a broader (population context). The selection
of participants in non-probability sampling is usually done *in situ* by the interviewer and
consequently an unknown amount of bias can enter the sample. The *Tourism and
Recreation Research Unit* (1993) recommend the use of the 'first to pass' system for administering surveys at recreational or tourist sites. Basically, the interviewer asks the first
person to pass them to participate in the survey, until they are successful. On completion
of the first questionnaire, the next person is interviewed and so on until completion. While
procedures of this kind help to overcome some of the bias they do not eliminate it, nor
do they give everyone in the population an equal chance of being included. The resulting sample may reflect the population from which it is drawn but this is not necessarily
the same as the survey population. The 'first to pass' system works best at sites where
there are formal entry/exit points and where there is a relatively small and steady flow of
visitors. At mass attractions and events the utility of such a system will be limited. There
are a number of different forms of non-probability sampling but all have been heavily
criticised in the methodological literature.

Figure 7.7
Surveying visitors
to attractions,
parks and other
recreational sites.

These surveys are often administered on a face-to-face basis and the sampling methodology is simply to interview the first person to pass the interviewer and thereafter the first person/group to pass after the previous interview had been completed. Some randomisation could be introduced in terms of determining the starting point but in reality these remain forms of non-probability sampling. The work of Prentice et al. (1998) is typical of this *genre*:

> Fieldwork was undertaken during the summer of 1993. The main survey, using a fully structured interview schedule, involved a sample of 403 visitors to the park, 207 of whom were interviewed during the school holiday month of August, and the remainder during the late summer when the school holidays were over. This period of structured interviewing was preceded by semi-structured interviewing from which the structured interview schedule was derived. For both sets of interviews, very few visitors declined to be interviewed when asked...
>
> (Prentice et al. 1998: 7).

These samples are usually quite large (to attempt to compensate for the lack of randomness) and are administered over a suitable period of time and at different times within that period in order to attempt to obtain a representative cross-section of visitors.

Source: Prentice et al. (1998)

Haphazard (convenience or availability) samples are simply those that fortuitously present themselves for study. For example, volunteer subjects from fortuitous sample elements. Samples of items from the past are similar due to selective decay and retention. For example, stone grave markers are more likely to be sampled than those made of wood, since the former will outlast the latter. Visitor surveys fall into this category in the sense that only those visitors who are available to the interviewer at a given moment in time and space are likely to be included.

Homogeneous samples are taken from a relatively narrow range of some theoretical variable. They are of two types: extreme case samples where only the extreme values of a variable are included and rare element samples where items with low frequencies are included. Such samples may be useful if a researcher is interested in studying the 'extreme' rather than the 'normal'.

Heterogeneous purposive samples may be divided into representative and quota samples. Ouchida (1980) conducted research into the broadest possible spectrum of excitement seeking, and hence had to rely on quite heterogeneous purposive samples. For instance, she sought data on excitement-seeking behaviour within and outside groups, among skiers, in a classroom, before and after sexual intercourse, and so on. Ouchida's sample is a representative sample. That is, she attempted to draw a variety of purposive samples which represent all values present in excitement-seeking behaviour.

Quota samples are a special case of 'representative' sample where the variable representation is made proportionate to the working population. Quota sampling is much used in market research because it provides some assurances of representativeness with reduced cost, since all it involves is decisions before sampling as to the numbers or percentages of a unit one wishes to sample. For example, if a researcher was interested in the effects of ethnicity and gender on leisure behaviour, then the numbers in each category ought to be similar to that in the population. Quota sampling tends to ensure proportionate heterogeneity of the sample. Nevertheless, it does have several major drawbacks. Firstly, it is difficult to sample on more than three variable dimensions. For instance, if we wished to sample proportionate numbers of persons by sex, three social classes and two age divisions, we would have $(2 \times 3 \times 2 =)$ 12 categories of respondents to select; if we add two categories of religion, the number of categories would double!

Secondly, the interviewer's freedom to choose which individuals with which to fill these quotas ensures that non-random biases will influence the decision of what to sample. For instance, it is well known that quota samplers tend to over-sample houses on corner lots (which tend to be more expensive); this over-sampling ensures over-representation of the more affluent than is typical.

Structured samples, unlike the previously defined purposive samples, are selected because of specific relational properties such as position in a dominance hierarchy, socio-metric network or communication chain. Thus, structural samples use as their units of selection, units connected with some specified relationship. Organisational researchers in leisure and tourism are likely to use such purposive samples, as are those examining the planning or policy-making process.

Two sub-types of strategic informant sample are *snowball sampling* and *expert choice sampling*. In snowball sampling the researcher builds up a sample of a special population by asking an initial set of informants to supply names of other potential sample members. For instance, members of deaf populations, elites and foreign expatriates often know about each other while outsiders would tend not to have such information. Expert choice sampling asks judgements of experts to choose 'typical' individuals, 'representative' cities, or to postulate the parent universe of a sample the researcher has already taken! Sociology is replete with expert judgement samples. The problem is that experts often 'hold differing views on the best way to choose representative specimens, or to decide which are the most representative' (Kish 1965: 19).

Sources of error with sampling

There are two main types of error associated with sampling:

- The sample used was only one of a large number of potential alternative same size samples, each one of which would give a different estimate of the population characteristic being measured (see Figure 7.8). This variation in sample estimates is referred to as *sampling error*.

Figure 7.8
Sampling error.

Discussion of the statistical principles associated with sampling error is beyond the scope of this text but the following exercise can serve as an illustration.

Say, the following represents the age of each member of the local squash club. This data represents the population.

24,21,23,16,17,56,60,64,58,57,60,47,42,41,40,22,35,38,40,41,49,48,19,19,20,35,27,28,29,30,71, 66,21,23,26,27,30,31,45,55.

The average (mean) age of this population is 37.5 years. Given that the membership is small ($n = 40$), then there would not normally be a requirement to sample this group, rather a complete enumeration would be undertaken. However, to illustrate the point the following represent estimates of the average age of the population taken from five separate samples of ten members:

35.7
39.5
23.1
51.3
30.3

Each sample produces different estimates of the average age. In this instance, we can check the accuracy of the result by comparing the sample estimate with the population parameter. However, knowledge of the population being surveyed is usually pretty fuzzy and the accuracy of the sample needs to be determined using sampling theory.

● Other sources of error are referred to as *non-sampling errors* and could be due to data processing, poor questionnaire implementation, ill-defined sampling frame and so on. These latter sources of error cannot be readily quantified but do introduce bias. For example, a 45 per cent non-response to a questionnaire survey raises questions about the characteristics of the non-respondents viz. those who responded. Likewise, use of an incomplete sampling frame can introduce similar bias in the estimation of the population parameters.

Sampling error can be measured for probability samples only but it is a useful tool as we shall see shortly. Sampling error cannot be calculated for non-probability samples and therefore it is not possible to comment on the precision or accuracy of such sample results (relative to the population). Non-sampling errors are discussed later but are really part of survey design, discussed in Chapter 6.

Therefore, data gathered from surveys will probably not be 100 per cent accurate as there will always be a sampling error or a difference between the true value in the population and the estimate or value in the sample. It is quite common when survey results are presented for the degree of error to be quantified thus:

56% of visitors were more than satisfied with service quality; this estimate is subject to a 2% error either way.

The 2 per cent error is called the standard error and can be calculated for sample estimates obtained from random/probability samples. The standard error is a measure of the statistical reliability of the sample – the larger the standard error the less reliable the sample. The calculation of standard error is outlined in Figure 7.9.

The largest possible sample that can be drawn will be the population. In this instance, the standard error will clearly be zero, since the sample is the same as the population! The smallest possible sample size would be one and the degree of error the greatest, but who would base an estimate on a sample of one? Thus, the standard error decreases as the sample size increases. Therefore, sample size is an important determinant of sampling error. Generally speaking, the larger the sample and the smaller the standard deviation in the sample, the lower the sampling error.

Degrees of confidence

Although the standard error presented in Figure 7.9 is useful it still leaves us with that nagging question – how likely is it that the estimate is correct? The problem is that, as presented so far the standard error does not tell us the probability or likelihood, that this estimated range is correct. This is where the properties of the normal distribution are of paramount importance. In Figure 7.9 it was pointed out that the distribution of sampling means approximates to the normal distribution. In the case of the normal distribution, 95 per cent of all cases fall within two standard deviations of the mean. The same applies to the distribution of sample means. The standard error is the standard deviation of sample means. Using the basic principles of the normal distribution we can say that 95 per cent of all sample means lie within two standard errors of the population mean. Or, if we take one sample then 95 times out of 100 the sample mean will lie within two standard errors of the population mean. In order to say how confident we are in our sample estimate we need to follow the procedure in Figure 7.10.

In using two standard errors we have a 95 per cent chance of being correct in locating the range within which the population mean falls; we will be correct 19 times out of 20! If we thought that the 5 per cent chance of being incorrect was too great, then we

Figure 7.9
Calculating
standard error
of the mean.

Reliability was one of those evaluative criteria introduced earlier in this text. Reliability of samples depends upon the minimisation of sampling error, but how do we calculate the standard error? In Figure 7.2 the principles of standard error were introduced. If we continued to take many more random samples, then the means of those samples would approximate to the normal distribution illustrated below:

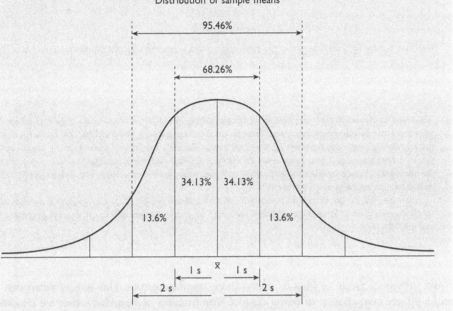

In statistical terms, the standard error is the standard deviation of the sampling means above. If the average of the sample means was calculated then this would be the same as the population mean. Clearly, taking a large number of consecutive samples is normally impractical. In practice any individual sample mean cannot be expected to be exactly the same as the population mean; some will be less, others will be more as the example in Figure 7.2 illustrated. It would be ridiculous if a researcher had to take a large number of samples in order to calculate the standard error of the sample mean! Indeed this is not necessary since it has been shown by statisticians that:

The standard error of the sample mean $= s_e = \dfrac{s}{n}$

where s = standard deviation of sample mean
 n = sample size

So, if a random sample of 50 visitors indicates that the mean age is 23.4 and the standard deviation is 9.7, the standard error may be calculated:

Standard error $= s_p = \dfrac{9.7}{50} = 1.4$

Bear in mind that the purpose of the standard error is to give some indication of how different or similar the sample mean is likely to be from the population mean; or more correctly to estimate the range of values within which the population mean will lie. In the above case, we can indicate that the population mean is likely to be 23.4 plus or minus 1.4 years; or in the age range 22–24.8 years. Thus the standard error adds some precision to our estimate.

Figure 7.10
Adding
confidence levels
to the standard
error.

> In the example in Figure 7.9 the standard error was 1.4 and the sample mean was 23.4. If we wish to
> be 95% confident in our estimate then we would use two standard errors. Using two standard errors,
> it is possible to estimate that the population mean is 23.4 plus or minus (1.4 × 2), or:
>
> Population mean lies within the range: 23.4 + (2 × 1.4).
>
> $$= 23.4 +/- (2.8)$$
>
> $$= 20.6 \text{ to } 26.2$$
>
> Thus, we can be 95% confident that the population mean is between 21 and 26 years.

Figure 7.11
Setting
confidence levels.

> According to statistical theorem, 68% of all sample means would fall within a range of plus or minus 1
> standard error of the population mean. Thus, in the previous example we could be 68% confident that
> the population mean was between 22 and 24.8 years. The 68% confidence level is usually inappropri-
> ate as it basically means that there is a 32% chance of being incorrect. Suppose that you were using
> the information from a sample survey to inform an investment plan and your client was investing £100,000,
> would they be content with such a risk?
> Likewise, 90% of the all sample means will fall with a range of plus or minus 1.6 standard errors of
> the population mean. The 90% confidence level may be more comfortable but it is usual practice to
> use the 95% level.

could provide a range of plus or minus three standard errors. This would mean that we had a 99 per cent chance of being correct. The number of standard errors we choose or the degree of confidence needed is known as setting the confidence level. Normally we are happy to use the 95 per cent confidence level. Figure 7.11 provides more detail. We can never be 100 per cent confident that the figure in a probability sample holds good for the population, though the confidence level can be quite high.

To recap, we have established that:

- Samples are used to make estimates about the population.
- Samples can be drawn from sampling frames where the population is known and is listed.
- Sampling error is inherent within the sampling process. Non-sampling errors can be reduced by good survey design.
- Sampling error is related to sample size; larger samples yield smaller errors.
- Sampling error can be measured using the standard error – but note that this only applies to probability samples
- The degree of confidence in the sample estimate can be expressed using confidence levels – but once again this only applies to probability samples.

The accuracy of the estimates derived from a sample depends to a large extent on the sample size and how the sample was taken. In other words, sampling strategy.

Sampling theory rests on the assumptions of a normal distribution. However, there may be instances when the population parameters are not normally distributed. Ryan (1995: 168) makes the point that given the nature of attitudinal research into holidays, and because people generally go on holiday to enjoy themselves, scores on Likert scale questions are likely to be skewed (see Chapter 8). Moreover, responses producing dichotomous nom-inal data will produce a binomial distribution.

Determining sample size

Sample size is usually determined by the level of resources available to the researcher – the sample is a more cost-effective method than a survey of the whole population. Decisions have to be made within a given resource envelope. Inevitably (and despite sampling theory) determining sample size will involve a number of pragmatic considerations. Firstly, you need to consider the purpose of the data you intend to collect. If the purpose is to collect some descriptive information on specific attitudes of visitors as a whole then a relatively small sample would surfeit. If you wished to analyse variations in behaviour or attitudes by social or demographic characteristics then a larger sample would be required. Consider the data in Table 7.2.

In Table 7.2 the intention is to compare levels of satisfaction between males and females. In order to do this it is important that you have sufficient numbers of each sex and levels of satisfaction, in order to capture the variation within the population. Therefore, it is important to ensure that there are sufficient responses in each of the cells. Assuming that there is an equal distribution of responses, no cell should contain less than five cases. In Table 7.2 this translates as a minimum sample size of 60. If you are examining customer satisfaction then, hopefully, the final results will be skewed towards the very satisfied, rather than those in Table 7.2! These pragmatic considerations for determining the minimum sample size are true for probability and non-probability samples.

Optimum probability sample sizes can be determined using the procedure in Figure 7.12.

Sample size is determined by the *degree of precision* and the *level of confidence* desired in the study. The precision is the degree of error that can be tolerated, whereas the level of confidence is the degree to which one can feel confident that the sample estimates approximate to the population parameters. The larger the sample, the more precise your estimates are likely to be and the more confident you can be in your analysis. This is why you should always sample as large a group as possible within the context of the previous discussion. In the example in Figure 7.12, it was demonstrated that reducing the level of precision also reduced the required sample size. It should be noted that the relationship between sample size and precision is not a straightforward linear one. Moreover, the laws of diminishing returns soon set in – that is the attainment of further precision requires incommensurate increases in sample size. Consider Figure 7.13.

The method of determining sample size discussed above only applies to random and systematic probability samples. When using other forms of probability sample you will need

	Male	*Female*	*Total*
Very satisfied	5 min	5 min	10
Satisfied	5 min	5 min	10
Neither satisfied nor dissatisfied	5 min	5 min	10
Dissatisfied	5 min	5 min	10
Very dissatisfied	5 min	5 min	10
No response	5 min	5 min	10
Total	30	30	60

Table 7.2
Cross-tabulation of satisfaction and sex of respondent: minimum sample size

Figure 7.12
Calculating the
sample size at
the 95 per cent
confidence level
when estimating
proportions.

There are a number of methods of establishing the optimum sample size but we will be concerned with just one of these. This method assumes that:

- you do not have access to information (about the standard error) from a previously conducted survey
- the size of the population is known
- you will employ a form of random or systematic sampling
- you are going to use the sample to estimate proportions i.e. what percentage of customers are satisfied.

The sample size is determined by the following formula:

$$n = \frac{z^2}{H^2}\pi(1 - \pi)$$

where: n = the sample size needed to achieve the specific level of reliability
π = the population proportion
H = desired level of precision
z = standard error corresponding to desired level of confidence (when using the 95% confidence z = 2)

To illustrate, suppose you were sampling customers with a travel agency who purchased a winter holiday, in order to assess levels of customer satisfaction.

1. The travel agency has a complete record of the names and addresses of all these customers (a sampling frame). We want to estimate the percentage of customers who are satisfied within +/–2%, so:

    H = 0.02

    NB: To convert percentages into levels of precision you divide the percentage by 100.

2. Next, you have to estimate what proportion of the population are satisfied and how reliable an estimate is needed. Yes this is true! Strange as it may seem you have to do this. It is usual practice to assume that there is a 50/50 split in the key variable, unless you have firm knowledge otherwise from previous studies, pilot surveys or published data. So we can assume that half are satisfied, which means that,

    $\pi = 0.5$

3. Working at the 95% level of confidence:

    z = 2

4. Therefore the sample size is determined by:

    $$n = \frac{2^2}{0.02^2}\ 0.5\ (1 - 0.5)$$

    $$= 10,000 \times 0.25$$

    $$= 2500$$

5. The chosen sample size is 2,500. You would now pick 2,500 customers using a random number table to form a random or a systematic random sample. This sample size is quite large and you may wish to consider a smaller sample size but tolerate a larger percentage error. In the above case changing the value of H to 0.05 (a 5% error either way), reduces the sample size to 400!

6. The confidence interval (plus or minus 2%) only holds true if the sample result is that 50% are dissatisfied. If the sample percentage is different then the confidence interval will also be changed. For example, if the sample percentage, p, was actually 0.4 (or 40%), then the sample standard error of the proportion is given by:

    $$s_p = \sqrt{\frac{pq}{n}}$$

7. where p is the proportion who are satisfied in the sample, q the proportion who are dissatisfied (q = 1 – p), which in this case is 0.60 (60%) and n the number in the sample (2500).

Figure 7.12
(*cont.*)

$$s_p = \sqrt{\frac{0.4(0.6)}{2500}} = 0.0098$$

The confidence interval (at 95%) for the population proportion is given by:

$$p +/- zs_p = 0.4 +/- 2(0.0098) = 0.4 +/- 0.019$$

8. That is, we can be 95% confident that the population percentage lies between 38.1 and 41.9%. This is smaller than we originally desired because the sample proportion turned out to be less than what we estimated. If it had turned out to be larger then the error would be greater than desired.

Churchill (1992: 510–40) provides an extended discussion of this issue and further consideration of:

● establishing the sample size when estimating the mean
● establishing the sample size when the population is relatively small.

Figure 7.13
Sample size and
precision.

Taking the example in Figure 7.12, we can see the effects on the required sample size of changes in the desired level of precision:

Level of precision	Sample size at 95% level	Sample size at 90% level of confidence (z = 1.6)
2%	2500	1600
3%	1111	711
4%	625	400
5%	400	256

If your resources only allow you to sample 256 units then you can only be 90% confident that the population percentage is within +/–5% of the sample estimate.
    See Smith (1995: 52) for a more elaborate table.

to use more complex methods of determining sample size and more advanced texts will need to be consulted (Ryan 1995: 185; Cannon 1994). Moreover, the above example assumes that the survey is only interested in a single estimate – such as customer satisfaction. However, most surveys will be seeking to make a number of estimates and even in the case of the travel agent in Figure 7.13 satisfaction would be broken down into a series of measures associated with different aspects of the service. In theory, the above exercise should be repeated for each estimate as different measures may produce different proportions, required levels of precision and desired levels of confidence. In reality, you would choose the largest required sample, which would be associated with the highest levels of precision and confidence, so you can get away with doing the exercise just the once!

There are two other considerations to take into consideration when determining sample size: the size of the population and the structure of the key variables. When the population is large the sampling error is a function of sample size. When the population is small and the sample comprises a significant proportion of that population then the standard error can be adjusted to reflect this. Basically, if you are surveying a small population, the sample size can be smaller to achieve the same standard error (see Churchill (1992) for further details).

It is not possible to determine an optimum sample size when using non-probability samples. In these instances the researcher has to fall back on the pragmatic considerations given earlier. Some indication of an appropriate sample size could be obtained by assuming that probability samples were to be used and the above procedure followed, but the levels of precision and degrees of confidence would be relatively meaningless.

Sample size is also influenced by the manner in which you intend to analyse your data. This applies to non-probability as well as probability samples. If you are analysing levels of satisfaction by gender, then you need sufficient numbers of each gender type in your sample. This means that each sub-group is treated as a separate sample and implies that the sample will need to be larger than if such data disaggregation was not necessary. If you intend to analyse responses according to model of market segmentation then you will need to ensure that your sample contains sufficient of each segment. When the key explanatory variables are identifiable before you commence your study then some kind of stratified sampling is in order, but you should be aware of the consequences this may have on other variables (see above).

The effect of non-sampling errors

Sampling errors can be reduced by increasing the sample size and if there are no other errors in the survey then the accuracy of the sample estimate can be quantified for probability samples. Non-sampling errors are more complex, their precise effect cannot usually be calculated and they can occur in probability and non-probability samples. Types of non-sampling errors are:

- non-observation errors, that is failing to obtain data from certain segments of the population either due to non-response or exclusion. Sample estimates are consequently biased
- observation errors result in inaccurate information being obtained from the samples or because errors crept in during the data processing, analysis or reporting stages.

These non-sampling errors are associated with survey design and implementation and are covered in the previous chapter. The effect of non-sampling errors on the standard error are difficult to quantify. Quoting a confidence interval associated with a sample estimate when there is a known bias due to non-sampling error is simply incorrect. Thus sampling method and questionnaire design and implementation are equally important aspects in survey methodology.

The effect of non-response should be built into consideration of the sample size. Questionnaire surveys rarely achieve a 100 per cent response rate (see Chapter 6) and if you need a sample of 200 and expect a response rate of 40 per cent then you should consider sampling 500. Likewise, if you are interested in those people who attended a special event, and only 30 per cent of your sample actually did so, then you should also consider increasing your sample size. Although this gives you a larger sample size, if the response rate remains poor then non-sampling errors retain their significance.

Summary

Sampling strategy revolves around these key issues:

- selecting an appropriate sampling method
- determining sample size
- considering the intended data analysis when determining sample size, particularly data disaggregation

- anticipating non-sampling errors associated with response rates
- minimising non-sampling errors through effective survey design and accurate data analysis.

In this chapter we have examined probability and non-probability sampling techniques. Probability sampling provides the researcher with considerable analytical scope, whereas non-probability samples bring a range of analytical restrictions. Sample size will be determined by:

- the degree of precision and level of confidence required
- the purpose of the data collection
- the nature of the data analysis to be performed
- the likely response rate
- the level of available resources.

We have seen in our evaluations of published research that too often researchers treat data obtained from non-probability samples incorrectly or do not provide sufficient detail in their methodology to allow their research to be taken at anything other than face value. Researchers should be ethically obliged to report any known limitations with the sample or sampling frame and discuss the implications for the research findings.

The potential of probability sampling in leisure and tourism research is restricted by the lack of appropriate sampling frames. Visitors to heritage attractions or customers at a leisure centre are not known before their visit and their personal details are seldom recorded afterwards. This suggests that non-probability sampling will always be popular amongst such researchers. However, quite often the justification is based not on the lack of sampling frames but the unwillingness of the researcher to assemble them.

In the next chapter we begin to explore the ways in which survey data can be analysed. These analytical techniques are relevant to non-probability as well as probability samples. Those analytical techniques covered in Chapter 11 should only be applied to data obtained from probability samples.

Many types of research utilise a sample of some kind or other. The purpose of a sample is to get a 'handle' on the characteristics of the population. However, the characteristics of any sample are likely to differ from those of the population; there will be sampling error. Two types of sampling have been introduced: probability and non-probability. Probability sampling has the advantage of allowing the degree of error to be calculated and the level of confidence to be stated. There are many instances when probability sampling cannot be used, in such cases non-probability sampling is an alternative. However, wherever possible probability sampling must be the preferred technique.

Student Activities

Activity 1

Use the procedure outlined in Figure 7.5 to extract a random sample of 20 cases from the Hadrian's Wall data file. Carry out Activities 1 to 5 at the end of Chapter 9 using this sample of 20 and compare the results with those obtained from the complete data file. ▷

Activity 2

The following listing gives details of all tourist attractions in the county of Lincolnshire, UK. As such it is a useful sampling frame. The first column contains the name of the attraction, the second the town in which the attraction is located, the third the type of attraction and finally a reference number for sampling.

1. Take a simple random sample of 50 attractions and calculate the percentage of each attraction type and the percentage of attractions in Lincoln. Compare this with the equivalent population percentages.

2. Take a systematic random sample of 50 attractions and calculate the percentage of each attraction type and the percentage of attractions in Lincoln. Compare this with the equivalent population percentages.

3. Take a stratified random sample of 50 attractions and calculate the percentage of each attraction type and the percentage of attractions in Lincoln. Compare this with the equivalent population percentages.

4. Compare the results from the first three tasks.

Name	Town	Facility Type	Reference
Gainsborough Model Railway Society	Gainsborough	Leisure	1
Scunthorpe Museum and Art Gallery	Scunthorpe	Museums	2
Normanby Hall Country Park	Scunthorpe	Country Parks	3
Baysgarth House Museum	Barton-upon-Humber	Museums	4
Elsham Hall Country & Wildlife Park	Brigg	Animals & Wildlife	5
Elsham Wrawby Moor Art Gallery	Brigg	The Arts	6
Elsham Hall Barn Theatre	Brigg	The Arts	7
Sargent's Ice Cream	Brigg	Leisure	8
Richmond Park	Gainsborough	Country Parks	9
Trinity Arts Centre	Gainsborough	The Arts	10
Gainsborough Old Hall	Gainsborough	Houses and Castles	11
Old Hall Farm Ice Cream Manufacturers	Gainsborough	Leisure	12
Mount Pleasant Windmill	Kirton-in-Lindsey	Windmills and Watermills	13
Brandy Wharf Cider Centre	Gainsborough	Leisure	14
Hemswell Craft Centre	near Gainsborough	Crafts	15
Hemswell Antiques Centres	Gainsborough	Antique Centres	16
Freeman Street	Grimsby	Leisure	17
Freshney Place Shopping Centre	Grimsby	Leisure	18
Abbeygate	Grimsby	Leisure	19
Alexandra Retail Park	Grimsby	Leisure	20
National Fishing Heritage Centre	Great Grimsby	Industrial Heritage	21
Back O'Doigs Museum	Grimsby	Museums	22
'Salt in the Air'	Grimsby	Special Events	23
Grimsby Leisure Centre	Grimsby	Leisure	24
Swingtime Golf	Grimsby	Leisure	25
Grimsby Auditorium	Grimsby	Leisure	26
Alfred Enderby Traditional Fish Smokers	Grimsby	Industrial Heritage	27

Name	Town	Facility Type	Reference
Grimsby Seafood Festival	Grimsby	Special Events	28
Fish Dock Carnival	Grimsby	Special Events	29
Fuchsia Fantasy and Lakeside Plant Centre	Cleethorpes	Show Gardens	30
Jungle World – The Mini Beast Zoo	Cleethorpes	Animals & Wildlife	31
Cleethorpes Coast Light Railway	Cleethorpes	Leisure	32
Ten Pin Bowling Centre	Cleethorpes	Leisure	33
Cleethorpes Leisure Centre	Cleethorpes	Leisure	34
Pleasure Island Theme Park	Cleethorpes	Leisure	35
Cleethorpes Discovery Centre	Cleethorpes	Animals & Wildlife	36
Grimsby International Jazz Festival	Grimsby	Special Events	37
St. James Festival	Grimsby	Special Events	38
Cleethorpes Carnival	Cleethorpes	Special Events	39
Waltham Windmill	Grimsby	Windmills and Watermills	40
Immingham Museum	Immingham	Museums	41
The Old Rectory	Doncaster	Historic Buildings	42
Humber Bridge	Barton-Upon-Humber	Industrial Heritage	43
Rutland Water	Oakham	Leisure	44
Torksey Leisure Cruises	Torksey	Leisure	45
Lincoln Guildhall	Lincoln	Historic Buildings	46
Snipe Dales Country Park	Horncastle	Country Parks	47
Bransby Home of Rest for Horses	Lincoln	Animals & Wildlife	48
Lincoln Castle	Lincoln	Houses and Castles	49
Cobb Hall Craft Centre	Lincoln	Crafts	50
Incredibly Fantastic Old Toy Show	Lincoln	Museums	51
Lincoln Archaelogy Centre	Lincoln	Historic Buildings	52
The Lawn	Lincoln	Leisure	53
John Dawber Garden	Lincoln	Show Gardens	54
Sir Joseph Banks Conservatory	Lincoln	Show Gardens	55
National Cycle Museum	Lincoln	Museums	56
Ellis Mill	Lincoln	Windmills and Watermills	57
Museum of Lincolnshire Life	Lincoln	Museums	58
Jubilee Park	Woodhall Spa	Leisure	59
Ostlers Plantation	Woodhall Spa	Country Parks	60
Woodhall Spa Cottage Museum	Woodhall Spa	Museums	61
Bainland Country Park	Woodhall Spa	Leisure	62
Manby Showground	Louth	Leisure	63
Alvingham Pottery and Crafts	Louth	Crafts	64
Alvingham Watermill	Louth	Windmills and Watermills	65
Alvingham Forge	Louth	Crafts	66
Louth Museum	Louth	Museums	67
Appleby's Farm Ices	Louth	Leisure	68
Legbourne Railway Museum	Louth	Museums	69
Hedgehog Care	Louth	Animals & Wildlife	70
Kids Kingdom	Louth	Leisure	71
Cadwell Park	Louth	Leisure	72
Mablethorpe Animal Gardens	Mablethorpe	Animals & Wildlife	73
Ye Olde Curiosity Museum	Mablethorpe	Museums	74
Woodthorpe Hall Leisure Park	Alford	Leisure	75

Name	Town	Facility Type	Reference
Claythorpe Watermill & Wildfowl Gardens	Alford	Animals & Wildlife	76
Alford Manor House Museum	Alford	Museums	77
Alford Windmill	Alford	Windmills and Watermills	78
Mawthorpe Museum	Alford	Museums	79
Waterside	Lincoln	Leisure	80
Enigma Zone	Lincoln	Leisure	81
Lincoln Theatre Royal	Lincoln	The Arts	82
Jews' Court	Lincoln	Historic Buildings	83
Usher Gallery	Lincoln	The Arts	84
Lincoln Bishop's Palace	Lincoln	Historic Buildings	85
Lincoln Cathedral	Lincoln	Churches	86
Lincolnshire Poultry Park	Lincoln	Animals & Wildlife	87
Rand Farm Park	Lincoln	Animals & Wildlife	88
Benniworth Springs Academy of Offroad Driving	Lincoln	Leisure	89
Metheringham Airfield Visitor Centre	Lincoln	Aviation Heritage	90
North Ings Farm Museum	Lincoln	Industrial Heritage	91
Timberland Art and Design	Timberland	Crafts	92
Billinghay Children's Farm and Rare Breeds Centre	Sleaford	Animals & Wildlife	93
Timberland Pumping Station	Timberland	Industrial Heritage	94
Tattershall Castle	Lincoln	Houses and Castles	95
Tattershall Park Country Club	Lincoln	Leisure	96
Battle of Britain Memorial Flight	Lincoln	Aviation Heritage	97
Teddy's Farm	Lincoln	Animals & Wildlife	98
City of Lincoln Bus Tours	Lincoln	Leisure	99
St Mary's Guildhall	Lincoln	Historic Buildings	100
Aubourn Hall	Lincoln	Houses and Castles	101
RAF Waddington Viewing Area	Lincoln	Aviation Heritage	102
Hartsholme Country Park	Lincoln	Country Parks	103
Lincolnshire Road Transport Museum	Lincoln	Industrial Heritage	104
Doddington Hall	Lincoln	Houses and Castles	105
Daisy Made Real Dairy Ice-Cream	Lincoln	Leisure	106
Whisby Nature Park	Lincoln	Country Parks	107
Market Rasen Racecourse	Market Rasen	Leisure	108
Wickentree Crafts Coffee and Tea Shop	Market Rasen	Animals & Wildlife	109
Chambers Farm Wood Forest Nature Reserve	Wragby	Country Parks	110
Horse World	Market Rasen	Animals & Wildlife	111
Horncastle Golf and Country Club	Horncastle	Leisure	112
Ashby Park Touring/Camping Site	Horncastle	Leisure	113
Pureland Japanese Garden & Meditation Centre	near Newark	Show Gardens	114
Newark Air Museum	Newark	Aviation Heritage	115
Belvoir Castle	Grantham	Houses and Castles	116
Grantham Museum	Grantham	Museums	117
The Guildhall Centre	Grantham	The Arts	118
Harlaxton Manor	Grantham	Houses and Castles	119
Harlaxton Manor Gardens	Grantham	Show Gardens	120

Name	Town	Facility Type	Reference
Arena UK Multi Function Event Centre	Grantham	Leisure	121
Belton House	Grantham	Houses and Castles	122
Fulbeck Hall	Grantham	Houses and Castles	123
Manor Stables Craft Workshops	Grantham	Crafts	124
Boothby Pagnell Norman Manor House	Grantham	Houses and Castles	125
Willoughby Memorial Trust Gallery	Grantham	The Arts	126
Woolsthorpe Manor	Grantham	Houses and Castles	127
Geeson Bros Motor Cycle Museum and Workshop	Grantham	Industrial Heritage	128
Cogglesford Mill	Sleaford	Windmills and Watermills	129
Cranwell Aviation Heritage Centre	Sleaford	Aviation Heritage	130
The Pearoom Craft Centre	Sleaford	Crafts	131
Tupholme Abbey Ruins	Tupholme	Historic Buildings	132
Grimsthorpe Castle, Park and Gardens	Bourne	Houses and Castles	133
South Holland Centre	Spalding	The Arts	134
Pinchbeck Engine & Land Drainage Museum	Spalding	Industrial Heritage	135
Ayscoughfee Hall Museum	Spalding	Museums	136
Ayscoughfee Gardens	Spalding	Show Gardens	137
Spalding Tropical Forest	Spalding	Show Gardens	138
The Spalding Bulb Museum	Spalding	Show Gardens	139
Gordon Boswell Romany Museum	Spalding	Museums	140
Springfields Gardens (World of Flowers)	Spalding	Show Gardens	141
Baytree Owl Centre	Spalding	Animals & Wildlife	142
Museum of Entertainment	Spalding	Museums	143
Butterfly and Falconry Park	Spalding	Animals & Wildlife	144
Blackfriars Arts Centre	Boston	The Arts	145
Boston Guildhall Museum	Boston	Museums	146
Fydell House	Boston	Houses and Castles	147
St Botolph's Church (Boston Stump)	Boston	Churches	148
Maud Foster Windmill	Boston	Windmills and Watermills	149
Allied Forces Military Museum	Boston	Aviation Heritage	150
Adventure Afloat	Boston	Leisure	151
Bolingbroke Castle	Spilsby	Historic Buildings	152
Lincolnshire Aviation Heritage Centre	Spilsby	Aviation Heritage	153
Stockwith Mill	Spilsby	Crafts	154
Northcote Heavy Horse Centre	Spilsby	Animals & Wildlife	155
Spilsby Theatre	Spilsby	The Arts	156
Gunby Hall and Gardens	Spilsby	Houses and Castles	157
Magdalen Museum	Skegness	Museums	158
Batemans Brewery	Skegness	Industrial Heritage	159
Ridgequest (Art Foundry) Ltd	Skegness	The Arts	160
Gibraltar Point National Nature Reserve	Skegness	Country Parks	161
Burgh-Le-Marsh Windmill	Skegness	Windmills and Watermills	162

Name	Town	Facility Type	Reference
Robin Hood Leisure Park	Skegness	Leisure	163
Anderby Drainage Museum	Skegness	Industrial Heritage	164
Skegness Natureland Seal Sanctuary	Skegness	Animals & Wildlife	165
Skegness Water Leisure Park	Skegness	Leisure	166
Hardy's Animal Farm	Skegness	Animals & Wildlife	167
Butlin's Funcoast World	Skegness	Leisure	168
Fantasy Island	Skegness	Leisure	169
North Shore Holiday Centre	Skegness	Leisure	170
Church Farm Museum	Skegness	Museums	171
Panda's Palace	Skegness	Leisure	172
Skegness Electric Tramway	Skegness	Leisure	173
Skegness Model Village	Skegness	Leisure	174
Richmond Leisure Complex	Skegness	Leisure	175
Crowland Abbey	Crowland	Churches	176
Peakirk Waterfowl Gardens	Peterborough	Animals & Wildlife	177
Browne's Hospital	Stamford	Museums	178
Stamford Museum	Stamford	Museums	179
Stamford Arts Centre	Stamford	The Arts	180
Burghley House	Stamford	Houses and Castles	181
Stamford Shakespeare Company	Stamford	The Arts	182
Tallington Lakes Leisure Park	Stamford	Leisure	183
Fantasy World	Cleethorpes	Leisure	184
Sibsey Trader Mill	Boston	Windmills and Watermills	185
Willingham Woods	Market Rasen	Country Parks	186
Lincoln Shakespeare Company	Lincoln	The Arts	187
Billinghay Old Vicarage Cottage	Sleaford	Houses and Castles	188
Grantham House	Grantham	Houses and Castles	189
Tattershall College	Tattershall	Historic Buildings	190
Thornton Abbey	Thornton Curtis (Ulceby)	Historic Buildings	191
Bomber County Aviation Museum	Gainsborough	Aviation Heritage	192
Dogdyke Pumping Station	Tattershall	Industrial Heritage	193
Alkborough Turf Maze	Scunthorpe	Leisure	194
Heckington Windmill	Heckington	Windmills and Watermills	195
Wrawby Postmill	Brigg	Windmills and Watermills	196

References

● Bramwell, B. (1998) 'User satisfaction and product development in urban tourism', *Tourism Management*, Vol. 19 (1), pp. 35–47.
● Cannon, J. C. (1994) 'Issues in sampling and sample design – a managerial perspective', in Brent Ritchie, J. R. and Goeldner, C. R. (eds) *Travel, Tourism and Hospitality Research: A Handbook for Managers*, Second Edition, New York: John Wiley and Sons, pp. 131–43.
● Churchill, G. A. (1992) *Basic Marketing Research*, Second Edition, London: The Dryden Press.
● Dimmock, K. (1999) 'Management style and competitive strategies among tourism firms in the Northern Rivers', *Tourism Management*, Vol. 20, pp. 323–39.

● Hull, J. (1998) 'Market segmentation and ecotourism development on the Lower North Shore of Quebec', in Hall, C. M. and Lew, A. (eds) *Sustainable Tourism: A Geographical Perspective*, Harlow: Addison Wesley Longman, pp. 146–58.

● Kish, L. (1965) *Survey Sampling*, New York: Wiley.

● Lawson, R. W., Williams, J., Young, T. and Cossens, J. (1998) 'A comparison of residents' attitudes towards tourism in 10 New Zealand destinations', *Tourism Management*, Vol. 19 (3), pp. 247–56.

● Ouchida, M. E. (1980) 'Activation, affect and desire for excitement', unpublished thesis, University of Wisconsin.

● Prentice, R. C., Witt, S. F. and Hamer, C. (1998) 'Tourism as experience: the case of heritage parks', *Annals of Tourism Research*, Vol. 25 (1), pp. 1–24.

● Ryan, C. (1995) *Researching Tourist Satisfaction: Issues, Concepts, Problems*, London: Routledge.

● Smith, S. L. J. (1995) *Tourism Analysis: A Handbook*, Harlow: Longman.

● Tourism and Recreation Research Unit (1993), *Recreation Site Survey Manual: Methods and Techniques for Conducting Visitor Surveys*, London: E and F Spon.

Chapter 8

The Analysis of Qualitative Data – Content Analysis and Semiological Analysis

Learning Outcomes

At the end of this chapter you will be able to:

- understand the use of content and semiological analysis
- appreciate the opportunities for content and semiological analysis in tourism research
- evaluate content and semiological analysis
- identify computer software packages that can be used to undertake qualitative data analysis

Introduction

In this chapter you will be introduced to two related research techniques, content analysis and semiological analysis. Worked examples of both methods will be provided by way of an introduction to these techniques. These will be supported by the inclusion of brief details from published research to illustrate good practice and the potential of content and semiological analysis in leisure and tourism research. The chapter concludes with an evaluation of both methods. This chapter also includes brief details of computer software packages that can assist in the use of content analysis and which are becoming increasingly important in qualitative data analysis.

What is content analysis?

There is no standard definition or universal agreement concerning the nature of content analysis as a variety of approaches to its use can be found in the literature. We can however state with some confidence that it is a technique that is applied to non-statistical material and that it allows you to analyse such material in a systematic way. Content analysis is thus a quantitative means of analysing qualitative data.

Approaches to content analysis range from the purely quantitative where frequencies are counted within categories through to an approach that focuses on meaning in which inferences are drawn from the data and the data is considered in context. For example, McNeill (1990: 112) defines content analysis as 'a method of analysing the contents of documents or other non-statistical material in such a way that it is possible to make statistical comparisons between them'. Krippendorff (1980: 21), on the other hand, is critical of an approach to content analysis that is based on the simple counting of qualities, be they words, attributes or whatever. He criticises those who approach content analysis as a way of extracting content from data, and who assume that the content is contained in the data in an objective manner. He defines content analysis as 'a research technique for making replicable and valid inferences from data to their context'. As Weber (1990) points out, these inferences can be about the sender of the message, the message, or the audience for the message. As to the context, Krippendorff (1980: 23) argues that content analysis 'must be performed relative to and justified in terms of the context of the data' and that 'all theories of meaning, all theories of symbolic phenomena, including theories of message content, are alike in concerning themselves with the relationship between data and their context'. Krippendorff's approach to content analysis is, therefore, one of seeking to understand data as symbolic phenomena and, as such, has much in common with semiological analysis as discussed later in this chapter.

What sort of material is amenable to this method? As content analysis refers in particular to the interpretation or analysis of products of communication, it can be applied to such things as newspapers, television, radio, books, letters, diaries, public documents such as local authority minutes or company annual reports and Official Reports such as the Taylor Report following the Hillsborough football tragedy. With its focus on secondary material in general, and media analysis in particular, content analysis is a technique that has applications in tourism research. One could, for example, analyse material such as tour company brochures, destination promotional material, the travel pages in newspapers, travel programmes on the television or radio, holiday photographs or postcards.

Conducting content analysis research

So how do we carry out this sort of research? A six-stage process is suggested here:

1. Identify the aims and objectives of the project, and develop research questions (hypotheses) that are to be addressed by the research. These will be developed by reference to relevant theory and previous research.

2. Select the sample to be utilised in the research. The sampling techniques used in content analysis research are the same as those used in other areas of enquiry (see Chapter 7).

3. Record. This will involve the selection and training of coders and, crucially, the creation and testing of a coding scheme (see Figure 8.1 for a development of this stage). This requires the development of a content analysis grid, examples of which are provided throughout this chapter. When defining your categories of analysis do not overlook previous work as the use of standard classifications or previously developed categories enables you to compare your work with that of other researchers. For example, categories of socio-economic status are well established in this country and are commonly used by survey researchers. There is no reason why they should not be used by the content analyst where appropriate. Similarly, the content analyst should be aware of the body of published work of other content analysts in their field and be prepared to utilise or adapt their categories of analysis.

4. Data reduction. This may or may not be an issue but data reduction may be required by adjusting the data to fit the analysis (by condensing some of the categories of

Figure 8.1
Procedure for developing a content analysis coding scheme.

Weber sets out an eight-step procedure for the creation and testing of a coding scheme:

1. **Define the recording units** i.e. the unit of text that is to be classified. This can be done by word, by word sense, by sentence, by theme, by paragraph and by whole text. The larger the unit of analysis the greater the problem of reliability, however.

2. **Define the categories** Here you will need to decide whether categories are to be mutually exclusive or whether an item can be categorised under more than one variable. You will also need to decide how broad or narrow the categories should be. A category such as 'impacts of tourism' is broad, a category such as 'economic impacts of tourism' is narrower and a category such as 'employment generated by tourism' narrower still.

3. **Pre-test the coding on a sample of text**, and make any alterations as necessary.

4. **Assess the accuracy of the coding** if done by computer and the reliability of human coders.

5. **Revise the coding rules in response to step 4**.

6. **Go back to step 3** until satisfactory levels of reliability and accuracy are achieved.

7. **Code the text**.

8. **Assess levels of reliability and accuracy** Remember that errors will occur in a project of any length as coders will tire and will introduce small, subtle changes to the coding rules as the project progresses. Computer coding should also be checked for accuracy.

Source: Adapted from Weber (1990)

analysis for example) or it may be required as a means of discarding data that is found to be of no relevance to the enquiry.

5. Analysis. The analysis of data generated by this method makes use of the statistical procedures discussed elsewhere in this book such as absolute frequencies, relative frequencies (percentages), cross-tabulations and the testing of associations. The analysis can also include measures of volume such as the proportion of broadcast time given to a certain topic or the proportion of column inches in a newspaper allocated to a particular issue.

6. The research report. The writing of a research report is discussed in detail in Chapter 12, and the stages involved are no different for a piece of content analysis research. It is, however, worth stressing the importance of the 'methodology' section of your report as in the academic community research findings are not considered independently of the process by which they were obtained. Particular attention should therefore be paid to the discussion of the coding instructions, to the process by which your content analysis grid was generated, and to how the issue of reliability was tackled.

To illustrate this procedure we will look at a piece of unpublished research carried out by the author of this chapter. The focus of the research was an analysis of gender roles as depicted on the front covers of UK holiday brochures, and in particular whether males and females are depicted in active or passive roles. The hypothesis was that there would be a significant difference in the ways men and women were depicted on the covers of the brochures with men being depicted in active roles and women in passive roles.

The brochures included in the research were selected by using a systematic sampling method utilising the racks of a travel agency as the sampling frame (see Chapter 7 for a detailed discussion of sampling). A section from the content analysis grid compiled for this research is shown in Table 8.1.

Table 8.1 Sample content analysis grid

Product	Setting	Males	Females	Activities	Active males	Active females	Passive males	Passive females
Country Holidays	Classic thatched cottage	1A 1C	1A 1C	Standing as a group outside cottage	0	0	2	2
Shropshire	River near castle	1A 1C	1A 1C	Rowing a boat	2	0	0	2
Irish Country Holidays	Collage of scenes: golf, fishing, sailing, gypsy caravan	10A 6C	6A 6C	As per setting	12	2	4	10
Brittany Ferries Holiday Homes	Dining in garden of gite	2A	2A	Waiting for meal to arrive	0	1	2	1
Drive France	Picture of a sunflower	0	0		0	0	0	0
Ireland '96	Collage of scenes: fishing, sailing, cottage	2A	2A	As per setting	2	1	0	1

A = Adult
C = Child

Figure 8.2
Sample brochure
cover.

As can be seen from the grid in Table 8.1, a number of categories were used for the analysis. First of all the product was recorded, that is to say the name of the brochure. Brief comments were then recorded on the setting(s) depicted on the brochure covers. The number of males and females were then recorded, and this was broken down into adults (A) and children (C). The fourth column in the grid recorded the activities of the people depicted on the brochure covers, which was clearly important given the primary focus of the research. The final four columns on the grid analyse these activities by counting the number of males and females in active or passive roles. Coding and analysis was conducted manually.

Figure 8.2 shows the first cover used in the research, that for Country Holidays. The setting recorded on the grid is a 'classic thatched cottage'. There is one male adult in the picture, one male child, one female adult and one female child. The activity is recorded as 'standing as a group outside the cottage', as a result of which we count two passive males and two passive females (although you will note that the boy is holding a football, which suggests recent or future activity. This is something about which we will have more to say later). These figures are then entered on the grid in the next four columns.

The research continued in similar fashion analysing all the brochure covers with males and females being counted in either active or passive roles. The next stage was then to total the final four columns, which produced the following cross-tabulation:

	Active	Passive	Total
Males	58	28	86
Females	28	60	88
Total	86	88	174

As can be seen from the table, the number of males and females depicted on the front covers of the brochures sampled were almost identical as was the depiction of people in active and passive roles. However, when we look at activity/passivity by gender we can see immediately that twice as many males were depicted in actives roles, and twice as many females were shown in passive roles. Is this difference a significant one? To answer this question we would need to carry out the sort of statistical testing detailed in Chapter 11, and so we will leave this analysis at the present stage.

This example illustrates how content analysis has been used in tourism research. A leisure researcher, for example, could utilise a similar framework but instead analyse the posters or leaflets produced by local authority leisure centres. The categories that are used for the analysis in the grid are not fixed, and will be determined instead by the research objectives, and by the nature of the data set being analysed. Getting a feel for your material in this way is part of your development as an insightful researcher.

One important issue to appreciate at this stage is the multi-layered nature of photographic images, and so it is not always a case of simply allocating one image to one category in the grid. For example, a picture of a middle-aged couple playing golf on a beautiful loch-side course projects three separate images – the middle-aged couple (the target segment), golf (the activity) and the loch-side setting (the scenery). Depending on the categories in your grid that image could thus be recorded three times.

The use of content analysis in tourism research

In this section we will briefly look at the use of content analysis in tourism research in order to further your understanding of the technique and its range of potential applications, and also to offer further categories for classification. This is not, therefore, a definitive literature review of the use of content analysis in leisure and tourism research. The aim is to stimulate your interest in content analysis and to help you generate ideas for your own research.

Postcards and content analysis

One particularly fruitful area of content analysis concerns the use of postcards. Albers and James (1988), for example, analysed postcards to study the relationship between tourism, ethnicity and photography. They put forward a four-stage process to achieve this:

- a discussion of the importance of photographs within tourism as a way of depicting ethnicity
- a focus on the pictures and messages transmitted by travel photography
- an analysis of methodological approaches i.e. content analysis and semiological analysis
- the location of the above within 'a wider discourse on tourist ideology'.

In doing so they suggest four content categories that tend to be significant and thus worthwhile using in analysis of this nature:

1. *The subjects of the postcards* – their number, age and gender.

2. *Dress* – are the subjects dressed in everyday clothing or are they wearing some form of festive clothing? Is the dress indigenous or alien?

3. *Presentation* – is it an active photo or a formal portrait? Is it natural or posed? What of the body language of the people in the photograph?

4. *Surroundings* – is the photograph taken in a studio or elsewhere? Is it taken in an outdoor indigenous location or at a tourist attraction? What artefacts are used in the composition?

Brochures and content analysis

There is a growing body of content analysis research in the tourism field utilising promotional literature such as destination brochures, two examples of which are briefly outlined here. Pritchard and Morgan (1996) focus on brand imagery and specifically on what they call 'destination specific icons' – national flags, national costume, language, culturally specific activities, famous personalities and emblems/symbols – in the brochures promoting Ireland, Scotland and Wales to US tourists. The aim of their research was to investigate the degree to which the marketing objectives of these three destinations were reflected in the brochure images used. They hypothesised, and subsequently concluded that, as Wales is an immature destination for US tourists, brochure imagery would be used to transmit a unique brand identity. Scotland on the other hand, being a more firmly established destination, would use imagery to reinforce brand identity thus allowing room for a focus on product features such as golf. Ireland, however, being a mature destination would not need to use destination imagery to such an extent, and so would have even greater latitude to stress product features such as sporting opportunities and Irish hospitality.

Using a content analysis of National Tourist Board brochures, the authors placed nearly 1,500 illustrations into seven categories – heritage, scenery and wildlife, activities, people, urban and rural life, consumption activities (such as shopping, eating and drinking) and destination specific icons. As stated earlier, it was this latter category which was of particular interest, and Pritchard and Morgan show how the three countries use them in different ways. Because Ireland is a mature destination for US tourists it already has a strong brand identity, and so has less need to utilise destination specific icons. In their analysis they found that only 4 per cent of Irish brochure images fell into this category. Scotland, as a more established destination, was found to use destination specific icons to enhance brand identity with 27 per cent of brochure images falling into that category; whereas the brochures for Wales, a new destination, were found to strongly use destination specific icons as a way of establishing a unique identity – 31 per cent of Welsh brochure images fitted the destination icon category. The authors conclude that:

> *from the evidence of these case studies it seems that the destination icon theory has*
> *some validity – 'new' destinations do make greater use of them. However further*
> *research is required on other emerging destinations in different markets to confirm*
> *this theory.*   (Pritchard and Morgan 1996: 363)

Another approach to the analysis of tourist brochures is taken by Dann (1996: 61) in which he explores 'the images employed by the media-makers as they attempt to bring together on the tourism stage two sets of actors – the hosts and the guests'. Dann's analysis is based on over 5,000 thousand pictures in 11 summer holiday brochures aimed at British tourists. His data, as we shall see, was subjected to both quantitative and qualitative analysis.

Given the research aims outlined in the previous paragraph, Dann developed seven categories of analysis for pictures of people in the brochures – single tourists only, two tourists only, three or more tourists only, single locals only, two locals only, three or more locals only, and, finally, locals and tourists. He found that 25 per cent of the pictures featured no people at all, reinforcing the notion of tourism as a means of escape. He also found that over 60 per cent of the pictures were of tourists only, which, as he says, emphasised 'advertisers' support for the normative segregation of hosts from guests' (Dann 1996: 63).

The next stage in his analysis was to cross-tabulate people by setting – see Table 8.2, which shows the results of this analysis and which provides another example of a content analysis grid in its final stage. From this data Dann identified four zones for tourists and locals:

- Zone A involved no people and covered the categories transport, sights, local scenes and animal scenes
- Zone B involved tourists only and covered beach, sports and hotel scenes
- Zone C depicted locals and tourists and covered hotels, entertainment and local scenes
- Zone D depicted locals only and covered entertainment, local scenes, transport, sights and animal scenes

For the moment we will leave Dann's analysis at that stage. We will return to it briefly in a later section on semiological analysis for, as Dann argues, there is a need for what he calls further 'semiotic ethnography', and so he subjects his data to qualitative analysis as well to support the quantitative analysis we have just discussed.

Analysing textual material

So far we have been considering the analysis of photographic images in brochures and on postcards. Content analysis can however be applied to textual material as well, thus opening up other forms of communication such as newspaper articles, letters, diaries, advertisements, radio broadcasts and television programmes. Here the researcher may count the number of times a pre-defined word, phrase or idea occurs in the text. The researcher, therefore, assumes that these words, phrases or ideas that are categorised together have similar meanings. As Weber (1990: 12) points out:

Table 8.2   Distribution of people by location

People category	Beach	Transport	Hotel	Sights	Local scene	Enter-tainment	Sport	Animal scene	Total %
No people (n = 1257)	7.6	2.9	50.8	18.0	16.8	0.2	0.3	3.4	100.0
Tourists (1)	16.9	0.5	38.5	1.2	4.6	0.3	37.0	1.0	100.0
Tourists (2)	24.7	1.7	47.7	1.8	6.7	0.5	15.8	1.1	100.0
Tourists (3+)	21.5	1.4	65.3	1.4	2.9	1.7	5.4	0.3	100.0
Tourists only (n = 3110)	21.5	1.3	58.5	1.5	3.8	1.3	11.5	0.6	100.0
Locals (1)	2.7	1.3	16.8	7.4	57.7	7.4	–	6.7	100.0
Locals (2)	4.5	2.3	–	6.8	59.1	18.2	2.3	6.8	100.0
Locals (3+)	3.2	2.6	3.9	7.8	61.1	15.6	3.2	2.6	100.0
Locals only (n = 347)	3.2	2.0	8.9	7.5	59.4	12.4	1.7	4.9	100.0
Tourist & locals (n = 458)	5.0	1.1	68.6	5.4	13.1	4.6	1.3	0.9	100.0
All (n = 5172)	15.5	1.7	54.2	6.2	11.5	2.1	7.2	1.6	100.0

Source: Dann, G. (1996) 'The people of tourist brochures', in Selwyn, T. (ed.) *The Tourist Image: Myths and Myth Making in Tourism*. Copyright John Wiley and Sons Limited. Reproduced with permission

Depending on the purposes of the investigator, this similarity may be based on the precise meaning of the words (such as grouping synonyms together), or may be based on words sharing similar connotations (such as grouping together several words implying a concern with a concept such as WEALTH or POWER).

While this may sound fairly straightforward, in practice it is a major challenge for the researcher as she/he strives to reduce a mountain of textual data into a few content categories.

To illustrate the use of textual analysis, a step-by-step guide is provided below. First of all, you need to read the article in Figure 8.3. This is the first six paragraphs of a four-page text and photo article that appeared in *The Sunday Times*. Here the journalist is reporting on a visit to Skibo Castle, situated on the Dornoch Firth in north east Scotland, and home of the exclusive Carnegie Club.

Step 1   Read the article and note down any trends that you notice in the text. The following themes are suggested:

- class by inheritance e.g. breeding, Lord Glenconner, Prince Alfonso
- class by wealth e.g. truly indolent rich, heiress, Donald Trump, Andrew Carnegie
- class by enterprise e.g. Donald Trump, film star, Peter de Savary, Andrew Carnegie, magnate
- class by aspiration e.g. hoi-polloi, encroaching masses, here-today-gone-tomorrow celebs
- exclusivity by class e.g. redoubt, private clubs, sanctuary, waiting list, select

Figure 8.3
Sample text for
textual analysis.

The fairytale castle

Roddy Martine visits Skibo, where an exclusive club offers a privileged few the chance to relax in luxury and tranquillity, in the glorious style of Carnegie.

In an age when even the hoi-polloi can lay their hands on serious money, and in a society so busy striving to be 'classless' that breeding means nothing, there are fewer and fewer places left for the truly, indolently rich to disport themselves in peace. Today, a suite at the Georges Cinq in Paris, the delights of a beach club on Martinique or an exclusive ski chalet in Aspen are just a lottery or pools win away. Only one last redoubt remains to protect the congenitally urbane from the encroaching masses, the private club. They are curious institutions attracting both envy and ridicule. The enduring image is of establishments that are trenchantly elitist, snobby and stuffy; with attractions that rarely run beyond smoking rooms and leather armchairs; and a membership composed entirely of ageing, gouty gentlemen.

Private clubs are back in vogue, and their characters are as divergent as the aspirations of the social sub-species they cater for. At the lower end, with its membership of media hacks and the here-today-gone-tomorrow celebs of popular culture, is the Groucho Club in London's Soho.

Across the Atlantic, and at the top of the scale, the ever-apparent Donald Trump is ploughing his resources into developing Mar-A-Largo, the Florida home of the late American heiress Marjorie Merryweather Post, as an exclusive beach club. Then there is the Mount Kenya Safari Club at Nanyuki, north of Nairobi, founded by Ray Ryan and William Holden, the film star, which continues to flourish as a sporting sanctuary.

Back in the 1970s, Lord Glenconner, then the Hon Colin Tennant, had a go at creating an island paradise on Mustique, and imported his friends. Then there was Prince Alfonso's Marbella Club in Spain, now transformed into an hotel. For those wanting to join Life at Key Club in the Bahamas there is a 25-year waiting list.

No less select, if not quite as exotic, is the Carnegie Club at Skibo Castle, on the shores of the Dornoch Firth in north east Scotland, which opened in April.

In this unlikely location Peter de Savary, whose entrepreneurial ventures in the past have encompassed shipping, oil and property development, has thrown open the doors of this mansion which once belonged to the Scots-born American steel magnate and philanthropist Andrew Carnegie.

Source: The Sunday Times, 20 August 1995

- inclusivity by class e.g. classless, encroaching masses
- description of place by desirability e.g. relax in luxury and tranquillity, island paradise, exclusive, sporting sanctuary, mansion
- description of place by fantasy e.g. living the dream (accompanying photo caption not included here), exotic, fairytale castle
- personalities by gender.

You should note that, in this instance, these categories have been developed inductively from a reading of the text. An alternative deductive approach would have involved prior development of categories with the text analysed within this pre-determined framework.

Step 2 You now need to decide if all these trends, which can be used as categories in your content analysis grid, are manageable or useful. For the purpose of this illustration the themes are going to be clustered, and so the nine initial categories are condensed into five broader but related ones:

1. class by wealth (wealth, inheritance and enterprise are clustered, since they share a common theme in this article of having money)
2. class by aspiration (some of the people mentioned in the article have achieved wealth by winning the lottery or pools, but have not been seen as having 'made it' in the journalist's terms – they are still the 'hoi-polloi')

3. exclusivity by class

4. inclusivity by class

5. description of place by desirability (this category has been clustered with fantasy, since the fantasy descriptions are strongly attractive).

The initial category of personalities by gender is dropped as notions of class and class positioning predominate in this article.

Step 3 Having condensed the categories into five manageable ones, we can now construct a content analysis grid. A simple method of counting references within each category is to number them and mark the text with that number each time a related reference occurs. Thus, your annotated text will look something like this:

> Roddy Martin visits Skibo, where an exclusive[5] club[3] offers a privileged few[1,5] the chance to relax in luxury and tranquillity[3,5], in the glorious style[5] of Carnegie[1].

Note that some references overlap categories. While it is desirable that discrete categorisation occurs, it is not always possible with text. You then need to total your textual references in each of your categories, and place them in a content analysis grid:

Class by wealth	Class by aspiration	Exclusivity by class	Inclusivity by class	Description of place by desirability
19	7	19	3	21

Step 4 The exercise so far has been useful in quantitatively analysing the first impressions which the reader will have had of the text – namely, that it is redolent in ideas about class, wealth and exclusivity. To measure the results, we can convert the raw count to a proportion or percentage of the text in order to see how saturated it is with any given category of ideas. The section of the article we have been using amounts to approximately 400 words. We can now express the numbers in the grid as percentages, although these are approximate as some references are composed of more than one word:

Class by wealth	Class by aspiration	Exclusivity by class	Inclusivity by class	Description of place by desirability
19	7	19	3	21
5%	2%	5%	1%	5%

Step 5 Draw inferences from the results and make your interpretation. In this case we can confirm that the introduction to the article contains twice as many references to wealth and exclusivity as it does to aspiration and inclusivity. Since desirable places are linked to the exclusive and wealthy, we can see that around 15 per cent of the text contains references to a wealthy upper class having exclusive access to desirable places of their own.

There are of course a number of questions that are not answered by a content analysis of this article. While the categories of analysis used in the grid are quite sophisticated, the level of analysis must remain somewhat superficial. A further understanding of what is going on here would be achieved by considering issues such as:

- The market segments targeted by *The Sunday Times*. Is the newspaper aimed at wealthy readers?
- How does this readership react to articles concerning the extremely rich?
- How do the 'hoi-polloi', who may have become rich through winning the football pools or National Lottery for example, feel about their exclusion from such clubs?

- How is suitability for entry to such clubs established?
- Are there really only two classes of people in society as implied by the article?
- How does the host community at Skibo relate to the Club?

To put it succinctly, what is the real meaning behind this article? To answer these sorts of questions you will need to go beyond a content analysis and utilise some of the qualitative techniques such as interviews and observations that are discussed in Chapter 5.

The use of textual analysis in tourism research

In this section brief details are provided of research projects in the area of tourism that have utilised a content analysis of textual material. Markwell and Basche (1998) describe their research on the dynamics of nature-based tourism, and on satisfaction levels of an ecotour. In both cases diaries were analysed, the material providing the basis for subsequent post-tour interviewing. This is another use of content analysis that has not so far been considered, its application at the early stages of a research project to provide material that informs other techniques.

Elsewhere, Stevens (1997) utilised content analysis in an examination of hotel ethical codes, which are written documents through which organisations express their ethical policies. They are important in terms of establishing organisational culture and articulating core values. Stevens was concerned with investigating these codes in order to identify those issues seen as important to hospitality managers, and also the topics that were most often addressed in the codes. In addition, she was interested in comparing the content of hotel ethical codes with the codes used in other business sectors in America.

Using a sampling frame of hotel and motel companies listed in two American directories, she approached 204 hotel and management companies requesting a copy of their ethical code. Usable replies were received from 26 hotel companies and 16 management companies. These codes were then analysed by two researchers trained in the technique who had undertaken practice analysis on a different set of ethical codes. Their rate of agreement in their analysis of the hotel ethical codes was 95 per cent. This is an important point and one that indicates how reliability can be built into the technique by using more than one researcher, and by cross-checking their analysis for levels of agreement. We will return to the issue of reliability and content analysis at the end of this chapter.

Two grids were used in the analysis, one analysing conduct on behalf of the firm, the other looking at conduct against the firm i.e. actions that might harm the firm. The categories of analysis within the grids, and the results produced can be seen in Table 8.3, which shows the results for just the hotel companies. As can be seen from these tables, each topic was analysed at four levels – 'not discussed' i.e. the ethical code made no mention of the topic; 'discussed' i.e. the ethical code devoted only a couple of sentences to the topic; 'discussed in detail' i.e. between two sentences and two short paragraphs; and 'emphasised' i.e. two or more lengthy paragraphs were allocated to the topic.

As Stevens acknowledges, the categories of analysis were adapted from ones used previously by Cressey and Moore (1983) and by Mathews (1987), and the four levels of analysis were borrowed directly from Mathews. It is a perfectly legitimate research technique to utilise directly or to adapt the work of other researchers (as long as it is properly acknowledged of course!). Replicating the work of others can be an important way of establishing the reliability and validity of research findings and, as in this case, it allows you to contrast results in different circumstances. Stevens, for example, compared her findings from the hotel sector with similar work on ethical codes conducted in other sectors of American business.

Table 8.3 Content analysis grid – ethical codes for hotels

	Content of ethical codes for hotels: conduct on behalf of firm						
	Not discussed		Discussed		Discussed in detail		Emphasized	
City/State/US Govt. Relations	17	65%	5	19%	3	12%	1	4%
Customer relations	8	31%	13	50%	4	15%	1	4%
Employee relations	19	73%	4	15%	2	8%	1	4%
Competitor relations	13	50%	7	27%	3	11%	3	12%
Investor relations	21	81%	3	12%	0	0%	2	8%
Civic and community affairs	25	96%	1	4%	0	0%	0	0%
Environmental affairs	23	88%	0	0%	1	4%	2	8%
Guest safety	25	96%	0	0%	0	0%	1	4%
Product quality	21	81%	4	15%	1	4%	0	0%
Payments or political contributions to govts, govt officials or other influential people	12	46%	3	12%	6	23%	5	19%
Personal character	8	30%	12	46%	3	11%	3	12%
Hospitality ethics	21	81%	4	15%	1	4%	0	0%

Number of codes examined: 26.

	Content of ethical codes for hotels: conduct against firm						
	Not discussed		Discussed		Discussed in detail		Emphasized	
Conflict of interest	5	19%	5	19%	3	12%	13	50%
Divulging trade secrets	11	42%	7	27%	2	8%	6	23%
Insider trader information	11	42%	9	35%	2	8%	4	15%
Other conduct against firm	16	61%	7	27%	1	4%	2	8%
Integrity of books/records	11	42%	8	31%	2	8%	5	19%
Payments/gifts	9	34%	3	12%	2	8%	12	46%
Laws cited	22	84%	2	8%	0	0%	2	8%
Federal agencies referred to	26	100%	0	0%	0	0%	0	0%
Compliance mentioned	10	38%	12	47%	0	0%	4	15%
Penalties for illegal behavior	15	58%	9	34%	1	4%	1	4%
Affidavit	Yes		14	54%	No		12	46%
Basis of code	Legal		20	77%	Ethical		6	23%

Number of codes examined: 26.

Source: Reprinted from *International Journal of Hospitality Management*, Vol. 16, Stevens, B., 'Hotel ethical codes: a content analysis', pp. 261–71, Copyright 1997, with permission from Elsevier Science

We need not be concerned here with a detailed consideration of Stevens' results, her work is included here to illustrate the potential of content analysis to the leisure and tourism researcher as a means of analysing textual material. Tourism and hospitality students may however be interested to know that she found a relatively low incidence of the use of ethical codes in the hotel sector – 57 per cent of the hotel companies and 21 per cent of the management companies were found to have such codes compared with a rate of between 70 per cent and 90 per cent of companies in other sectors of American business. As can be seen from the data in Table 8.3, conflict of interest was the most frequently mentioned category, which matched the findings from other corporate studies.

Another example of textual analysis is provided by Nickerson (1995) who was interested in the role of gambling as a means of tourism and economic development in small communities. Nickerson studied the mining town of Deadwood, South Dakota as it introduced limited stakes gaming in 1989. Three research objectives were established:

- the gaming-related issues raised in newspapers
- the emphasis given to tourism and economic regeneration issues in newspaper stories in areas that had or were about to introduce gaming
- the trends apparent in newspaper stories dealing with gaming by tracking these over a five-year period.

The methodology was to carry out a content analysis of three newspapers in the area. No sampling techniques were used in this project. Instead, every edition of the three newspapers was analysed for a period of just under five years, which covered a period both before and after the introduction of gaming. Three keywords – gambling, tourism, Deadwood – were used to conduct a headline search. Any article with one of these three keywords in the headline was then selected for inclusion in the study. This produced 712 articles in total. An initial reading of the articles produced 21 content categories for analysis. All articles were then reread and allocated to just one of these categories. This meant that articles raising several issues were allocated to the category dealing with the main issue discussed. Finally, for ease of analysis, these 21 topics were condensed to five final general categories.

These five categories were economic issues (32 per cent of the articles), regulatory concerns (21 per cent), initial questions on gaming (19 per cent), logistical and planning matters (15 per cent) and negative issues associated with gaming (13 per cent). Nickerson then provides in her results section a more detailed account of each of the topics as she addresses her three research objectives. For example, a content analysis grid dealing with the economic issues related to gambling includes categories such as tourism and the economy, tourism and gambling, and land value. The number of newspaper articles dealing with these topics is provided for each of the five years of the study, thus allowing the researcher to track the relative importance of issues over time. Similarly, the analysis grid looking at the negative issues associated with gambling provides figures for the five-year period on articles dealing with social issues, crime and gambling near schools. Nickerson concludes by considering a number of questions concerning gaming as a means of economic development, and points out that the social issues surrounding gaming only come to the fore after it has been introduced.

An interesting example of content analysis research combining graphical and textual analysis is provided by Gamradt (1995). Her research was concerned with examining how Jamaican children perceive tourists and tourism. Her specific research objectives were twofold. Firstly, she was concerned to 'simply "give voice" to some of Jamaica's young hosts'; and, secondly, 'to examine the feasibility of using children's drawings and written commentaries as a way to study the interrelationship between proximity to touristic activities, other kinds of economic development, and patterns of culture acquisition and identity formation in a developing nation' (Gamradt 1995: 735).

Gamradt's research instrument was a self-completion activity booklet, and her analysis is based on responses to three items from the booklet:

- 'Here is what I think about people who visit Jamaica . . .'
- 'What people from other countries should know about Jamaica . . .'
- 'Draw a picture of some visitors who have come to Jamaica from far away'. (A space was also included for the children to add comments on their drawing.)

We can see, therefore, that two of the items involved content analysis of the written responses to the completion of open-ended questions, and the third required the content analysis of drawings as a way of investigating how children depicted visitors. The sample consisted of 316 children, predominantly in the 11–12 age group, from six schools. A reliability check was built into the methodology by re-analysing the data. For example, the drawings were re-categorised by the same researcher one week later, and this produced a level of agreement ranging from 81 to 90 per cent. The drawings were then assessed by two independent researchers, which produced a level of agreement ranging from 78 to 93 per cent.

As with the other examples of content analysis research that we have looked at, we are not concerned here with a detailed consideration of the findings but instead with exploring the potential of this technique for leisure and tourism researchers. A brief consideration of Gamradt's findings is, however, instructive as they offer additional examples of content analysis grids as well as pointing to further issues and problems with this approach. To analyse the Jamaican children's views of visitors a content analysis grid was constructed. This grid identified the positive traits mentioned by the sample as a whole (41 per cent) as well as the negative traits (5 per cent). These responses were also analysed by school so that differences could be observed between children attending schools near to tourism centres and those attending schools in remote areas. Comparisons were also made between types of school e.g. between an elite private preparatory school and different types of public school as a way of examining possible differences in the socialisation process. A similar grid was constructed to analyse responses to the second question concerning what visitors should know about Jamaica. Again a distinction was drawn between positive comments (31 per cent) and negative attributes (3 per cent).

The grid used to analyse the drawings used categories such as people only, friendship/affiliation, beachlife, entertainment and commercial activities. The analysis of the drawings was, however, more problematic. Drawings can clearly cut across content categories. The categories developed were mutually exclusive and so the researchers had to allocate each drawing to just one category according to what was thought to be its primary focus. Another problem with interpreting the drawings was that the meaning of the drawing was unclear. As Gamradt acknowledges, it would have been beneficial if the researchers had been able to discuss the drawings with the children to gain a clearer understanding of what was going on. This suggests the need to use host culture researchers, perhaps as part of a longer-term ethnographic project. The issue of cultural differences is clearly a potentially important one in a project of this nature, and points to the need for researchers undertaking work of this nature to be culturally aware if the interpretation of such research findings is to be an accurate one.

Finally, in this section, although not strictly speaking textual material of the sort we have been discussing so far, content analysis can be applied to the responses gathered from semi-structured/depth interviews in order to identify those words and ideas common to respondents in the research programme. For example, let us assume that you have carried out a piece of research looking at the motivations for playing squash among a small sample of members of a private sector squash club. Because you not only want to explore motivations, but also to try and understand the meaning behind the responses, you have chosen a qualitative approach using a programme of semi-structured interviews. Each interview has lasted approximately half an hour, and 20 members have been included in the study, giving a total of ten hours of taped conversation. Let us also assume that you have produced a transcript of these interviews. This will give you a daunting amount of material. How do you begin to analyse it? How can you identify the key motivations for playing squash? Again, content analysis can be used to sift and sort the material in order to identify groups of ideas, which can then be located onto a content analysis grid. While your respondents will not necessarily use the same words, common themes are likely to emerge that will form the categories in the grid. In this case these themes might include relaxation /stress reduction, getting/keeping fit, fun/enjoyment, social contact and competition.

Depending on the size of your sample, this can be a time-consuming process (making a transcript certainly will be!), and so researchers are increasingly turning to software packages that allow them to conduct a more sophisticated and speedier analysis of their data. A brief discussion of these software packages is provided in a later section. This is not to imply that your analysis of semi-structured interviews will be reduced solely to quantitative measures in this way. The reporting of such interviews typically includes a great deal of verbatim evidence to support the analysis. Content analysis can, however, provide you with one way of making sense of your data. Indeed, if we think of content analysis in this way then the coding of answers to open-ended questions in surveys is yet another application of this technique.

Content analysis, emerging as it does from a positivist paradigm, is a descriptive approach concerned with quantification, with counting frequencies utilising categories such as age and gender, and thus with describing the basic features of a data-set. It is therefore concerned with the surface level meaning. From the content analysis grid one can begin to infer certain things, and inferential statistics can be applied to the data (see Chapter 11) but, as Albers and James (1988: 146–7) point out:

> *In order to determine whether these inferences have any validity, however, the research must move beyond the level of content description. For no matter how comprehensive and detailed a content analysis may be, it can never determine the symbolic meaning of a specific set of pictorial appearances, nor can it explain their existence.*

To do this, to take the research on to a different level, we need to conduct an interpretative semiological analysis, and it is to this that we turn in the next section.

What is semiological analysis?

Semiological analysis is a way of getting below the surface of a piece of communication to discover what lies beneath the obvious content of the communication, and, as MacCannell (1989: 3) reminds us, 'Within semiotics, the term "communication" is unbounded. It can refer to intentional or unintentional, direct or mediated communication between human beings'. MacCannell defines semiotics as:

> *a technical perspective for close analysis of the forms and processes of communication . . . Anything that can be treated as a question of communication and/or the problem of discovering the meaning of signs is appropriate to semiotic analysis. A sign is half fact and half concept or idea.*

Harvey and MacDonald (1993: 46) define semiology more succinctly as 'the science of signs'. As they point out, 'any sign, be it a word, a picture, a flag or a piece of fashion clothing, communicates a meaning to us'. The meaning is however neither constant or simple. Furthermore, this meaning exists at two levels:

1. The *denotative level.* This is the surface level. To take a very basic example of what is meant here, consider a picture of a red rose. At the denotative level this picture represents a prickly, sweet-scented flower.

2. The *connotative level.* This is the second level of deeper meaning i.e. what in different contexts the sign might stand for. And so, returning to our picture of a red rose, in different contexts this might stand for Lancashire County Cricket Club (the red rose county), the Labour Party (which uses the red rose as its logo), love (an emotion traditionally represented by a red rose) and the English Rugby Union team (who have a red rose on their shirts).

The example is a simple one to illustrate a complex point. Media output is clearly more sophisticated than a single sign. It does however operate at both levels, and so semiology is an approach concerned with analysing not just what goes on at the surface level (the denotative level), but also what lies behind the message (the connotative level). In other words, semiotic analysis is concerned with the meanings that are embedded in communication. We will look at some brief examples of semiological analysis shortly.

While Harvey and MacDonald talk of the connotative and denotative levels, Albers and James use the terms 'metanym' and 'metaphor'. Albers and James (1988) argue that a photograph (postcard) can operate at the level of a metanym (a sign) or a metaphor (a symbol). At the metanymic level the photograph is an objective recording of that which is real. At the metaphoric level however the photograph, by analogy, stands for something else, there is a hidden message. According to Albers and James (1988: 141):

Pictorial elements are represented as symbols; they are devices that allude to meanings and understandings outside the picture. In both art and advertising the intent of photography is largely metaphoric. The camera becomes a means to fabricate illusions and to convey subjective messages.

Postcards, for example, contain both metaphoric and/or metanymic images, and Albers and James argue that a key challenge for the tourism researcher is to establish which type of image is being used and to what end.

Cohen (1993) suggests that the use of metanym and metaphor can be applied to images in all kinds of media such as souvenirs, the arts and touristic events. He argues that the authenticity of the image is a key issue. At the metanymic level this is not an issue as the image is neutral, it is authentic. Cohen reminds us however of the potential for authenticity to be 'staged', and for ideological bias to be introduced.

The language of semiotic analysis can be daunting, and the situation is not helped by the fact that there is no universal vocabulary of semiotics, and so different writers use the same term in slightly different ways. In the following section we introduce you to the meaning and usage of key terms in semiotic analysis before applying them to a tourism advertisement. This section is drawn in part from an article by Mick (1986) and students interested in developing their understanding of semiotics are referred to this source as Mick provides a brief history of semiotics along with definitions and discussion of key terms. For a more detailed discussion of the history and vocabulary of semiotics see, for example, Noth (1990).

Mick starts out by discussing the work of Saussure who argued that language is a system of signs, and that a sign is the relationship between the signified (the object, a bridge for example), and the signifier (the spoken word 'bridge' or its equivalent in other languages). Meaning is thus established and communicated through this relationship between the signified and the signifier. As Mick (1986: 197) points out:

Saussure sought to overthrow the traditional view of linguistics wherein language was seen as an aggregation of separate units (words), each with a distinct meaning. From Saussure's perspective, the relationships and interaction between words take precedence over individual words when meaning is formed or derived.

Signs can be organised in two ways – there can be *paradigmatic relations* or *syntagmatic relations*. Saussure used the term 'paradigm' in this context to refer to a set of signs, and so 'Paradigmatic relations are those that reveal the oppositions and contrasts between signs in a set' (Mick 1986: 197). Mick utilises the example of the setting for an advertisement to illustrate the point. The advertiser has to choose from a range of settings (the 'paradigm'), and, in developing the message, meaning is transmitted through the difference between the sign that is selected and those that are rejected. If we take as another example the images used in postcards, many of these depict indigenous people in festive dress. The fact that they are not shown in everyday dress is as significant as the fact that they are shown in festive dress. A syntagm, on the other hand, is the message that emerges through signs from various paradigms, and so 'Syntagmatic relations are evident in the combinations of paradigmatic choices, revealing the rules or conventions that facilitate sign combinations to form messages . . .' (Mick 1986: 197). In other words, syntagmatic relations are about how meaning is established through combination. A resort may be described in a brochure as 'restful and peaceful'. The relationship between the two adjectives and the noun is a syntagmatic relationship. The choice of adjectives – 'restful and peaceful' rather than 'lively and bustling' – is paradigmatic. When conducting semiotic analysis we are, therefore, concerned with both syntagmatic relations (i.e. with combinations) and with paradigmatic relations (i.e. with choice).

Mick also refers to the work of Peirce. Unlike Saussure, who was a linguist and thus concerned with words as sign systems, Peirce applied semiotics to non-verbal as well as verbal sign systems. Peirce developed his triangular model of semiotics (see Figure 8.4). In this model meaning is acquired through the relationship between three elements – the object signified, the sign (that is to say the signifier being used to represent the object) and the interpretant (i.e. the person interpreting the sign in question). Peirce's model is thus a development on the work of Saussure in that he argued that semiotics concerns the relationship between three elements rather than two by introducing the concept of the 'interpretant'. However, as Mick points out, what Peirce meant by the interpretant is the subject of debate among academics. Here it is being used in the sense of the person

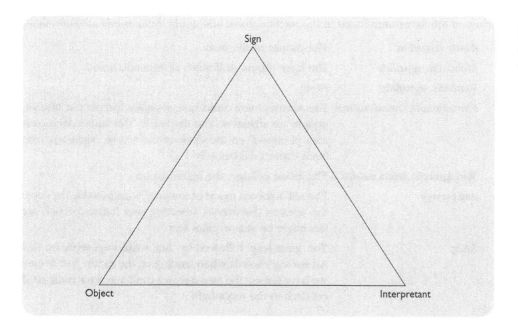

Figure 8.4
Peirce's triangular model of semiotics.

interpreting the sign (as advocated b͜ ͜a͜ ke͜s (1' 77), for example), but this is not a position that Mick holds.

When considering the work of Peirce we also need to take on board his three major sign categories – *iconic* signs, *indexical* signs and *sy nbolic* signs. An iconic sign is one that represents its object in that it replicates the object. The tourist returning from Italy with a miniature Leaning Tower of Pisa has purchased an iconic sign. An indexical sign correlates with something more, and so a picture of Sydney Harbour Bridge is an index for Australia. An indexical sign has a causal relationship to its object. A symbolic sign requires the recipient to use their referent systems to interpret it as the sign itself relates to its object in a straightforward way – there is no causal relationship. Symbolic signs are thus fully connotative in character, and so may be interpreted in different ways. Symbolic signs such as major tourist sites and national flags, for example, are frequently used in destination marketing to represent a destination. In this sense there is clearly an overlap between these three categories, as a picture of the Forth Road Bridge can be an icon, but can also be a symbol representing Scotland.

Finally, in our brief tour of the language of semiology, we need to take on board two additional terms from the work of Barthes (1977), *anchorage* and *relay*. Anchorage refers to the process by which the picture and the caption in an advertisement, for example, work together to anchor the desired signified. Relay refers to how

> *'text (most often a snatch of dialogue) and image stand in a complementary relationship; the words, in the same way as the images, are fragments of a more general syntagm and the unity of the message is realized at a higher level, that of the story . . .'.*
>
> (Barthes 1977: 41)

So the reader is moved back and forth between the words and the image.

The use of semiological analysis in tourism research

Let us now look at a couple of examples of semiological analysis in the tourism sector. We have already made the point that advertisements are a rich source of material for this form of analysis, and readers are directed to the advertisement in Figure 8.5. We now take many of the terms introduced in the section above and apply them to this advertisement:

Iconic signifiers	The picture of the boat
Indexical signifiers	The large moon, indicative of romantic mood
Symbolic signifiers	None
Paradigmatic relationships	The advertisement could have shown actual people. Instead, people are absent so that the reader can author their own idea of 'mood' on the deck of the vessel. Night-time has been chosen deliberately
Syntagmatic relationships	The moon is large, the lights are on
Anchorage	The self-authored mood of romance is anchored in the copy: the 'greatest discoveries' (meeting your future spouse?) are still made by sea: a 'giant leap'
Relay	The 'giant leap' followed by 'one small step' replicate Neil Armstrong's words when landing on the moon. Just in case we have not got the message, we can have 'a romantic stroll on deck in the moonlight'.

Figure 8.5
Semiotic analysis
– sample
advertisement.

Figure 8.6
Dann's four-quadrant model of touristic paradise.

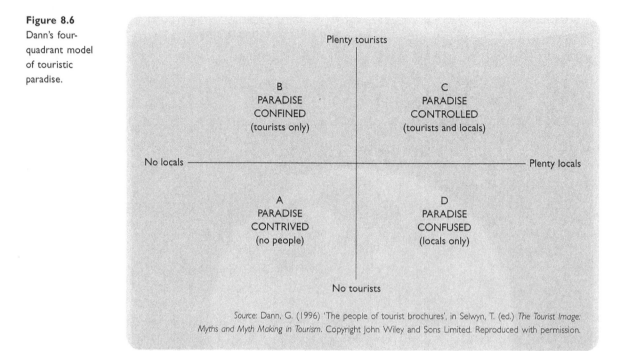

Plenty tourists

B
PARADISE
CONFINED
(tourists only)

C
PARADISE
CONTROLLED
(tourists and locals)

No locals ——————————————————————————— Plenty locals

A
PARADISE
CONTRIVED
(no people)

D
PARADISE
CONFUSED
(locals only)

No tourists

Source: Dann, G. (1996) 'The people of tourist brochures', in Selwyn, T. (ed.) *The Tourist Image:*
Myths and Myth Making in Tourism. Copyright John Wiley and Sons Limited. Reproduced with permission.

Turning to Dann's work on tourist brochures, he went on to identify four forms of holidays (see Figure 8.6) that match the four zones we discussed earlier.

Utilising this model, a qualitative semiotic analysis of the data was undertaken using textual material as well as the pictures. This developed his understanding of the four quadrants and, while we need not concern ourselves here with the detail of that analysis, it was undertaken under the following headings:

PARADISE CONFINED
The tourist ghetto

PARADISE CONTROLLED
Natives as servants
Natives as entertainers
Natives as vendors

PARADISE CONTRIVED
Absence of people
Natives as scenery
Natives as cultural markers

PARADISE CONFUSED
Natives as seducers
Natives as intermediaries
Natives as familiar
Natives as tourists
Tourists as natives

(Dann 1996)

Finally, in this section, let us return to the front cover of the brochure with which we started this chapter (see Figure 8.2), and subject this to a semiological analysis. What can we say about this image at the denotative level? The family group depicted on the cover is assumed to be the segment targeted by the company. They represent the typical nuclear family of two parents of the same age and their two children. The boy is wearing shorts and trainers, while the girl has on a pretty floral dress. The parents' clothing can best be described as smart casual. The father has on brown lace-up shoes, jeans and a polo shirt, while the mother is wearing a plain skirt and top. The father is holding the daughter in his arms, and the son stands slightly in front of the rest of his family holding a ball. The family group is photographed outside the thatched cottage where they are assumed to be staying. And that is all we can really say about this image at the surface denotative level.

What though is going on at the connotative level? What else is this image actually saying to us? How might it be decoded? The following connotations could be allocated:

- The two-parent, two-child unit is the dominant and 'natural' family form (although we know that this is not actually the case, most people do not live in family units of this kind).

- Marriage and heterosexual relationships are the norm. While there is no 'evidence' in this picture that the couple are married, we just 'know' that they are.

- Middle-class families of this type are the intended consumers for this company's product. Their clothing suggests a more affluent middle-class background, and we can assume that the property they are staying in does not come cheap (together forming a powerful syntagmatic relationship).

- The father has taken on a position of dominance within the family. Not only is he taller but he holds his daughter in a protective way.

- The position of the wife is revealing. She has a sweet smile on her face, and her hand rests lightly and lovingly on her husband's arm. Her demeanour and, crucially, her head tilt, suggest submission.

- The position of the boy is similarly interesting. He stands apart, there is no physical contact as there is between the other family members, suggesting perhaps early developing male independence. He is holding a ball, which suggests recent or future activity of a typical male sort. We cannot see the daughter engaging in such 'rough' activity.

- Overall, this image supports a view of society structured on patriarchal principles where the males are seen as active and naturally dominant, whereas women are viewed as passive, nurturing and forbearing.

There is therefore quite a lot that the researcher can say by way of an analysis of one image, although any conclusions drawn on the basis of one person's analysis of one cover would have to be cautious, to say the least. In the full research project a similar analysis was conducted on all of the brochures included in the original content analysis stage, and the final report challenged the notion that these images were representative of actual or ideal society. Ideally one would want to take this research further by interviewing the companies involved to understand more about the messages encoded in their brochure covers. One would also want to interview the customers of these companies to see if they do indeed match the target audience implied by the brochure covers, and to investigate how they decoded the transmitted messages. One would also want to investigate how customers react to the values implied by the cover images. All of this would provide a fuller understanding of what was going on, and would help establish the reliability and validity of the initial findings.

This discussion of tourism and semiological analysis has, of necessity, been a brief one. Readers who are interested in developing their understanding of this approach and its potential within tourism research are referred to the paper by Echtner (1999). In this paper the author not only includes a useful discussion of the vocabulary of terminology but also provides a valuable literature review of the use of semiology within tourism research, focusing particularly on tourism marketing.

In conclusion, semiological analysis is not straightforward. Leaving aside the very real difficulties of the terminology, it must be appreciated that, unlike content analysis, semiology is not a method. While Echtner also acknowledges that semiology need not be a linear procedure, she does offer a useful six-stage process for semiological enquiry (see Figure 8.7).

Figure 8.7
Six stages of
semiological
enquiry.

Stage 1   Select a representative data set e.g. a set of destination postcards

Stage 2   Establish the units of analysis – this could be types of picture or words

Stage 3   Count frequencies

(Stages 1–3 are, in effect, a content analysis)

Stage 4   Examine the syntagmatic and paradigmatic relationships

Stage 5   Develop a taxonomy of element combinations within and between cases. Understand the rules that determine this system

Stage 6   Get through the surface meaning (the denotative level) to draw out the deeper level of meaning (the connotative level)

Source: Adapted from Echtner (1999)

The identification of these stages is valuable in reminding us of what goes into research of this nature. You should appreciate, however, that semiology allows significant freedom in terms of developing a research design geared to meeting your specific research aims.

The use of computers in qualitative data analysis

It is not intended in this section to provide a detailed account of all the software packages on the market, what they do and how to use them. This is beyond the scope of this text. Readers who are interested in developing their knowledge in this area are referred, for example, to the work of Miles and Huberman (1994), Weitzman and Miles (1995), Gahan and Hannibal (1998) and Fielding and Lee (1998). Instead, we hope to give you a flavour of what is available by briefly introducing you to some of the packages that analyse qualitative data. All are relatively inexpensive, and all run in a Windows environment. As the cost of these packages come down, as they become increasingly powerful and sophisticated in their application, and as researchers become increasingly comfortable with computer analysis of all sorts, it is clear that qualitative data analysis using computer software will become more widespread in leisure and tourism research.

QSR's NUD.IST software – Non-numerical Unstructured Data Indexing, Searching and Theory-building – allows you to process imported plain text files from, for example, interviews, focus group discussions, answers to open-ended questions in surveys, business correspondence or media extracts or external documents of any sort that have been typed or scanned into your computer. QSR NUD.IST can also handle material such as photographs, maps and even videotapes. You can then search the imported text for words, phrases, patterns or relationships and automatically code the results. Patterns of codes and categories can then be searched for, and so the meanings within the data can be questioned. Such searches can be saved for further exploration, thus enabling you to develop and test theories. Version 4 of NUD.IST includes QSR Merge, which allows you to merge any number of NUD.IST databases into one. Finally, you can also import and export tables so statistical analysis can be conducted using SPSS for Windows.

ATLAS.ti works not only with text but also graphical and audio data, allowing you to analyse and interpret such data. As the publicity material for this package says, using it you can 'build unique networks which allow you to "connect" visually selected passages, memos, and codes, so enabling you to construct concepts and theories based on visible relations and to reveal other relations'. As with NUD.IST, this package codes automatically, and allows you to export your data into SPSS for statistical analysis.

Finally, DICTION is a text analysis package that analyses a passage of text in order to determine the tone of a verbal message utilising five general features plus 35 sub-features. The general features are:

- *certainty* – language indicating determination and inflexibility
- *activity* – language that is to do with change and the realisation of ideas
- *optimism* – the language of endorsement or language that accentuates the positive
- *realism* – language that connects with people's everyday lives
- *commonality* – language that focuses on the accepted values of a group.

DICTION produces reports on the text and writes the results to numeric files so that they can be subjected to statistical analysis using SPSS for Windows. The package also provides comparative statistics based on a wide sample of public texts so that the researcher can compare their data with a normative range of scores.

An important advantage of using computer software packages like these is that they allow you to more easily explore the context. To do this manually would be a time-consuming and laborious affair. Data analysis packages, however, have a keyword-in-context facility that prints the sentences surrounding a keyword. This allows you to check the semantic validity (see below) of the analysis as one of the problems with undertaking computer analysis is the inability of the software package to distinguish between the use of the same word in different contexts. Another advantage of carrying out computer analysis is that the procedures for coding text are clear and consistent and so reliability should not be an issue here. This has the added advantage, assuming that the same software has been used, that results from different studies are comparable.

It is appreciated that not all researchers will have access to the sort of software packages discussed here. Most will, however, have use of word-processing software and this too can be used to conduct some basic textual analysis by using the 'find' option to conduct keyword searches and counts. A potential problem with analysis of this nature is that it does not consider words in context, but, as Anderson and Shaw (1999) point out, this is not an insurmountable problem as cases can be removed at a later stage of analysis if the context is deemed to be inappropriate.

Finally, an example of the use of computers in tourism research to conduct qualitative data analysis is provided in the paper by Anderson and Shaw (1999). While this is essentially a methodological paper concerned with comparing different forms of qualitative data analysis, it provides an example of NUD.IST in action. In this case, the programme is used to analyse the responses to an open question in a survey of volunteer staff motivation at a heritage attraction.

Evaluating content and semiological analysis

In this section we will apply the three key evaluative concepts of validity, reliability and representativeness, which have been introduced earlier in the book, as well as considering some of the various strengths and weaknesses associated with content and semiological analysis. Establishing validity is crucial, but the term is confusing as it has several different applications. We will look briefly at some of these applications, and consider their relevance to the evaluation of content analysis.

It is accepted that the minimum a researcher should settle for is *face validity*, which refers to the extent that a measure actually reflects the concept it is meant to measure. The weakness of face validity is that it refers to a single variable, and Weber (1990) argues that many content analysis studies can only offer face validity and so are easy to criticise. Any claim to validity is strengthened if multiple variables are involved and if data generated by content analysis can be compared with external criteria. This leads us into other forms of validity. *Construct validity* is established if a measure can be shown to be correlated with another measure of the same construct. As Weber (1990: 19) puts it, 'construct validity entails the generalizability of the construct across measures or methods'. Construct validity can be broken down into *convergent validity* and *discriminant validity*. If a measure correlates with other measures of the same construct it is said to have convergent validity, whereas if a measure is not correlated with measures of different constructs it is said to have discriminant validity.

Another type of validity is *predictive validity*. Weber (1990: 20) defines this as 'the extent that forecasts about events or conditions external to the study are shown to correspond to actual events or conditions'. Weber argues that content analysis studies rarely demonstrate predictive validity, not because there is an inherent weakness in the method, but because such considerations are not considered at the research design stage. The final type of validity to be discussed here is *semantic validity*, which is achieved when agreement is reached that the words that have been categorised together do have similar meanings. This is a particular problem with language, which can clearly be ambiguous and can have symbolic meaning. As Krippendorff (1980: 157) writes, 'In content analysis high semantical validity is achieved when the semantics of the data language corresponds to that of the source, the receiver, or any other context relative to which data are examined'.

Another problem with language occurs if the study is cross-cultural in nature or if foreign-language documents are being analysed. Typically, one will want to translate any such documents before content analysis begins, but a problem is likely to arise concerning the accuracy of the translation. One common way of tackling this problem is to use back-translation. Let us assume, for example, that you wish to study sections from a sample of German tour operator brochures. The required text will first of all be translated into English, and this will then be translated back into German. A comparison is then made between the back-translation and the original document, and if they are identical then the English translation can be said to be valid. Linguistic problems can also arise with computer analysis as some programs are unable to discriminate between the same word having quite different meanings. If this were the case then any count of keywords would lack semantic validity.

This discussion of validity may have appeared a little daunting not only because writers refer to different forms of validity (see Chapter 13 of Krippendorff for a more detailed typology of validation for example), but also because the types of validity referred to are defined in different ways in the research methods literature. You should, however, appreciate that validity is crucial. An unreliable measure (see below) must lack validity but a reliable measure is not necessarily a valid one. A measurement could be 100 per cent reliable but would be invalid, and thus useless, if it was actually measuring the wrong thing.

The issue of representativeness is also an important one, but is one that can be addressed by content analysis researchers. In our earlier discussion we noted how the author of this chapter used the racks of a travel agency as a sampling frame from which a systematic sample of brochures was selected. Reference was also made to the work of Stevens (1997) who used directories as a sampling frame from which she selected the hotel and motel companies for inclusion in her research. Probability sampling methods can therefore be used in this type of research, and so the issue of representativeness can be addressed. In similar vein, this sort of research has been criticised as it typically uses small samples. While this may be true, the amount of material generated can be considerable. We saw earlier that, although Dann used just 11 summer holiday brochures in his research, over 5,000 pictures were analysed. Similarly, Pritchard and Morgan's work involved nearly 1,500 illustrations.

Another criticism that can be levelled at this sort of research is that it is impressionistic, and therefore unreliable. In other words, would another researcher faced with an identical set of postcards or whatever else is being analysed produce an identical, or broadly similar, content analysis grid? The answer to this question will depend in part on the categories for analysis. Categories such as gender are usually unproblematic but age and other more contestable categories may well give rise to problems with the reliability of the method. Detailed and unambiguous coding rules need, therefore, to be developed.

Reliability is clearly a key concern for content analysis research, and so you need to ensure that, as far as possible, your categorisation procedures are reliable and consistent. Let us, therefore, take a more detailed look at this concept. Krippendorff discusses three types of reliability that are relevant to the evaluation of content analysis – stability, reproducibility and accuracy. 'Stability is the degree to which a process is invariant or unchanging over time' (Krippendorff 1980: 130). In other words, stability is established if the same researcher repeats their analysis of the same material at different times. We saw an example of this earlier in the work of Gamradt where the categorisation of the children's drawings was repeated a week later by the same researcher. However, because only one researcher is involved in this process, stability is, Krippendorff argues, 'the weakest form of reliability'.

Reproducibility is defined by Krippendorff (1980: 131) as 'the degree to which a process can be recreated under varying circumstances, at different locations, using different coders'. Some writers refer to this as *intercoder reliability*, and we saw an example of this in the work of Stevens (1997) who used two researchers trained in this technique, and who cross-checked their analysis of the ethical codes. They achieved a high rate of intercoder reliability of 95 per cent. Weber argues that high rates of intercoder reliability such as this are a minimum requirement for content analysis because reproducibility measures shared understanding or meaning.

The third type of reliability is accuracy, which is defined by Krippendorff (1980: 131) as 'the degree to which a process functionally conforms to a known standard, or yields what it is designed to yield'. Both Weber and Krippendorff argue that accuracy is the strongest form of reliability. However, as Weber acknowledges, standard classifications within texts are uncommon, and so researchers using this method rarely claim accuracy when evaluating the reliability of their work. This is perhaps an unfortunate term, as to suggest that a piece of research lacks accuracy is to imply that it is a pretty poor piece of work. We need, therefore, to appreciate the specific meaning of the word 'accuracy' in this context. In practice, reproducibility or intercoder reliability is the best that the researcher can hope for.

When we move on to an interpretative semiotic analysis then it may well be just that, one person's interpretation of what is going on at the connotative level. In such circumstances any claims of reliability are difficult to substantiate. In our earlier discussion of semiotics we saw that communications have semiotic meanings encoded into them, and that these are decoded by readers or viewers through the use of their referent systems. However, just because a message has been sent does not mean that it will have been received as the decoding of a message depends on the referent systems of recipients. Similarly, the reading of a message is not proof that the message was sent as the reader may well have interpreted a message in ways that were unintended by those responsible for the message. In addition, different recipients of the same message may well decode that message in different ways.

For example, a number of connotations were allocated by the researcher to the advertisement in Figure 8.2. That decoding of the message is unlikely to correspond with the message sent by brochure designers – that would have to be tested by other methods. Crucially, the researcher cannot claim reliability for these connotations as, without testing, we cannot assume that other readers of the brochure will have decoded the cover message in the same way. This is not an objective process as you cannot deny the contribution of the researcher to the interpretation of the message; indeed in this instance this is precisely what we are evaluating – the researcher's interpretation of the message. Meanings are, however, not necessarily shared – if they are then this will only likely occur at the manifest level or amongst people from similar cultural backgrounds.

This discussion of validity, representativeness and reliability should be applied to the evaluation of all research methods as they are common and key issues. You should not, therefore, dismiss content and semiological analysis as techniques simply because such issues are raised. Hopefully, you have appreciated from the discussion so far that they have much to recommend them. Indeed, the very nature of this sort of research makes it attractive in that it is unobtrusive as the data collection does not interfere with the phenomenon being observed and so there is no contamination of the data.

Another advantage of content/semiological analysis is that it is cheap in the sense that it costs very little to gather together the material for analysis. The fact that documents are available that cover lengthy periods of time means that content analysis is a particularly useful technique for tracking changes over time in things like attitudes, values and beliefs. Following on from this, we can also explore cross-cultural differences, although the point has already been made that you need to use researchers familiar with the 'host' culture. Another appeal of content analysis is its flexibility in that it can be used in the initial stages of research as a means of developing hypotheses for testing by other methods; or it can be used in the later stages of research as a means of testing hypotheses developed by other methods. Data collected by the use of content analysis can also be compared with data generated by other research methods. This approach, known as 'triangulation', is an important way of establishing the validity of research findings.

On the down side, the analysis stage can certainly be time-consuming, particularly if undertaking the analysis of textual material, but that is an issue with all research methods. The amount of initial material needed is, however, not always great, and in our experience impressive dissertations have been written using no more than ten travel brochures, for example, as a basis for the work. Having said that, it is clear from the examples discussed in this chapter that a considerable amount of material can be handled using these techniques.

As with all research methods there are potential ethical considerations to be taken on board, particularly if analysing personal documents such as letters or diaries in which case the principle of 'informed consent' applies. The historical nature of such documents may of course make the obtaining of such consent difficult, if not impossible.

Summary

This concludes our discussion of content and semiological analysis. In this chapter worked examples of both methods have been provided, and mention has also been made of the potential for using computer software packages to assist with the process of qualitative data analysis. A detailed evaluation has been included to enable the reader to develop an appreciation of the strengths, weaknesses and issues involved in this type of research. A brief review has also been conducted of the use of content and semiological analysis within the tourism literature to further your understanding of the potential of these methods for leisure and tourism researchers. Researchers in the disciplines of leisure and tourism have arguably been slow to realise the potential of these twin techniques. However, an increasing interest in forms of communication and media analysis is likely to result in much more work being done in this area.

The last thoughts on the topic are left to Weber (1990: 69), who wrote that, *there is no single right way to do content analysis. Instead, investigators must judge what methods are appropriate for their substantive problems . . . One reason content analysis is not used more widely is that it is difficult and time-consuming to do well. Computers eliminate some of the drudgery, but time, effort, skill, and art are required to produce results, interpretations, and explanations that are valid and theoretically interesting.*

Student Activities

Activity 1

Undertake a content analysis of one of the holiday programmes on television. It is suggested that you use the same research hypothesis as the one applied to the holiday brochures discussed earlier in this chapter i.e. there is a significant difference in the ways men and women are depicted in these programmes, with men being depicted in active roles and women in passive roles. You are encouraged, however, to develop your own research objectives and to analyse the programmes accordingly.

To carry out this research you will need to:

● develop a content analysis grid in line with your research objectives

● videotape the programme (it is suggested that your analysis should cover more than one week's output)

● complete your content analysis grid (you should consider working with a colleague as a way of measuring intercoder reliability)

● subject your findings to appropriate statistical analysis.

Activity 2

Carry out a textual analysis of a holiday programme on either television or radio to research the ways in which destinations are portrayed through the use of language. You will need to construct a content analysis grid using categories such as 'ways of escape', 'fun', 'activity', 'sexual encounter' etc.

Activity 3

Using the categories of analysis developed by Pritchard and Morgan (1996), analyse the destination brochures of former Soviet Bloc countries or emerging Third World countries. What kind of brand identity is being portrayed? Analyse the use of destination specific icons in these brochures.

Activity 4

Conduct a 'time series' content analysis of a destination's postcards. How has 'the message' changed over time?

Activity 5

Obtain the brochures for a cruise company over the past 60 years and carry out a content analysis of the marketing messages over time.

References

● Albers, P. C. and James, W. R. (1988) 'Travel photography. A methodological approach', *Annals of Tourism Research*, Vol. 15, pp. 134–58.

● Anderson, M. A. and Shaw, R. N. (1999) 'A comparative evaluation of qualitative data analytic techniques in identifying volunteer motivation in tourism', *Tourism Management*, Vol. 20 (1), pp. 99–106.

● Barthes, R. (1977) *Image Music Text*, London: Fontana.

● Cohen, E. (1993) 'The study of touristic images of native people. Mitigating the stereotype of a stereotype', in Pearce, D. G. and Butler, R. W. (eds) *Tourism Research: Critiques and Challenges*, London: Routledge.

● Cressey, D. and Moore, C. A. (1983) 'Managerial values and corporate codes of ethics', *California Management Review*, 25 (53), pp. 53–77.

● Dann, G. (1996) 'The people of tourist brochures', in Selwyn, T. (ed.) *The Tourist Image: Myths and Myth Making in Tourism*, Chichester: John Wiley.

● Echtner, C. M. (1999) 'The semiotic paradigm: implications for tourism research', *Tourism Management*, Vol. 20 (1), pp. 47–57.

● Fielding, N. G. and Lee, R. M. (1998) *Computer Analysis and Qualitative Research*, London: Sage.

● Gahan, C. and Hannibal, M. (1998) *Doing Qualitative Research Using QSR NUD.IST*, London: Sage.

● Gamradt, J. (1995) 'Jamaican children's representations of tourism', *Annals of Tourism Research*, Vol. 22 (4), pp. 735–62.

● Harvey, L. and MacDonald, M. (1993) *Doing Sociology*, Basingstoke: Macmillan.

● Hawkes, T. (1977) *Structuralism and Semiotics*, London: Methuen.

● Krippendorff, K. (1980) *Content Analysis: An Introduction to Its Methodolgy*, Newbury Park, California: Sage.

● MacCannell, D. (1989) 'Introduction' to special issue of *Annals of Tourism Research*, Vol. 16 (1), pp. 1–6.

● Markwell, K. and Basche, C. (1998) 'Using personal diaries to collect data', *Annals of Tourism Research*, Vol. 25 (1), pp. 228–31.

● Mathews, M. C. (1987) 'Codes of ethics: organizational behavior and misbehavior', *Research in Corporate Social Performance*, Vol. 9, pp. 107–30.

● McNeill, P. (1990) *Research Methods*, Second Edition, London: Routledge.

● Mick, D. G. (1986) 'Consumer research and semiotics: exploring the morphology of signs, symbols, and significance', *Journal of Consumer Research*, Vol. 13, pp. 196–213.

● Miles, M. B. and Huberman, A. M. (1994) *Qualitative Data Analysis: An Expanded Sourcebook*, Thousand Oaks, California: Sage.

● Nickerson, N. P. (1995) 'Tourism and gambling content analysis', *Annals of Tourism Research*, Vol. 22 (1), pp. 53–66.

● Noth, W. (1990) *The Handbook of Semiotics*, Bloomington, Indiana: Indiana University Press.

● Pritchard, A. and Morgan, N. J. (1996) 'Selling the Celtic Arc to the USA: a comparative analysis of the destination brochure images used in the marketing of Ireland, Scotland and Wales', *Journal of Vacation Marketing*, Vol. 2 (4), pp. 346–65.

● Stevens, B. (1997) 'Hotel ethical codes: a content analysis', *International Journal of Hospitality Management*, Vol. 16 (3), pp. 261–71.

● Weber, R. P. (1990) *Basic Content Analysis*, Second Edition, Newbury Park, California: Sage.

● Weitzman, E. A. and Miles, M. B. (1995) *Computer Programs for Qualitative Data Analysis: A Software Sourcebook*, Thousand Oaks, California: Sage.

Chapter 9

Summarising Data – Descriptive Statistics and the Graphical Presentation of Data

Learning Outcomes

At the end of this chapter you will be able to:

- understand the four 'levels of measurement'
- set up an SPSS data file
- summarise data using tables and frequency distributions
- use SPSS to generate frequency distributions
- construct a range of graphical presentations to summarise data, and understand their appropriate use
- use SPSS to generate graphs
- use SPSS to select cases for analysis
- use SPSS to compute a new variable
- identify the various measures of location and understand their appropriate use
- identify the various measures of dispersion and understand their appropriate use
- understand the importance and properties of a normal distribution, and the notion of 'skewness'
- use SPSS to calculate measures of location, measures of dispersion and skewness

Introduction

Chapter 4 of this book looked at the collection and analysis of quantitative secondary data, and Chapter 6 dealt with the generation of primary data through the use of questionnaires. In this chapter we look at ways of summarising the quantitative data generated by such techniques so that it can be more easily understood. In Chapters 10 and 11 we then move on to a consideration of more complex statistical procedures.

For many students the thought of working with numbers and conducting statistical tests is intimidating. This need not, however, be the case, particularly as most students will have access to statistical analysis software packages that will do all the calculations for you. In this chapter and Chapters 10 and 11 we will, therefore, be providing step-by-step instructions on how to use SPSS to carry out the statistical tests as they are introduced. The version we will be using is the latest one at the time of writing, SPSS 8.0 for Windows. Older versions of SPSS will work in broadly similar ways, although minor modifications may have to be made. You should consult the 'Help' menu within SPSS for guidance if you do experience difficulties.

SPSS is a powerful statistical analysis and data management package, and is the standard statistical package used by governments, businesses and academic institutions around the globe. SPSS can take data that is inputted directly or that is imported from another package such as EXCEL. It can then generate charts, plot distributions and trends, produce descriptive statistics, as well as carrying out complex statistical analysis. SPSS will not, however, tell you which statistical test is appropriate for your needs nor will it interpret the results for you. Before using SPSS you need a clear idea of what you want to know, which tests to use in which circumstances and how to interpret the test statistic. These issues are discussed throughout the next three chapters.

The data file that we are going to use was generated from a research project undertaken by one of the authors of this book. The aims of this project were to analyse the expectations of holiday-makers visiting Hadrian's Wall, a World Heritage Site situated in the north of England, and to assess the extent to which their experience and interpretations matched their expectations. The main questionnaire used in that research can be found in Appendix 2 at the end of the book. A follow-up questionnaire was also used in this project. This generated additional variables that are mentioned in Chapters 9, 10 and 11, and that are included in the data file, although the follow-up questionnaire itself has not been reproduced. A section of the final data file (101 of the 371 respondents) is included in Appendix 4. This has been included so that you can set up your own SPSS data file and follow the procedures discussed in this chapter and the next two. The data file can also be used to answer the questions at the end of this chapter and Chapters 10 and 11, and for further data analysis of the reader's choosing. It should be noted that not all the variables from the main questionnaire can be found in the data file. A selection has been included to illustrate the techniques discussed.

Types of variable

Before we proceed with the discussion of ways of summarising data, it is vital that you appreciate the different types of variable that exist because this determines the form of analysis that can be undertaken. Most writers on statistics refer to four types of variable – nominal, ordinal, interval and ratio. These are often referred to as the four *levels of measurement*, and they are discussed below.

Nominal variables

Nominal variables involve categories such as gender (male/female), and so some books refer to nominal level variables as 'categorical' variables. Such variables must be mutually exclusive; in other words, it should not be possible for a case to fall into more than one category. Nominal variables thus include a number of categories that the researcher can then use to classify cases and to count frequencies. For example, in a sample survey of

100 visitors to a museum you might count 71 women and 29 men; or 54 people who answered 'yes' to a question about whether they would be prepared to pay an entrance fee to the museum, and 46 people who answered 'no'.

In the Hadrian's Wall survey (see Appendix 2), the variable 'travel' (Question 2.a) is an example of a nominal variable as it is classifying respondents according to their mode of travel to Hadrian's Wall. Each respondent (case) in the survey can only be allocated to one of these eight categories, and in terms of analysis all we can really do with this variable is to count the frequencies in each category or perhaps express them as a percentage of the sample. For this reason, nominal level variables are said to contain the least information.

Ordinal variables

Ordinal variables allow us to go beyond simply measuring the presence or absence of a particular characteristic and, instead, to measure the intensity or degree of something by ordering categories. The classic example of this in questionnaire design is the use of the Likert scale (see Chapter 6). Question 2.b in the Hadrian's Wall survey is an example of an ordinal variable. A question has been put – 'If used Hadrian's bus, to what extent do you agree or disagree that it was value for money?' – and possible responses are ordered on a five-point scale ranging from 'strongly agree' through to 'strongly disagree'. So, in this question there is more than just a series of categories, as is the case with a nominal variable, as there is clearly an order to these categories. Ordinal variables are thus used to 'rank' things. However, it cannot be assumed that the distance between ranks is the same. Finishers in a horse race are ranked first, second, third and so on, but we cannot assume that the distance between the first and second horse was the same as the distance between the second and third horse. Limitations are thus still placed on what we can say about ordinal variables, although they clearly contain more information than nominal variables.

Interval/ratio variables

While there is a difference between interval and ratio variables, which will be explained shortly, for the purpose of the procedures discussed in this chapter and the next two, the difference can be ignored as tests that are appropriate for interval variables are also appropriate for ratio variables.

With interval/ratio variables we can say a lot more about our data as their use overcomes the main limitation of ordinal level data by allowing us to measure the differences between values. Temperature is an example of an interval scale as here numbers on the scale are not only ordered but the intervals along the scale are of equal size. The difference in temperature between 25 and 26 degrees Fahrenheit is the same as the difference between 95 and 96 degrees Fahrenheit.

The main feature that distinguishes the interval scale from the ratio scale is that it has an arbitrary zero point. On a ratio scale there is an absolute, a logical zero point. A value of zero means that there is a total absence of that variable e.g. income. We could then say, for example, that someone earns twice as much as someone else. Age would be another example of a ratio variable, and so we could say that someone who is 50 is twice as old as someone who is 25 and that the difference in their ages is 25 years.

If you look at Question 20 in the Hadrian's Wall survey, you will see that age was recorded as a variable. Having just said that age is an interval/ratio variable, in this case age has been grouped into categories – 16–24 years, 25–34 years, 35–44 years, 45–59 years and

Table 9.1

Types of variable

Variable type	Description	Example from Hadrian's Wall survey
Nominal	Classification of responses into mutually exclusive categories	Question 2.a – travel
Ordinal	Categories are rank ordered	Question 2.b – hwvalue
Interval/ratio	Distances between items on scale are equal	Question 3.a – lenhol

over 60 years. In this instance age is now an ordinal variable as the age categories have been placed in order. While important detail may be lost by grouping data in this way, the analysis of data by categories can aid presentation and lead to more easily understandable findings. There is also the particular issue of sensitivity when it comes to age. Some people are not prepared to give their actual age but might be prepared to indicate which category their age falls into.

Ratio variables contain the most information and nominal variables the least. As a result, more statistical tests can be performed on interval/ratio variables than on the other two types. It is important that you appreciate the characteristics of the three main types of variable (see summary in Table 9.1) and can identify them, as the type of data places limitations on the type of analysis. You need to think very carefully at the research design stage about the implications for the nature of the subsequent data analysis arising from the types of variables you develop.

Given the limitations placed on nominal and ordinal data there is a move among researchers to treat ordinal data as interval data where multiple-item scales are involved. For example, you may have measured tourists' satisfaction with various aspects of their holiday hotel using a number of statements in conjunction with a five-point attitude scale. Each statement, on its own, constitutes an ordinal scale. However, scores from these statements could be combined to give an overall satisfaction score. Some researchers argue that it is legitimate to treat multiple-item measures of this nature as interval data because of the large number of categories involved and because the tests that are run utilise numbers rather than the words/categories that those numbers represent. Bryman and Cramer (1997), for example, argue that if a variable is made up of a small number of categories such as the five in a typical scale then it should be treated as an ordinal variable. If, however, the number of categories is significantly increased to say 15 or 20 by combining several scales then, they argue, it is legitimate to treat such a variable as an interval level one. An example of this can be found in the Hadrian's Wall data file. This includes an interval level variable called SATSCORE. This is a computed measure of overall satisfaction with the visit. It was arrived at by combining 12 separate measures of satisfaction, which were initially measured on a five-point Likert scale.

Setting up an SPSS data file

SPSS requires a lot of memory to run properly and so it is advisable not to have other programs open when using it. To open SPSS click on the SPSS icon. You can enter data directly into a spreadsheet in SPSS or you can enter data into any program from which SPSS can import. Data that is already in numerical form can be inputted as it is. Data that is in the form of words or categories must be given a numerical code before inputting. This is why code boxes appear on questionnaires.

When you open SPSS 8.0 for Windows you are asked what you would like to do e.g. run the tutorial, type in data or open an existing data file. For those of you who would like to know more about SPSS, this would be a good opportunity to do so by looking at the tutorial. As we are setting up our own SPSS data file, you should select the **type in data** option, and then click on **OK**. This produces the SPSS Data Editor window, which is in a spreadsheet format, and which we use to set up our data file. This window can be maximised by clicking in the grey square in the top right-hand corner. If you wish subsequently to return this window to its original size, then click in the square with the overlapping boxes in the top right-hand corner of the screen.

For the purpose of this exercise it is recommended that you input the raw data directly into SPSS. Each record is stored in a separate row, in SPSS this is known as a 'case', and all data for a single variable is stored in a column. Each respondent in a questionnaire survey would thus constitute a case. Notice that case numbers are already provided by SPSS in the left-hand column.

Defining the variables

Before entering your data you need to define each of the variables in your research. To do this a number of stages have to be followed, and these are set out in Figure 9.1. This takes you through the stages involved in defining the variable 'travel' from the sample data file in Appendix 4. Once you have done this you simply follow the same procedure for the remaining variables.

Data entry in SPSS

Now that the variables have been set up, the data can be entered from the data file in Appendix 4. This is done in exactly the same way as you would enter data on any spreadsheet, using the arrow keys or the mouse to move around. At first the cursor will be in the first row of the first column. The frame of the cell is shown in bold to indicate that it is the active cell. Once all the data has been entered, check it for accuracy, and then save the data file in the usual way i.e. by selecting **Save** from the **File** menu.

If you make any errors in entering values they can be corrected by highlighting the appropriate cell, entering the correct value, and moving to another cell. If you want to delete the contents of a cell and leave it empty, move to that cell and press the Backspace or Delete key and move to another cell. This will leave a full stop (.) in the cell to denote a missing value. To leave SPSS select **Exit** from the **File** menu.

Summarising data: tables and graphs

Having collected the raw data in a questionnaire survey for example, consideration needs to be given to ways of summarising that data in order to make your research findings more easily understood. Two approaches are considered in this chapter – the use of descriptive statistics, which will be discussed in a later section, and the use of tables and graphs. The tabular and graphical presentation of data is a common feature of student work but both approaches must be used with care. For example, the level of measurement of your data will limit the range of graphical options. Some forms of presentation are more

Figure 9.1
Defining variables
in SPSS.

Before you commence defining variables in SPSS you need to have ready, for all your variables, three key pieces of information: the name that you are giving the variable, the variable type in SPSS terms and any value labels. These are explained below as we go through the procedure.

1. Place the cursor at the top of the first column on the word 'var' and double click the left-hand mouse button. The **Define Variable** dialog box appears. This defaults to the variable name VAR0001. Press the delete key to remove this, and then type in the variable name. This can be up to eight characters long and must begin with a letter (this will be **travel** in this example). If you have difficulty double clicking the mouse an alternative is to select **Data** from the SPSS for Windows applications menu. This produces a drop-down menu from which you select **Define Variable** to produce the **Define Variable** dialog box. Note that whenever three dots (. . .) appear after an item on a drop-down menu this signifies that a dialog box will appear if that option is chosen.

2. Next click on **Type**. This defaults to Numeric 8.2 i.e. the variable is a number comprising up to eight digits and two of these are decimal places. This should be sufficient for most numeric variables but you can be more precise if you wish by specifying the maximum width of the data you will be entering for the numeric variable. SPSS offers a range of variable types. The most frequently used types are likely to be 'numeric' and 'string'. The numeric option is used for interval/ratio data as you will be entering the actual numeric values for that variable. The string option is used for category variables i.e. nominal and ordinal data where you will be entering a code (either a letter or a number) to represent the category of response. Travel is a string variable so select that option with the mouse. Click on **Continue** to return to the **Define Variable** box.

3. The next step is to assign a value label to each category. To do this click on **Labels** in the **Define Variable** box – the **Define Labels** box will now appear. In the **value** box type 1 and then click in the **Value Label** box and type HW Bus. If you then click on the '**Add**' button 1 = 'HW Bus' should now appear in the box next to it. Follow the same procedure for Public Bus with the code number 2, Coach with the code number 3, and so on. SPSS now knows that for the variable 'travel' the numerical code 1 refers to people travelling by the Hadrian's Wall bus, and that the code 2 refers to people travelling by public bus etc. If you subsequently wish to remove a value label, select it with the mouse and then select **Remove**. If you want to change a value label, select it, make the necessary change and then select **Change**.

4. Using the **Define Labels** box you can also define each variable more fully if you wish by entering further information into the **Variable Label** section e.g. means of travel. Such labels can be up to 120 characters long, although most output will not print labels of this length so keep them as short as possible. This variable name will then appear on any subsequent output from statistical tests.

5. Finally, select **Continue** to return to the **Define Variable** box and click on **Column Format** – change the column width setting to 6 (i.e. the number of characters in the variable name 'travel'). Select **Continue** to return to the **Define Variable** box and then click on **OK**. After a few seconds the variable name appears at the top of the column.

6. Note: another option in the **Define Variable** box is **Missing Values**. It is likely that in most surveys you will have some missing values as not all respondents will answer all the questions. In your data file these can either be ignored, in which case SPSS leaves a full stop in the cell to denote a missing value or you can use the Missing Values option to assign a numerical code to the missing value. We discuss later how SPSS treats missing values in its calculations.

7. At this stage you should save your data file. To do this, select **Save As** from the **File** menu. Give the file a name e.g. HADRIAN.sav, and enter this in the File name section. You should note that SPSS for Windows recognises data files by the file extension 'sav'. Click on **Save**. The words **Running SAVE** should now appear at the bottom of the screen. Wait until the message **SPSS Processor is ready** appears before continuing.

appropriate than others depending on what it is you are trying to show; and there will be occasions when a table or graph is simply not necessary and the point can more easily be made in a line or two of text. You should, therefore, always be clear in your own mind what it is you are trying to show, and ask yourself whether the table or graph gets across the essential features of the data.

Socio-economic status of respondent or main earner (n = 308)	Overseas holiday-makers (%)	UK holiday-makers (%)	All holiday-makers (%)
A	24	11	15
B	35	31	33
C1	20	18	18
C2	8	14	12
D	0	2	2
E	1	1	1
Retired	8	21	16
Other	4	2	3

Table 9.2
Socio-economic profile of holiday-makers to Hadrian's Wall area

Tables

The most straightforward way of summarising quantitative data is through the construction of a table, which is facilitated by the use of word-processing or spreadsheet packages. A table serves two basic purposes – it acts as a storehouse of information and, properly constructed, shows the reader what is going on. Tables can, however, be confusing. This is usually due to poor table construction, which in turn results from failing to ask at the outset a fundamental question, 'What am I trying to show in the table?'. Tables can be constructed for a variety of purposes e.g. to summarise the data or to show patterns in the data, and so you need to be clear about the purpose behind the table and make sure that its construction meets that purpose.

An important technique in achieving clarity in table construction is the use of the percentage. Rather than simply including the raw scores in tables, the use of percentages clarifies and facilitates comparison particularly if the table includes more than one variable calculated using different units of measurement. Expressing all variables using a common system (the percentage) makes comparisons more easily intelligible. Question 21 in the Hadrian's Wall survey asked for the respondents' occupation with a view to establishing a socio-economic profile of holiday-makers to the area. Answers to that question are summarised in Table 9.2.

This table clearly shows that the socio-economic profile of holiday-makers is skewed towards the higher socio-economic groups with 48 per cent of visitors in the AB groups and 16 per cent retired. However, the table also reveals significant differences between overseas and UK holiday-makers. Overseas visitors are more likely to be in the AB category (59 per cent) than UK holiday-makers (42 per cent), whereas UK holiday-makers are more likely to be retired (21 per cent) than overseas holiday-makers (8 per cent).

Frequency distributions

Question 3.a in the Hadrian's Wall survey recorded the length of holiday of the respondents. The answers of the first 100 respondents are shown in Table 9.3. There are, in fact, only 93 figures in Table 9.3 as seven respondents did not answer this question.

As it stands, this is a fairly meaningless jumble of figures. The first step that we can take to clarify the picture is to construct a *univariate frequency distribution* where the

Table 9.3
Length of holiday
of people visiting
Hadrian's Wall

7 17 7 21 7 42 30 70 7 7 7 7 21 8 21 14 16 120 15 60 7 7 14 24 12 7 8 7 14 14
35 28 7 10 14 14 7 28 10 14 24 10 14 7 7 24 1 14 7 14 25 7 30 10 14 75 7 20
24 7 14 28 10 1 19 1 28 7 1 1 7 21 14 42 10 7 3 30 7 30 7 14 4 21 3 90 21 56
13 7 180 3 3

various holiday lengths are listed along with their frequency in the distribution. This produces the following:

Length (days)	Frequency	Length (days)	Frequency
1	5	21	6
2	4	24	4
4	1	25	1
7	25	28	4
8	2	30	4
10	6	35	1
12	1	42	2
13	1	56	1
14	14	60	1
15	1	70	1
16	1	75	1
17	1	90	1
19	1	120	1
20	1	180	1

This procedure can, however, be taken further to improve presentation and analysis as this is still a fairly long list of categories and numbers, and the pattern is still not immediately apparent. The next stage is to group the data in order to construct a *grouped frequency distribution* (see Table 9.4).

The choice of classes used when converting a frequency distribution into a grouped frequency distribution is left to the researcher. The classes must, however, be exhaustive (i.e. they should cover all the cases) and mutually exclusive (i.e. it should not be possible for a case to fall into more than one category). From the grouped frequency distribution in Table 9.4 we can see more clearly that the majority of respondents (51.6 per cent) were on holiday for two weeks or more.

Two extra columns have been added to this table, the relative frequency and the cumulative frequency. The relative frequency is simply the frequencies for each category expressed as a percentage of the total sample. As already stated, the conversion of the raw scores into percentages aids comparison. The cumulative frequency is calculated by simply adding each relative frequency to the proceeding one.

Table 9.4
Grouped
frequency
distribution
showing length
of holiday of
respondents

Length of holiday	*Frequency*	*Relative frequency (%)*	*Cumulative frequency (%)*
1–6 days	10	10.8	10.8
7–13 days	35	37.6	48.4
14–20 days	19	20.4	68.8
Over 21 days	29	31.2	100
Total	93	100	

Using SPSS to generate frequency distributions

SPSS will generate frequency distributions and will also transform raw data into groups using the Recode procedure. In other words, we can use SPSS to transform the raw data in Table 9.3 into the grouped data in Table 9.4. The procedure for doing this is set out in Figure 9.2. Remember that whenever you carry out any form of work in SPSS such as using the Recode procedure, drawing graphs or calculating statistics, the relevant data file must be open.

The procedure for generating frequency distributions in SPSS is shown in Figure 9.3. In this example we are utilising the new variable 'Lenhol2' described above. The SPSS output is, of course, identical to the results calculated in Table 9.4. Note, however, that the SPSS output has a column headed 'per cent' and another column headed 'valid per cent'. The percentage column expresses the frequencies as a percentage of the total sample (100), whereas the valid percentage column expresses the frequencies as a percentage of those who answered the question (93 in this case as there are 7 missing values).

Figure 9.2
Using the Recode procedure in SPSS.

1. Select **Recode** from the **Transform** menu.
2. Select **Into Different Variables** to open the **Recode into Different Variables** dialog box.
3. Place the variable to be recoded (Lenhol in this case) into the **Input Variable→Output Variable** box.
4. Enter Lenhol2 in the **Output Variable Name** box.
5. Select **Change**. This places the new variable name (Lenhol2) alongside the old variable name (Lenhol) in the **Numeric Variable→Output Variable** box.
6. Select **Old and New Values** to open the **Recode into Different Variables: Old and New Values** dialog box.
7. Select **Range: Lowest through** and enter 6.
8. Enter 1 in the **Value** box in the **New Value** section.
9. Select **Add**. Lowest thru 6→1 will appear in the **Old→New** box.
10. Select **Range** and enter 7 in the first box and 13 in the box after **through**.
11. Enter 2 in the **Value** box in the **New Value** section.
12. Select **Add**. 7 thru 13→2 will appear in the **Old→New** box.
13. Select **Range** and enter 14 in the first box and 20 in the second box.
14. Enter 3 in the **Value** box in the **New Value** section.
15. Select **Add**. 14 thru 20→3 will appear in the **Old→New** box.
16. Select **Range: through highest** and enter 21 in the box.
17. Enter 4 in the **Value** box in the **New Value** section.
18. Select **Add**. 21 thru highest→4 will appear in the **Old→New** box.

In other words you have now instructed SPSS to recode all holiday lengths of 6 days and under with the value 1; all holidays between 7 and 13 days with the value 2; all holidays between 14 and 20 days with the value 3; and all holidays of 21 days and over with the value 4.

19. Select **Continue** to get back to the **Recode into Different Variables** dialog box and then select **OK**.
20. The new variable (Lenhol2) will then appear in the Data Editor window.

Define this variable in the usual way (see Figure 9.1) by giving each category a value label.

Figure 9.3
Generating
frequency
distributions
in SPSS.

1. Select **Summarize** from the **Statistics** menu.

2. Select **Frequencies** from the sub-menu to open the Frequencies dialog box.

3. Place 'Lenhol2' in the **Variables** box.

4. Click on **OK**.

The message **Running Frequencies** appears at the bottom of the screen until the output appears. SPSS output appears in the **SPSS Output Navigator** window. You can easily switch between this window and the **SPSS Data Editor** window where your data file can be found by selecting the **Window** menu and clicking on the appropriate name. The results of this output are shown below.

		Frequency	Per cent	Valid per cent	Cumulative per cent
			Length of holiday		
Valid	1–6 days	10	10.0	10.8	10.8
	7–13 days	35	35.0	37.6	48.4
	14–20 days	19	19.0	20.4	68.8
	over 21 days	29	29.0	31.2	100.0
	Total	93	93.0	100.0	
Missing	System missing	7	7.0		
	Total	7	7.0		
Total		100	100.0		

Simple bar charts

Bar charts can be presented either horizontally or vertically. Simple bar charts are made up of a number of separate bars, and the height or length of the bar represents the size of the data. For example, the data generated by Question 13 in the Hadrian's Wall survey (Appendix 2) can be shown in the form of a bar chart (see Figure 9.4). This figure shows that most people got information on the area from a guidebook or from friends and family when planning their visit.

Compound bar charts

This form of diagram is useful in demonstrating proportions or to illustrate the relative size of groups. If we return to the data in Table 9.2 showing the socio-economic profile of visitors to Hadrian's Wall, this data could be displayed in a compound bar chart. Compound bar charts showing percentage proportions in this way will always have bars the same height as each bar will naturally show 100 per cent.

Finally, both forms of bar charts can be combined so that actual values can be shown by the heights of individual bars, and the proportions within bars can also be depicted. Bar charts do, however, become difficult to follow where there are a large number of component parts. In such circumstances it is preferable to use a pie chart (see below).

Using SPSS to draw bar charts

SPSS will easily draw all of the diagrammatic forms discussed in this chapter, and they can be accessed via the Graphs menu. To draw a bar chart using SPSS follow the procedure outlined in Figure 9.5.

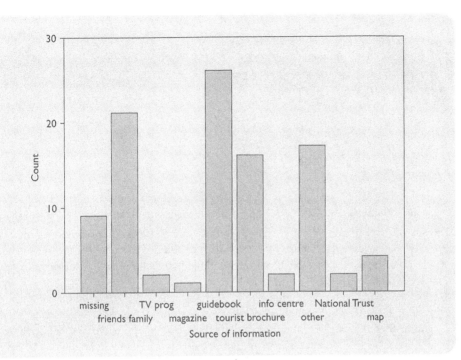

Figure 9.4
Sources of visitor
information.

Figure 9.5
Drawing bar
charts in SPSS.

1. Select **Bar** from the **Graphs** menu.
2. This opens the **Bar Charts** dialog box.
3. Select **Simple** and check that **Summaries for groups of cases** is selected.
4. Click on **Define** to open the **Define Simple Bar: Summaries for Groups of Cases** dialog box.
5. Place the desired variable in the **Category Axis** box.
6. Make sure that **N of cases** beneath **Bars Represent** has been selected.
7. Click on **OK**.

Histograms

A histogram is a graphical presentation of a frequency distribution. A histogram will show the amount of variation in a variable and, as we shall see later, is a useful way of checking whether the data approximates to a normal distribution or is skewed. Histograms are similar to bar charts except that when bar charts are drawn the bars are kept separate, whereas with histograms the bars are connected to depict the continuous nature of the categories.

Using SPSS to draw histograms

The procedure for generating a histogram in SPSS is shown in Figure 9.6.

Figure 9.6
Drawing
histograms in
SPSS.

1. Select **Histogram** from the **Graphs** menu.
2. This opens the **Histogram** dialog box.
3. Place the desired variable in the **Variable** box.
4. Click on **OK**.

Pie charts

An alternative way of showing the relative size/importance of groups is to use a pie chart. The data showing the socio-economic profile of visitors to Hadrian's Wall could also be presented in the form of a pie chart (see Figure 9.7). Here each segment or slice of the pie represents the percentage of cases falling in each socio-economic group. The SPSS Chart Editor makes it possible to show the percentage values and/or the actual values for each segment of the pie.

Pie charts are better than compound bar charts where there is a large number of categories but even here the ability to decipher information and to label and colour/shade the segments becomes more difficult as the number of segments increases. While there is no rule here, a pie chart containing more than six segments will become difficult to decipher. It may, therefore, be necessary to collapse categories for ease of presentation and understanding, although in doing so you should ensure that important detail is not lost. Having said that you can have too many segments in a pie chart, you can also have too few. You should not, for example, produce a pie chart showing the proportion of respondents answering yes/no to a particular question. Charts should be used to summarise and clarify – in this case this can easily be achieved in a line of text. Neither should pie charts be used where time series analysis is involved, as it is difficult to compare a number of pie charts even if they are placed alongside each other.

Figure 9.7
Socio-economic
profile of visitors
to Hadrian's Wall.

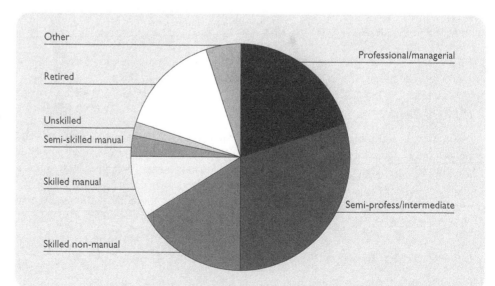

Figure 9.8
Drawing pie
charts in SPSS.

1. Select **Pie** from the **Graphs** menu.

2. This opens the **Pie Charts** dialog box.

3. Select **Summaries for groups of cases** and click on **Define**.

4. This opens the **Define Pie: Summaries for Groups of Cases** dialog box.

5. Place the required variable in the **Define Slices By Box** and make sure that **N of cases** is selected under **Slices Represent**.

6. Click on **OK**.

Note: SPSS will produce a pie chart with each segment a different colour. Assuming that you do not have access to a colour printer, you will need to edit the pie chart so that each segment is clearly differentiated when printed in black and white. This is achieved in the following manner:

1. Double click within the chart to bring up the **SPSS Chart Editor**.

2. Select a segment of the chart in the Chart Editor window (dots will appear around the edge of the segment), and select the **Color** icon.

3. A colour chart will then appear.

4. Select **Fill**, select chosen colour (select colours that contrast sharply so that they are distinguishable when printed in black and white), select **Apply**.

5. Repeat above for each segment of the pie.

6. Click on **OK**.

You can also highlight one of the segments of the pie for effect by 'exploding' it. To do this, simply select the segment, and select the **Explode Slice** icon.

Using SPSS to draw pie charts

The procedure for drawing pie charts in SPSS is set out in Figure 9.8.

Line graphs

Line graphs are most appropriate for showing trends over time. Figure 9.9 shows trends in football league attendance figures since England won the World Cup in 1966. The graph clearly shows a dramatic slump in attendance figures in the early 1980s with a steady recovery since the 1985/86 season. Not only do line graphs show peaks and troughs but also the slope of the line gives an indication of the rate of any increase/decrease. Another advantage of the line graph is that, unlike the other diagrammatic forms discussed above, it can show more than one variable at a time. For example, another line could have been added to this graph showing the unemployment rate during the same period. This could then be used to indicate a possible relationship between the two variables. The procedure for drawing line graphs in SPSS is set out in Figure 9.10.

Care must be taken in not including too many lines on a graph, particularly if they are close together and/or overlap. If they are more widely dispersed on the graph then more lines are possible. When constructing a graph the independent variable should always go on the horizontal axis and the dependent variable on the vertical axis (see Chapter 10 for a discussion of these terms). Time is always an independent variable and so will always go on the horizontal axis.

In summary, bar charts, histograms, pie charts and line graphs can be easily produced using spreadsheet packages such as EXCEL or, as in this case, by using SPSS. Better graphics can, however, be produced in EXCEL than in SPSS. On occasions this ease of chart

Figure 9.9
Football
attendance
figures 1966–97.

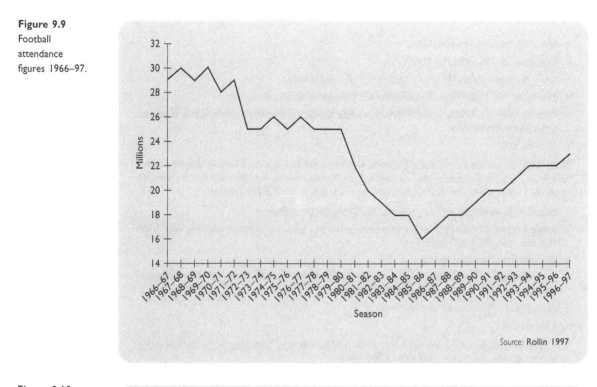

Source: Rollin 1997

Figure 9.10
Drawing line
graphs in SPSS.

1. Select **Line** from the **Graphs** menu.
2. This opens the **Line Charts** dialog box.
3. Select **Simple** and make sure that **Summaries for groups of cases** is selected.
4. Click on **Define**.
5. This opens the **Define Simple Line: Summaries for Groups of Cases** dialog box.
6. Put the required variable in the **Category Axis** box and make sure that **N of cases** is selected under **Line Represents**.
7. Click on **OK**.

production is regrettable as it encourages researchers to produce over-elaborate charts at the expense of clarity. Tables and charts should be clear and appropriate and should be chosen with a purpose in mind. Do not just include charts for the sake of them. Think about whether your data needs summarising in this way, think about what you are trying to show from the data, and consider the most appropriate form of presentation.

Whatever form of presentation you use, there are a number of items that must be included – a title, all axes must be labelled, there must be a key that explains the different segments of a compound bar chart for example, the units of measurement must be clearly identified, and the source of the data must be acknowledged if secondary sources are being used. Charts can easily be edited in SPSS to include all this information. To do this simply double click within the chart to produce the SPSS Chart Editor, and then select edit options as required.

All tables and charts must be referenced in the text and be discussed. While every picture does tell a story, do not assume that the picture is clear to everyone. In other words, you must interpret and discuss all charts.

Table 9.5
Levels of
measurement
and graphical
presentations

Variable type	Bar chart	Pie chart	Line graph
Nominal	Yes	Yes	No
Ordinal	Yes	Yes	No
Interval/ratio	Yes (if grouped)	Yes (if grouped)	Yes

Finally in this section, we return to our discussion of levels of measurement. The data that you are working with will place restrictions on the forms of graphical presentation that are possible (see Table 9.5).

Selecting cases for analysis

So far in this chapter it has been assumed that we will be analysing all the cases in our data file. There may be occasions, however, on which you do not wish to analyse the whole sample but only certain sections of the sample. SPSS allows you to select certain cases for analysis. Let us assume that we only want to analyse the characteristics or the views of those people in the Hadrian's Wall survey who are on holiday staying away from home (see Question 3 on the questionnaire – this variable has been named 'trip' and those on holiday staying away from home have been coded 1). The procedure for selecting these cases only for analysis is set out in Figure 9.11.

Using SPSS to calculate a new variable

As well as selecting cases for analysis, you can also use SPSS to calculate a new variable that was not in the original survey. In the SPSS data file from the Hadrian's Wall survey there is a variable called 'length'. This refers to the total length of time respondents were in the Hadrian's Wall area, and was calculated by adding together the length of time respondents had already been in the area (Question 3.b – durhw) with the length of time they still had in the area (Question 4 – furstay). In the survey, the responses to both these questions were eventually recorded in hours. The procedure for doing this is set out in Figure 9.12.

Figure 9.11
Using SPSS to
select cases for
analysis.

1. Select **Select Cases** from the **Data** menu.

2. This opens the **Select Cases** dialog box.

3. Select **If condition is satisfied** and then select **If**.

4. This opens the **Select Cases: If** dialog box.

5. Place trip = 1 in the box by using the variable list and the available symbols and numbers. You have now established the condition that must be satisfied for a case to be selected.

6. Select **Continue** to return to the **Select Cases** dialog box and then select **OK**.

Any subsequent analysis will now only be carried out for those cases who meet the condition that you have established – in this instance the people who are on holiday staying away from home. This condition will remain in force until you alter it, and so if you wish to go back to analysing the whole sample you will need to select **All cases** in the **Select Cases** dialog box. To remind you that you have selected certain cases for analysis SPSS places the message **Filter On** in the bottom right-hand corner of the screen. This disappears when you go back to the **All cases** mode.

Figure 9.12
Using SPSS to compute a new variable.

1. Select **Compute** from the **Transform** menu to open the **Compute Variable** dialog box.
2. Type the new variable name, 'length', in the **Target Variable** box.
3. Select **Type & Label** and make sure that this new variable is set as a numeric one.
4. Double click on 'durhw' from the list of variables to place it in the **Numeric Expression** box (alternatively you can single click on the variable name to highlight it and use the pickup arrow key [>] to place the variable in the box).
5. Select an operator from the list shown, which in this case will be the + sign. This automatically appears in the **Numeric Expression** box once selected.
6. Double click on 'furstay' from the list of variables to place it in the **Numeric Expression** box.
7. Click on **OK**.

You have now instructed SPSS to calculate a new variable, length, by creating the numeric expression durhw+furstay. The values for the newly computed variable appear at the end of the data file.

Statistical ways of summarising data

While graphs and tables are useful devices, it is often valuable and necessary to summarise data by calculating a single statistic that conveys one of the essential features of the distribution. This process is particularly valuable in allowing comparisons to be made between data sets. Let us assume that we have conducted a study of employment conditions in the travel sector. One of the things that we have measured is the wage levels of 500 employees. Readers of your research will not want to plough through 500 individual values as that would be laborious and ultimately confusing. What they would find of value is the use of a few summary statistics that put across the essential features of the wage distribution. Firstly, they would like to know about the *location* of the distribution of wages – whereabouts on the wage scale are wage values concentrated? Secondly, they would like to know about the distribution of wages – are wages spread out, are there big wage differentials or are they clustered closely together on the scale? In other words, it would be useful to provide a single statistic that summarises the *dispersion* of the data. Thirdly, readers would want to know if the majority of wages are to be found at one end of the distribution or whether they are to be found symmetrically either side of the middle of the distribution. To use a statistical term, we are interested here in the *skew* in the distribution of wages. These three issues – location, dispersion and skew – are discussed below.

Measures of location (the average)

A useful tool in our statistical toolkit is to calculate what is sometimes referred to as a 'measure of location', sometimes as a 'measure of central tendency' and more commonly as 'the average'. The term 'average' is, however, imprecise as there are in fact three different types of average, and each of these makes different assumptions about the data, is calculated in a different way and is used for a different purpose. This is why our initial discussion concerning the types of variable was so important as the type of variable you are working with will determine the type of average you can calculate. Let us now look at each of the three types in turn, starting with the mode. To illustrate the discussion we will use the example of salaries below:

VIRTUAL VISION TRAVEL CONSULTANCY
The salaries of the ten employees of Virtual Vision are:
£79k, £75k, £22k, £20k, £20k, £14k, £14k, £11k, £10k, £8k

The mode

The mode is the simplest measure of central tendency as it is the value that occurs most frequently, and so the mode is valuable in identifying the typical item in a data set. The use of the mode is implied when we talk about 'the average holiday being two weeks' when we mean that the typical length of holidays taken is two weeks. The mode can be used with variables at any level of measurement. It can be misleading, however, if the mode is found at the end of a range of data i.e. the mode is an extreme value. Using the mode in such circumstances would give a distorted picture. The other problem with using the mode is that you might have more than one. This is the case in the Virtual Vision example where there are two modes as £20k occurs twice as does £14k. This is known as a bimodal distribution.

The median

The median is the middle value in a set of data so that half the scores are below and half the scores are above the median. To calculate the median you must be able to arrange your data in order from lowest to highest, and so the median can only be used with ordinal data or with interval/ratio data. The advantage of the median is that it is unaffected by the values at either end of the range and so will not be distorted by extreme values. Another advantage of the median is that it can be calculated even if you do not have a complete data set. If the two highly paid managers of Virtual Vision had refused to reveal their salaries it would still have been possible to have calculated the median salary as the value of the median is not affected by the actual value of these two salaries.

Calculating the median with an odd number of values is straightforward. However, in our Virtual Vision example there are ten salary values in our data set, an even number. Remember that we want the middle value, and so we are interested in this instance in the 5.5th item as this lies half way between the 5th and 6th case. In other words, the median salary is £17k as this is half-way between £14k and £20k.

The mean

The mean, or the arithmetic mean, is what most people are usually referring to when they talk about the average in everyday speech. It is the sum of the values divided by the number of values in the data set. The strength of the mean is that, unlike the other two measures, it uses all the values in the distribution for its calculation. Its limitations are that it can only be used with interval/ratio data, and that it too can be distorted by extreme values, particularly when there are few values in the data set. The mean is less likely to be distorted by extreme values when there is a large number of cases.

As the mean can be distorted by extreme values, it is best used when numbers cluster closely around a central value. The mean wage for Virtual Vision is £27,300 (£273,000 ÷ 10), but eight out of the ten employees are earning less than the mean salary, which is being distorted by the two extreme values at the top of the range. A distribution that has a few very large values, as is the case here, is said to be *positively skewed*, and we will return to the subject of skewness later in this chapter. A positively skewed distribution will have a mean that is greater than the median – £27,300 compared with £17,000 in this case. As the mean is affected more by skewness, the median is a more appropriate statistic for skewed distributions. Some writers (e.g. Clegg 1982) argue that with skewed distributions you should provide all three forms of average.

In conclusion, we have looked at the three measures of central tendency and seen that they are calculated in different ways, and can only be used with certain variable types. The mean can be calculated for interval/ratio data; the mode can be calculated for any level of measurement; and the median can be used with ordinal or interval/ratio data. Crucially, you need to consider the appropriate use of each form of central tendency and in calculating an average you should always ask yourself which of the measures provides the most accurate representation of the data. The inappropriate choice of average can obscure; the task of the researcher is to clarify.

Measures of dispersion

In our fictitious survey of employment conditions in the travel company sector we have found that the mean salary for junior managers is £15k. In isolation that figure does not tell the reader all that much. How useful is that average figure as a summary statistic? Are the salaries in the distribution clustered together or are they more widely spread? What is the range of salaries among junior managers? Is that average figure distorted by extreme values?

While the mean is a useful summary statistic, people reading your research findings may want to know more than just the average – they may want to know the spread of your data and how representative the average is. Just quoting the average does not indicate this.

Consider the following data that shows salaries in two travel companies:

SALARIES IN THE PRIMERA TOUR COMPANY AND GLOBAL VIEW TRAVEL

Primera Tour Company
£11k, £15k, £15k, £18k, £25k, £30k, £32k, £38k
Mean salary = £23k (£184k ÷ 8)

Global View Travel
£20k, £21k, £22k, £23k, £23k, £24k, £25k, £26k
Mean salary = £23k (£184k ÷ 8)

The mean salary in both companies is the same, £23k, but a quick visual examination of the data shows that these companies are far from similar in the way that they pay their junior managers. The key point is that there is variability in the salaries for each organisation, they differ considerably in their 'dispersion' or 'variation' around the 'average'. The variability of data is at the heart of much research and, while that variability can be demonstrated graphically (by drawing a histogram, for example), there are a number of statistical measures known as *measures of dispersion* that we can use. These allow us to measure dispersion and to express it as a single statistic.

The range

This is the simplest and crudest measure of dispersion. The range indicates over how many numbers a distribution is spread i.e. you subtract the smallest from the largest, having first placed your values in ascending order. In our example above the range of salaries in the Primera Tour Company is £27k whereas for Global View Travel the range is £6k. The problem is that extreme values clearly have an effect, indeed in one sense the range depends on extreme values for its calculation, but having one extreme value in a data set will give a false picture of the data as a whole. As a result, the range should only be used when all the values in a data set are clustered closely together.

In the example above, providing details of the range of your data will give the reader a feel for the spread of your data. If you were to simply report that the mean salary was £23k, the reader would probably assume from this that salaries were all in the area of £20–30k, but we know that in one company this was far from the case and that the salaries were more widely dispersed. Computing and reporting the range gives a greater insight into your data but gives no indication of the clustering of the individual values in your data set.

The inter-quartile range

If you are working with ordinal data, the most appropriate measure of dispersion or spread is one using quartiles. As the name suggests, using quartiles the distribution is divided into four equal parts (see Figure 9.13). This is an extension of the idea of the median. You will recall that the median is the mid-point in the data so that 50 per cent of the values lie above this figure and 50 per cent lie below it. The inter-quartile range is a representation of the middle 50 per cent of the data or the values that fall between the first and third quartiles.

The strength of the inter-quartile range is that it is not affected by any extreme values in the data set. The disadvantage of utilising the inter-quartile range is that it does not utilise all the values in the data set, indeed it discards 50 per cent of the values. It therefore provides a limited picture of the degree of clustering of the data.

Standard deviation

This is the most useful measure of dispersion in that it utilises all the data in the distribution. The standard deviation compares each value in a distribution with the mean. In other words, it examines the variance of the data around the mean, and so says something about the representativeness of the mean for the data set. Generally speaking, the smaller the standard deviation the more concentrated the data is around the mean; the greater the standard deviation, the greater the dispersion. But remember that the size of the standard deviation is in part a reflection of the size of the mean itself. A large standard deviation may simply be the product of a large mean, and so both figures should be quoted. If you put together a measure of central tendency and a measure of dispersion in this way, you will provide some useful insights into the nature of a distribution. While it is true that the standard deviation can also be distorted by extreme values, the amount of distortion is

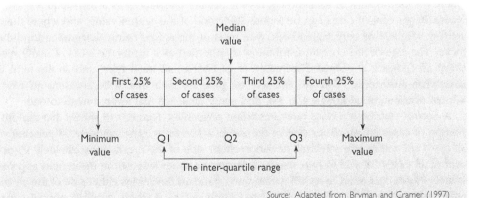

Figure 9.13
The inter-quartile range.

Source: Adapted from Bryman and Cramer (1997)

	Nominal data	*Ordinal data*	*Interval or ratio data*
Examples	Male/female Yes/No	1st/2nd/3rd Strongly agree Strongly disagree	Temperature Age Speed
Measure of location	Mode	Median	Mean
Measure of dispersion	Not applicable	Inter-quartile range	Standard deviation

less than in the case of the range. The standard deviation is, therefore, a measure of dispersion that is widely used in research findings of a quantitative nature.

In our salary example the standard deviation for the Primera Tour Company is much higher (9.68) than that of Global View Travel (2.00). In this case the standard deviation is telling us that, while the mean is the same in both cases, the salaries in the Primera Tour Company are more widely dispersed than those in Global View Travel. The mean is more representative in the second set of figures, even though it is the same for both sets. As it utilises the mean, the standard deviation can only be used with interval/ratio data. It does, however, allow us to compare the amount of dispersion in two data sets that use the same unit of measurement.

In summary, and going back to our discussion of levels of measurement, the standard deviation can only be used with interval/ratio data. If you are working with ordinal data then the range or the inter-quartile range can be calculated. Measures of dispersion cannot be calculated for nominal data. The appropriate use of measures of location and measures of dispersion are summarised in Table 9.6.

The normal distribution and skewness

Throughout the last two sections we have been talking about the distribution of data and the patterns that distributions take. A distribution is said to be symmetrical if the mean, median and mode coincide and the shape of the distribution is the same either side of these central values (see Figure 9.14).

As can be seen in Figure 9.14, such a distribution is known as a normal distribution where the distribution is symmetrical (this is usually referred to as a bell-shaped curve), where 50 per cent of cases can be found either side of the central value, and where there are few very low or very high scores, with most of the scores being clustered around the mean. The idea of the normal distribution is important as it forms the basis of many statistical procedures. A normal distribution is, of course, an ideal type, and so the term is somewhat misleading. You are unlikely to generate data that will represent an exact normal distribution, although you will find many data sets that approximate to one.

A normal distribution does have important properties. Figure 9.15 shows that the proportion of cases falling either side of the mean is known – approximately 68 per cent of all cases fall within one standard deviation either side of the mean; approximately 95 per cent of all cases fall within two standard deviations either side of the mean; and approximately 99 per cent of all cases fall within three standard deviations either side of the mean. Other percentage values can be calculated using statistical tables showing normal curve values. These tables can be found in most standard statistical texts. This predictability of

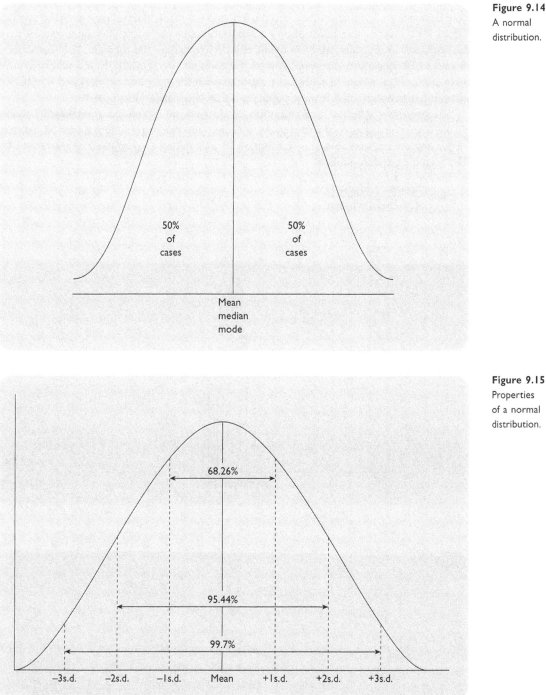

Figure 9.14
A normal
distribution.

Figure 9.15
Properties
of a normal
distribution.

the normal distribution is important and is used in sampling and hypothesis testing, both of which are discussed in Chapters 7 and 11.

The normal distribution is, therefore, a model against which data sets can be compared. There will be occasions when data sets do not match a normal distribution. Consider the distribution in Figure 9.16. This distribution is said to be *positively skewed*. It has a few very large values, most cases cluster to the left, and the mean will be larger than the median. Figure 9.17, on the other hand, shows a distribution that has a few very small values, most cases cluster to the right, and the mean will be lower than the median. This distribution is said to be *negatively skewed*. Skewed distributions are typically found where sample sizes are small or where bias has been introduced in the sampling process and so a biased sample has been selected from a population that is normally distributed.

To determine whether a distribution is skewed can often be established visually through the construction of a histogram. It is also possible to provide a statistical measure of the amount of skewness in a distribution by calculating a *co-efficient of skewness* (sk). The formula for doing this is:

$$sk = \frac{3(\text{Mean} - \text{Median})}{\text{Standard deviation}}$$

Figure 9.16
A positively skewed distribution.

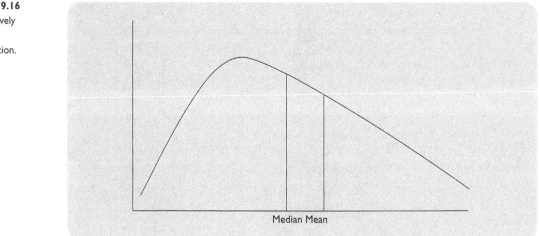

Median Mean

Figure 9.17
A negatively skewed distribution.

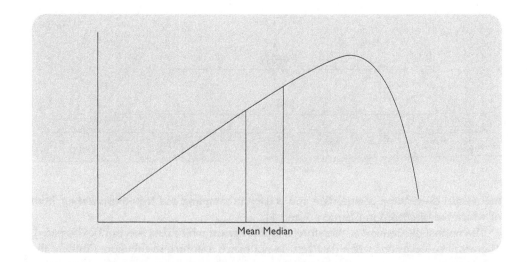

Mean Median

This allows you to compare the degree of skewness in data sets as the higher the co-efficient the greater the amount of skew. The co-efficient of skewness also tells you the direction of the skew as a positive value indicates a positive skew and a negative value indicates a negative skew. A perfectly normal distribution will, of course, have a co-efficient of skewness of zero. SPSS also provides a measure of skewness – see Figure 9.18 for the procedure used to produce this. However, this measure of skewness is not easy to interpret and so it is recommended that you tackle this problem diagrammatically through the construction of a histogram.

This discussion of normal distributions and skewed distributions is of particular relevance for the material covered in the next two chapters. In Chapter 11 you will encounter non-parametric and parametric tests, but parametric tests can only be used if the sample data have been drawn from a normally distributed population (see Chapter 11 for a complete discussion of the assumptions behind the use of parametric tests).

Using SPSS to calculate measures of location, measures of dispersion and skew

In Figure 9.18 we take you through how to use SPSS to calculate the different forms of average and the various measures of dispersion discussed above. At the end of the chapter you will find some questions to test your understanding of these issues and your ability to construct an SPSS data file.

Summary

This chapter has been concerned with univariate data analysis. In other words, it has dealt with the analysis of a single variable. We started out by introducing the notion of levels of measurement, and you should now appreciate that the type of variable you are working with will restrict/determine the forms of analysis that are possible. That analysis has taken two forms in this chapter. First of all we looked at ways of summarising data in the form of tables and various graphical presentations. We then moved on to look at statistical ways of summarising single variables through the use of measures of location, measures of dispersion and skew.

Figure 9.18
Using SPSS to calculate averages, measures of dispersion and skew.

1. Click on the **Statistics** menu.
2. Select **Summarize**.
3. Select **Explore** to bring up the **Explore** dialog box. All your variables will be listed on the left.
4. Place the variable(s) you wish to analyse in the **Dependent List** box. This can be done by double clicking on each variable. Alternatively, you can single click to highlight the variable, and then use the right-arrow key (>) to place the variable in the box.
5. Click on **OK**.
6. The message **Running Examine** will appear at the bottom of the screen.

The analysis will then appear in the SPSS Output Navigator window. This will include the variable name, the number of cases (which should equal the sample size as long as there are no missing cases), the maximum and minimum values, the range, the mean, the median, the standard deviation, the interquartile range and a measure of skewness among other things.

Univariate data analysis has its place but will only take you so far. It is, of course, quite possible that, given your research objectives, this is as far as you wish to go. In leisure and tourism research we will often want to go further. Is there a relationship between gender and levels of sports participation? Is there a difference in hotel occupancy rates following the construction of a by-pass? Here we are concerned with bivariate data analysis. In other words, we wish to explore the differences between variables or to measure the nature and strength of association between variables. This is the subject matter of the next two chapters.

Student Activities

You can check your understanding of the material introduced in this chapter by using SPSS to answer the following questions based on the Hadrian's Wall study. To tackle these questions you will need to construct your own SPSS data file following the procedures set out in Figure 9.1. The data can be found in Appendix 4. This shows the responses to some of the questions in the Hadrian's Wall study for the first 101 cases. Do not restrict yourself to just answering these questions but explore the data file by answering your own questions and at the same time developing your understanding of how SPSS works.

1. Calculate the percentage of people travelling on their own, and the percentage of people travelling with friends.

2. Calculate the mean length of time that respondents had been in the Hadrian's Wall area. Assuming that this data is normally distributed, what is the range of values that will lie within one standard deviation of the mean, and what percentage of cases should fall within that range?

3. Calculate the mean journey time to Hadrian's Wall from where respondents were staying the previous night.

4. Calculate the mean length of holiday of respondents, the median length of holiday, the range of holiday duration and the inter-quartile range.

5. What was the modal age group of respondents in the survey?

6. In what circumstances is the inter-quartile range a more appropriate measure of dispersion than the standard deviation?

7. Is the length of holiday of respondents in this survey an example of a positively skewed or negatively skewed distribution? Use SPSS to calculate a measure of skewness.

References

● Bryman, A. and Cramer, C. (1997) *Quantitative Data Analysis with SPSS for Windows*, London: Routledge.
● Clegg, F. (1982) *Simple Statistics*, Cambridge: Cambridge University Press.
● Rollin, G. (ed.) (1997) *Rothmans Football Yearbook 1997/98*, London: Headline.

Chapter 10

Bivariate and Multivariate Analysis

Learning Outcomes

At the end of this chapter you will be able to:

- analyse quantitative data systematically
- select and critically apply appropriate quantitative techniques
- interpret and critically evaluate the outputs of quantitative methods/models
- implement forecasting methods to tourism activity and organisations
- carry out regression and correlation analysis on appropriate tourism data and reach valid conclusions
- carry out and interpret multiple regression analysis

Introduction

The first chapter of this book argued that research is about asking and attempting to answer questions. So far we have essentially been concerned with methods which can be used to collect data and with ways of summarising the data collected. The data collected is used to answer the questions set. The way in which the questions are asked, or conceptualised, influences the techniques used to answer them.

The analytical techniques covered in the previous chapter are basically used for answering descriptive questions; such as how many people visited, what is the average age of visitors and so on. These questions are *univariate* in nature; that is in order to answer them they only require information on a single variable. Quite often research poses questions which are more complex than this. For example, are younger visitors more satisfied than older ones? In order to answer this question you need to examine two variables simultaneously – age of visitor and level of satisfaction. This question would require *bivariate* analysis. Interestingly, this simple question could be expressed in two slightly different ways:

- Are there differences in levels of satisfaction between younger and older visitors? or
- Is there a relationship or connection between age of visitor and level of satisfaction?

A bit obtuse perhaps, but the way the question is posed suggests, as we shall see, different analytical means. The former implies a relationship between two variables, whereas the latter states it explicitly! The former question is more appropriately examined using tests of difference or *inferential statistics*, whereas the latter would require *measures of association*. This chapter looks at measures of association, whereas inferential statistics are examined in Chapter 11.

This chapter covers some of the main procedures used to answer those questions which refer to two or more variables. We will be concerned with the statistical analysis of data – in particular data which are likely to be created by a questionnaire survey. Questionnaire surveys usually yield data which are categorical or nominal in nature and this usually restricts the analysis to some form of cross-tabulation. However, there will be times when interval or ratio data are collected or where such data are obtained from other sources. To this end, this chapter provides details on how to analyse different types of data. Details of calculation will seldom be given as the emphasis is on the interpretation of the answers provided by the statistics; where appropriate, instructions are given on how to compute the statistics using SPSS for Windows. More detailed accounts of the various procedures can be found in Cramer (1998).

Research design and data analysis are interrelated – one is not independent of the other. It may be an obvious point, but to design research which creates data that cannot be analysed will produce nothing but frustration. This chapter is concerned with providing a number of ways in which data can be analysed. The focus is on examining the relationships between things or variables using measures of association; providing answers to questions such as, 'is length of stay related to distance travelled?'.

What is 'association'?

In Chapter 9 we introduced ways of summarising various types of data. The focus was on describing one particular attribute of a data, through the 'average' length of stay, for example. We learnt, in other words, how to represent one particular characteristic in statistical terms, using graphs or by using measures of central tendency and dispersion. It is more usual in social research to go beyond simple description and to investigate whether two (or more) variables are related or associated, for example, to see whether holiday habits vary across different social groups. Two variables are said to be associated if one variable differs in accordance with the other. So, if different age groups display different holiday preferences, then there is an association between age and holiday preference; in the past older people tended to prefer coach tours and younger people tended to prefer 18–30 'style holidays'. If there is no difference in holiday preference by age then there is no association, or in other words, holiday preference is independent of age – the latter having no effect on the former.

The purpose of this chapter is to introduce ways in which association can be measured statistically. The examples used will initially be bivariate, examining the effect of one variable on another i.e. involving two variables. This may seem strange given the complexities of leisure and tourism. Clearly, most phenomenon are multi-dimensional, being affected by many factors, however, in most cases it is useful to start with an examination of bivariate relationships.

Independent and dependent variables

In statistical work it is normal to define the dependent and the independent variables. Quite simply, the dependent variable is the one that is influenced by changes in the independent variable. So if one hypothesised that there was an association between gender and level of customer satisfaction, then the dependent variable would have to be satisfaction, since your level of satisfaction cannot affect your gender! So, the dependent variable is the one that is influenced and the independent variable is the one that influences.

Cross-tabulation and the percentage difference

The technique of cross-tabulation is widely used in the analysis of recreation research data. This simple technique is an extension of the principles of tabulation and the percentaging of data covered earlier in the book. Cross-tabulation is simply a method of displaying data so that associations can be readily observed and measured. Table 10.1 is an example of a cross-tabulation of two variables.

Here we are interested to see if there is an association between origin of visitor (independent variable) and the extent to which their expectations (dependent variable) were met by the visit. Note how the table is constructed – the dependent variable is placed at the top (forming the columns) and the independent variable is placed down the side (forming the rows), in this instance. Moreover, note how the rows and columns are totalled – this is important information as we shall see later. Interpretation of this table is difficult. We can see that for 37 out of the 152 domestic visitors their expectations were exceeded and that this compares with 17 out of the 54 overseas ones! This illustrates the point made in Chapter 7 on sampling, that the sample size should ensure a sufficient number of respondents in each sub-category or group. It is immediately apparent that the number of overseas visitors is far exceeded by domestic ones. This calls for the use of percentages, but do we percentage down or across the table? We need to think about what we are aiming to achieve here. As we wish to compare overseas with domestic visitors, we need to compare down the table. In order to compare down the table we must percentage across, that is calculate the percentage of visitors in each group who fall into each expectation category. This is completed in Table 10.2.

	Extent to which expectations were met				
Origin	*Exceeded expectations*	*Met all expectations*	*Met some but not all expectations*	*Fell short of expectations*	*Total*
Domestic	37	92	22	1	152
Overseas	17	28	8	1	54
Total	54	120	30	2	206

Source: Elliott-White and Cuthill (1998)

Table 10.1
Origin of visitor and the extent to which the visit to Hadrian's Wall met their expectations

	Extent to which expectations were met				
Origin	*Exceeded expectations*	*Met all expectations*	*Met some but not all expectations*	*Fell short of expectations*	*Total (number)*
Domestic	24%	61%	14%	1%	152
Overseas	31%	52%	15%	2%	54

Table 10.2
Cross-tabulation of origin of visitors to Hadrian's Wall and the extent to which their expectations were met (percentaged)

Figure 10.1

Format for

cross-tabulation.

There are two general rules of thumb about cross-tabulations:

1. If you wish to compare down a table then percentage across the rows, while if you wish to compare across the rows then percentage down the columns.

2. If the independent variable is down the side and the dependent across the top, then percentage across the rows. If the independent is across the top then percentage down the columns.

Cross-tabulation in SPSS for Windows

1. With your data file open, select **Summarize** from the **Statistics** menu.

2. Now select **Crosstabs** and the following dialogue box will appear.

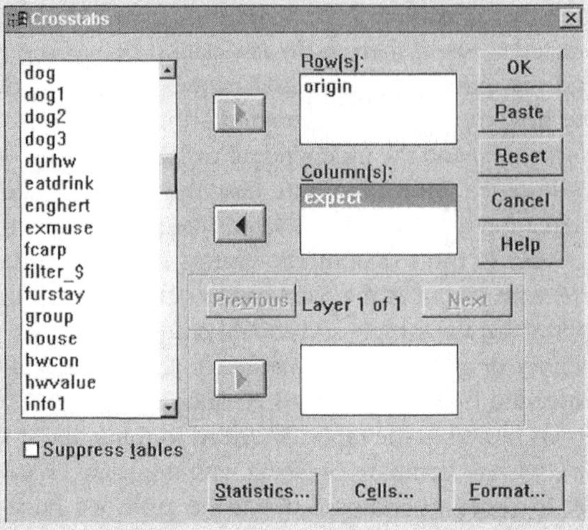

3. Select the **independent** variable from the left-hand list and place it in the **Rows** box using the button provided.

4. Select the **dependent** variable and place it in the **Columns** box.

5. Select **Cells** and make sure that the **Rows** check box is ticked in the percentages section.

6. Click on **Continue**, and then **OK**.

7. The Crosstabs will be placed in the output window.

By percentaging, the cross-tabulation interpretation is made easier. The purpose of cross-tabulation is the investigation of association, to see whether or not an association exists between the independent and the dependent variables. Was there an association between the origin of visitor (independent variable) and the respondents' level of expectation (dependent variable)? Table 10.2 remains somewhat difficult to interpret because there are so many groups. However, it is possible to say that origin did not determine respondents' level of expectation. In order for this to be the case then the differences between the two rows in each column would be large, whereas the greatest difference between domestic and overseas visitors is recorded in the second category and is onl21y 9 per cent! This suggests that the association between the two variables is weak. This becomes even more apparent if we collapse the table into one based on dichotomous variables (Table 10.3). This is done by merging the data in the four columns into two; easily done in SPSS using the recode option.

Collapsing the categories is a useful option where there are no or only a small number of cases in a few cells. However, care should be taken to ensure that the integrity of

| Visitor origins | Extent to which expectations were met | | Total |
	Met or exceeded expectations	Did not meet all expectations	
Domestic	85%	15%	152
Overseas	83%	17%	54

Table 10.3
Cross-tabulation of origin against expectation met (dichotomous variables)

| Independent variable | Dependent variable | | Total |
	First category	Second category	
Group A	*A*	*C*	
Group B	*B*	*D*	

Table 10.4
Calculating the percentage difference

the data is not lost i.e. by collapsing dissimilar categories. If we compare down the table it is now clear that the difference between the two groups of visitors is exceptionally small. Indeed a useful tool for a two-by-two table is the percentage difference. The percentage difference is simply calculated as in Table 10.4. The percentage difference = *A* minus *B* or *C* minus *D*.

In the case of Table 10.3 the percentage difference is 2 per cent. The size of the percentage difference is an indication of the strength of that association. The closer the figure is to 100 per cent (the maximum) then the stronger the association, 100 per cent meaning a perfect association. The closer the percentage difference is to 0 per cent the weaker the association, zero meaning no association. So, in the above case the association is very weak.

So the cross-tabulation, together with the computation of the percentage difference, informs us whether or not an association exists. When examining your own cross-tabulations those in Table 10.5 may be useful points of reference.

Alternative measures of association for contingency tables

The percentage difference is a useful indicator of the strength of an association. However, it is more usual in research to quote a *coefficient of correlation*. This is simply a summary measure of association, which provides a condensed overview of the properties in the table, or more technically it measures the degree to which the two variables co-vary; for example, the extent to which levels of holiday satisfaction co-vary or are correlated with the weather! If levels of satisfaction fell as the amount of rainfall (an indicator of poor weather) increased, then the two variables could be said to co-vary. There is a broad range of coefficients of correlation and the appropriateness depends upon the nature of the data. The data in cross-tabulation is always in the form of categories – either nominal or ordinal categories. It seems pertinent, therefore, to introduce two coefficients of correlation which are appropriate to nominal (and also ordinal) data: the phi coefficient and Cramer's *V*. These correlation coefficients take values between zero and one and their interpretation is similar to the percentage difference.

Table 10.5
Cross-tabulations:
some useful
comparisons

Perfect association: percentage difference = 100%

Independent variable	Dependent variable		
	First category	*Second category*	*Total*
Group A	100%	0%	E
Group B	0%	100%	F

Moderate association: percentage difference = 50%

Independent variable	Dependent variable		
	First category	*Second category*	*Total*
Group A	75%	25%	E
Group B	25%	75%	F

No association: percentage difference = 0%

Independent variable	Dependent variable		
	First category	*Second category*	*Total*
Group A	50%	50%	E
Group B	50%	50%	F

The phi coefficient

The phi coefficient (ϕ) is included here because it is usually applied to 2×2 tables (two categories on the dependent and two on the independent) and because it is very simple to compute and can be included in the output from SPSS. The phi coefficient is a measure of the strength of the statistical association. It ranges in value from 0 to +1 and is similar to the percentage difference in interpretation:

- a value of +1 indicating a perfect association
- a value of 0.5 indicating a moderate association
- a value of zero is taken as indicating no association.

Hence, the closer the value of the coefficient is to zero, the weaker the association, the closer to one the stronger. A useful example is provided by some research conducted on the relationship between visitor expectation and satisfaction. Observe the data in Table 10.6.

Using SPSS to calculate phi, we get a coefficient of:

$$\phi = 0.203$$

The research demonstrated that the association between expectation and satisfaction was very weak. Interestingly this figure compares with a percentage difference of only 13 per cent.

Cramer's V

The phi coefficient is used with 2×2 tables; when tables are larger than this then an alternative coefficient should be used. Cramer's *V* is just such an alternative. This coefficient is

Dependent variable –	Independent variable – expectation		
satisfaction	High	Low	Total
High	1512	2406	3918
	(16%)	(3%)	
Low	7780	85,574	93,354
	(84%)	(97%)	
Total	9292	87,980	97,272

Table 10.6
Phi coefficient correlating expectation and satisfaction

To calculate phi or Cramer's *V* in SPSS for Windows, proceed as for **Cross-tabulations**.

1. With your data file open, select **Summarize** from the **Statistics** menu.

2. Now select **Crosstabs**.

3. Select the **independent** variable from the left-hand list and place it in the **Rows** box using the button provided.

4. Select the **dependent** variable and place it in the **Columns** box.

5. Select **Cells** and make sure that the **Rows** check box is ticked in the percentages section.

6. Make sure that the appropriate box is ticked in the **Statistics** dialog box.

7. Click on **Continue**, and then **OK**.

8. The Crosstabs will be placed in the output window.

Figure 10.2
Using SPSS to calculate phi and Cramer's *V*.

standardised so that it always takes values between 0 and +1. In this sense it can only indicate the strength of the association. Take Table 10.7 for example. In this case the independent variable is across the top of the table and as we, therefore, need to compare across the columns, so the percentage is calculated downwards. Is there an association between satisfaction and occupational group? It is not immediately clear from the table whether an association exists or not, let alone the strength of that association. Some initial points could be made here, particularly that low levels of satisfaction are apparent amongst blue-collar workers (groups 111M to V). Calculation of Cramer's *V* will assist us in this case. Using SPSS for Windows, Cramer's *V* is calculated as:

$$V = 0.12$$

So, there is only a weak association between satisfaction and occupation, since Cramer's *V* is only 0.12. As in all correlation coefficients the strength of the association is indicated by the comparison with the maximum (1) and minimum values (0); as the calculated value approaches 0, so the association weakens and as it approaches 1 it strengthens. Cramer's *V* is particularly useful since it can be applied to cross-tabulations involving variables with more than two categories.

We have seen how we can investigate associations between two categorical variables. The methods of cross-tabulation, percentage difference and associated coefficients of correlation are important, not least because data which is at the interval/ratio level of measurement can be readily transformed into a series of categories. This is particularly useful

Table 10.7
Visitor
satisfaction and
occupational
group

Level of satisfaction	Occupational group				
	I/II	III (N.M)	III (M)	IV/V	Total
High	38 (38%)	63 (42%)	53 (42%)	84 (42%)	238
Medium	41 (41%)	51 (34%)	35 (28%)	44 (22%)	171
Low	21 (21%)	36 (24%)	37 (30%)	74 (36%)	168
Total	100	150	125	202	577

Note: Groups I, II and III (N.M) are 'white-collar' occupations whereas the others are manual or 'blue-collar' workers.

where one variable is categorical and the other is numerical, the latter being transformed into a series of classes. However, there are times when both variables are at a higher level of measurement than nominal – when they are at the interval or ratio levels.

Looking at associations with numerical data

Consider the data in Table 10.8. The table shows visitor numbers and the accommodation levels for all districts in a region; together with the mean and the standard deviations. Clearly there is a difference between the two variables – the average number of visits appears to have been somewhat lower than accommodation available. However, the question is whether or not the amount of accommodation bears any relation to the number of visits. This is a simplistic idea, but one which will serve as an illustration. The simplest and usually the first step in attempting to see whether there is a relationship between two numerical variables is to construct a scatter diagram as in Figure 10.3.

We would expect that the amount of accommodation would influence the number of tourism visits. Therefore accommodation (beds) is the independent variable and visits the dependent variable. The dependent variable is always placed on the vertical or y axis and the independent on the horizontal or x axis, hence x is said to influence y. The interest here lies in the pattern or scatter which the points take. As might be expected there is no perfect one-to-one relationship between the two variables. On the other hand, there does appear to be a general relationship in that, taking the data as a whole, the lower quantities of accommodation do tend to be associated with the lower numbers of visits and the higher quantities of accommodation with larger numbers of visitors. Also, if we draw a line through the scatter of points we find, with one or two exceptions, they are clustered fairly close to the line.

The tendency for a set of data to approximate to a straight line is fairly important and lies at the centre of the concept of a correlation coefficient. Figure 10.4 demonstrates a number of alternative scatter diagrams.

The spread of points in Figure 10.3 indicates that there is not a one-for-one relationship between the two variables; if this was the case then the diagram would have looked like that in (A) in Figure 10.4. This would have been a perfect positive correlation, since all points are in a line and the scatter of points goes from bottom left to top right, or high

District	Visitor numbers	Bed-spaces
1	308	370
2	211	283
3	264	360
4	242	361
5	260	386
6	252	361
7	257	307
8	225	326
9	300	309
10	194	256
11	221	312
12	263	361
13	177	274
14	208	283
15	204	275
16	201	284
17	191	264
18	223	329
19	252	334
20	249	334
21	294	285
22	224	276
23	237	297
24	223	290
25	232	350
26	238	315
Mean	237	315
Standard deviation	33	37

Table 10.8
A comparison of tourism visits with quantity of accommodation available

Figure 10.3
Scatter diagram of amount of accommodation against tourism visits.

Figure 10.4
Scatter diagrams
for comparison.

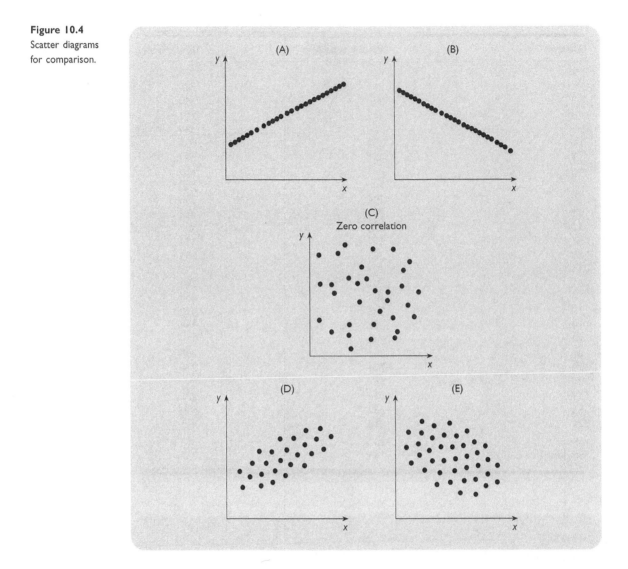

values of x are associated with high values of y. The graph in Figure 10.4(B) also indicates a perfect correlation, but this time it is negative – a perfect negative association, as high values of x are associated with low values of y. These two extremes are useful for comparative purposes. The strength of the association between two variables is indicated by the concentration of the points about an imaginary straight line. The more concentrated the points the stronger the statistical association – the higher the correlation. The strength of an association cannot be stronger than that in a perfect association; whether positive or negative. If there is no discernible linear trend between x and y, as in Figure 10.4(C), then there is no association or zero correlation; here low values of x are equally likely to occur with low and high values of y. The scatter in Figure 10.4(D) represents a strong positive correlation; the points show a trend from bottom left to top right and are quite tightly clustered. On the other hand, the scatter in Figure 10.4(E) represents a weak negative association.

Figure 10.5
Using SPSS
to generate
scattergrams.

Plotting a scatter diagram indicates:

(a) The direction of the relationship as indicated by the scatter of points; positive or negative.

(b) The strength of the correlation; measured by the concentration of points round an imaginary straight line.

Scattergrams can be produced in SPSS using the following instructions:

1. **Open** your data file.

2. Select **Scatter** from the **Graphs** menu.

3. Make sure **Simple** is highlighted in the dialog box, then click on the **Define** button.

4. Select the **independent** variable from the list and add it to the **x-axis** box using the button provided.

5. Select the **dependent** variable and add it to the **y-axis** box.

6. Titles and labelling can also be added using the options provided. Click on **OK** and a scattergram will be produced.

Correlation coefficients

The scatter diagram is a useful starting point in correlation analysis, but what we really need is a means of measuring the strength of the association. This would be helpful in comparing one correlation with another and would simplify and standardise description. Such a measure would be provided by the correlation coefficient, a precise and numerical summary of the degree of statistical association. The properties of the correlation coefficients for numerical variables are somewhat different from those introduced earlier. In the case of interval/ratio data the correlation coefficients take values between -1 and $+1$, thus indicating the direction as well as the strength of the association, as Figure 10.6 indicates.

Thus, a value of -1 indicates a perfect negative association (or (B) in Figure 10.4) and $+1$ a perfect positive association (or (A) in Figure 10.4). A value of zero indicates there is no association. The closer the value is to $+1$ or -1 the stronger the correlation, the closer to 0 the weaker the association. Using SPSS on the data in Table 10.8 produces the following result:

$$r = 0.6$$

So the correlation coefficient indicates that there is a moderately strong association between the amount of accommodation available and the number of tourism visits. This relationship is positive rather than negative. A positive correlation indicates that as the number of bed-spaces increase, so too do the number of visitors. A negative correlation would suggest that an increase in the number of bed-spaces is associated with a declining number of visitors!

Figure 10.6
The range of
values for
correlation
coefficients.

Perfect negative association		Moderate negative		No association		Moderate positive		Perfect positive association
-1	-0.7	-0.5	-0.1	0	0.1	0.5	0.7	$+1$
	Strong negative		Weak negative		Weak positive		Strong positive	

Figure 10.7
Calculating
Pearson's
correlation
coefficient using
SPSS.

1. Select **Correlate** from the **Statistics** menu, followed by **Bivariate**.

2. Select and then add the two variables to the **Variables** list.

3. Make sure that **Pearson's** is ticked and then click on **OK**.

SPSS produces a correlation matrix like the one below. This is the result of correlating length of stay at Hadrian's Wall with the time taken to travel from home to the destination (ex. Overseas visitors). SPSS gives us the following correlation matrix:

	LENGTH	TIMEHOME
LENGTH	1.0000	0.2680
	(76)	(76)
	P = .	P = 0.019
TIMEHOME	**0.2680**	1.0000
	(76)	(76)
	P = 0.019	P = .

(Coefficient / (Cases) / 2-tailed Significance)

This matrix forms a mirror image about a diagonal from top left to bottom right. We are only interested in the one highlighted cell (or rather one of two) which contains the correlation of Length against Timehome. This gives us three pieces of information:

● The first value in the cell is the correlation (0.2680) and in this case, the correlation is weak but positive, which suggests that there is a weak positive association between the two variables.

● The second value is the number of cases used to compute the statistics, in this case 76.

● The final value is used for testing the statistical significance of the result and will be referred to in the next chapter.

The result is interesting as it suggests that length of stay at Hadrian's Wall is weakly connected to distance travelled from home. Further work may have revealed that in most instances Hadrian's Wall was part of a tour of Northern England and Scotland and that most visitors simply called on the way to somewhere else.

The correlation coefficient is an informative measure which tells us how strongly two variables are related. In this sense the strength of the correlation gives the tourism manager an indication of how a change in one variable will impact on another. The higher the correlation, the more likely the independent variable is to impact significantly on the dependent. In other words, the strength of the correlation lends weight to the assumption that the two variables are causally linked. In the example discussed above, the link between accommodation and tourism visits is moderately strong, suggesting the likelihood of a causal link.

The assumptions of Pearson's Product Moment Correlation Coefficient (PPMCC)

The Pearson's Product Moment Correlation Coefficient (PPMCC) is a powerful statistical measure. However, the PPMCC is a parametric measure and makes a number of assumptions:

● that the data is numerical

● that both variables come from populations that are normally distributed. One of the pre-conditions for this is that the data in the two variables approximates to the normal distribution. This can be tested through the construction of a histogram

● that the relationship between the two variables is linear. This can be tested through the construction of a scatter diagram.

Ideally, if any of these assumptions are not met then an alternative measure should be used (see Cramer 1998). Fortunately, the product moment correlation is very robust and these assumptions are not always strictly applied. If, however, the data is ranked, then the Spearman's Rank Correlation Coefficient should be used.

The Spearman's Rank Correlation Coefficient

If the data is at the ordinal scale of measurement or if you are unwilling to accept the assumption of a normal distribution then the Spearman's Rank Correlation Coefficient may be used. This is a non-parametric measure and as such does not make the assumption about the normality of the distribution. As Spearman's coefficient requires ordinal data the numerical data in Table 10.8 has been ranked and is presented in Table 10.9.

Spearman's Rank Correlation Coefficient is given by SPSS as:

$r_s = 0.735$

So, Spearman's Rank Correlation Coefficient is 0.735 in this case. This means that there is a strong positive association between visitor numbers and bed-spaces in these districts, since the coefficient is interpreted in the same way as Pearson's. It is interesting to note

District	Visitors (ranks)	Bed-spaces (ranks)
1	1	2
2	2	14
3	3	18
4	4	4
5	5	4
6	6	1
7	7	14
8	8.5	4
9	8.5	7.5
10	10	7.5
11	11	4
12	12	11
13	13	15
14	14	6
15	15	10
16	16	21
17	17.5	9
18	17.5	16
19	18	12
20	19	19.5
21	20	19.5
22	21	22
23	22	18
24	23	25
25	24	24
26	25	23

Table 10.9
Bed-spaces and visitor numbers as ranked data

Figure 10.8
Calculating
Spearman's
correlation
coefficient using
SPSS.

Follow the instructions detailed in Figure 10.7, but check **Spearman's** rather than Pearson's.

that Spearman's gives a different result than Pearson's for the same set of data; the Spearman coefficient is higher than the Pearson (0.6). Such differences highlight variations in the precision and sensitivity of different techniques and also how choice of technique can influence the result obtained!

The difference between correlation and causation

One fundamental problem that applies to correlation coefficients is the quite common error of confusing correlation with causation. It is important to remember that a correlation coefficient is simply a number, a mathematical construct which shows a statistical relationship between two sets of measures. It does not in itself imply any causal relationship. The confusion between causation and correlation has given rise to many instances of 'nonsense' or spurious correlations such as the strong correlation between size of feet and the quality of handwriting. The correlation is high simply because both are related to a third variable – the size of feet and handwriting are both related to age of children. That is as children grow older their feet grow larger and their handwriting tends to improve. To draw any conclusions that association is due to causation requires evidence and analytical judgement beyond what the coefficients can provide. The case for causation is strengthened if:

1. The association is repeated in different circumstances, reducing the chance that it is due to confounding factors.

2. A plausible explanation can be offered showing how changes in one variable could cause changes in the other.

3. No equally plausible third variable could cause changes in both variables together.

Regression

While correlation tells us the statistical strength of the relationship between two variables and gives some indication of the likelihood of a causal relationship, it does not tell us the impact of the independent variable on the dependent variable. While it may be useful to know the correlation between two variables, knowing the size of the impact of one variable on the other is more practical. In other words, we may wish to know how many more tourists would visit a district if we increased the supply of accommodation. Such an application is an example of forecasting – one variable (tourism visits) can be predicted from another correlated one (accommodation supply). This can be achieved through regression analysis.

If we return to our earlier example of the correlation between tourism visits and the supply of accommodation, we can see that there is a trend in the distribution of points on the graph (see Figure 10.9).

Clearly, the points do not fall on a straight line (hence the correlation does not have the value 1) but there is a distinct upward trend from left to right. This can be summarised by a best fit or regression line which approximates to the trend identified. Regression analysis basically calculates the equation for the best fit line, which in the case of linear regression takes the form:

$$y = a + bx$$

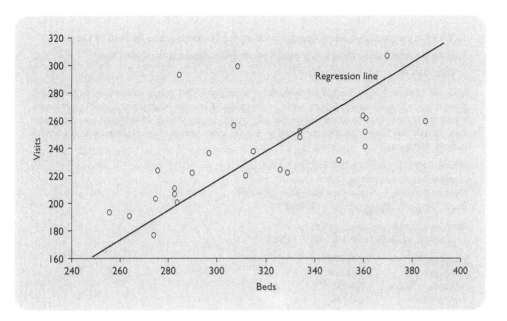

Figure 10.9
Tourism visits and
accommodation.

where
a = a constant representing the point at which the line crosses the y axis (tourism visits)
b = a coefficient representing the gradient of the slope and can be positive *or* negative
y and x are the dependent and independent variables, respectively.

In this book we will not examine how the regression equation is calculated because computer software is available which will do this for you (see Figure 10.10). Rather our concern is with the interpretation of the resultant equation. In the case of the above example the regression equation is:

$$y_i = 63 + 0.552 \; x_1$$

The values of the coefficients are therefore clear. The first (a = 63) represents the number of tourism visits that would result if there were no accommodation provided. The second (b = 0.552) represents the extra tourism visits generated by an additional bed-space. Clearly, in this equation an extra two (0.552 multiplied by 2) accommodation units would need to be provided in order to yield one extra tourism visit.

Evaluating the success of the regression model

If we examine the scatter diagram and regression line in more detail (Figure 10.9), we can see that the regression line is a summary of the relationship between the two variables on the whole. As such, it is only an estimate for each value included in the diagram; in some cases the line is a better estimate than in others. This is illustrated in more detail in Figure 10.11.

We can see that for each case there is a difference between the actual value and the value predicted by the regression line. The more closely the actual values lie to the regression line the more accurate the model becomes. If all the values fell on the regression line there would be zero error in the sense that the estimated values would be the same as the actual values. You will recall how the distribution of points on the scatter diagram related to the correlation coefficient (r). In regression analysis, the success of the model is evaluated

Figure 10.10
Using SPSS to
carry out
regression
analysis.

1. With the datafile **Open**, select **Regression** from the **Statistics** menu, followed by **Linear**.

2. Place the appropriate variables in the **dependent** and **independent** variables box.

3. Click on **OK**.

SPSS will produce output like the following for the Hadrian's Wall survey referred to earlier. In this instance it was hypothesised that there would be a relationship between length of stay (length) at Hadrian's Wall and the total duration of the holiday (lenhol). Length of stay (measured in hours) was the dependent variable and it was thought that those on longer breaks would spend more time at the wall (a positive relationship).

M U L T I P L E   R E G R E S S I O N ****
Listwise Deletion of Missing Data
Equation Number 1   Dependent Variable.   LENGTH
Block Number 1. Method: Enter   LENHOL

Variable(s) Entered on Step Number
1. LENHOL   LENGTH OF HOLIDAY – DAYS

Multiple R   **0.92970**
R Square   **0.86434**
Adjusted R Square   0.86255
Standard Error   48.25748

Analysis of Variance
                DF   Sum of Squares   Mean Square
Regression   1   1127641.90386   1127641.90386
Residual   76   176987.62478   2328.78454

F = 484.21908   Signif F = 0.0000

--------------------------Variables in the Equation--------------------------

Variable   B   SE B   Beta   T   Sig T
LENHOL   **0.986032**   0.044809   0.929698   22.005   0.0000
(Constant)   23.116986   5.583399   4.140   0.0001

This seems daunting but the results which we are interested in are highlighted in bold. We can make a number of comments:

1. The correlation between the two variables is indicated by the multiple *r* value. In this case at +0.92970 it is a strong positive relationship.

2. The *r*-squared value (0.86434) suggests the model is successful and that 86% of the variance in length of stay has been accounted for by this model (explained later).

3. The regression equation is:

   $y = 23.1 + 0.986x$, where *y* is the length of stay and *x* is length of holiday

This suggests that one day's holiday will result in 24 hours (rounding 0.986 to 1 and adding to 23.1) being spent in the area of Hadrian's Wall! But that on average each extra day on holiday will only result in an additional hour spent in the area.

   This model is quite successful but before we get carried away we should realise that it is based on the analysis of only 77 visitors.

using the square of *r* or r^2. The statistical theory underpinning this measure is more than adequately covered in the statistical texts (Cramer 1998). At this stage suffice it to say that the r^2 value represents the proportion of the variance in the dependent variable (tourism visits) explained (statistically) by the independent variable (supply of accommodation). The r^2 value is standard print out from most computer packages but is simply the correlation coefficient squared. So in the example in Figure 10.10 the value is:

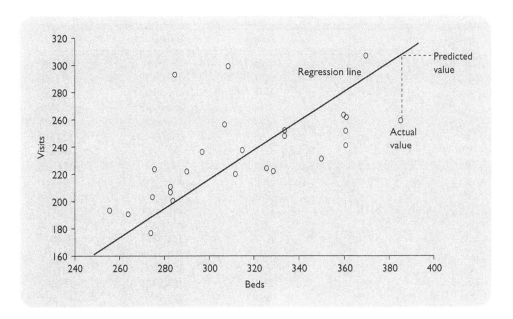

Figure 10.11
Exploring the
accuracy of the
regression model.

$r^2 = 0.864$

This means that just over eight-tenths of the variance in length of stay at Hadrian's Wall is accounted for by the duration of the holiday. By multiplying the r^2 value by 100, we can express this as '86 per cent of the variance in the amount of time spent by holiday-makers in the area of Hadrian's Wall being explained by the length of their holiday'. This figure is quite good for a simple bivariate relationship and lower values are normally expected given that tourism visits are determined by the complex interaction of many factors.

Exploring the residuals and improving the model

Returning to Figure 10.11, differences between actual and predicted visits to any district is known as the residual. Analysis of the residuals can be quite useful if the model is to be developed by adding more variables. As can be seen from Table 10.10 some cases have larger residuals than others.

The size of the residuals indicates the size of the estimation error for that particular case. The smaller the residual the better the estimate for that case. Clearly, those with large residuals will be those cases where the model does not provide an accurate estimate – they do not fit the model developed thus far and are known as *outliers*. Examination of those districts that do not fit into the model (i.e. have large residuals) may suggest ways in which the model may be improved. In other words, if we form two groups – the large positive and negative residuals – we may find that members of each group have something in common. The main question is how do we decide when a residual is large enough to be called an outlier? This is quite straightforward and is normally done through the computation of standardised residuals – that is each residual is given a standard score based on its size in relation to the average residual value. These are listed in Table 10.11. Outliers are normally defined as those having standardised residual values in excess of two standard deviations either side of the mean; these are based on the concept of the normal distribution curve which states that 5 per cent of the values lie outside two standard deviations either side of the mean. In the above example, the outliers are shown in Table 10.11.

Table 10.10
Actual, predicted
and residual
values

District		Visits	*PRED	*RESID
1	. * .	308	267.0665	40.9335
2	. * .	211	219.0454	−8.0454
3	. * .	264	261.5468	2.4532
4	. * .	242	262.0988	−20.0988
5	. * .	260	275.8980	−15.8980
6	. * .	252	262.0988	−10.0988
7	. *	257	232.2926	24.7074
8	. * .	225	242.7799	−17.7799
9	. * .	300	233.3965	66.6035
10	. * .	194	204.1422	−10.1422
11	. * .	221	235.0524	−14.0524
12	. * .	263	262.0988	0.9012
13	. * .	177	214.0777	−37.0777
14	. * .	208	219.0454	−11.0454
15	. * .	204	214.6296	−10.6296
16	. * .	201	219.5973	−18.5973
17	. * .	191	208.5580	−17.5580
18	. * .	223	244.4358	−21.4358
19	. * .	252	247.1957	4.8043
20	. * .	249	247.1957	1.8043
21	. * .	294	220.1493	73.8507
22	. * .	224	215.1816	8.8184
23	. * .	237	226.7729	10.2271
24	. * .	223	222.9091	0.0909
25	. * .	232	256.0271	−24.0271
26	. * .	238	236.7083	1.2917

Visits = Actual number of visitors.
*PRED = Number of visitors predicted by the regression line.
*RESID = Difference between actual and predicted.

Table 10.11
Outliers

District		Visits	*PRED	*RESID
9	. .. * .	300	233.3965	66.6035
21	. .. * .	294	220.1493	73.8507

If we examine these districts more closely and seek additional information, it may be that we can identify additional factors to put into our regression model in order to increase the accuracy of the predictions it makes.

Multivariate extension of the model

The regression model we have discussed so far is a simple linear bivariate one; that is it involves one dependent and one independent variable. This model can be extended by adding more independent variables to form a multivariate model. Such multiple regression models are much more appropriate to tourism management where activities/demand are likely to be determined by a large number of factors rather than a single cause. Detailed

Figure 10.12
Residuals in SPSS.

1. Proceed as in Figure 10.10, but this time click on the **Plots** button before clicking on **OK**.

2. Check the **Casewise** box and change the **Outliers** outside to **2** standard deviations.

3. Click on **Continue**.

4. Click on **OK**.

To continue with the analysis detailed in Figure 10.10, the following residuals were produced:

Casewise Plot of Standardized Residual
Outliers = 2.   *: Selected   M: Missing
         −5. −2. 2. 5.

Case #	O:.......: :.......:O	LENGTH	*PRED	*RESID
35	. .. * .	244.00	36.9214	207.0786
105	. ..* .	145.00	30.0192	114.9808
159	. ..* .	169.00	30.0192	138.9808
355	. .. * .	244.00	36.9214	207.0786
361	. ..* .	171.00	32.9773	138.0227

In this case the *r*-squared value was high so there are few outliers. Examination of other details about these respondents could suggest ways in which the model could be improved.

discussion of this extension is far beyond the scope of a text like this, but there are many excellent texts on the subject (Black 1999, Cramer 1998 and Lewis-Beck 1993). However, we will briefly examine the basic linear multivariate model and indicate key elements for interpretation.

We can extend the data on tourism visits to include two further variables, the number of tourism attractions in each district and environmental quality (taking employment in heavy industries as an indicator), consistent with the analysis of residuals discussed above. The data is shown in Table 10.12.

A multivariate regression model has the following equation:

$$y = a + b_1 x_1 + b_2 x_2 + b_3 x_3$$

the main additions being b_2 and b_3 which are the regression coefficients for the number of attractions (x_2) and the percentage employed in heavy industry (x_3), respectively. SPSS for Windows produces the results of the model as follows:

$$y_i = 152 + 0.245 \ x_1 + 6.5 \ x_2 - 1.22 \ x_3$$
$$r^2 = 0.90426$$

The first thing to note is that the success of the model (as measured by r^2) has increased tremendously – over 90 per cent of the variance in tourism visits is now explained by the model. Secondly, the *a* coefficient is now 152 – 152 visits would result if all the independent variables were set to zero! Thirdly, we can see that the impact of accommodation has been reduced by the addition of the other two variables; this is probably due to the fact that the quantity of accommodation is also related to the number of tourism attractions in a district – this would require further investigation. We can see that an extra attraction will generate an extra 6.5 tourists and that an increase of 1 per cent in those employed in heavy industries will depress the number of tourists by 1.22. Comparisons between the regression coefficients, in order to ascertain which is the most significant in terms of effect, is impossible in the above equation because the unit of measurement varies in each variable. Normal regression coefficients are expressed in the unit of measurement used for that particular variable. Where different units of measurement are used for different variables

Table 10.12

Data for multiple regression

District	Accommodation (No beds)	Visits (persons)	Number of attractions	% Employed in heavy industry
1	308	370	8	11
2	211	283	2	20
3	264	360	4	12
4	242	361	4	13
5	260	386	5	12
6	252	361	5	11
7	257	307	6	10
8	225	326	1	18
9	300	309	11	4
10	194	256	0	20
11	221	312	2	17
12	263	361	7	15
13	177	274	0	25
14	208	283	2	19
15	204	275	1	17
16	201	284	1	19
17	191	264	1	26
18	223	329	2	14
19	252	334	7	13
20	249	334	4	12
21	294	285	14	9
22	224	276	3	14
23	237	297	2	15
24	223	290	2	11
25	232	350	5	9
26	238	315	3	4

in a multivariate model comparisons using normal regression coefficients are impossible. Therefore, it is common practice to use standardised beta coefficients which enable comparisons to be made. Thus, the regression equation becomes:

$$y_i = \beta_1 x_i + \beta_2 x_{ii} + \beta_3 x_{iii} + e_i$$

where

$\beta_1 - \beta_3$ = beta regression coefficients for each variable ($x_i - x_{iii}$).

Beta regression coefficients are the equivalent of the slope coefficient (b) mentioned in bivariate regression in the sense that they indicate the impact of that particular variable on the dependent variable. However, they are different in the sense that they measure the effect of that particular variable on the dependent variable with the effects of all other variables held constant i.e. it measures the effect of that variable alone. Furthermore, beta coefficients are standardised and can therefore be compared with each other to ascertain which variable has the greatest impact. Inputting the above data into SPSS for Windows produces the following model:

$$y_i = 0.274\ x_i + 0.655\ x_{ii} + -0.197\ x_{iii}$$

Interpretation of the model proceeds as before:

Figure 10.13
Multivariate
regression in
SPSS.

The procedure is as detailed earlier for bivariate regression. The only difference being that you add more than one independent variable. Below are the results of a multivariate extension of the model outlined in Figure 10.10. In this instance two additional variables have been added – number of children (KIDS) and origin of visitors (ORIGIN). The former is a numerical variable whereas ORIGIN is a categorical one (either UK or overseas). These were chosen after examining the outliers mentioned earlier. Categorical variables can be added to the regression equation as *dummy variables*; that is they can be recoded to become dichotomous variables taking the values 0 or 1. In this instance overseas visitors were given a value of 1, with UK visitors given a value of 0.

```
****MULTIPLE REGRESSION****
Listwise Deletion of Missing Data
Equation Number 1   Dependent Variable.   LENGTH
Block Number 1. Method: Enter   LENHOL   ORIGIN   KIDS
Variable(s) Entered on Step Number
1. KIDS    how many of your group are under 16?
2. LENHOL  LENGTH OF HOLIDAY – DAYS
3. ORIGIN
```

Multiple R	0.93977
R Square	0.88317
Adjusted R Square	0.87742
Standard Error	49.29412

Analysis of Variance

	DF	Sum of Squares	Mean Square
Regression	3	1120481.34730	373493.78243
Residual	61	148224.52020	2429.91017

F = 153.70683   Signif F = 0.0000

-------------------------- Variables in the Equation --------------------------

Variable	B	SE B	Beta	T	Sig T
LENHOL	0.982823	0.045950	0.937059	21.389	0.0000
ORIGIN	-25.513596	29.180964	-0.038317	-0.874	0.3854
KIDS	-8.214156	8.466138	-0.042484	-0.970	0.3358
(Constant)	29.136513	7.393080		3.941	0.0002

End Block Number 1 All requested variables entered.

We need to note the following:

1. The r and r-squared values have increased but only slightly – the model remains successful, but the addition of two new variables has only added a small amount to the 'explanatory power' of the model.

2. The beta values indicate that LENHOL retains its importance and the other two variables have only a small effect on the length of stay, but this is negative. This implies that the greater the number of children in the party, the less time the group will spend at Hadrian's Wall. Moreover, if the visitors are from overseas they will spend less time at the wall. However, we must not *overinterpret* the effects of these last two variables as the effects are quite small, and as we shall see in the next chapter *statistically insignificant.*

3. The number of outliers was reduced to 4.

1. Examination of the coefficient of determination: over 90 per cent of the variance in tourism visits is explained by the model – this remains the same when using beta coefficients.

2. Examination of the regression coefficients: the number of attractions in a district has the greatest impact on tourism visits, with the quantity of accommodation having a lesser impact. The amount of heavy industry in a district does tend to depress the number of tourism visits.

Final comment on linear regression models

Prior to discussing forecasting models based on trend analyses, it is worth mentioning a further issue associated with linear regression models. Although we have some indication of the accuracy of the model in the r^2 value, the validity of the prediction requires further comment. The r^2 value gives an indication of the accuracy of the model for the range of the data inputted; it does not say anything about the accuracy of predictions outside the range of data included in the model. If we return to the sample data graphed in Figure 10.9, then we can see that the range of the Beds variable is from about 240 to 400 units. The model is clearly a valid tool for making predictions within that range (a process known as *interpolation*), but would have limited validity for figures outside that range, or *extrapolation*. Extrapolation beyond the range of data inputted into the model is uncertain and there must come a point where the law of diminishing returns sets in i.e. an extra accommodation unit would produce no net gain in terms of tourism visits. Extrapolation just outside the range of data is considerably less uncertain than extreme extrapolation.

Trend extrapolation

The above models were based on the assumption that trends are best explained by reference to underlying 'causes', and hence predictions are best predicated on the basis of an identification of those causes. There are many situations when the tourism manager does not have the time to discover what the main causes are or where data referring to plausible causes are unavailable. In such cases, the manager has little alternative but to fall back on intuition or use an alternative forecasting model – time series. Time-series models are much simpler than regression models and are based on the assumption that past trends will continue. Forecasts are therefore based on the extrapolation of past trends. There are a large number of potential methods, but we will just consider trend curve analysis.

All these models are essentially univariate and are non-causal – they assume that forecasts can be made without reference to any other variable than past trends. Clearly, the application of such models to volatile industries such as tourism and leisure must be treated with caution since they assume that those factors causing past trends will continue to operate in the same way and in the same places as they have in the past. It is therefore wise not to extrapolate too much into the future using such models.

Trend curve analysis

We shall begin with this model simply because it follows on from the regression models discussed earlier. This analysis uses the regression model to fit a line or curve to the time-series data and then uses that curve to project the trend forward through time. This type of forecasting is quick and simple. The basic trend curve model is based on the linear equation:

$$y = a + bT$$

where a and b are coefficients (as in the regression model)
    T is the time period
    y is the forecast variable.

To illustrate, examine the data in Table 10.13.

Clearly, tourism demand has grown significantly during the 1970s and 1980s. While this growth has not been steady, the general trend is evident enough, as Figure 10.14 illustrates.

Year	Arrivals
1970	159.7
1971	172.2
1972	181.9
1973	190.6
1974	197.1
1975	214.4
1976	220.7
1977	239.1
1978	257.4
1979	274.0
1980	284.8
1981	288.8
1982	287.0
1983	284.4
1984	311.2
1985	325.9
1986	333.9
1987	358.9
1988	390.0
1989	405.3

Source: World Tourism Organization (1990)

Table 10.13
World international tourism arrivals, 1970–89 (millions)

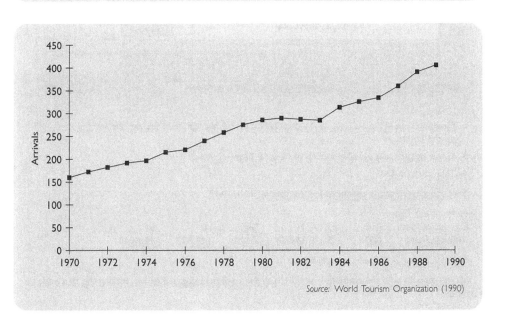

Source: World Tourism Organization (1990)

Figure 10.14
World tourism demand: 1970–89.

The more or less upward and linear trend suggests that the linear regression equation discussed above is an appropriate model to fit to this data set. Using trend curve analysis it is possible to compute a forecast for the following year(s). The statistical principles are similar to regression and SPSS for Windows produces the following equation for the best fit line:

Figure 10.15
Time series in
SPSS.

To compute a time series in SPSS the year need not be entered (as in the above case), rather time can be used as the independent variable. When time is used then it is assumed that for the first case within the data set $t = 1$ and each subsequent case is one time period further on; i.e. in the second case t is 2, in the third case $t = 3$ and so on.

1. With the data file **open**, click on **Regression** in the **Statistics** menu, and then **Curve Estimation**. The following dialogue box appears:

2. Place the time-series variable in the **dependent** box – highlight it in the variable list and then click on the button.

3. In the independent variable section make sure **Time** is ticked.

4. Then click on **OK**.

The following output is produced for the data in Table 10.13.

Independent: Time

Dependent	Mth	Rsq	d.f.	F	Sigf	b0	b1
ARRIVALS	LIN	0.975	18	690.77	0.000	**142.823**	**12.0040**

Hi-Res Chart # 3: Curvefit for arrivals

b0 corresponds with the constant a and, b1 with the coefficient detailed earlier, making the time-series model:

$$Y = 142.823 + 12.004t$$

where t is the next time interval.

The forecast for 1990 ($t = 21$) is **394** million and still represents a decline!

SPSS also produces a chart showing the actual and the predicted trends for the inputted data.

$y_t = -23493 + 12T_t$

Having computed the equation it is now a relatively straightforward matter to generate a forecast for 1990:

$-23493 + (12 \times 1990) = 387$ million

The prediction of a fall in demand is an interesting one given the previous constant upward trend. This is a reflection of the length of the time series and the fact that the rates of growth were not as high in the earlier period as in the late 1980s. Herein lies a problem with this type of forecasting model and is discussed in the specialist literature (Box and Jenkins 1970, Martin and Witt 1989, Saunders, Sharp and Witt 1987, Witt 1989). The linear trend line outlined above is only one of many alternatives. The choice of trend curve and associated equation depends upon the pattern of points comprising the trend. The important point is to choose a trend line that fits the trend in the past and alternatives are discussed in more specialist texts (Saunders *et al.* 1987).

The above analysis of time series was based on a simple linear trend and a yearly data series and, as such, is potentially problematic in the context of tourism, when it is applied to monthly or quarterly data series. Adjustment for seasonal variations is clearly important in an industry such as tourism and leisure (Saunders *et al.* 1987; Witt 1989).

Final comment on general linear multivariate models

Correlation and regression, as discussed above, are based on the general linear model; that is they make the assumptions outlined for Pearson's Product Moment Correlation. Of prime concern is that the relationships are linear in form, as indicated in the scattergrams, for example. If the relationship is not linear then you are faced with a choice:

- either transform the data in some manner to establish a linear relationship, or
- use a non-linear model

In which case you will need to examine more detailed texts (Cramer 1998; Manly 1986). Multivariate models have been used extensively in leisure and tourism research and this chapter has concentrated on just one such technique. Cluster and factor methods are also quite common and are covered in more specialist texts. The article by Lawson *et al.* (1998) referred to in Chapter 7 makes use of a multivariate technique known as factor analysis and should be examined further by those who are interested. The article by Prentice, Witt and Hamer (1998), also referred to in Chapter 7 makes use of cluster analysis.

Summary

In this chapter we have examined a range of quantitative methods which should be of use to the tourism researcher and practitioner. You should be able to apply these techniques to your own study and workplace context. In this chapter you have learnt:

- the meaning of statistical association
- how to differentiate between independent and dependent variables
- how to investigate and measure association at nominal, ordinal and interval/ratio levels
- the difference between causality and association
- how to carry out and interpret bivariate and multivariate analysis
- how to do time-series analysis.

Make sure that you understand and can apply the methods covered prior to moving on. If you have not grasped something or if you are further inspired, try exploring the reading listed – someone may have explained it better.

Student Activities

Activity 1

Using the data set for the Hadrian's Wall survey, choose an appropriate procedure to calculate correlation coefficients between overall level of satisfaction (SATSCORE) and length of stay (LENGTH). Are people who stay longer more or less satisfied with their visit?

Activity 2

Using the Hadrian's Wall survey data again, is there any relationship between age of visitor (AGE) and the purpose of their visit (MAINPURP)?

Activity 3

Let us assume that you have been appointed as marketing manager for a theme park, and you have been allocated a budget for this year's advertising. You know already from the company's own statistics how much the company has spent on advertising in the last ten years. From the amounts of visitors entering your theme park in the last ten years, you have been asked whether there is a correlation between the size of advertising budget and number of visitors.

The table below shows the basic data.

Year	X (Advertisement budget is measured in £1000)	Y (Total number of visitors is measured in 1000)
1	75	85
2	80	85
3	60	65
4	55	60
5	85	80
6	95	95
7	70	60
8	75	80
9	80	80
10	65	60

Work out the correlation coefficient for the above data. How strong is the relationship between advertising and the number of visitors? What are the implications of this?

Activity 4

Using the data from Activity 3, compute the regression equation.

1. What are the meanings of the coefficients (*a* and *b*)?
2. How successful was the model as a whole?
3. Are there any outliers? If so which years? What do outliers tell us?
4. If this year's advertising budget is £70,000, how many visits is this likely to result in?

Activity 5

Using the data below compute the equation of the best-fit trend line. Produce a graph indicating the nature of the trend.

Total visits of Japanese tourists to the UK, 1978–90

Year	Visitors ('000)
1978	132
1979	140
1980	162
1981	164
1982	159
1983	170
1984	201
1985	211
1986	205
1987	297
1988	388
1989	505
1990	571

Source: British Tourist Authority (1991)

1. What is the equation for the trend line?
2. What is the forecast for 1991?
3. What are the problems with extrapolating beyond 1993?

References

● Black, T. R. (1999) *Doing Quantitative Research in the Social Sciences*, London: Sage.
● Box, G. E. P. and Jenkins, G. M. (1970) *Time Series Analysis*, London: Holden Day.
● British Tourist Authority (1991) *Digest of Tourist Statistics*, London: BTA.
● Cramer, D. (1998) *Fundamental Statistics for Social Research*, London: Routledge.
● Elliott-White, M. and Cuthill, V. (1998) *Image and Expectation of a World Heritage Site*. Report for the Hadrian's Wall Tourism Partnership. Unpublished.
● Lawson, R. W., Williams, J., Young, T. and Cossens, J. (1998) 'A comparison of residents' attitudes towards tourism in 10 New Zealand destinations', *Tourism Management*, Vol. 19 (3), pp. 247–56.

● Lewis-Beck, M. S. (1993) *Regression Analysis*, London: Sage.
● Manly, B. F. J. (1986) *Multivariate Statistical Methods*, London: Chapman Hall.
● Martin, C. A. and Witt, S. F. (1989) 'Tourism demand elasticities', in Witt, S. and Moutinho, L. *Tourism Marketing and Management Handbook*, London: Prentice Hall.
● Prentice, R. C., Witt, S. F. and Hamer, C. (1998) 'Tourism as experience: the case of heritage parks', *Annals of Tourism Research*, Vol. 25 (1), pp. 1–24.
● Saunders, J. A., Sharp, J. A. and Witt, S. F. (1987) *Practical Business Forecasting*, London: Gower.
● Witt, S. F. (1989) 'Forecasting international tourism demand: univariate time series methods (non causal quantitative techniques)', in Witt, S. and Moutinho, L. *Tourism Marketing and Management Handbook*, London: Prentice Hall.
● World Tourism Organization (1990) *Yearbook of Tourism Statistics*, Geneva: WTO.

Chapter 11

Inferential Statistics

Learning Outcomes

At the end of this chapter you will be able to:

- test the statistical significance of correlation coefficients
- determine which tests are appropriate to particular data sets
- carry out parametric and non-parametric statistical tests
- interpret inferential statistics and associated significance levels
- interpret statistically significant and insignificant outcomes

Introduction

In the last chapter we learnt about identifying and measuring statistical association. In other words, how to set about discovering whether something is influenced (statistically) by something else, whether a change in one variable produces a change in the other. The discovery of a correlation can often lead us to generalise about the result. In short we make an inference about the relationship that was found to exist in our particular set of data to all cases at large, to the population. Generally our research rests on data which was obtained from a sample rather from all known cases; if we generalise we make an inference from our sample to the population. In a sample of holiday intentions we may find that 70 per cent of British respondents intended to holiday in the UK. If this sample represents the entire population of holiday-makers, then we might conclude that the majority of British holiday-makers would take their holiday in the UK. However, such an inference necessitates the use of inferential statistics.

Inferential statistics

Inferential statistics are values calculated from a sample and used to estimate the same value for a population. In other words, inferential statistics are simply estimates of the qualities or quantities existing in a population. We have already seen how these can be applied to descriptive statistics in Chapter 9. These particular statistics are based on the Central

Limit Theorem – a mathematical principle which is beyond the scope of this book. However, it is important to note that this theorem rests on the basic prerequisite that the sample has been selected by random selection.

Earlier in this book it was stated that samples are used to estimate to the population, and that if the sample is obtained through probability sampling then the margin of error in that estimate can be calculated. Inferential statistics are essentially a means of calculating that amount of error in the sample estimate; or to put this another way, the likelihood that the sample statistic can be applied to the population.

Strictly speaking inferential statistical tests should only be applied if the sample was obtained using probability sampling. However, as we discovered in Chapter 7 much research in leisure and tourism is based on non-probability sampling. This suggests that inferential statistics are inappropriate in such instances. However, if you examine published research critically you will soon discover that this rule is frequently flaunted and inferential statistics are applied to non-probability samples. This is controversial among statisticians and although social researchers have to be more pragmatic, inferential statistics should only be used with probability samples.

Types of inferential statistics

Our earlier work on descriptive statistics made it clear that data can take different forms: nominal, ordinal and interval/ratio. The scale of measurement acts as a restriction on how the data can be analysed. There are basically two types of inferential statistics:

1. *non-parametric statistics* – these use ordinal (ranked) or nominal data, and are relatively new compared to the older parametric tests
2. *parametric statistics* – these use interval/ratio data.

Parametric statistics also make additional assumptions about the data:

1. The sample data have been drawn from a normally distributed population (as opposed to a skewed one, for example).
2. The two samples have the same variance (the square of the standard deviation). In this situation a sample is a group. So if, for example, you were exploring leisure differences between rural and urban areas, then one sample would be the rural group and the other the urban group.
3. The results are applicable to interval/ratio data only.

Parametric and non-parametric statistics both assume that the sample has been obtained through probability sampling. Parametric tests have more information available to them (because the data is at the interval/ratio level) and therefore they are more precise and sensitive than non-parametric tests; the latter, being based on cruder levels of measurement, are inevitably less precise and comparatively insensitive!

What do inferential statistics do?

Inferential statistics tell us the likelihood of obtaining the results due to chance factors. If the statistical test tells us that the result (the correlation, say) was probably not due to chance, the result is said to be statistically significant. If the test tells us that the result was probably due to chance then the result is said to be statistically insignificant. A 'significant' result is probably repeatable. So, inferential statistics are basically a tool for informing the researcher whether or not the result is statistically significant, and so, in the case of

Probability as %	Probability on a 0–1 scale (p)	Confidence level
5	0.05	95%
1	0.01	99%
0.1	0.001	99.9%

Table 11.1
Probabilities and percentages

correlation coefficients, whether or not the sample correlation can be generalised to the population. This is clearly useful as most research will seek to make some generalisations beyond the sample upon which it is based.

Thus, the statistical tests tell us the probability that the result occurred by chance, in other words, that the correlation coefficient is due to sampling error rather than a reflection of true association in the population! Probabilities can be expressed in terms of percentages or as probabilities (see Table 11.1).

If the probability of p is small, as in the above table, then the result is unlikely to be due to chance i.e. the result in the sample is likely to exist in the population. At what point is p small? There is no absolute answer to this, but the most common level is 0.05. This means that if our inferential statistics yield a value of 0.05 or less then the result is said to be significant; it is unlikely to have occurred by chance. If p is greater than 0.05 then the result is said to be not statistically significant; the result obtained in the sample is likely to be due to chance.

This table implies a choice – which probability level do we choose? A probability level of $p = 0.05$ suggests that we will be wrong 5 times out of 100 (5 per cent of the time). In other words, our estimate would be 'incorrect' 5 per cent of the time. This is not a bad level of accuracy, particularly in the social rather than the mathematical world. Suppose that we found a difference in the assignment marks between two groups in favour of the group which had been issued with this research methods book (the other having another book) and that the probability that this difference could have occurred by chance was 0.05, or 5 times out of 100. Normally we would accept that the difference is significant and abandon the standard text in preference to this one. On the other hand, suppose that in testing the effects of a powerful new performance enhancing drug we found that the difference between the control and the experimental group, in terms of effect, was significant at the 5 per cent level, but that the drug also adversely affected the health of the athlete. Given that such drugs will be used by human beings then we may not be content with this result. For 1 in 20 cases the drug may be doing no good at all, but would have nasty side-effects. In medical research it is common to use the 1 per cent level or less. Most research in leisure and tourism is not concerned with life or death and so the 5 per cent level is appropriate. Another way of looking at this problem is to consider how confident you would like to be in your generalisation. In Table 11.1, significance levels have been equated with confidence levels – the 0.05 significance level equates to 95 per cent confidence. For most work in tourism and leisure the 95 per cent confidence level is satisfactory (see Chapter 7 for more details).

The hypothesis testing procedure

Inferential statistics are used to test whether or not a given sample statistic (i.e. mean, correlation) is likely to have occurred by chance (due to sampling error) or not. The testing process is known as the hypothesis testing procedure. In the statistical hypothesis testing procedure it is the *null hypothesis* (H_0) that is tested. The null hypothesis is:

> *the negative or the no difference or the no association hypothesis, and a statistical test in inferential statistics is commenting on the likelihood of the null hypothesis being true.*

An example of a null hypothesis would be:

> *there is no statistical association between gender and participation in the sport of golf.*

It is only when the null hypothesis has been rejected that the alternative or research hypothesis can be accepted. The research hypothesis will state that the difference or the correlation is statistically significant, that it is unlikely to have occurred by chance. Testing the null hypothesis is rather like a criminal trial. The jury must decide whether or not the defendant is guilty; you must decide whether there is an association in the population, based on the evidence collected for only a sample of that population. Prior to the trial, the assumption is that the defendant is innocent and it is the job of the prosecuting counsel to provide enough evidence to overrule this assumption of innocence; indeed the prosecutor must prove the guilt beyond all reasonable doubt. In research the assumption is that there is no association or difference (the null hypothesis) and it is the job of the researcher to prove beyond all reasonable doubt that this is not the case (i.e. to disprove the null hypothesis). In inferential statistics 'beyond all reasonable doubt' translates into the probability of being wrong or the likelihood of being right. Normally in social research, the null hypothesis is tested at the 5 per cent level; if it has a greater than 5 per cent chance of being correct then it has to be accepted.

Hypothesis testing is normally either directional or non-directional. In non-directional hypothesis testing the research hypothesis simply states that there is a statistical difference or association. In a directional test, then the direction of the association (positive or negative) or difference is stated. For example, the statement that 'men are more likely to participate in football than females' could form the basis of a directional research hypothesis. Directional tests are usually referred to as *one-tailed tests,* whereas non-directional tests are known as *two-tailed tests.*

In the case of the testing of a correlation coefficient then inferential statistics are useful tools in determining whether values of the sample coefficients indicate some association between the two variables in the population. In other words, a PPMCC of 0.420 obtained from a sample of ten cases, may appear at first sight to indicate a moderate degree of association, but formal testing using inferential statistics could reveal that this value could have occurred by chance and is therefore taken as zero. The crucial factor is that, while the coefficient is moderate, the sample size is only ten – the sample size is an important determinant of sampling error, as Chapter 7 made clear.

Testing the significance of Pearson's Product Moment Correlation Coefficient

Pearson's Coefficient is a parametric statistic, the significance of which can be tested using a hypothesis testing procedure. This procedure will ascertain whether the value of the correlation obtained from a sample can be applied to the whole population from which the sample was taken (i.e. is statistically significant) or whether it could have occurred by chance (i.e. taken as zero or not statistically significant). In order to test the significance of the coefficient it is important that the following procedure is used:

1. State the null hypothesis:

   H_0 = there is no association between the two variables, the observed coefficient is simply due to chance.

2. State the research hypothesis:

   H_1 = there is an association between the two variables and such an association is likely to exist in the population.

3. State the significance level. Normally this is set at 0.05.

   $p = 0.05$

4. Calculate the correlation coefficient.

5. Examine the significance of the coefficient using the information provided in SPSS (see Figure 11.1). If the probability of the calculated (sample) coefficient is less than or equal to 0.05 then the null hypothesis is rejected; if it is greater than 0.05 then the null hypothesis must be accepted. If the null hypothesis is rejected then the research hypothesis may be accepted.

For example, in the previously mentioned study of visitors to Hadrian's Wall we may think that there is a relationship between the distance travelled and the length of stay at the Heritage Site. We could use SPSS to compute and test the correlation coefficient as detailed in Figure 11.1.

So, the statistical significance of PPMCC can be calculated. In other words, it is possible to ascertain whether or not the association observed in the sample is likely to exist

Figure 11.1
Testing the correlation coefficient using SPSS.

The procedure for calculating the correlation coefficient using SPSS was detailed in the previous chapter.

The coefficient would be tested in the following way:

H_0 = There is no association between time taken to travel to Hadrian's Wall and length of stay. The observed correlation is simply due to chance.

H_1 = There is an association between time taken to travel to Hadrian's Wall and length of stay.
$p < 0.05$

Note how the research hypothesis is non-directional and therefore two-tailed.

SPSS gives us the following correlation matrix:
----------CORRELATION COEFFICIENTS----------

	LENGTH	TIMEHOME
LENGTH	1.0000	0.2680
	(76)	(76)
	P = .	P = 0.019
TIMEHOME	0.2680	1.0000
	(76)	(76)
	P = 0.019	P = .

(Coefficient / (Cases) / 2-tailed significance)

The *p* values are highlighted. The correlation is positive but weak (at 0.2680) but the probability, at 0.019 is less than the critical 0.05. We can therefore reject the null hypothesis and accept the research hypothesis. Note that SPSS calculates the actual probability that the association is due to chance rather than stating that the result is statistically significant. You need to compare the calculated probability with the probability level you have established (usually 0.05).

Therefore, there is likely to be a weak association between distance travelled (using time as an indicator) and length of stay at Hadrian's Wall or, to be more accurate, we are 95% confident that it applies to the whole population from which it was drawn. That is, we can be confident in our generalisation.

in the population. The above example illustrates that the coefficient does not need to be strong in order for it to be significant; indeed bivariate correlations are infrequently strong in social research.

Significance tests of difference

In the last section, we tested the significance of a correlation coefficient to see if it would apply to the whole population from which the sample was drawn. In this section we are going to focus on differences between two sets of sample data. If you think back to the basic design of the experimental method, you will realise the particular value of these tests. In an experiment, the independent variable is manipulated and the results of the two groups, the experiment and the control group, are investigated for differences, significant differences. The central purpose is to ascertain whether the difference between the two groups is small enough to have occurred by chance or large enough to apply to the whole population. If the difference is large then we can argue that the independent variable has an effect on the dependent variable. We can never be 100 per cent certain that the results of the experiment were due to the effects of the independent variable, but we can state that the probability of our result occurring by chance was so small that we are prepared to take the risk of rejecting the null hypothesis, accepting the difference between experimental and real conditions.

Tests of difference can be used in a similar way in survey data, where you wish to ascertain whether there are differences between sub-groups on a particular attribute – whether there is a difference between participation in team sports between men and women, for example. Choice of statistical test depends upon the nature and origin of the data used.

The student's t-test

So far we have talked about accepting or rejecting the null hypothesis, but have not said how we can ascertain whether or not differences are significant. Student's *t*-test is one method of determining whether or not there is a difference between two groups, when:

1. the groups have been randomly selected
2. the population variances are equal
3. the population distributions are normal – though if the sample is large ($n > 30$) then this assumption may be relaxed
4. the dependent variable is at the interval/ratio scale of measurement.

In statistical terms the *t*-test examines the likelihood of both groups being part of the same population (i.e. no difference) or whether they can be viewed as coming from different populations.

Consider the following set of data in Table 11.2; here we have data which constitutes a random sample of district councils with the number of visitors given for each district. Each district is classified as having an active (A) or a passive (P) tourism policy. The purpose of this data is to ascertain whether there is a statistically significant difference in visitation levels between districts in terms of their policy towards tourism.

Here there are two variables – policy and number of visitors. The research hypothesis is that:

there is a statistically significant difference in visitation levels between districts with an active tourism policy and those with a passive one.

Table 11.2

No visitors	Policy
391	A
386	A
349	P
381	P
386	P
314	P
303	P
345	A
297	P
317	P
296	P
348	A
318	A
371	A
399	A
309	A

Table 11.2
Random sample of visitor numbers by tourism policy

Passive	Active
349	391
381	386
386	345
314	348
303	318
297	371
317	399
296	309
Mean = 327	Mean = 354

Table 11.3
Average visitor numbers and tourism policy

The null hypothesis is that there are no differences between the two groups. In this situation it is argued that visitation is influenced by type of policy, that visitation is the dependent variable. So the dependent variable is measured at the ratio level of measurement, the distribution of the population is normal, and there is no real difference in the variance between the two groups (active and passive). We could rearrange the data in the form of Table 11.3.

The initial calculation of the means for the two groups suggests that passive policies are associated with lower levels of visitation, whereas active policies produce higher numbers of visitors. However, this is quite a small sample and the difference could be due to chance so we need to test this difference more rigorously. So the hypothesis testing procedure is as follows:

H_0 = There is no difference between the two groups.

H_1 = There is a difference in visitation levels between active and passive districts.
Rejection level is $p < 0.05$.

Figure 11.2
Calculating
student's *t*-test
using SPSS.

We will be using an independent samples *t*-test. This procedure is used when the two groups are unrelated and ascertains whether they have significantly different means. A paired-sample *t*-test is usually used when the two groups are related – for example, in an experiment where the same group were tested before and after. SPSS assumes that you have two variables – the dependent variable is measured at the interval/ratio level and the independent variable is categorical.

1. Select **Compare Means** from the **Statistics** menu.

2. Select **Independent Samples *t*-test.**

3. The numerical variable (visitation) forms the **test** variable, whereas the categorical one (Policy) is the **grouping** variable.

4. You will need to click on the **Define Groups** button to set the group codes – simply type in the codes corresponding to each group in the dialog box. These codes correspond with the codes you used for the independent variable. Click on **Continue.**

5. Click on **OK.**

The following is produced by SPSS:

t-tests for Independent Samples of Policy

Variable	Number of Cases	Mean	SD	SE of Mean
VAR00001				
VAR00002 1	8	353.7500	31.950	11.296
VAR00002 2	7	327.7143	38.943	14.719

Mean Difference = 26.0357
Levene's Test for Equality of Variances: F = 0.562 P = 0.467

t-test for Equality of Means

Variances	*t*-value	df	2-Tail Sig	SE of Diff	95% CI for Diff
Equal	**1.42**	13	**0.178**	18.295	(−13.489, 65.560)
Unequal	1.40	11.68	0.187	18.554	(−14.514, 66.586)

Quite complex! However, we are only interested in two pieces of information: the *t*-value and the significance. These are highlighted and we can see that *t* equals 1.42 and the significance is greater than 0.05. What does this mean? Well, *t* is just a measure of difference between the two independent groups. We have already established that we are undertaking a two-tailed test at the 5% significance level. This means that:

the null hypothesis is accepted – that the difference between the two policies is so small that it could have occurred by chance.

So, it is safe to assume that there is no difference in visitation levels between active and passive districts.

Strictly speaking there is a need to state whether we are undertaking a one- or a two-tailed test. Basically a one-tailed test is directional (i.e. that one group will have higher visitation than the other) and a two-tailed test in non-directional (simply that there is a difference). However, SPSS assumes that the tests are two-tailed.

The *t*-test results in a dramatically different interpretation of the data. Prior to testing you would have wrongly concluded that policy type makes a difference to visitation. Thus, such testing is important as it allows you to make more informed decisions based on probabilities. The result is no less interesting as it suggests that policy is having statistically insignificant impacts on visitation and further investigation is needed as to why this is the case.

Different types of t-*test*

In the above example we carried out a *t*-test which compared the means of two independent samples. This simply means that the subjects for the two samples are different: eight were active and eight were passive. This type of *t*-test is also known as the unrelated or independent test. Such a test would be used in experimental designs with two conditions testing one independent variable (training method, for example), when different subjects are doing the two conditions (say athletes only training at altitude compared with those training at sea level).

An alternative experimental design may necessitate the use of a paired or correlated *t*-test. In such a design the same subjects are exposed to different conditions, the measurements relate to the same variable, or the subjects may be measured before and after 'treatment'. The way in which '*t*' is calculated is slightly different from the method used for independent samples. Computer programs are normally sensitive to this, but readers who wish to develop this further are directed to the work of Cramer (1998).

Analysis of variance (ANOVA)

The *t*-test is fine for those instances where there are only two groups in the data. When there are more than two groups, you can transform both variables into nominal or ordinal data and carry out a cross-tabulation as outlined previously, or you can use analysis of variance (ANOVA). ANOVA is a parametric test which requires that the dependent variable is at an interval/ratio level of measurement and that the independent variable is categorical. In this sense it is similar to the *t*-test. The main difference is that in ANOVA you can have more than two samples or groups, meaning that you can test for differences between four or five occupational or age groups, for example.

The mathematical details of the procedure are left to more specialist texts on the subject (Black 1999; Bryman and Cramer 1997). However, the assumptions made by the test are the same as those of the *t*-test: random samples, normal distribution and equal population variances. Basically, the procedure compares the amount of variation *within* the groups, with that *between* the groups and uses this to compute the *F*-ratio; the latter is a measure of the difference between the two. If the amount of variation within the groups exceeds that between the groups then the result is unlikely to be significant. This later point is hardly surprising because it suggests that the groups themselves are not homogeneous.

The ANOVA test can be applied to the Hadrian's Wall survey data. The respondents were interviewed at different times of the year and it is possible to distinguish between three different groups: off-peak late spring/early summer (group A), off-peak autumn (group B) and peak summer (group C). It was considered that those travelling in spring/autumn would not stay as long at the Heritage Site due to shorter holidays and uncertain weather. However, the following mean length of stays do not confirm this:

Group	Mean	Standard deviation	Number
Group C	15.789	30.2820	112
Group B	20.2589	38.3740	93
Group A	20.8218	38.0672	94

Summer visitors stay for an average of 16 hours in the vicinity of Hadrian's Wall, whereas off-peak visitors stay for over 20 hours. Are these differences significant? We test this in Figure 11.3.

Figure 11.3
Calculating
ANOVA using
SPSS.

SPSS requires two variables to perform this analysis, the dependent variable (length of stay) must be interval/ratio data, whereas the factoring variable must contain categories (time of year). However, the data in the factoring variable must be numeric – that is the different groups must be represented by different numbers as string variables cannot be inputted into the procedure.

1. With the data file open, select **Compare Means** from the **Statistics** menu, followed by **One Way ANOVA**.

2. Add the **dependent** variable (length of stay) to the appropriate box, and the grouping variable (time of year) to the **factor** box.

3. Click on **OK**.

4. The output from SPSS for Windows is as follows:

Variable LENGTH
By Variable TIME

Analysis of variance

Source	D.F.	Sum of squares	Mean squares	F Ratio	F Prob
Between Groups	2	1596.7117	798.3559	**0.6352**	**0.5306**
Within Groups	296	372030.1340	1256.8586		
Total	298	373626.8457			

The *F*-ratio is the inferential statistic and the *F*-Prob is the probability that the differences are due to chance. The probability (0.5306) is in excess of 0.05, so we must accept the null hypothesis that there is no difference between the three groups.

The principles of inferential statistics are always the same and ANOVA is no different. A measure of difference is calculated and the probability of this occurring by chance is stated. In this case the differences between the groups is statistically insignificant.

ANOVA and *t*-tests are parametric tests which make assumptions about the population from which the sample is drawn and use interval/ratio data. There are times when the researcher is unwilling to make the normality assumption and/or when the data is at the ordinal scale of measurement. If, for example, the data is at the interval scale of measurement but does not fulfil the assumptions of the parametric test, the data may be ranked and the Mann Whitney *U* test applied.

The Mann Whitney U test

The Mann Whitney is a non-parametric test which does not make assumptions about the population, and uses ordinal data. The Mann Whitney tests for the difference between two means. The same hypothesis testing procedure is used. Consider the data in Table 11.4.

Table 11.4
Satisfaction
scores from an
urban and a rural
locality

Urban	Rural
15.2	8.4
10.7	9.3
8.6	8.7
9.3	10.2
12.4	10.0
11.1	
$n_1 = 6$	$n_2 = 5$

The data must be entered into SPSS in the form of two variables:

Figure 11.4
Calculation of
Mann Whitney U
using SPSS.

Score	Locality
15.20	U
10.70	U
8.60	U
9.30	U
12.40	U
11.10	U
8.40	R
9.30	R
8.70	R
10.20	R
10.00	R

1. Select **Nonparametric** tests from the **Statistics** menu and then **2 Independent Samples**.

2. Make sure **Mann Whitney U** is ticked as the test type.

3. The numerical variable (satisfaction score) is the **test** variable and locality is the **group** variable. **Define** the groups as in the *t*-test above. Click on **Continue** and **OK**.

The following is produced by SPSS:

------ Mann-Whitney U – Wilcoxon Rank Sum W Test

Score
by Locality

Mean Rank	Sum of Ranks	Cases	
4.30	21.50	5 Locality =	1.00
7.42	44.50	6 Locality =	2.00
	—		
	11 Total		

Exact**

U	W	2*(One-Tailed P)	Z	2-Tailed P
6.5	21.5	0.1255	−1.5554	0.1198

** This exact *p*-value is not corrected for ties.

Take the smaller of the two *U* values (6.5) and the 2-tailed probability ($p = 0.1198$). We can see that the probability is greater than the crucial 0.05 and therefore we cannot reject the null hypothesis. There are no differences in levels of satisfaction between urban and rural areas.

A local politician is convinced that rural dwellers are significantly less satisfied with local leisure provision than urban dwellers. This data relates to satisfaction with leisure provision and a key consideration is whether there are differences between urban and rural localities.

H_0 = There is no difference in satisfaction between urban and rural areas.

H_1 = There is a significant difference between urban and rural areas (two-tailed).
   Rejection level is $p > 0.05$.

The data is measured on an interval scale but we cannot assume they are derived from a normally distributed population. Thus, the interval data is converted to ordinal data (by SPSS); this is done by ranking the values out of the total set of data (from lowest to highest).

The chi-square test

The chi-square test is a much used and highly flexible non-parametric test which can be applied in one-sample, two-sample and multi-sample situations. Data for the chi-square test must be in the form of frequencies or at the nominal level of measurement.

A one-sample test

In this type of test we are comparing an observed set of frequencies, produced by a sample investigation, with an expected frequency distribution. The expected frequencies are usually input by the computer but could be based on prior knowledge or theory. SPSS assumes in a one-sample test that each category would be expecting the same number of cases. In the following example, a leisure department examined the mode of travel to a leisure centre used by a representative sample of 132 customers. The results are shown in Table 11.5. The department wished to know whether any one form of transport is favoured significantly more than others. As in all significance tests this is stated in the form of a null hypothesis, that there is no significant difference in the customers' choice of transport.

Table 11.5
Method of travel
to leisure centre

	Foot	Bus	Train	Car	Bike	Motor bike
Number of customers	50	19	17	30	9	7

Figure 11.5
One-sample
chi square using
SPSS.

SPSS would require the raw data in order to calculate this – that is a variable by case matrix for all 132 cases. Once the data file is **open** then the following procedure is followed:

1. Select **Nonparametric** tests from the **Statistics** menu, followed by **Chi-square**.

2. Add the required variable to the **test** variable box, and make sure that **All Categories Equal** is checked, then click on **OK**.

The following is produced:

```
-----Chi-Square Test
Chi-Square    D.F.    Significance
57.9          5       0.000
```

SPSS often returns significance values of 0.000 – this means that the probability is very low. In this case the significance of the result is less than 0.05. We would therefore reject the null hypothesis and accept the research hypothesis that '*there are statistically significant differences in customers' choice of transport*'. The result would be written like this:

$\chi^2 = 57.9$ df. $= 5$ $p < 0.05$

This means that the calculated value was 57.9 with five degrees of freedom; the probability of this result occurring by chance is less than 5 in 100. We can be 95% confident that the result could not have occurred by chance. In fact, if you glance back at the significance value, our calculated value is much less than the critical value of 0.05 level. Thus, the result would be best summarised thus:

$\chi^2 = 57.9$ df. $= 5$ $p < 0.001$

There is less than 1 in 1000 probability of this being a chance result.

	Type of image			
Sample	*Map-like*	*Verbal*	*Pictorial*	*Total*
Tourists	14	6	8	28
Visitors	31	24	17	72
Total	45	30	25	100

Table 11.6
Visitors' image of the town

Two-sample test

The chi-square test can be used to test whether there is a difference between two samples of data expressed in a frequency form. A survey of a random sample of 100 visitors was carried out to find out how they perceived the town which they were visiting. Two groups of visitors (or samples) are being tested, tourists and day visitors. The respondents' image of the town is put into one of three categories: map-like, verbal or pictorial. The results are illustrated in Table 11.6.

The null hypothesis would be that there is no significant difference between tourists and day visitors in the types of images of the town, testing at the 5 per cent level. However, there is another way of stating the null hypothesis – that there is no significant association between type of visitor and type of image held of the town.

As in the one-sample test, chi-square compares the observed with the expected frequencies; expected frequencies are calculated by SPSS. The end result is:

$\chi^2 = 1.368$ df = 2 $p > 0.05$ (not significant)

The null hypothesis is accepted – there is no difference in the kind of image held by the two groups.

Multi-sample test

The chi square for three or more samples is simply an extension of the two-sample case. We can use an example from the Hadrian's Wall survey, but note that this is not strictly speaking appropriate as the sample is not random. The data was examined to see if there was an association between age of visitor and the time of visit (peak/off-peak). A cross-tabulation and associated chi-square test were conducted in SPSS (see Figure 11.6).

Restrictions in the use of the chi-square test

There are a number of restrictions in the use of chi square:

1. The data must be in frequencies, not proportions or percentages. SPSS assumes that the data is in a raw form and computes frequencies from this. All categories must be mutually exclusive, so that one individual cannot be counted in more than one category.

2. There should not be many categories where the expected frequency is small. If the number of categories is greater than two, no more than 1/5 of the expected frequencies should be less than five (none should be less than one). If the number of categories is two, both expected frequencies should be five or larger.

3. Data must normally have been obtained by random sampling.

Figure 11.6
Multi-sample
chi square using
SPSS.

Chi-square was printed out as part of the crosstabs procedure:

1. With the data file **open**, select **Summarise** from the **Statistics** menu, followed by **Crosstabs**.
2. Place the independent variable (age) in the **columns** and the dependent (month) in the **rows**.
3. Click the **Statistics** button and check **chi-square** and **Cramers V**. Click **Continue**.
4. Click the **Cells** button and check the **column percentages**. Click on **Continue**.
5. Click on **OK**.

SPSS outputs the following table:

Cross-tabulation
MONTH by AGE

Month	Age group					
	a 16–24	b 25–34	c 35–44	d 45–59	e 60+	Row total
Peak Count	11	26	50	46	14	147
Expected value	6.0	28.4	39.5	53.9	19.2	39.9%
Col Pct	**73.3%**	36.6%	**50.5%**	34.1%	29.2%	
Off-peak Count	4	45	49	89	34	221
Expected value	9.0	42.6	59.5	81.1	28.8	60.1%
Col Pct	26.7%	63.4%	49.5%	**65.9%**	**70.8%**	
Column	15	71	99	135	48	368
Total	4.1%	19.3%	26.9%	36.7%	13.0%	100%

Chi-square	Value	DF	Significance
Pearson	**16.16408**	**4**	**0.00281**
Likelihood ratio	16.10247	4	0.00288

Minimum expected frequency – 5.992

Approximate statistic	Value	ASE1	Val/ASE0	Significance
Phi	0.20958			0.00281
Cramer's V	**0.20958**			**0.00281**

The chi-square value (16.16) and associated significance value (< 0.05) indicate that there are statistic-ally significant differences between age groups in the times of their visit. The Cramer's V coefficient is also statistically significant but weak. We would conclude that there is a statistically significant weak association between age and time of visit. The table could be analysed further – interesting figures are highlighted in bold. Younger visitors are most strongly associated with the peak summer months, whereas the older visitors are associated with the off-peak season.

The example illustrated in Figure 11.6 violates the fourth assumption of the test. The survey was based on a face-to-face questionnaire administered on site using the first to pass technique. This is a form of non-probability sampling and as such is not random. The example was used here purely to illustrate the technique.

Where assumption three is violated, groups may be collapsed into a smaller number of categories to increase the counts in each cell. Combining classes can change the value of chi square as well as the number of degrees of freedom. Is it legitimate to tamper with the classes? This depends upon the justification:

YES: if the combination of classes is logical. The researcher has a duty to combine classes to obtain the highest probability that the differences are real and not due to sampling error. Many classes yielding non-significant differences may mask a few classes yielding significant differences.

NO: if juggling with the data undermines the randomness of the sample and prejudices the outcome of the test. It is tantamount to cheating as a combination of classes can always be found that is statistically significant.

An intermediate position would be that the classes are determined without reference to the data and changed only if the expected frequencies are small.

Social significance and statistical significance

So far the term significance has been used in a statistical sense. It means there is a statistical difference between the two samples or between expected and observed frequencies. Statistically insignificant findings should not be dismissed by the researcher. If you are following the hypothesis testing procedure then such results are potentially of great intellectual or social significance. If when setting up the null and research hypotheses you expected to find significant differences but found none, then this merits some comment. Can you explain the absence of differences or association? Does this suggest that published research is no longer valid, or at least not in the context of your own research? In other words, statistically insignificant results can be *socially* very significant.

However, many statistically significant differences may be trivial. In the Hadrian's Wall work referred to earlier, statistically significant differences in length of stay were ascertained between different groups, but these only amounted to a few minutes on average! On the other hand, in a large-scale survey a difference of 1 per cent may involve thousands of people! So it is important to bear in mind the social meaning or relevance of the results.

Summary

Inferential statistics are simply tools which are used to make estimates from a sample to a population. Inferential statistics should only be used on data obtained by probability sampling; this is a key reason for preferring this kind of sampling. There are two types of inferential statistic – parametric and non-parametric, and both make assumptions about the data which should be checked prior to use and considered at the data collection stage. Table 11.7 may help you make decisions about appropriate tests.

Inferential statistics tell us the statistical significance of the sample statistics – the probability that differences or correlations are simply due to chance and whether we can generalise to the survey population. These techniques make use of the hypothesis testing procedure – this involves the null hypothesis, the research hypothesis and the rejection level. The null hypothesis is simply the hypothesis of no difference; the rejection level for research in leisure and tourism is usually $p \leq 0.05$.

Inferential statistics are potentially powerful tools and enable the researcher to clarify and interpret the data collected. Statistically significant results are often difficult to obtain – quite often the differences observed between various groups on key questions are small and therefore statistically insignificant. There is a difference between statistical and social significance. While you may obtain statistically insignificant results, these are often in themselves significant as they suggest that the differences or the relationships you expected, from prior reading of published literature, were not manifest in your research. Such findings, if based on a sound methodology, begin to question the validity of published work in particular contexts. Quite often statistically insignificant results are just as important and noteworthy as statistically significant ones.

Table 11.7
Choosing an
appropriate
statistical
procedure

Level of measurement of dependent variable	Level of measurement of independent variable		
	Nominal	Ordinal	Interval/ratio
Nominal	Cramer's V Phi Chi-square test	Chi square if the data is in categories, if not then convert to categories	Convert to categorical data and then do a chi square
Ordinal	Mann Whitney	Test significance of Spearman's Rank	Convert to ordinal data and then do Spearman's Rank
Interval/ratio	t-test ANOVA	t-test/ANOVA can be used if the data can be formed into appropriate sub-groups	Test significance of Pearson's Product/Regression Analysis

Note: The assumptions of parametric and non-parametric tests should be met where appropriate

Student Activities

The Hadrian's Wall data set can be used for these exercises, but do remember that it is not based on a random sample.

Activity 1

Using the Hadrian's Wall data (and assuming that it was collected by random sampling):

1. Are there significant differences between overseas and UK visitors in terms of their expectations?

2. Are there significant differences between overseas and UK visitors in terms of their length of visit (LENGTH)?

3. Are there significant differences between overseas and UK visitors in overall levels of satisfaction (SATSCORE)?

Activity 2

Consider the table below. This contains data which was obtained by random selection as part of an investigation into fitness performance and shows the results by sex. Are there differences between the two sexes? Set out the hypothesis testing procedure, compute an appropriate inferential statistic and comment on the significance of the result.

▷

Performance scores	
Females	Male
35	67
73	58
65	54
39	47
54	20
70	71
53	52
57	63
45	55
61	48

References

● Black, T. R. (1999) *Doing Quantitative Research in the Social Sciences*, London: Sage.
● Bryman, T. R. and Cramer, D. (1997) *Quantitative Data Analysis With SPSS for Windows*, London: Routledge.
● Cramer, D. (1998) *Fundamental Statistics for Social Research*, London: Routledge.

Chapter 12

Writing a Research Report

Learning Outcomes

At the end of this chapter you will be able to:

- produce a well-structured research report
- correctly utilise the Harvard system of referencing
- construct an accurate list of references
- appreciate the importance of time management, language, style and presentation in the report writing process

Introduction

Having spent so much time planning your research, conducting your research and analysing your findings, it would be a shame if all this hard work was let down by the writing-up process. Yet, in our experience, this happens all too often, and students end up with a grade lower than anticipated due to an inaccurate, incomplete or sloppily presented research report. This is a shame because the mistakes are usually easy to avoid. In this chapter we set out the principles and procedures of good research report writing. A word of caution however – it is impossible to provide a definitive guide to this subject as there are many different types of report. A report submitted to a client organisation as part of a student research project will differ from a final year undergraduate dissertation, for example, as the client is unlikely to want to read lengthy literature reviews or chapters on academic theory. They instead are more likely to require executive summaries containing key findings and recommendations. The notion of 'the audience' for your research report is therefore a key one. In other words, who are you writing the report for, and what do they require from you? If you are writing a research dissertation, for example, then no doubt your tutors will have provided you with detailed instructions on the sections to be included. If you are still unsure of what is required, then check. Ignorance is no excuse.

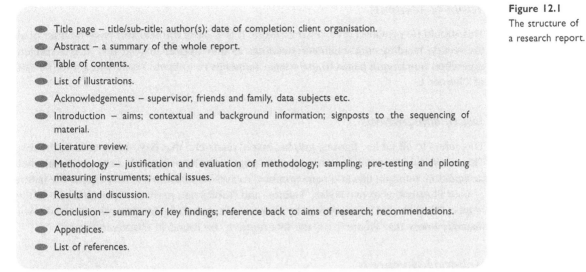

Figure 12.1
The structure of
a research report.

- Title page – title/sub-title; author(s); date of completion; client organisation.
- Abstract – a summary of the whole report.
- Table of contents.
- List of illustrations.
- Acknowledgements – supervisor, friends and family, data subjects etc.
- Introduction – aims; contextual and background information; signposts to the sequencing of material.
- Literature review.
- Methodology – justification and evaluation of methodology; sampling; pre-testing and piloting measuring instruments; ethical issues.
- Results and discussion.
- Conclusion – summary of key findings; reference back to aims of research; recommendations.
- Appendices.
- List of references.

Structuring your research report

It is perhaps a little simplistic to suggest that a research report consists of just three ideas – tell them what you are going to say, say it and remind them about what you have said. This notion does, however, get across the need for an ordered and logical structure consisting of three key sections i.e. the introduction, the main body of the report and the conclusion. You will, of course, have to include other sections in your report, and a suggested structure is summarised in Figure 12.1 and discussed in more detail below.

Title page

The title of your report must be succinct (usually no more than a single sentence), unambiguous and accurate. Many writers use a short, attention-grabbing title. On their own such titles are rarely sufficient, and so a sub-title is used to clarify the nature of the project. Whatever format you choose, the title/sub-title must convey the content of the report. On the title page you will also typically include the name of the author(s), the month and year of completion, and the name of the client organisation where applicable. A research report in the form of a dissertation is likely to require additional information on the title page such as the name of the university, the name of the supervisor and a phrase similar to this – *A dissertation submitted in part fulfilment of the requirements of the degree of Bachelor of Arts with Honours in European Tourism.*

Abstract

This is a very difficult section to write well. It is a summary of the whole report. The abstract stands alone and thus must make sense if read without the report. In other words, anyone reading just the abstract should understand the aims of the research, its methodology and its key findings and conclusions. It is your report in miniature, and is typically 200–300 words in length. The purpose of the abstract is to allow other researchers to quickly determine whether your report would be worth following up. It is, if you like, another service that academics and researchers provide for each other.

Table of contents

This should be provided on a separate page. It is a list of the title and page number of all the section headings and main sub-headings as they appear in your text. It is a convention when numbering pages to use roman numerals (i, ii, iii etc.) until you get to the start of Chapter 1.

List of illustrations

This refers to all tables, figures, graphs, maps, plans etc. that have been used in the text. This too should be provided on a separate page, with items listed in order, and with their designation, number, title and page number. To avoid confusion it is best to limit the nature of your illustrations to two styles, 'Figures' and 'Tables' are perhaps the most useful in this respect. They should be numbered by chapter/section and so, for example, the reader will instantly know that Figure 4.1 is the first figure to be found in chapter/section 4.

Acknowledgements

Assistance given to students in the course of their research should, as a matter of courtesy, always be acknowledged. Typical acknowledgements would be to the dissertation supervisor, to other academic staff who may have provided specialist help, to people within organisations that might have provided assistance, to friends and family who might have commented on drafts of the report or helped with the typing, and to the subjects of the research. For those of us involved in the marking of research reports this is often the most entertaining section. It would, of course, be unprofessional to acknowledge that our marking of a report is influenced by the glowing tributes given to us in this section!

The introduction

This section will include your reasons for choosing the topic; the aims of the project, expressed perhaps as a hypothesis or series of hypotheses that you have set out to test; and the scope or limit of your investigation. Acknowledging the limitations of a project is not an admission of failure. Nobody will expect a student researcher working on their own to conduct a comprehensive research programme involving a sample of thousands. You should, instead, acknowledge the limits of your investigation in this section by, for example, commenting on the representativeness of your findings.

The introduction will also include any relevant contextual or background information. Finally, it will also be used to define key concepts, and to signpost the reader to the sequencing of material. This signposting is achieved in the introduction by providing a summary of each chapter in the order that they appear in your report. It is not, however, sufficient to leave it at that – you should constantly remind your reader of your objectives. Each chapter should therefore begin with a summary of what the chapter is going to achieve, and should conclude with a reminder of what the chapter has achieved.

The literature review

It is important in any research project to establish the current state of knowledge of the subject under investigation, and in so doing to maximise your understanding of the topic by becoming familiar with the theory, concepts, ideas, key issues, debates and language surrounding your chosen research topic. This process will also highlight any gaps in our knowledge and will place your research in context. All of this is achieved through the literature review.

So what is a literature review? In answering that question it is necessary to make clear what a literature review is not. It is not an annotated bibliography. In other words, it is not a list of references of everything that you have managed to find that has been written indirectly or directly about your topic. That serves little purpose. Instead, a literature review allows you to demonstrate your ability to read critically and analytically, and to summarise the work of other writers clearly and briefly. It is defined by Hart (1998: 13) as:

> *The selection of available documents (both published and unpublished) on the topic, which contain information, ideas, data and evidence written from a particular stand-point to fulfil certain aims or express certain views on the nature of the topic and how it is to be investigated, and the effective evaluation of these documents in relation to the research being proposed.*

Hart's definition indicates that the literature review serves a number of crucial purposes and is not a stage that has to be reluctantly worked through to give work academic credibility.

Not only does the literature review provide the reader with an understanding of the present state of knowledge of the subject through your analysis and summary of previous work, but it also helps you the researcher in the design of your research by highlighting how other researchers have approached similar investigations. Appropriate methods for your study will thus be suggested. There is also a 'snowball' effect in any literature review, as the sources you identify will themselves list other sources not originally uncovered. The literature review process might also forewarn you of potential problems with your study, and suggest ways of overcoming them.

Finally, there is one particularly important practical benefit of undertaking a comprehensive literature review. The single most common problem that we encounter with student researchers is not a lack of ideas, far from it, but an inability to develop a clearly focused and manageable proposal. All too often students develop proposals that are far too broad and over-ambitious and that could not be completed by a team of experienced researchers working for a year yet alone a single student researcher with perhaps six months at their disposal. The literature review therefore facilitates the process of progressive focusing and allows you to refine your ideas into a realistic project with clear objectives that can be completed on schedule. The need to complete the literature review at an early stage should be apparent.

Conducting a literature review is not easy. It requires time, thought, effort and a diligent approach to the tracking down of sources. You need to be familiar with the full range of information sources at your disposal, both electronic and hard-copy sources. We assume, however, that by the time you come to conduct research in your academic careers the use of abstracts, indexes and bibliographies etc. will be second nature. Detailed guidance on the conduct of a literature review is beyond the scope of this chapter. This is, however, comprehensively addressed in the work of Hart (1998). While written primarily for masters and doctoral level students, there is much in this book that will be of value to the undergraduate student researcher.

Methodology

At this stage you will need to include a section describing your methodology. The importance of this section cannot be over-emphasised, and a separate section/chapter should be devoted to this in your report. A useful rule-of-thumb is to assume that the person reading your report knows nothing about your work. In other words, your methodology section should be sufficiently detailed so that the reader knows exactly how the research was carried out. In theory they could then replicate your research, and test your findings, albeit at a different time and possibly a different place. All too often we come across accounts of methodology that are just a few sentences in length stating in the blandest terms the methods used. This is not good enough.

So what should be included in the methodology? Let us assume that you have used a questionnaire survey as your research instrument. You will need then to provide answers to a variety of questions. Why was this method chosen? So, justify your approach. With hindsight, was this the best approach to take or would you use different research methods next time? In other words, evaluate your approach. While we would naturally hope that your initial choice of research methods was appropriate, evaluating aspects of your own work is part of the process of becoming a reflective practitioner.

Alternatively, this reflection on your methodology could be left to the 'Conclusion' (see below), as one of your recommendations may be the need for further research along with suggestions concerning how that research might best be carried out. Other questions to address in the methodology include, did you pre-test your questionnaire? If so, what changes were made to the final questionnaire, and why? What sort of questionnaire survey was used – postal, self-completion, interviewer administered?

You will need to discuss sampling (see Chapter 7). What was the sample size? What was the response rate? How were sample members selected? What was the composition of the sample? What are the implications arising from your choice of sampling method? Answers to these questions are important as they allow the reader to assess the representativeness of your research.

You will need to describe the measuring tools used in your survey. What sort of questions were included in the questionnaire, and why? Remember that you will need to include a copy of your final questionnaire as an appendix. You will need to cover how the questionnaires were analysed. Were there any ethical issues arising from your choice of research methods and, if so, how were they addressed?

One question that students often ask is how long should these introductory sections be? You will not be surprised to hear that there cannot be a definitive answer to this. However, you will have gathered that the introductory sections are important and seek to cover a lot of ground. They can, therefore, easily take up between 10 and 20 per cent of the report.

In summary, it can be argued (Karran 1992) that the introductory sections have four main objectives in that they are about 'Purpose' (what are you trying to achieve?), 'Reason' (why are you doing it?), 'Content' (the relationship of your research to the existing body of knowledge) and 'Summary' (how will you carry out the work? What is your methodology?).

Results and discussion

This section deals with the findings and analysis of your own research utilising the techniques discussed in Chapters 5, 8, 9, 10 and 11. The results should be presented clearly and concisely. Only that which is important, and no more, is a useful guide when deciding what to include. The nature of the research will in part determine the format of the presentation of the results, and you will need to consider the appropriate use of tables and graphs as a means of summarising complex data. The key word here is 'appropriate'. It is unlikely that your report will need to include detailed analysis of every question from your questionnaire, for example. You are going to have to exercise some judgement about what data to include, and the order in which data is included. It is tempting to simply produce your results in the same order as questions appear on your questionnaire. This should be avoided. You need to group your findings around the research aims as outlined in the introduction, and produce and discuss your results accordingly. Assuming you can make such a judgement, it is usual to present your most important findings first.

The means of data presentation should also be appropriate. The point of diagrams, for example, is to simplify what would otherwise be a complex data set. Do not, therefore, include pie charts showing the split between people answering yes/no to a particular question. A diagram is not needed here as this can be covered in one line of text. Think also about the most appropriate form of diagrammatic presentation. What are you trying to show? A line graph, for example, is best for showing trends over time. All tables and diagrams must be numbered and given a title, as they will have to be referenced in your 'list of illustrations' (see above). Remember also to label the axes, to provide a key where appropriate, and to acknowledge the source of your data, although it is not necessary to include the data source if it is your own primary research. The use of tables requires particular care, and you will need to exercise some judgement here. Lengthy and complex tables containing lots of statistical information can be confusing and off-putting. It may, therefore, be better to include the full tables in an appendix with simplified summary tables providing the key data included in the main body of the report. Such decisions will be guided in part by the nature of your audience. The results of any statistical tests will also be reported in this section, and you will need to be familiar with the conventions used to do this.

If you have used qualitative techniques of data collection, do not simply provide transcripts of your interviews, for example. Of course verbatim evidence is required, and this can be very powerful indeed, but you will need to sift and sort such data, and use appropriate and manageable extracts. Methods of analysing qualitative data are discussed in Chapters 5 and 8.

Some books recommend that you separate your findings and the discussion of your findings into two distinct sections. This needs consideration and handling with care. If your results section is a brief one, consisting perhaps of a few tables and three or four paragraphs of text, then this separation of results and discussion is workable. If, however, your results section is a detailed one, we advise you not to separate these sections in this way. The danger is that it can lead to a tediously presented list of tables, graphs, statistics, quotes or whatever, completely out of context and with no bridge to the aims of the project. We recommend, therefore, that the interpretation of the data be carried out as it is introduced, taking care of course not to confuse fact and opinion. However you handle this section, the need to interpret your data is vital.

While it is true that every picture tells a story, you need to tell the reader what that story is. The facts, on their own, do not speak for themselves. Do not, for example, simply refer the reader to Table 1 by saying something like 'Table 1 shows the different reasons given for playing squash at the Victoria Leisure Centre, broken down by gender and age-group'. For a start, Table 1 may not be as clearly presented as you would like to think it is – it is, after all, showing quite a complex picture involving three variables. Even if it is well constructed, you need to draw out the main points in the text. This does not mean that you should slavishly describe every table or figure in the text, but you do certainly need to highlight the significant points. A useful rule-of-thumb here is that 'the text of your report should still make sense even if you take the data out' (Harvey and MacDonald 1993: 233).

Conclusion

In this section you will need to refer back to the introduction as it gives you the opportunity to demonstrate how successful you have been in meeting your objectives. You may need to qualify some of your findings i.e. provide a critical evaluation of your own work.

You may wish to compare your findings with those of other researchers. Have you confirmed what others before you found? Have you added to the body of knowledge and, if so, how? It may be appropriate, given the nature of your research, to make recommendations. This is likely to be the case if you are doing a project for a client where they will want to know the policy and/or management implications of your findings. If this sort of research is undertaken then it may be appropriate to include your recommendations as a separate section. One of your recommendations may well be the need for further research, in which case you should be specific about the aims of this research, and you should suggest appropriate methods to tackle it. One golden rule in the conclusion is not to introduce any new material. There is a temptation to hold back a key finding until almost the last word. You should resist this. All findings should appear in the main body of the report.

Appendices

These must be used with caution. There is an attraction in gathering company reports, promotional literature, maps, club rules and constitutions etc. and throwing them into appendices at the back of the report. The suspicion will always be that this is done to pad out a thin piece of work. The first question you must ask yourself is whether the material really is necessary. Is it adding something important to your report? If it is necessary then can it be placed in the text? Computer scanning techniques make it relatively straightforward to scan material into a word-processed document. If this is not possible or desirable (e.g. it would disrupt the flow by cluttering up the report) then you must always number each appendix and reference this material in the text (e.g. see Appendix A). If you do not reference the material in the text, the reader will not look at it. Ideally all tables and graphs should be included in the text at the appropriate point, and the use of word-processing and spreadsheet packages make this a relatively straightforward procedure. If this is not possible, then they should be included as numbered appendices and referenced in the text. Typical items found in the appendices of research reports include a copy of any questionnaire used, and an interview schedule, if one is used. As suggested earlier, if you have used a questionnaire survey then you should give consideration to the inclusion of a full statistical appendix. This includes tables giving the findings from all your questions in the order in which they appear on your questionnaire. You will have included what, for you, are the key findings in your results section. Readers may, however, be interested in other aspects of your survey, and they can get full details from your statistical appendix.

List of references

These usually come at the end of the report, although some writers put references at the end of each chapter or section. Textual referencing and the correct way of constructing a list of references are discussed below.

In this section we have considered the structure of the research report. The requirements will, however, vary both in content and emphasis depending on the nature of the report and for whom it is being written. The point has already been made, but is worth repeating, you must clarify at an early stage what is required of you in terms of report structure and content.

Referencing your sources

A research report is no different from any other piece of written work that you submit at college or university in that it must be correctly referenced. In other words, you must always cite your sources of information. Whenever you use ideas, words, data etc. that emanate from other people or organisations, you must always reference your source in the text, and then provide full details in a properly constructed list of references at the end of your work. Information citation of this nature is an important part of academic practice, and it is important that you get this right for three good reasons (Lewis and Rushworth 1997):

1. It gives your work credibility. As a student, you are expected to research the work of other people by perhaps providing a literature review of your topic or by considering different theoretical approaches to a subject. This is good academic practice, and you need to demonstrate to the reader that you have carried this out. Referencing your sources of information allows you to do this. Your tutor will know when ideas, words or evidence are not yours. By correctly referencing the material you are acknowledging where the information has come from.

2. It avoids a charge of plagiarism. Plagiarism is a serious offence, and the penalties in some academic institutions are draconian. Plagiarism involves using the work of other people or organisations without acknowledgement. It involves more than just copying therefore, and includes the paraphrasing of words and ideas, which are then presented as if they were your own. In other words, plagiarism is theft of intellectual property. All sources of information have the potential to be plagiarised. Fortunately it is easy to avoid. It is avoided by the use of correct referencing, which is why you should follow the procedures and tips suggested here. You cannot have too many references. This is why plagiarism is so stupid. Why try to present other people's work as if it were your own when you will be rewarded for showing off the extent of your research and thus coverage of other people's work?

3. It allows your readers to trace and check material. People reading your research may well want to go back to an original source, cited by you, for further information. In a sense, this is part of the service that academics and researchers provide for each other. Your list of references should therefore contain sufficient information for the reader to go to a library or bookshop to obtain a copy of the original source. Details of how to construct a list of references are provided later in this chapter.

Which system of referencing should I use?

There are several forms of referencing that you may have come across. Some people use the Oxford system, which is a numerical method of referencing utilising numbers provided in superscript in the text. A full list of references in numerical order is then provided at the end of the chapter or the book. Alternatively, the full reference may be provided as a footnote at the bottom of the page on which it occurs. This can create problems, particularly if you add a new reference and therefore have to re-number all the subsequent ones, although word-processing packages make the use of footnotes easy, and will automatically re-number if new references are added or other ones are deleted. If the next reference in your list comes from the same source, rather than repeat the full reference, you just put the word 'ibid' (short for 'ibidem' – meaning in the same place). You would also need to include the page number if this is different from the previous one. If you wish to repeat a reference later on, but it is not the next one on your list, then you use the term 'op. cit.' instead. This is short for 'opere citado' – meaning in the work quoted – and so you would put, for example, Bull op. cit. The reader now knows that you are referring to the work of Bull, the full details of which you have provided earlier.

Arguably the most widely used system, and certainly the easiest to use as a writer and the easiest to follow as a reader, is the one known as the Harvard system of referencing.

It is this system that we strongly urge you to use in your report writing. The Harvard system avoids the use of footnotes, which can be a distraction, and the potentially confusing use of the words 'op. cit.' and 'ibid'. Using this system a full list of references is provided in alphabetical order at the end of the work or at the end of the section/chapter. Textual references are then provided by placing in brackets the author's surname and the year of publication at the appropriate point in the text. For example:

Henry (1993) considers the impact of New Right ideology on leisure policies during the Thatcher era.

The date of publication (1993) is recorded on the first occasion that mention is made of the author's work. It would only be repeated if you wished to distinguish between two works by the same author. The reader will therefore assume, unless you indicate otherwise, that every time you refer to the work of Henry it is his 1993 publication you are talking about. Full details of Henry's book would then appear in the list of references (see below). If you happen to reference two sources by the same author in the same year, then they are distinguished by the use of alphabetical lettering e.g. Henry (1993a) and Henry (1993b). Note that you do not need to use initials with the Harvard system. The only time you would do this would be if you needed to distinguish between two authors with the same surname.

If the source you are referencing is by two authors then the surnames of both authors should appear in the text. If, however, your source is by several authors, you note them all the first time:

Finn, Elliott-White and Walton (2000) have argued that . . .

Any subsequent reference would be to Finn *et al.* (2000) – '*et al.*' being an abbreviation of '*et alia*' meaning 'and others'.

Often when conducting leisure and tourism research you will be using sources that do not have an identifiable author, in which case you should treat the organisation responsible for the publication as the author, and reference them accordingly e.g. (The Rank Organisation 1998). If, in the final analysis, you cannot identify an author, be it an individual or an organisation, then you should use the term 'Anon' (short for anonymous).

If you want to utilise material that you have not read, but a source you are using discusses it, then you must acknowledge that fact. For example:

Henry (1993) cites the work of Glyptis and Pack whose research on sports schemes for the unemployed supports the notion of leisure policy as a means of reinforcing social order.

This is known as 'second-hand referencing' and also occurs if you are using a quotation that has been provided in another source i.e. you have not read the original source of the quotation. The question now arises as to whether you should include the reference for Glyptis and Pack in your list of references. While it has been made clear in the above example that the work of Glyptis and Pack has not been consulted directly, Veal (1997: 93) argues that 'it is misleading, somewhat unethical, and dangerous, to give a full reference to the original if you have not read it directly yourself'. He maintains, therefore, that you should not reference the original source but the second-hand source. As he points out, this is also safer in the case of quotations 'since any inaccuracy in a quotation then rests with the second-hand source' (p. 93). If you were to reference the work of Glyptis and Pack in this example, then you are implying that you have consulted it directly.

Finally, if you are referencing a direct quote using the Harvard system, then the only difference is that you include the page number(s) in your textual reference. For example:

In considering different feminist perspectives on leisure, it has been argued that 'the radical feminist position is premised in part on the rejection of other ways of viewing the world as ideologically flawed.'

(Henry 1993 p. 53 or Henry 1993: 53)

The reader now knows that this quotation can be found on page 53 of Henry's book, full details of which can be found in the list of references. Note, however, that you should also provide the page reference if you are drawing heavily on another person's ideas, and these can be precisely referenced by the addition of a page number. Again, this allows the reader to go directly to the appropriate part of the source material where these ideas are introduced.

If words are omitted from the quotation, then you should signify this by the use of three full stops. For example, as Henry (1993: 209) says, 'The attracting of high-technology industry . . . through the development of an attractive cultural infrastructure is a zero sum game'. Where the quotation is short, it can be included in the text with inverted commas. Longer quotations are usually indented so that they stand out better, in which case inverted commas are not necessary.

In this section we have recommended that you use the Harvard system of referencing for your report writing. We do so for three main reasons – it is the easiest system to use, it involves an alphabetical list of references that can be an important resource for your readership, and it is the most widely used academic system of referencing. The word 'academic' is the key one here, however, and this system may not be appropriate for reports of a more practical nature where your reader(s) may not be used to this convention. The notion of the 'audience' for your report is, therefore, again an important one. Another problem with the Harvard system is that excessive referencing can swamp the text and make it difficult and irritating to read. This is something that you need to guard against in your writing style, as clarity should always be your aim.

A list of references or a bibliography?

There is often confusion between these two terms, and they are on occasions incorrectly used inter-changeably. Strictly speaking, a list of references is a composite list of those items you have referenced in the text. A bibliography, however, as Bell (1987: 129) reminds us,

> *has several meanings. It can be used to mean a publication listing the details of material about a subject, place or person. It can be a list of works by a specific author or it can be a list of sources consulted during the preparation of an essay, project or dissertation.*

A bibliography can therefore include items not referenced in the text but which you have consulted during the course of your research, and which have therefore influenced your thinking and the progress and nature of your research. Which form you use is a matter of personal choice to a certain extent, although you may be directed towards one or the other. A word of warning however. If you do use a bibliography, and you are required to undertake a presentation or a viva on your research, then the examiners may well ask you how items in your bibliography have informed your thinking. Be prepared therefore, and make sure that your bibliography is an accurate record, and that you are familiar with the content of the material listed.

Unless instructed otherwise, we recommend that you use only a list of references i.e. you list those sources referenced in your report.

Constructing a list of references or a bibliography

In this section we look at how to reference the more common sources of information. Whether you are using a list of references or a bibliography, items should be put in alphabetical order.

Books

When referencing a book, the following details are required:

- author's surname, followed by their initials
- year of publication (in brackets)
- title of publication – either in *italics* or **emboldened**
- edition (if not the first edition)
- place of publication
- publisher

Our worked example above would therefore appear in the list of references as:

Henry, I. P. (1993) *The Politics of Leisure Policy*, Basingstoke: Macmillan.

Chapters in a book

Where a book is an edited collection of chapters by different authors, and you wish to reference one of the chapters, then the following information is required:

- chapter author's surname and initials
- year of publication (in brackets)
- chapter title in quotation marks, followed by 'in'
- surname and initials of the editor, followed by (ed.)
- title of publication – either in *italics* or **emboldened**
- edition (if not the first edition)
- place of publication
- publisher
- page numbers of chapter – usually abbreviated to pp

Bramham, P. (1994) 'Community arts', in Haywood, L. (ed.) *Community Leisure and Recreation*, Second Edition, Oxford: Butterworth-Heinemann, pp. 83–110.

Journal articles

- author's surname and initials
- year of publication (in brackets)
- title of article in quotation marks
- title of journal – either in *italics* or **emboldened**
- volume number – usually abbreviated to Vol
- part or issue number (in brackets)
- page number(s) – usually abbreviated to p/pp

Witt, C. A. and Muhlemann, A. P. (1994) 'The implementation of total quality management in tourism: some guidelines', *Tourism Management*, Vol. 15 (6), pp. 416–24.

Newspaper articles

- author's surname and initials (in newspaper articles there is often not a named author, in which case use the title of the newspaper)

- year of publication (in brackets)
- title of article in quotation marks
- name of newspaper – either in *italics* or **emboldened**
- day and month of publication
- page number(s) – usually abbreviated to p/pp

Selvey, M. (1998) 'Caught by the pitch and toss', *The Guardian*, 23 June, Sport p. 5.

Many journals and newspapers are now available on CD-ROM. If you are referencing such a source we recommend that you put [CD-ROM] after the title of the journal or newspaper.

Published conference papers

- author's surname and initials
- year of publication (in brackets)
- title of paper in quotation marks, followed by 'in'
- surname and initials of the editor of the conference report, if known, followed by (ed.)
- title of conference report either in *italics* or **emboldened**
- name, place and date of conference
- place of publication
- publisher
- page numbers – usually abbreviated to pp.

Chak-keung, S. W. (1996) 'Cross-cultural management in the Hong Kong hotel industry', in Prosser, G. (ed.) *Tourism and Hospitality Research: Australian and International Perspectives*, Proceedings from the Australian Tourism and Hospitality Research Conference, Coffs Harbour, February 1996, Canberra, ACT: Bureau of Tourism Research, pp. 249–63.

Referencing electronic sources of information

As students increasingly turn to electronic sources of information in general, and the use of the Internet and e-mail in particular, then these too will have to be cited. No clear academic conventions have yet emerged here, but we recommend the following approach. As with all referencing, it is important that you are consistent in the way electronic sources are referenced.

Internet sites

- author's surname and initials (if not named, use the name of the organisation responsible for the site)
- year (if no publication date, put 'No date')
- title [on-line]
- available from: URL (the address of a Web site is called the Universal Resource Locator)
- [Access date].

Rough Guides (No date), Australia [on-line], Available from: http://www.hotwired.com/rough/australia [accessed 13 April 2000].

Electronic journals

- author's surname and initials
- year of publication (in brackets)
- title of article in quotation marks
- title of journal – either in *italics* or **emboldened** followed by [on-line]
- volume number – usually abbreviated to Vol
- part or issue number (in brackets)
- page number(s) – usually abbreviated to p/pp
- available from: URL
- [access date].

Tietjen, M. A. and Myers, R. M. (1998) 'Motivation and job satisfaction', *Management Decision* [on-line], Vol. 36 (4), pp. 226–231. Available from: http:www.emerald-library.com/pdfs/00136db2.pdf [accessed 30 June 1998].

Personal e-mail

If you enter into e-mail correspondence or perhaps even conduct interviews by e-mail, then any material from these sources should be referenced accordingly. Remember that if you are conducting interviews by e-mail, you will need to get the interviewee's permission to use such material, as you would with any form of interview. You should also get permission if you intend to reference a person's e-mail address.

- sender (sender's e-mail address)
- day, month, year
- subject
- e-mail to recipient (recipient's e-mail address).

Finn, M. (mfinn@lincoln.ac.uk), 1 July 1998. Book proposal. E-mail to M. Walton (mjwalton@lincoln.ac.uk).

Finally, there are a number of guides to referencing electronic sources available on the Internet. A good example is the one provided by South Bank University – http://www.sbu.ac.uk/lis/helpsheets/lrc2.html.

Organising your references

It is very tempting when you use a piece of information from a book or journal, for example, to simply jot down the author's name and to promise yourself that you will remember exactly where it came from when you come to construct your bibliography or list of references. A word of warning – you won't remember! Two consequences are likely to arise. Either you will then spend precious hours going through the library catalogue of works by that author to try and trace the source, or you will give up and include the information in your report unacknowledged and thus leave yourself open to a charge of plagiarism. As you are going to have to record the full information at some stage for your list of references then you should get into the habit of doing this systematically as soon as you use a source. As well as recording full bibliographic details, it is also useful if you include a one-paragraph summary of the content of the reference. Some people use a box of file index cards for this but, as most students now have access to computers for their work, we strongly advise you to utilise a computer file for recording full references as they occur. The advantage of this is that the sort facility will easily allow you to finally organise your references in the required alphabetical order. If you use a database program for storing references you then have the added facility to search your references by topic, key word or whatever.

Managing your time

As is the case with other aspects of your studies, effective time management is a critical success factor. There is a real danger in underestimating the time needed to carry out the report writing stage of the project. Harvey and MacDonald (1993) suggest that you consider a research project as consisting of three distinct stages – first, planning (which includes all the background work such as the literature review); second, data collection; and third, analysis and write-up – and that you should divide your time equally among all three stages. This is not to say that these three stages always of necessity follow sequentially, and that each must therefore be completed before the next stage can commence. Sections of the early stages of the report can be written in draft form as they are completed (most of the introduction e.g. the aims of the research, the literature review, the theoretical sections and the methodology) and before you commence or complete data analysis. The hardest part of writing is often getting started, and so writing early in this way gets you going and can give you confidence as you see your work taking shape.

It is impossible to provide definitive advice on time management and the writing process as we all have our own preferences and, often peculiar, personal habits. In this section some tips on time management and the report writing process are offered (see Figure 12.2).

People seem to divide into one of two camps – larks and owls. Larks are people who start work early in the morning and gradually slow down as the day progresses, often unable to do useful work much beyond 5.00pm. Owls on the other hand, and for some unfathomable reason many students seem to fit this category, come alive after dark, and produce their best work in the evening and late at night.

Some people write in short sharp bursts, and need to intersperse this activity with frequent breaks. These people often have several projects on the go at the same time, needing this variety to keep them interested and motivated. Other writers prefer lengthy sessions, perhaps working on one project through to completion before starting another. Some people have a favourite location for working, and feel as if they can concentrate and do their best work there. Bell (1987: 125) refers to the desirability of creating a 'rhythm of work'. In other words, if you are on a roll and the writing is flowing, do not break off to check the accuracy of a reference (this can wait till later) or because you have completed the thousand word target that you had set for yourself in the session. Keep the rhythm going is Bell's advice. The main point of this discussion, however, is that we are

Figure 12.2
Time management and the writing process.

- Appreciate the three key stages in a research project – planning, data collection and analysis/write-up – and allocate time accordingly.
- Recognise when, where and how you write effectively.
- Write in drafts.
- Check your work thoroughly.
- Allow time for printing and binding.
- Work to a timetable and meet deadlines.

all different. You need to recognise what works for you, and to manage your time and space accordingly.

You should certainly be working to a timetable, which should have been constructed at the research proposal stage, and you should stick to this as closely as possible. While deadlines within the project do have a degree of flexibility, the deadline for completion and submission does not. There is a temptation to prolong the data collection stage by assuming that just a little bit more data will make all the difference. Resist that temptation at all costs. Time taken here is time lost to the analysis and report writing stage and, as mentioned earlier, good research can easily be let down by poorly prepared and hastily written reports.

Remember too that you will need to write at least two drafts of your work, and so you should allocate time accordingly. As you produce drafts of your work you may find that the structure of your report changes from that originally envisaged. What you perhaps thought deserved a chapter of its own may now feel better merged into another chapter. This is perfectly acceptable; you are not bound by your original planned structure, as long as the key sections are there in a logical order.

Drafts should be shown to fellow students and/or your tutor for comment. Ask friends to check for clarity of expression and logical sequencing. Whether you have the time for a third or fourth draft is debatable, but the point is that you will not be able to produce a satisfactory document at the first attempt. Allow time to thoroughly check your final document. Have you run it through the spell-checker and grammar checker? Remember that the spell-checker will not pick up all errors i.e. the wrong word spelt correctly, and so you should physically check it yourself. Are the pages numbered and in the correct order? Have you checked your referencing? Is there a match between the textual referencing and the list of references? Does the list of references contain all the necessary information? Is the line spacing correct? Are the margins set at the required size? In other words, have you satisfied all the report writing criteria? Ideally, someone else should also check your final copy. The problem, you will find, is that you will have become so familiar with your work you will simply be unable to spot any errors. This is why it is such a good idea to work with another student on this, checking each other's work.

It has been assumed so far that you will be typing or word-processing your own report. You may feel, however, that your typing skills are not up to the challenge of producing such a lengthy and important document, in which case you should consider paying a professional typist. No doubt the noticeboards at your university are covered with advertisements from people in your area offering such a service. A few words of caution, however. If you do employ a typist check how much they will charge, and shop around to compare prices. Ask to see examples of their work, and check what they can and cannot do. Not all typists will be able to scan in documents or produce complex tables or charts, for example. Find out in what form they will accept material – hand-written, typed, on floppy disk? Will they accept part-work as it is completed? Crucially, for this section on time management, you will need to confirm how long they will take to complete the work. You will need to build in time to allow for checking of their work, and for any subsequent revisions to be made. All of this should be included in your initial timetable.

Language, style and presentation

In this section some suggestions are offered about language, style and presentation. The key points are summarised in Figure 12.3 and discussed more fully below.

The style of your writing will be influenced by the audience for your report. However much as we might like to pretend otherwise, all organisations, all professions, in fact all of us speak in jargon to a certain extent. Words, phrases, abbreviations and concepts that

Figure 12.3
Language, style
and presentation
in report writing.

- Appreciate the 'audience' for your report, and write accordingly.
- Strive for clarity, and avoid jargon.
- Keep within any word limits.
- Number paragraphs/sections as required.
- Follow local conventions on the use of the first person.
- Avoid discriminatory language.

we are comfortable with may not be so obvious to the outsider. While you may be confident talking about the implications of postmodernity for contemporary marketing practices, the manager of your local leisure centre may not. You need to understand your readership therefore and, as far as possible, write in a style accessible to them. You are trying to present what may well be a complex picture and so 'clarity' is the key challenge.

You may feel that some of the points made in this section are more to do with presentation than with substance, and to a certain extent you would be right. You should appreciate, however, that people feel positive about and respond to a report that is well presented. A report that has been nicely bound and looks good on the page will immediately get the reader on your side. Binding is a relatively inexpensive procedure and most college libraries will have machines that allow you to simply and cheaply spiral-bind your report. You should also consider the use of colour. Colour photocopying can be expensive, but increasingly students are getting access to colour printers. Colour can be particularly important in the use of graphs and other charts. The problem with these if reproduced in black and white is that the patterns used to differentiate the different sections in a pie chart, for example, do not always reproduce clearly in black and white.

Perhaps a more important reason for paying close attention to the presentation of your report is that the marking criteria for a college-based project always, in our experience, include a category for 'presentation', and between 15 and 20 per cent of the marks can be allocated to this. These are marks that can easily be gained, and so the implications should need no stressing. Of course the material, the substance, is the most important thing, but if you do not present your findings and your analysis in a clear and appropriate manner then you are not doing them justice, and you are certainly not maximising the potential of your report. In this section, therefore, some miscellaneous, but nevertheless important, concluding points are made about language, style, presentation and the academic conventions surrounding these.

First of all, you will know that one particularly important academic convention is that you keep within word limits. If you are writing a research report at college or university then your tutors will no doubt have given you a word limit. It is important that you keep within that limit as the penalties for falling outside can be severe! Most word-processing packages have a word count facility, and so it is easy to keep track of this. Reports written for clients are unlikely to have a word limit imposed on them. In such circumstances, however, those involved are unlikely to have the time or inclination to read lengthy documents. They will want you to get straight to the point with your findings and recommendations in the form of an executive summary of key points. You should always clarify such points with the client at the outset.

Most reports use a numbering system for sections and sub-sections. For example, Section 9 of the dissertation briefing document that we use with our students is headed '9.0 How to avoid failing your dissertation'. Sub-sections are then numbered as follows:

9.1 The pitfalls of work-based or personal interest dissertations

9.2 Analysing your data with care

9.3 Avoiding plagiarism

9.4 Listening to your supervisor's advice

9.5 Timetabling and organising your work.

Sections within each sub-section are then numbered 9.1.1., 9.1.2 etc. Some reports even number each paragraph. Local authority reports, for example, use this convention, one of the advantages being that paragraphs can be easily identified when they are being scrutinised in Committee. Care needs taking here as this can get messy and confusing, and can certainly distract the reader. Once again, you should check any requirements in this respect.

There are other academic conventions about presentation and writing style. It is a convention, although one which thankfully seems to be breaking down, that you do not write in the first person. Avoiding the use of the first person is not usually difficult and so, for example, instead of writing, 'in this dissertation I will look at the barriers to leisure participation faced by women . . .', you would instead write, 'this dissertation looks at the barriers to leisure participation faced by women . . .'. A problem usually arises, however, when you want to provide personal comment and observation, and so the use of the first person appears appropriate. Again, this can be overcome by writing in a passive tense e.g. 'it is argued here that the principle barriers to leisure participation by women are structural . . .'. Writing in this way may seem unnecessarily cumbersome to you, and you should check any requirements concerning this aspect of writing style.

Discriminatory language should be avoided at all costs, and work should be carefully checked for any examples, however unintentional. Indeed, you should try and ensure that the planning and conduct of your work as whole is non-discriminatory. It is beyond the scope of this chapter to deal with this issue in any depth, it is simply flagged up as an issue here. Readers are referred to the work of Eichler (1988), for example, for a detailed consideration of these issues.

Final thoughts

While the person who finds writing easy is a lucky and rare individual, the material discussed in this chapter is not difficult to take on board, and with practice most of it will become second nature. Getting the structure of your research report right is simply a matter of following some common sense routines and conventions, as is textual referencing and the construction of a list of references. In this chapter we have attempted to take you through those basic conventions. This is not to say that all reports must necessarily be structured in exactly the same way. Local conventions will differ, although we doubt in any significant way.

One way of developing an understanding of good report writing is to look at examples of published work. Journals such as the *Annals of Tourism Research*, *Tourism Management* and *Leisure Studies* regularly carry articles reporting on people's research. Organisations such as the Sports Council also publish research reports, and your library will no doubt stock many such sources. Look at these reports and see how experienced researchers have presented their findings. Read these reports critically, however. Who do you think is the audience for the report? Is the language used in the report appropriate for that audience? Does the style of the report clarify or obscure the findings? Could the report have been better presented?

Careful thought and attention given to the presentation of your report will reap dividends. While a poorly conceived piece of research can never be salvaged by a glossy report, good research deserves good presentation. This is likely to be one of the most satisfying and rewarding things that you do as a student. It is, after all, your own work; you have discovered something new. The sense of achievement that this brings can be considerable. Good luck!

References

- Bell, J. (1987) *Doing Your Research Project*, Buckingham: Open University Press.
- Eichler, M. (1988) *Nonsexist Research Methods: A Practical Guide*, London: Allen & Unwin.
- Hart, C. (1998) *Doing a Literature Review. Releasing the Social Science Research Imagination*, London: Sage.
- Harvey, L. and MacDonald, M. (1993) *Doing Sociology*, Basingstoke: Macmillan.
- Henry, I. P. (1993) *The Politics of Leisure Policy*, Basingstoke: Macmillan.
- Karran, T. (1992) *University of Humberside, BA (Hons) Contemporary Studies – Dissertation Guidance Notes*, unpublished.
- Lewis, D. and Rushworth, S. (1997) *The Effective Learning Programme Portfolio*, Hull: University of Lincolnshire and Humberside.
- Veal, A. J. (1997) *Research Methods for Leisure and Tourism*, Second Edition, London: Financial Times Pitman Publishing.

Appendix 1: Random numbers

16 16	57 04	81 71	17 46	53 29	73 46	42 73	77 63	62 58	60 59
98 63	89 52	77 23	61 08	63 90	80 38	42 71	85 70	04 81	05 50
01 03	09 35	02 54	51 96	92 75	58 29	24 23	25 19	89 97	91 29
29 07	16 34	49 22	52 96	89 34	17 11	06 91	24 38	55 06	83 59
72 61	80 54	70 99	24 64	11 38	83 65	27 23	40 37	84 58	48 53
71 11	41 82	79 37	00 45	98 54	52 89	26 34	40 13	60 38	08 86
61 05	66 18	76 82	11 18	61 90	90 63	78 57	32 06	39 95	75 94
81 89	42 34	00 49	97 53	33 16	26 91	57 58	42 48	51 05	48 27
10 24	90 84	22 16	26 96	54 11	01 96	58 81	37 97	80 98	72 81
14 28	33 43	01 32	58 39	19 54	56 57	23 58	24 87	77 36	20 97
35 41	17 89	87 04	28 32	13 45	59 03	91 08	69 24	84 44	42 83
07 89	36 87	98 73	77 64	75 19	05 61	11 64	31 75	49 38	96 60
27 59	15 58	19 68	95 47	25 69	11 90	26 19	07 40	83 59	90 95
95 98	45 52	27 35	86 81	16 29	37 60	39 35	05 24	49 00	29 07
12 95	72 72	81 84	36 58	05 10	70 50	31 04	12 67	74 01	72 90
35 23	06 68	52 50	39 55	92 28	28 89	64 87	80 00	84 53	97 97
86 33	95 73	80 92	26 49	54 50	41 21	06 62	73 91	35 05	21 37
02 82	96 23	16 46	15 51	60 31	55 27	84 14	71 58	94 71	48 35
44 46	34 96	32 68	48 22	40 17	43 25	33 31	26 26	59 34	99 00
08 77	07 19	94 46	17 51	03 73	99 89	28 44	16 87	56 16	56 09
61 59	37 08	08 46	56 76	29 48	33 87	70 79	03 80	96 81	79 68
67 70	18 01	67 19	29 49	58 67	08 56	27 24	20 70	46 31	04 32
23 09	08 79	18 78	00 32	86 74	78 55	55 72	58 54	76 07	53 73
89 40	26 39	74 58	59 55	87 11	74 06	49 46	31 94	86 66	66 97
84 95	66 42	90 74	13 71	00 71	24 41	67 62	38 92	39 26	30 29
52 14	49 02	19 31	28 15	51 01	19 09	97 94	52 43	22 21	17 66
89 56	31 41	37 87	28 16	62 48	01 84	46 06	04 39	94 10	76 21
65 94	05 93	06 68	34 72	73 17	65 34	00 65	75 78	23 97	13 04

13 08	15 75	02 83	48 26	53 77	62 96	56 52	28 26	12 15	75 53
03 18	33 57	16 71	60 27	15 18	39 32	37 01	05 86	25 14	35 41
10 04	00 95	85 04	32 80	19 01	85 03	29 29	80 04	21 52	14 76
23 94	97 28	60 43	42 25	26 48	48 13	34 68	39 22	74 85	03 25
35 63	42 90	90 74	33 17	58 77	83 36	76 22	00 89	61 55	13 17
42 86	03 36	45 33	60 77	72 92	10 76	22 55	11 00	37 60	47 73
67 26	92 87	09 96	85 37	82 61	39 01	70 05	12 66	17 39	99 34
91 93	88 56	35 76	97 35	19 37	14 66	07 57	24 41	06 90	07 72
37 14	73 35	32 01	07 94	78 28	90 33	71 56	63 77	89 24	24 28
07 46	50 58	08 73	42 97	20 42	64 68	48 35	04 38	28 28	36 94
92 18	09 46	94 99	17 41	28 60	67 94	26 54	63 70	84 73	76 61
00 49	98 43	39 67	68 40	41 31	92 28	49 57	15 55	11 81	41 89
08 59	41 41	33 59	43 28	14 51	02 71	24 45	41 57	22 11	79 79
67 05	19 54	32 33	34 68	27 93	39 35	62 51	35 55	40 99	46 19
24 99	48 06	96 41	21 25	29 03	57 71	96 49	94 74	98 90	21 52
65 86	27 46	70 93	27 39	64 37	01 63	21 03	43 78	18 74	77 07
52 70	03 20	84 96	14 37	51 05	63 99	81 02	84 56	17 78	48 45
32 88	29 93	58 21	71 05	68 58	79 08	86 37	98 76	70 45	66 23
54 16	39 40	98 57	02 05	65 15	73 23	51 51	75 06	38 13	51 68
95 22	18 59	54 57	44 22	72 35	81 24	14 94	24 04	42 26	92 14
93 10	27 94	90 45	39 33	50 26	88 46	90 57	40 47	71 63	62 59
19 20	85 20	15 67	78 03	32 23	50 59	24 83	64 99	18 00	78 50

Appendix 2: Questionnaire used in the Hadrians' Wall Survey 1997

Location: Date: Time:

Hadrian's Wall Survey 1997

1. Is this your first visit or have you been before?

First visit ☐
Repeat visit ☐

If repeat, when did you last visit?

☐

2.a. How did you travel here today?

1. Hadrian's Wall bus ☐
2. Public bus ☐
3. Coach ☐
4. Car ☐
5. Bicycle ☐
6. Foot ☐
7. Train ☐
8. Other (or combination) ☐

2.b. *If used Hadrian's bus*, to what extent do you agree or disagree that it was value for money?

strongly agree	agree	neither agree nor disagree	disagree	strongly disagree
☐	☐	☐	☐	☐

2.c. *If used Hadrian's bus*, how convenient was it?

very convenient	convenient	neither convenient nor inconvenient	inconvenient	very inconvenient
☐	☐	☐	☐	☐

2.d. *If not used Hadrian's bus* – are you aware of the Hadrian's Wall bus service?

YES/NO

If yes, do you plan to use it during your stay?

YES/NO

If no, why not?

☐

3. Are you here today?

On holiday staying away from home ☐
On a leisure day trip from your home ☐
Other ☐
Please specify ☐

3.a. *If on holiday*, how long is your holiday?

☐ days

3.b. *If on holiday*, how many days have you been in the area of Hadrian's Wall? (Use a map of the area to prompt – by the Hadrian's Wall area we mean.....)

☐ days

3.c. *If on holiday*, where did you stay last night and how long did it take you to travel here?

place	time

4. How much longer will you spend in the area of Hadrian's Wall? (Use a map of the area to prompt – by the Hadrian's Wall area we mean.....)

	hours or days

5. Is your home?

Outside UK
UK based

country:
town:
postcode:

If UK based, could you estimate how long it took to travel from home to Hadrian's Wall?

	hrs/mins

6. Which of these best describes the main purpose of your trip today?

1. Going for a short walk (up to 2 hours)
2. Going for a long walk (over 2 hours)
3. Visiting the Wall
4. Visiting a World Heritage Site
5. Sitting and relaxing, enjoying the view
6. Passing through
7. Visiting tourist/historic attractions
8. Education to increase knowledge
9. Visiting friends and relatives
10. Enjoyment / Fun day out
11. Travelling round and sight-seeing
12. Attending an event
13. Other
(please state)

(If a combination, ask the respondent to rank)

7. Where are you going next?

8. Before you came here what did you expect it to be like?

9. To what extent do the following describe your expectations of the Hadrian's Wall area?

For each pair of adjectives, state the number which reflects the extent to which the description matches your expectation:

	1	2	3	4	5	
unattractive countryside						beautiful countryside
wild & spectacular scenery						dull & boring landscapes
polluted air						fresh air
warm weather						cold weather
rich in wildlife						without wildlife
unfriendly people						friendly people
unspoilt						tourist trap
crowded						uncrowded
easy to get to						difficult to get to
safe						unsafe
inspiring						uninspiring
noisy						peaceful

10. To what extent do you expect to find any of the following:

1 – strong expectation
3 – some expectation
5 – not expected

	1	2	3	4	5	Don't know
information on the Romans						
long stretches of wall						
information on the Reivers						
ruins						
information on the Borderlands						
excellent museums						
information on natural history						
plentiful accommodation						
convenient public transport links						
good choice of places to eat and drink						
information centres						
free car parking						
lots of things to do						
good walks						
outdoor sports/activities						
children's activities						
attractive small towns/villages						
value for money						
good touring base						

11. Which of the following attractions have you visited already?

Birdoswald		Housesteads	
Roman Army Museum		Corbridge Roman site	
Once Brewed		Tullie House	
Vindolanda		Chesters	

12. Which other attractions or places must you see before you go home?

13. Which sources of information did you use when you were planning your visit?

1. Friends and family
2. Radio
3. TV programme
4. Newspaper
5. Magazine
6. Guide book
7. Travel agent
8. Tourist brochure
9. Information Centre whilst on holiday/trip
10. Other
(please specify)

If more than one, which was the main source of information?

14. Which aspects of your visit have you most enjoyed so far?

15. Which aspects of your visit have been most disappointing so far?

16. How would you describe the typical visitor to Hadrian's Wall?

1. Very much like me
2. Similar to me
3. Not sure
4. A bit like me
5. Not at all like me

17. Before today, were you aware that Hadrian's Wall is a World Heritage Site?

YES/NO

Respondent Details

17. Are you on this holiday/trip:

on your own
with family
with friends
with friends and family

18. How many people, including yourself, are with you on this holiday/trip?

19. How many of your group are under the age of 16?

20. Which of these age groups are *you* in?

a 16–24
b 25–34
c 35–44
d 45–59
e 60+

21. What is your occupation, or the occupation of the main earner in your household?

22. Note characteristics of respondent:

Male   Female

23. Note whether dog owner:

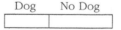

Dog   No Dog

We are very interested in what people think when they go home – what memories they have of the area and how satsified they are with their visit. Would you be so kind as to complete this follow up questionnaire and return it to us either when you get home or before you leave the UK? You will be entered into a Prize Draw.

Thank you very much.

Appendix 3: Variables used in the sample data file

Note: the first two columns of the data file are 'number' which is simply the sequential code number of the questionnaires. Month refers to the month in which the interview was conducted – J=June, A=August, P=September and S=October.

Question number	Variable name	Value labels
1	visit	1=First visit 2=Repeat visit
2.a	travel	1=HW bus 2=Public bus 3=Coach 4=Car 5=Bicycle 6=Foot 7=Train 8=Other (or combination)
2.b	hwvalue	1=Strongly agree 2=Agree 3=Neither agree nor disagree 4=Disagree 5=Strongly disagree 7=N/A
3	trip	1=Holiday away 2=Leisure day trip 3=Other
3.a	lenhol	None
3.b	durhw	None
3.c	timetohw	None
4	furstay	None
5	origin	1=UK 2=Overseas

Question number	Variable name	Value labels
5	timehome	None
6	mainpurp	1=Short walk
		2=Long walk
		3=Visiting Wall
		4=Visiting WHS
		5=Sit and relax
		6=Pass through
		7=Visit tourist attraction
		8=Education
		9=VFR
		10=Enjoyment
		11=Sightseeing
		12=Event
		13=Other
9	cside	1=Unattractive
		5=Beautiful
9	scenery	1=Wild and spectacular
		5=Dull and boring
9	air	1=Polluted
		5=Fresh
9	weather	1=Warm
		5=Cold
9	wildlife	1=Rich
		5=Without wildlife
9	people	1=Unfriendly
		5=Friendly
9	spoilt	1=Unspoilt
		5=Tourist trap
9	crowded	1=Crowded
		5=Uncrowded
9	access	1=Easy
		5=Difficult
9	safe	1=Safe
		5=Unsafe
9	inspire	1=Inspiring
		5=Uninspiring
9	noisy	1=Noisy
		5=Peaceful
10	roman	1=Strong expectation
		3=Some expectation
		5=Not expected
		6=Don't know
10	longwall	as above

Question number	Variable name	Value labels
10	reivers	as above
10	ruins	as above
10	borders	as above
10	exmuse	as above
10	nathis	as above
10	accom	as above
10	pubtrans	as above
10	eatdrink	as above
10	infocen	as above
10	fcarp	as above
10	todo	as above
10	walks	as above
10	osport	as above
10	childact	as above
10	smvill	as above
10	value	as above
10	tour	as above
13	maininfo	1=Friends/family
		2=Radio
		3=TV programme
		4=Newspaper
		5=Magazine
		6=Guide book
		7=Travel agent
		8=Tourist brochure
		9=Information Centre
		10=Other
		11=National Trust
		12=Map
		99=Missing value
17	group	1=On your own
		2=With family
		3=With friends
		4=With friends and family
18	persons	None
19	kids	None
20	age	a=16–24
		b=25–34
		c=35–44
		d=45–59
		e=60+

Question number	Variable name	Value labels
21	occup	1=Professional/managerial 2=Semi profess/intermediate 3=Skilled non-manual 4=Skilled manual 5=Semi-skilled manual 6=Unskilled 7=Retired 8=Unemployed 9=Armed forces 10=Student
22	sex	1=male only 2=female only 3=mixed sex group
From follow-up questionnaire	expect	1=Exceeded expectations 2=Met all expectations 3=Met some but not all 4=Fell short of expectations 9=No response

Note: the two final variables, 'length' and 'satscore' are computed variables. These are discussed in the text. Length is a measure of the total length of stay in hours. Satscore is an overall measure of satisfaction.

Appendix 4: Sample data file

	number	month	visit	travel	hwvalue	trip	lenhol	durhw	timetohw
1	6	J	1	4	7	1	42	1.000	.25
2	11	J	1	4	7	1	7	1.000	1.00
3	18	J	1	4	7	1	120	2.000	.05
4	21	J	1	2	7	1	7	1.000	.10
5	24	J	1	4	7	1	24	.100	.
6	28	J	2	4	7	1	7	1.000	1.00
7	29	J	2	4	7	1	14	1.000	.
8	31	J	1	1	2	1	35	1.000	1.00
9	35	J	2	4	7	1	14	4.000	.10
10	47	J	1	4	7	1	24	.500	2.00
11	54	J	1	4	7	1	30	1.000	1.30
12	59	J	1	4	7	1	20	1.000	.20
13	65	J	2	4	7	2	1	.000	.00
14	66	J	1	4	7	1	19	3.000	1.30
15	67	J	2	4	7	2	1	.000	.00
16	70	J	1	4	7	2	1	.000	.00
17	73	J	2	4	7	1	21	.000	1.00
18	76	J	1	5	7	1	10	1.000	15.00
19	80	J	1	4	7	1	30	1.000	.10
20	81	J	2	4	7	1	7	1.000	2.00
21	86	J	1	4	7	1	21	3.000	1.00
22	91	J	1	4	7	1	21	1.000	1.00
23	99	J	1	4	7	1	3	3.000	.75
24	113	A	1	4	7	1	14	.500	3.00
25	114	A	2	4	7	1	7	7.000	1.00
26	118	A	2	4	7	2	1	.000	1.30
27	119	A	1	4	7	1	14	2.000	.20
28	122	A	1	1	1	1	28	1.000	.40
29	129	A	1	4	1	1	17	2.000	.30
30	130	A	1	4	7	1	7	1.000	1.00
31	131	A	1	4	7	1	17	6.000	.30

	number	month	visit	travel	hwvalue	trip	lenhol	durhw	timetohw
32	137	A	1	4	7	1	4	1.000	.30
33	139	A	2	4	7	2	0	.000	.00
34	141	A	1	4	7	1	7	1.000	1.30
35	144	A	2	4	7	1	3	1.000	.20
36	146	A	1	4	7	1	14	1.000	2.00
37	156	A	2	4	7	2	0	.000	.50
38	157	A	1	4	7	1	3	3.000	.20
39	158	A	2	4	7	2	1	.000	.40
40	159	A	2	4	7	1	7	1.000	.30
41	162	A	1	4	7	1	4	3.000	1.30
42	165	A	1	4	7	1	7	1.000	2.00
43	167	A	2	4	7	1	10	1.000	1.00
44	168	A	2	4	7	2	1	.000	.30
45	174	A	2	4	7	2	1	.000	.45
46	175	A	2	4	7	1	4	4.000	.30
47	176	A	1	4	7	2	1	.000	.00
48	177	A	2	4	7	2	1	1.000	.00
49	187	A	2	4	7	1	7	1.000	.30
50	189	A	1	4	7	1	14	2.000	1.00
51	190	A	1	4	7	1	8	.010	.70
52	191	A	2	4	7	1	4	1.000	1.25
53	197	A	2	4	7	1	14	10.00	.50
54	198	A	1	8	2	1	7	4.000	.30
55	202	A	1	4	7	1	5	.500	3.00
56	204	A	2	4	7	1	14	10.00	2.00
57	208	A	1	4	7	1	26	1.000	2.00
58	209	A	1	4	7	1	4	1.000	.50
59	210	A	2	4	7	1	5	5.000	.30
60	215	A	2	4	7	1	14	1.000	.10
61	218	A	1	4	7	1	8	1.000	.50
62	222	A	2	4	7	1	18	1.000	.10
63	224	A	1	4	7	1	7	1.000	.
64	228	A	1	4	7	1	5	.050	1.50
65	229	A	2	4	7	1	14	1.000	.30
66	233	A	2	1	4	1	21	1.000	.25
67	234	A	2	4	7	1	3	.100	.
68	237	A	1	4	7	1	14	1.000	2.00
69	239	A	1	4	7	1	5	1.000	1.00
70	245	A	2	4	7	1	2	1.000	.30
71	249	A	1	4	7	1	6	1.000	1.25
72	254	A	1	4	7	1	7	1.000	1.50
73	256	P	2	4	7	1	14	5.000	.08
74	260	P	1	4	7	1	14	.500	2.00
75	266	P	2	4	7	1	14	2.000	.30
76	267	P	2	4	7	1	10	.500	1.00
77	268	P	2	4	7	1	7	7.000	.60
78	272	S	1	4	7	1	2	1.000	.10
79	274	S	1	4	7	1	4	3.000	.75

	number	month	visit	travel	hwvalue	trip	lenhol	durhw	timetohw
80	275	S	1	4	7	1	3	1.000	.20
81	278	S	2	4	7	1	2	.500	1.00
82	283	S	2	4	7	1	2	.250	.
83	287	S	2	4	7	1	2	1.000	.
84	294	S	1	4	7	1	18	3.000	1.25
85	298	S	1	4	7	1	2	.250	.75
86	299	S	2	4	7	1	2	.300	.75
87	306	S	1	4	7	1	49	2.000	3.00
88	312	S	1	4	7	1	21	1.000	1.00
89	313	S	2	4	7	1	28	1.000	.50
90	319	S	1	4	7	1	7	1.000	
91	320	S	1	4	7	1	56	2.000	.10
92	321	S	1	4	7	1	3	1.000	.30
93	324	S	1	4	7	1	88	1.000	.10
94	325	S	1	4	7	1	10	1.000	2.00
95	327	S	1	4	7	1	7	1.000	1.50
96	334	S	1	4	7	1	42	1.000	.30
97	341	S	1	4	7	1	4	2.000	.16
98	342	S	1	4	7	1	90	1.500	.50
99	343	S	1	4	7	1	7	3.000	.50
100	355	S	1	4	7	1	7	2.000	1.00
101	357	S	2	4	7	1	3	2.000	1.00

	furstay	origin	timehome	mainpurp	cside	scenery	air	weather
1	4.00	2	.	7	3	1	5	1
2	1.00	1	4.00	1	5	1	5	1
3	1.00	2	.	4	5	1	5	5
4	12.00	2	.	3	5	2	4	5
5	12.00	2	.	1	4	2	5	1
6	24.00	1	.	3	5	1	5	5
7	1.00	1	2.50	3	5	2	5	4
8	12.00	2	.	3	5	2	5	5
9	240.00	1	6.50	1	5	1	5	2
10	.00	2	.	3	5	2	5	4
11	1.00	2	.	3	4	3	5	5
12	24.00	2	.	3	5	1	5	5
13	2.00	1	.30	3	5	1	5	5
14	6.00	2	.	3	5	1	5	5
15	2.00	1	3.00	3	3	1	5	3
16	4.00	1	1.00	3	4	3	.5	4
17	3.00	2	.	3	5	1	5	5
18	12.00	1	.	13	4	2	5	4
19	12.00	2	.	3	3	3	5	3
20	.	1	3.00	3	4	2	4	4
21	2.00	2	.	3	5	1	5	2
22	3.00	2	.	3	4	2	5	2
23	12.00	1	4.00	10	4	2	5	2

	furstay	origin	timehome	mainpurp	cside	scenery	air	weather
24	.50	1	.	3	5	1	5	3
25	2.00	1	3.00	3	5	1	5	5
26	24.00	1	1.30	13	5	1	5	5
27	1.00	1	.	3	5	1	4	4
28	72.00	1	.	3	5	1	5	3
29	3.00	2	.	3	5	3	5	1
30	6.00	1	.	3	5	1	5	1
31	.00	1	.	3	3	5	5	4
32	6.00	1	.	3	5	2	5	5
33	.00	1	.10	1	5	1	5	5
34	4.00	2	.	3	4	3	4	4
35	12.00	1	2.00	9	4	3	5	2
36	2.00	1	.	3	5	1	5	3
37	.00	1	.50	2	5	1	5	3
38	.00	1	3.00	4	4	1	5	5
39	.00	1	.40	2	5	1	5	1
40	168.00	1	46.00	2	5	2	5	3
41	24.00	1	5.00	3	5	3	5	4
42	6.00	1	6.00	3	5	3	5	5
43	6.00	1	.	3	5	1	5	1
44	.00	1	.30	1	4	1	5	3
45	.00	1	.45	4	5	1	5	3
46	12.00	1	4.30	3	5	1	5	5
47	.00	1	.	3	5	1	5	1
48	.00	1	.	1	5	5	5	3
49	12.00	2	.	2	5	2	5	3
50	6.00	1	.	3	5	1	5	5
51	6.00	1	40.00	1	4	2	3	3
52	6.00	1	.	3	5	1	5	3
53	98.00	1	5.00	3	5	1	5	3
54	72.00	1	.	3	5	1	5	3
55	12.00	1	3.00	6	4	4	5	3
56	.00	1	.	9	4	3	4	5
57	.00	2	.	3	5	1	5	3
58	.	1	10.00	3	5	1	5	3
59	.50	1	4.00	3	5	3	5	4
60	.00	1	.	3	5	1	5	5
61	12.00	2	.	3	4	3	5	4
62	48.00	2	.	3	4	3	5	5
63	2.00	1	.	3	5	1	5	3
64	48.00	1	.	3	4	2	5	4
65	.00	1	.	3	4	2	5	1
66	2.00	1	.	2	4	1	5	4
67	1.00	1	4.50	3	3	1	5	5
68	6.00	2	.	3	5	1	5	5
69	1.00	1	.	3	5	2	5	3
70	6.00	1	2.00	3	3	1	5	5
71	1.50	1	.	3	3	1	5	5

	furstay	origin	timehome	mainpurp	cside	scenery	air	weather
72	.00	1	.	3	5	1	5	5
73	48.00	1	.	3	5	1	5	3
74	6.00	1	.	3	5	1	5	5
75	96.00	1	.	3	3	1	5	3
76	6.00	2	.	3	4	2	5	5
77	12.00	1	2.00	3	3	1	5	3
78	6.00	2	2.00	3	4	1	5	2
79	2.00	1	4.00	3	5	1	5	5
80	.	2	.	3	4	1	5	3
81	24.00	1	.	10	5	1	5	4
82	2.00	1	3.50	1	4	2	5	4
83	12.00	1	3.50	2	4	1	5	4
84	.50	2	.	3	4	2	5	5
85	.15	1	2.50	3	4	2	5	3
86	.15	1	2.50	3	5	1	5	5
87	12.00	2	.	3	5	1	5	3
88	12.00	2	.	1	3	3	5	4
89	12.00	2	.	3	4	2	4	4
90	12.00	1	5.50	3	5	3	4	4
91	1.00	2	.	3	5	2	5	5
92	12.00	1	5.00	3	5	1	5	5
93	12.00	2	.	2	5	3	5	3
94	12.00	2	.	13	4	2	5	3
95	.	1	5.50	3	4	2	5	4
96	6.00	2	.	3	3	4	5	5
97	48.00	1	4.50	3	5	1	5	5
98	36.00	2	.	7	3	2	3	5
99	96.00	2	.	3	5	1	5	5
100	24.00	1	7.00	3	4	2	4	3
101	12.00	1	3.00	3	5	1	5	4

	wildlife	people	spoilt	crowded	access	safe	inspire	noisy	roman
1	5	5	4	1	1	4	5	4	1
2	2	5	3	3	1	1	1	5	1
3	3	5	3	4	3	1	1	5	1
4	3	4	2	4	3	1	2	5	3
5	3	4	2	2	2	2	1	5	1
6	3	4	5	5	1	1	2	5	2
7	1	3	2	2	1	1	1	5	1
8	3	5	5	1	1	1	1	5	2
9	1	5	1	2	1	1	1	5	1
10	3	5	3	4	1	1	1	5	3
11	3	4	3	3	1	1	3	3	1
12	3	5	3	3	1	1	1	5	1
13	3	5	1	3	1	3	1	5	1
14	1	5	1	5	5	1	1	5	1
15	1	5	4	1	2	1	1	5	3

	wildlife	people	spoilt	crowded	access	safe	inspire	noisy	roman
16	4	3	4	4	3	2	2	4	1
17	1	5	3	2	1	1	1	5	3
18	3	4	1	2	2	2	2	4	1
19	3	3	3	3	2	1	1	5	5
20	3	4	1	4	1	1	1	5	1
21	5	5	3	3	2	1	1	5	1
22	3	4	4	3	1	1	2	2	1
23	1	5	3	4	4	1	1	4	1
24	3	5	5	3	1	1	2	5	1
25	3	3	1	3	1	1	1	5	1
26	1	5	4	3	1	3	2	5	1
27	2	5	2	4	3	2	2	4	1
28	1	5	1	5	1	1	1	5	1
29	5	3	1	1	1	1	3	5	1
30	1	5	1	3	1	1	1	5	1
31	5	5	3	2	1	1	2	5	1
32	3	5	5	3	1	1	1	5	2
33	5	5	5	1	1	1	1	5	1
34	3	3	3	3	3	2	1	5	3
35	3	4	3	4	2	1	3	5	1
36	3	5	2	4	1	2	2	4	2
37	4	5	3	3	1	1	1	5	4
38	2	5	5	5	5	1	1	5	4
39	1	5	4	2	2	1	1	5	2
40	1	5	1	3	3	1	1	5	3
41	5	5	5	1	5	3	2	3	3
42	3	5	3	1	1	1	3	5	1
43	1	3	1	1	1	5	3	5	1
44	1	5	2	1	1	1	1	4	1
45	1	5	1	4	1	1	1	4	1
46	3	5	3	3	1	1	3	3	1
47	5	5	5	1	1	1	1	3	3
48	5	5	3	5	1	1	3	5	1
49	5	5	3	4	2	1	1	4	1
50	1	5	5	1	1	1	1	5	1
51	1	4	2	5	2	3	1	5	1
52	1	3	4	2	1	1	1	3	1
53	1	5	1	3	1	3	1	5	1
54	1	5	3	3	3	1	1	5	1
55	3	3	4	4	3	2	2	4	1
56	3	5	1	3	1	1	1	2	1
57	1	5	3	3	3	1	1	5	1
58	2	5	3	3	3	3	1	5	5
59	1	5	3	5	1	1	2	4	1
60	1	5	3	3	1	1	1	3	1
61	5	5	3	3	1	1	3	5	4
62	3	5	2	3	2	1	1	5	1
63	3	3	1	5	3	1	3	5	1

	wildlife	people	spoilt	crowded	access	safe	inspire	noisy	roman
64	3	3	2	3	1	1	2	4	1
65	2	5	4	2	1	1	1	5	1
66	2	4	1	5	1	1	3	4	2
67	3	4	2	4	2	1	1	5	1
68	5	5	1	5	1	1	1	5	3
69	2	5	1	3	1	1	1	4	1
70	1	5	3	3	3	3	1	3	4
71	1	5	5	4	1	1	1	5	5
72	3	5	3	5	4	1	1	5	1
73	1	5	2	5	1	1	1	5	1
74	3	5	3	5	4	1	1	5	4
75	4	5	1	3	1	1	1	3	1
76	3	5	5	3	1	1	2	3	1
77	5	5	1	5	1	1	1	5	1
78	3	5	2	5	2	2	2	5	1
79	2	5	4	4	1	1	1	5	1
80	4	5	2	5	3	1	2	5	2
81	2	5	3	4	1	1	1	4	3
82	3	4	2	2	2	3	2	4	1
83	3	3	4	4	2	2	1	5	2
84	4	5	3	1	1	1	2	5	1
85	3	5	3	5	1	1	2	4	1
86	3	5	4	3	1	1	3	3	1
87	2	5	3	3	1	3	1	5	1
88	2	5	3	3	3	1	1	5	1
89	3	4	3	4	2	1	3	4	2
90	4	4	1	2	3	1	2	4	1
91	2	3	5	1	1	1	1	5	2
92	3	4	1	5	4	1	3	4	5
93	3	4	3	4	2	1	1	5	2
94	5	5	3	5	1	1	1	5	1
95	2	4	2	4	1	1	3	5	1
96	4	4	3	5	5	1	2	5	1
97	1	5	1	1	3	1	1	5	1
98	5	4	5	4	3	1	1	5	1
99	3	4	2	5	2	1	2	5	2
100	5	3	3	3	4	3	2	4	1
101	2	4	2	5	3	1	1	5	1

	longwall	reivers	ruins	borders	exmuse	nathis	accom	pubtrans
1	2	6	1	2	3	2	3	5
2	1	6	1	5	1	3	5	5
3	1	6	1	3	5	5	5	5
4	2	5	2	2	4	2	3	4
5	1	5	1	2	2	1	5	5
6	1	5	2	5	2	5	3	5
7	1	5	1	5	2	5	1	5

	longwall	reivers	ruins	borders	exmuse	nathis	accom	pubtrans
8	1	1	1	1	2	1	5	1
9	1	5	1	5	1	3	4	1
10	4	6	1	5	5	5	5	5
11	1	6	1	2	1	2	2	5
12	1	6	1	2	5	5	2	5
13	1	6	1	3	1	3	5	5
14	3	6	1	3	3	1	1	3
15	3	6	1	5	3	3	1	1
16	3	6	3	5	5	3	3	5
17	1	5	1	5	1	2	5	6
18	1	5	1	5	5	3	4	5
19	1	5	1	5	5	5	5	5
20	1	5	1	1	2	1	5	5
21	1	5	1	5	2	2	5	5
22	1	5	1	2	2	4	5	5
23	3	2	1	2	2	5	1	5
24	1	1	1	5	1	5	3	5
25	1	3	1	1	1	1	1	5
26	3	5	1	2	3	5	5	5
27	3	4	1	2	2	2	2	5
28	3	6	1	1	5	3	1	4
29	5	6	1	6	5	5	1	1
30	5	6	1	1	3	3	1	5
31	4	6	1	5	1	2	5	5
32	4	6	1	3	2	5	1	1
33	3	5	1	1	1	3	5	5
34	2	5	2	5	5	5	6	3
35	2	2	1	1	3	4	2	3
36	4	5	2	5	3	4	5	5
37	1	2	1	5	1	2	4	4
38	1	6	1	5	5	1	1	5
39	1	5	1	5	5	5	5	6
40	1	6	1	1	3	3	3	5
41	1	6	1	1	4	1	1	1
42	1	6	1	1	1	4	1	5
43	5	2	1	3	1	3	1	1
44	2	5	2	5	3	5	5	5
45	1	5	1	4	1	5	1	5
46	1	6	1	5	1	5	1	3
47	3	6	3	3	2	2	6	6
48	1	3	1	1	1	5	5	5
49	1	6	2	1	3	3	2	4
50	1	1	1	5	1	1	1	1
51	2	5	1	4	2	5	5	2
52	1	5	1	2	1	3	4	5
53	1	6	1	1	1	3	1	1
54	1	2	1	1	1	1	1	1

	longwall	reivers	ruins	borders	exmuse	nathis	accom	pubtrans
55	4	6	1	3	3	3	6	5
56	1	6	2	3	1	1	2	6
57	1	6	1	6	1	5	1	1
58	3	6	1	5	4	5	1	5
59	1	5	1	5	1	5	4	5
60	2	5	1	1	1	2	1	5
61	5	6	1	5	1	1	1	1
62	3	5	1	2	1	3	3	2
63	3	5	1	3	3	3	1	6
64	3	5	1	3	5	5	5	5
65	3	6	1	1	1	5	1	5
66	2	6	1	3	4	3	4	5
67	1	6	1	4	1	5	5	6
68	1	6	1	5	3	3	5	5
69	3	6	1	3	4	3	1	3
70	2	6	1	4	4	4	3	5
71	1	6	1	1	1	4	1	1
72	1	5	1	1	3	5	4	3
73	1	3	1	3	2	2	3	3
74	1	5	5	5	5	5	4	5
75	2	5	1	5	3	5	5	3
76	2	6	1	5	1	5	5	3
77	1	5	1	4	4	4	3	5
78	2	5	1	5	3	3	3	5
79	4	5	1	2	2	1	1	3
80	2	5	1	3	1	2	1	2
81	4	5	1	3	5	5	1	5
82	1	5	1	1	1	3	1	4
83	1	3	2	4	2	4	1	5
84	1	5	1	2	1	5	1	5
85	2	5	1	3	5	5	3	5
86	1	5	1	3	4	3	3	5
87	4	5	1	1	1	1	2	2
88	3	5	1	1	3	3	3	5
89	1	5	1	4	3	3	2	5
90	3	5	3	5	3	1	1	5
91	1	5	1	1	3	5	1	3
92	3	2	1	2	5	5	5	5
93	1	5	1	5	2	1	1	4
94	5	3	1	2	1	1	1	1
95	3	5	1	3	2	5	5	5
96	1	6	1	1	5	3	3	1
97	1	6	3	5	1	5	5	1
98	1	6	1	3	5	5	3	1
99	3	6	2	3	3	3	5	5
100	3	5	1	3	2	4	4	3
101	3	5	1	3	2	2	1	5

	eatdrink	infocen	fcarp	todo	walks	osport	childact	smvill	value
1	3	1	5	1	1	5	1	2	5
2	3	1	5	5	1	5	5	1	3
3	3	1	1	1	1	1	5	1	1
4	4	2	5	3	1	5	5	2	3
5	5	5	1	2	1	5	5	1	1
6	1	1	5	3	1	5	5	1	3
7	2	1	1	1	1	5	1	4	1
8	5	2	1	2	1	5	1	5	1
9	4	2	2	2	1	4	4	1	1
10	5	2	2	5	4	5	5	1	2
11	2	1	1	1	1	6	6	1	3
12	5	6	1	3	1	5	5	1	1
13	5	1	5	5	1	3	5	1	3
14	1	1	6	1	1	3	5	1	1
15	3	1	5	3	1	3	3	1	1
16	5	3	1	1	1	3	3	3	3
17	3	2	5	5	1	5	5	1	3
18	5	2	1	4	2	5	3	1	2
19	5	5	5	5	2	5	5	2	1
20	5	1	1	5	1	5	5	5	1
21	4	1	1	3	1	5	5	1	1
22	4	2	2	3	1	2	3	3	4
23	2	1	5	3	1	2	1	2	2
24	3	1	5	5	1	3	5	1	1
25	1	1	3	1	1	5	5	1	1
26	1	1	1	4	1	4	2	1	1
27	4	1	5	2	1	1	2	2	1
28	1	1	5	5	1	5	4	1	1
29	1	1	5	5	1	5	5	1	3
30	4	3	3	1	1	4	5	1	1
31	5	1	3	3	1	5	5	6	1
32	1	1	1	1	1	5	5	1	1
33	5	1	1	5	1	5	5	5	1
34	5	3	2	5	3	5	5	3	3
35	4	2	1	3	1	4	4	3	2
36	5	1	3	5	1	5	5	1	1
37	5	1	2	4	1	3	5	5	1
38	3	1	2	4	1	5	5	1	1
39	2	1	1	2	1	1	5	1	1
40	1	1	5	1	1	3	3	1	1
41	5	1	1	5	1	5	5	5	3
42	5	1	2	5	1	1	1	3	1
43	2	1	5	5	1	5	5	1	2
44	3	1	5	3	1	5	5	1	1
45	1	1	5	3	1	5	5	1	1
46	6	1	1	1	1	6	5	1	2
47	1	1	3	5	1	5	5	1	1
48	1	1	5	1	1	5	5	1	1

	eatdrink	infocen	fcarp	todo	walks	osport	childact	smvill	value
49	3	2	1	3	1	3	3	1	1
50	1	1	1	1	1	1	5	1	1
51	5	2	1	3	1	4	3	2	2
52	3	1	2	3	1	4	3	3	1
53	2	1	1	1	1	1	3	1	3
54	1	2	1	3	1	1	4	1	1
55	3	4	5	3	1	6	2	1	2
56	6	1	1	3	1	1	1	1	1
57	1	1	5	1	1	1	3	1	1
58	2	1	4	5	3	1	5	1	1
59	4	1	1	1	1	1	5	4	1
60	5	1	1	3	1	5	5	1	3
61	5	1	1	5	1	5	5	1	1
62	3	1	1	5	1	4	5	1	1
63	3	1	5	1	1	5	5	3	3
64	3	1	4	5	1	3	5	3	3
65	1	1	1	1	1	5	3	1	1
66	3	2	1	3	1	3	4	2	3
67	4	3	1	5	1	5	4	1	6
68	5	1	1	5	1	5	5	1	4
69	2	1	1	2	1	6	5	1	2
70	3	3	3	5	1	5	5	3	5
71	1	1	1	4	1	5	5	1	1
72	3	1	4	5	1	5	5	2	1
73	2	2	3	2	1	4	3	2	2
74	1	1	1	5	1	4	5	1	1
75	1	1	3	5	3	5	5	1	1
76	2	1	1	5	1	5	5	1	1
77	2	1	2	5	2	5	5	1	2
78	4	2	1	2	1	5	5	1	1
79	3	1	5	1	1	4	4	2	3
80	1	1	1	3	2	5	5	1	1
81	2	1	5	3	1	3	5	1	1
82	2	2	2	2	1	5	5	1	1
83	2	1	1	5	1	5	5	1	1
84	1	1	1	5	1	5	5	1	1
85	4	2	1	5	1	5	3	1	2
86	4	2	1	5	1	2	4	1	2
87	2	1	1	3	1	4	4	1	1
88	3	3	3	3	1	3	3	1	3
89	4	2	2	2	1	5	5	2	1
90	4	1	1	5	1	3	5	1	2
91	2	1	1	4	1	4	5	1	1
92	3	5	5	3	1	5	5	5	1
93	5	1	1	4	1	5	5	1	1
94	1	2	1	3	1	2	5	1	1
95	3	3	1	5	1	5	5	2	5
96	1	1	5	3	1	5	1	1	1

·	eatdrink	infocen	fcarp	todo	walks	osport	childact	smvill	value
97	1	1	5	1	1	5	6	1	1
98	3	6	1	5	1	5	5	1	2
99	5	2	1	3	1	3	3	1	3
100	3	2	2	3	1	4	4	2	2
101	1	1	3	3	1	3	5	1	1

	tour	maininfo	group	persons	kids	age	occup	sex	expect	length	satscore
1	6	6	2	3	1	b	2	1	3	5.00	38.00
2	1	8	4	6	0	e	7	3	3	2.00	38.00
3	1	8	2	2	0	b	3	3	1	3.00	41.00
4	1	1	3	2	0	b	10	3	3	13.00	55.00
5	1	10	2	2	0	d	1	2	2	12.10	50.00
6	1	1	2	2	0	b	3	3	2	25.00	33.00
7	5	12	2	4	2	c	2	1	2	2.00	42.00
8	1	6	3	2	0	a	10	2	1	13.00	38.00
9	1	99	2	2	0	d	1	1	2	244.00	42.00
10	6	10	2	2	0	d	2	3	1	.50	18.00
11	1	8	2	2	0	b	4	3	2	2.00	42.00
12	3	99	2	4	1	d	1	1	2	25.00	40.00
13	1	10	4	4	0	c	1	2	2	2.00	42.00
14	1	1	1	1	0	c	3	1	2	9.00	45.00
15	1	10	1	1	0	c	5	1	2	2.00	49.00
16	3	10	3	2	0	b	10	2	2	4.00	51.00
17	3	10	2	5	2	d	2	2	2	3.00	43.00
18	2	12	2	2	0	b	1	3	2	13.00	57.00
19	3	1	1	7	3	d	1	2	1	13.00	31.00
20	5	99	2	5	1	d	4	1	2	.	35.00
21	5	1	2	5	3	c	1	1	2	5.00	48.00
22	5	1	3	4	1	d	2	2	2	4.00	60.00
23	3	8	2	3	1	c	1	2	1	15.00	39.00
24	1	6	2	2	0	d	2	3	1	1.00	41.00
25	1	5	2	3	0	d	3	1	2	9.00	39.00
26	1	10	2	3	1	c	1	3	2	24.00	38.00
27	2	10	2	4	2	c	2	3	3	3.00	42.00
28	1	1	2	2	0	d	2	3	1	73.00	34.00
29	5	6	3	2	0	d	1	3	2	5.00	45.00
30	1	1	2	4	2	c	1	3	2	7.00	40.00
31	5	8	3	2	0	b	2	3	2	6.00	43.00
32	1	6	2	2	0	a	3	3	2	7.00	41.00
33	1	10	2	2	0	c	2	3	2	.00	42.00
34	5	6	3	2	0	a	10	2	2	5.00	42.00
35	3	1	3	2	0	b	9	1	2	13.00	48.00
36	1	9	2	2	0	d	1	3	1	3.00	46.00
37	1	6	3	8	0	d	7	3	2	.00	45.00
38	1	8	2	3	0	d	4	3	2	3.00	36.00
39	1	1	3	2	0	b	1	3	3	.00	44.00
40	1	1	3	2	0	a	8	2	2	169.00	56.00

	tour	maininfo	group	persons	kids	age	occup	sex	expect	length	satscore
41	1	9	2	3	1	b	2	2	3	27.00	41.00
42	5	1	2	4	2	c	1	2	1	7.00	44.00
43	1	8	2	2	0	d	5	3	2	7.00	49.00
44	1	10	2	2	0	b	2	3	2	.00	50.00
45	1	10	2	2	0	c	3	3	2	.00	32.00
46	1	8	2	2	1	c	2	3	2	16.00	51.00
47	1	10	2	4	2	c	4	3	2	.00	49.00
48	1	1	4	5	1	c	6	3	2	1.00	38.00
49	1	6	3	2	0	b	1	3	2	13.00	47.00
50	1	10	2	5	3	c	4	3	3	8.00	64.00
51	5	12	3	2	0	a	2	3	2	6.01	44.00
52	1	12	2	4	2	c	2	1	2	7.00	52.00
53	1	1	2	4	2	c	10	2	2	108.00	36.00
54	1	5	2	2	0	b	6	2	2	76.00	40.00
55	5	11	2	4	2	c	1	1	1	12.50	46.00
56	1	10	2	7	3	e	7	1	2	10.00	42.00
57	1	1	3	2	0	c	3	3	1	1.00	25.00
58	1	10	2	2	0	d	3	3	2	.	43.00
59	1	11	2	2	0	d	2	3	1	5.50	48.00
60	1	12	3	2	0	d	2	2	2	1.00	46.00
61	2	5	3	2	0	d	3	3	2	13.00	42.00
62	3	1	2	2	0	c	3	3	1	49.00	33.00
63	1	6	2	4	2	c	3	3	3	3.00	43.00
64	5	8	2	3	1	c	2	3	1	48.05	53.00
65	1	6	3	2	0	b	2	3	3	1.00	48.00
66	2	6	2	4	0	b	2	3	1	3.00	47.00
67	1	10	2	2	0	c	2	3	2	1.10	50.00
68	5	5	2	2	0	c	3	1	4	7.00	45.00
69	1	1	1	2	0	d	3	3	2	2.00	49.00
70	3	10	2	2	0	c	3	3	2	7.00	48.00
71	1	99	4	8	3	d	10	1	2	2.50	48.00
72	1	8	2	6	1	c	2	3	2	1.00	49.00
73	1	8	2	4	2	c	4	2	2	53.00	38.00
74	1	1	2	2	0	d	4	3	1	6.50	38.00
75	1	9	1	2	0	d	7	3	3	98.00	41.00
76	1	8	3	2	0	d	2	2	1	6.50	50.00
77	2	8	2	3	1	c	3	3	3	19.00	32.00
78	5	6	2	3	0	d	1	2	3	7.00	48.00
79	2	99	3	4	0	e	1	1	2	5.00	38.00
80	1	99	1	1	0	c	2	1	2	.	41.00
81	1	99	2	4	2	c	2	3	9	24.50	36.00
82	1	9	2	3	0	d	7	1	1	2.25	47.00
83	1	99	4	7	0	e	7	3	2	13.00	24.00
84	1	6	3	3	0	e	7	2	3	3.50	48.00
85	5	1	4	2	0	c	2	2	2	.40	51.00
86	1	99	4	2	0	d	3	1	2	.45	55.00
87	1	9	2	4	2	d	2	2	1	14.00	42.00
88	3	6	2	2	0	c	2	1	1	13.00	36.00

	tour	maininfo	group	persons	kids	age	occup	sex	expect	length	satscore
89	2	6	2	2	0	b	2	3	1	13.00	45.00
90	2	4	4	4	0	d	7	3	1	13.00	51.00
91	1	6	2	2	0	d	3	3	2	3.00	47.00
92	1	6	2	2	0	e	3	3	1	13.00	41.00
93	1	8	2	2	0	d	7	3	2	13.00	45.00
94	1	5	1	1	0	d	4	1	3	13.00	41.00
95	2	9	2	2	0	e	7	2	2	.	56.00
96	3	8	3	2	0	b	10	1	2	7.00	43.00
97	1	10	2	2	0	b	4	3	1	50.00	25.00
98	1	6	2	2	0	e	2	2	3	37.50	46.00
99	2	1	2	5	3	c	2	1	2	99.00	44.00
100	4	8	3	2	0	b	2	3	1	26.00	34.00
101	1	6	2	2	0	c	2	3	2	14.00	30.00

Student Activities: selected answers

On the following pages we provide brief suggested answers and ways of approaching some of the Student Activities that can be found at the end of most chapters. These are offered as ideas and are not, in most cases, meant to be definitive answers. Restrictions of space and the nature of some of the activities mean that not all of the activities are dealt with here.

Chapter 1: Introducing Research

Activity 1

1. A small-scale research project would probably include the following features not found in an extended essay:

   - Research problem identified
   - Reference to the research process
   - A methodological section
   - The collection of primary data and/or secondary data analysis
   - Analysis of the data
   - Reflection on the research process

   An extended essay would use a range of secondary sources and would be structured in paragraphs with an introduction and a conclusion. The extended essay would probably be a coherent answer to a prescribed question. For a small-scale research project the focus of the research would probably be determined by the researcher.

2. Research is exploring the unknown where the outcome of the research depends upon the relationship between theory, method and analysis. A researcher with preconceived ideas of the outcome of the research may be blind to alternative techniques of data collection that may result in a different outcome. There would be a temptation to be selective in the interpretation of the results of the research to match the expected outcome i.e. bias the research. Research should not be seen as a self-fulfilling prophecy. The researcher may have hunches as to the outcome of the research, and these are usually expressed as hypotheses and tested by collecting and analysing data.

3. The key to answering this question is whether knowledge can be gained in a neutral and objective way. In methodological terms, the hypothetico-deductive method used by the natural scientists is seen by many as neutral and value-free. It is neutral because a set procedure is followed with the researcher detached from the research setting. But this objectivity is being questioned by some researchers, who argue that knowledge is 'situated'. What is meant by this is that knowledge is not out there waiting to be discovered but is socially constructed. It is argued that no matter how impartial the researcher feels, he or she comes to the research with personal 'baggage'. Research is researcher-orientated.

There are many stages in the research process where the values of the researcher can intervene. It begins with the choice of topic to research. Politically sensitive topics may be avoided due to problems of data collection. Research sponsored by an organisation may have its research focus determined by the sponsor. Even the research design may be chosen to suit the expertise of the researcher.

In contrast to this the ethnographer immerses himself/herself in the research setting and becomes involved in the research process. Neutrality is not a consideration for the ethnographer. A researcher adopting a more 'scientific' approach to research would probably describe the data from ethnographic research as 'subjective' and 'idiosyncratic'.

4. 'Good' research is where:

- The style of research is appropriate to the topic being researched and the problems under investigation.

- Strategic decisions on research design are made to help gain the best possible outcome from the research.

- Methodological choices are carefully considered in the light of the research aims and made explicit in the research report.

- The researcher reflects on the research process and recognises that the research is a social activity affected by the researcher's own motivations and values.

- Some contribution is made to understanding the world in which we live.

- Methodological triangulation is used to enhance the validity of the results.

- The researcher is sensitive to issues of reliability, validity and representativeness.

- Ethical issues are taken seriously.

5. Surveys and the use of questionnaires have tended to dominate research in leisure and tourism at both the demand and supply ends of the subjects. 'Hard', quantitative data has traditionally been viewed positively by people working in the leisure and tourism industries. With the recent emergence of Leisure and Tourism studies, computers and software programs for analysing vast amounts of statistical data have been available, encouraging researchers to 'number crunch'. The multi-disciplinary nature of leisure and tourism means that methodological developments in subjects like Sociology, Geography, Economics and Psychology have influenced research in tourism. There are strong, established traditions of positivist research in these disciplines that have been 'borrowed' by leisure and tourism researchers. For more information, the reader is recommended to consult:

Bramham, P. and Henry, I. (1996) 'Leisure Research in the UK', in Mommaas, H., van der Poel, H., Bramham, P. and Henry, I. (eds) *Leisure Research in Europe: methods and traditions*, Wallingford: CAB International.

Hemingway, J.L. (1995) 'Leisure Studies and interpretive social inquiry', *Leisure Studies*, Vol.14, pp. 32–47.

Smith, S.L.J. (1995) *Tourism Analysis: A Handbook*, Harlow: Addison Wesley Longman, Chapter 1.

6. To understand why there is a limited role for the field experiment in leisure and tourism research, an understanding of the experimental style of research is needed. An experiment involves setting up a research and control group to test the effect of an independent variable on a dependent variable where all other factors likely to affect the outcome are controlled. This is clearly possible in a laboratory experiment, but when applied outside the laboratory as a field experiment then it is virtually impossible to control outside, extraneous factors. In real life situations it is difficult and unethical to control and manipulate people to test a causal relationship.

7. This is a question best answered by the students themselves. Answers may include:

- Questionnaires are quick and easy to construct and administer.
- Cross-section of views is required at one point in time.
- More published research in leisure and tourism using the survey method.
- Other methods like interviewing and observation techniques are more time-consuming.
- Quantitative data are easier to analyse (computer packages available).
- Lack of confidence and experience of other methods.
- Plenty of specific advice on how to conduct surveys and construct questionnaires.

Chapter 3: Evaluating Research

Activity 2

Evaluation notes for:

Carr, N. (1999) 'A study of gender difference: young tourist behaviour in a UK coastal resort', *Tourism Management*, Vol.20 (2), pp. 223–8.

- Definition of a 'young' tourist discussed at the beginning of the article (16–35 years), yet a sub-group (18–24 years) was interviewed.
- Good literature review on gender differences in leisure activities (under-researched area).
- How typical was the choice of Torquay? To what extent can the research findings be generalised to other coastal resorts?
- Good response rate from a questionnaire survey administered face-to-face.
- Sampling method not discussed – random?
- More than one method was used. Data from the survey was combined with data from recall diaries and in-depth interviews – multi-method approach.
- Inferential statistical test used to identify any differences between the young men and women (assumption of a random sample).
- Qualitative data from interviews and diaries corroborated the statistical evidence from the survey (triangulation of methods).
- Comparison with previous research difficult as this study focused on young people specifically.

This is clearly a well thought out piece of research combining quantitative and qualitative data, although for many young students who have taken holidays with a group of friends, the results of this research may not seem surprising. But this should not detract from the sound methodology employed.

Was this a deductive or inductive piece of research? Support your answer with evidence from the research article.

Chapter 4: Secondary Data Analysis in Leisure and Tourism Research

Activity 1

The most comprehensive database available to answer this question is the General Household Survey (GHS), produced by the Office for National Statistics under the title Living in Britain. The question requires you to consider trends in leisure participation over the period 1977–1996, but as the chapter points out, changes in methodology were introduced in 1987, making comparisons with earlier years problematic. We cannot, therefore, answer the question as set – 1987 should be used as the new base year from which trends over time can be examined.

Questions on participation in sport and leisure activities have been included in their present format in the GHS every three years since 1987. We can therefore draw on data from 1987, 1990, 1993 and 1996 in answering this question. Participation rates for over 30 separate indoor and outdoor sports are recorded in the GHS. Some examples are provided below:

Trends in participation in sports, games and physical activities 1987–1996

	1987	1990	1993	1996
Walking	38	41	41	45
Swimming	13	15	15	15
Snooker/billiards/pool	15	14	12	11
Cycling	8	9	10	11
Running	5	5	5	5
Squash	3	3	2	1
At least one activity	61	65	64	64

NB: Figures show the % participating in the four weeks before the interview

As can be seen from these sample activities, there has been an overall increase in adult participation in at least one activity, rising from 61% in 1987 to 64% in 1996, although there was a high of 65% in 1990. Looking at individual activities we can see that some have gained participants, some have lost, and others have remained constant. Walking, which involves a walk for pleasure of two miles or more, went up from 38% in 1987 to 45% in 1996, whereas participation in cue sports declined in the same period from 15% to 11%. The participation rates for running remained constant at 5% throughout the period in question.

Whilst we do not have the space to cover this here, further analysis of the GHS data could be made by age, gender and socio-economic grouping.

Turning now to more sedentary leisure activities, the 1996 GHS provides data for the whole of the period in question, 1977–1996. Again, some examples are provided below.

	1977	1980	1983	1986	1987	1990	1993	1996
Watching tv	97	98	98	98	99	99	99	99
Listening to radio	87	88	87	86	88	89	89	88
Reading books	54	57	56	59	60	62	65	65
Gardening	42	43	44	43	46	48	48	48
Dressmaking/needlework/ knitting	29	28	27	27	27	23	22	22

Trends in participation in leisure activities 1977–1996

NB: Figures show the % participating in the four weeks before the interview

Participation in these leisure activities is generally higher than rates for the sports activities. The vast majority of people watch television and listen to the radio, and this has been a constant feature over the whole period. The percentage of adults reading books increased from 54% in 1977 to 65% in 1996. Gardening also increased from 42% to 48%. Participation rates for dressmaking etc. declined, however, from 29% to 22%. As with the sports activities, the GHS data allow us to conduct further analysis by gender, age and socio-economic group.

It should be noted that the figures included here are those for participation in the four weeks prior to interview. The GHS also provides participation rates for the previous 12 months. These figures are, not surprisingly, higher.

Activity 2

These questions are deliberately vague in order to highlight some of the problems of conducting secondary data analysis, and to make the point that anyone attempting them would have to develop clearer research objectives and establish appropriate indicators. For example, in answering the second part we need to be clear about what we mean by the North and South of the United Kingdom. Is it Scotland versus the rest? Or is it Scotland along with the North of England (assuming we can agree where that begins and ends) compared with the rest of the United Kingdom? How else might we tackle this issue? In similar vein, when we talk about tourism numbers do we mean domestic tourists, international visitors or a combination of both? Restrictions will certainly be placed on the level of analysis by the ways in which the data is presented. This is one of the frustrations/limitations of undertaking secondary data analysis.

Sources that can be used to tackle such a question include the International Passenger Survey. This provides annual visitor numbers to the UK. These figures are broken down by country – England, Scotland, Wales and Northern Ireland – and within England regional data is also given (e.g. Heart of England, West Country, and the South East). As the International Passenger Survey has been running since 1964 it can be used to tackle the period in question.

Turning to domestic tourism, the British National Travel Survey looks at the British on holiday in Britain, and also provides regional data. However, once again we come up against the problem of definition and thus the need to change the base year for comparison purposes. The 1997 British National Travel Survey adopted changes in definition of the regional boundaries. These included a new East of England region, with the Heart of England region being the subject of substantial re-definition. So, whilst the British National Travel Survey has been running continuously since 1960, we cannot use the same regional boundaries for comparison purposes.

Another source that is of potential value in answering this question given its regional focus is Regional Trends. Regional Trends 34 (1999) provides tourist numbers and expenditure for both UK residents and overseas residents, and compares 1997 with 1991. The data is provided by Tourist Board region and suggests that the North of England constitutes Northumbria, Cumbria, North West and Yorkshire; that Central England constitutes East of England and the Heart of England; and that the South is made up of London, Southern, South East England and West Country regions.

The first part of Activity 2 also requires clearer research objectives. What constitutes a heritage attraction – historic monuments, heritage theme parks, museums? In addition, the available data may also not be presented in the form the researcher would like, in which case you would have to go to the original source or the data archive (assuming that it is accessible). For example, the Annual Abstract of Statistics looks at trends in visitor numbers to a range of categories of attractions including historic properties and museums, both of which are clearly of value in tackling the question. However, rather than providing the actual numbers, it uses a system of index numbers to show trends with 1985 being the base year (1985 = 100). The 'historic properties' category shows considerable fluctuation in the period 1985–95 but actually peaks in 1995 with an index figure of 113.2. In contrast, the 'museums' category climbed steadily throughout the period before dropping for the first time in 1995 to an index figure of 113.8. So, whilst index numbers of this kind are useful in depicting trends, the researcher may require actual visitor numbers in which case s/he has to track down the original data source.

Chapter 6: Social Surveys

Activity 3

Some points to note:

- The instructions are too vague and unprofessional. This needs to be formalised so that the participants all receive the same information and can therefore make an informed decision on whether to participate.
- The age categories overlap. Demographic questions like this are best left to the end in most instances.
- Is marital status needed?
- Dependent children is not defined – be specific in terms of age.
- The question on residence is too vague – would house be better?
- Asking about possessions may get the participants suspicious – why do you want this information? Do you intend to burgle the place later?
- You need to specify the name of the local leisure centre.
- Frequency of visit can be handled using a closed question.
- Always? – since birth or what? The question remains too vague.
- Car ownership is not always useful – ask about access to a car during the day.
- Physical exercise is vague and its meaning will vary.
- The enjoyment of physical exercise depends upon what they regard as falling into that category. It may be better to rephrase such questions and introduce scaling at this point.
- The questions on 'what is on your mind?' is too vague and needs rewording. Such questions may be best left open rather than closed. If you use a closed question it should include an 'other' category.

- Class concept is unnecessary jargon and is lazy design.
- You need to use a model of social class and devise a way of measuring it. If occupation is the measure, ask for the occupation of the main earner. You will need to classify this later.
- The question on why people go to the leisure centre contains a number of separate items which need to be reformulated into separate questions.
- A leisure centre may be clean but not efficient. It may be expensive but not dirty. These two could be re-phrased as semantic differentials.
- The question on staff is actually several questions and needs re-working as such.
- The question on being known is poorly phrased and ambiguous.
- The question on stealing implies that the respondent is a thief and this is reinforced by the next question. You would need to re-phrase these in terms of personal security.
- The ending is poor and unprofessional.

Chapter 7: Sampling Techniques

Activity 2

There are no set answers but you may like to compare the sample statistics with those of the population below:

Type	Number	%
Animals & Wildlife	19	9.8
Antique Centers	1	0.5
Aviation Heritage	8	4.1
Churches	3	1.6
Country Parks	9	4.7
Crafts	8	4.1
Historic Buildings	10	5.2
Houses and Gardens	17	8.8
Industrial	11	5.7
Leisure	46	23.8
Museums	22	11.4
Show Gardens	9	4.7
Special Events	6	3.1
The Arts	14	7.3
Windmills	10	5.2

Chapter 9: Summarising Data – Descriptive Statistics and the Graphical Presentation of Data

1. This refers to Question 17 on the Hadrian's Wall questionnaire. The variable name is 'group'. 6.9% of the respondents were travelling on their own and 21.8% were travelling with friends.
2. This refers to Question 3.b (variable name 'durhw'). The mean length of time that respondents had been in the Hadrian's Wall area was 1.5 days. We know from the

properties of a normal distribution that approximately 68% of all cases can be found within one standard deviation either side of the mean. The standard deviation in this example is 1.8. This gives a nonsensical result, the reason being that this is not a normal distribution. It is a positively skewed distribution, and SPSS provides a skewness value of 2.662 for this variable.

3. Question 3.c asked respondents how long it took them to travel to Hadrian's Wall (variable name 'timetohw'). The mean journey time was 0.9 hours.

4. Question 3.a deals with the length of the respondents' holiday (variable name 'lenhol'). The mean holiday length was 13.8 days, the median holiday length was 7 days, the range was 120 days and the inter-quartile range 13.5 days.

5. Question 20 (variable name 'age') asked respondents to identify their age group. The modal age group (i.e. the most frequently occurring) was the 35–44 age group with 35 respondents.

6. To use the inter-quartile range you have to be able to place your data in order ranging from lowest to highest. It is, therefore, a useful measure of dispersion when working with ordinal data. The attraction of the inter-quartile range is that, as it discards the 25% of the data at either end of the range, it is not affected by extreme values. Unlike the standard deviation, it does not therefore utilise all the data in a distribution.

7. This refers back to Question 3.a ('lenhol') where we discovered that the mean length of holiday, 13.8 days, was higher than the median length of holiday, which was 7 days. This is a characteristic of a positively skewed distribution, and SPSS provides a skewness value of 3.391 for this variable.

Chapter 10: Bivariate and Multivariate Analysis

Activity 1

This requires a bi-variate correlation using Pearson's Product Moment Correlation Coefficient. SPSS computes this to be r = −0.064. This indicates that there is no statistical relationship between length of stay and level of satisfaction.

Activity 2

This requires the use of crosstabulation and of Cramer's V Correlation Coefficient. The data was re-coded to reduce the number of categories as shown in the crosstabulation below.

Crosstabulation of purpose of visit and age of respondent

			AGE 16–34	35–44	45+	Total
PURP	Walk	Count	6	3	7	16
		% within AGE	24.0	8.6	17.1	15.8
	Visit Wall/WHS	Count	16	28	31	75
		% within AGE	64.0	80.0	75.6	74.3
	Other	Count	3	4	3	10
		% within AGE	12.0	11.4	7.3	9.9
Total		Count	25	35	41	101
		% within PURP	24.8	34.7	40.6	100.0
		% within AGE	100.0	100.0	100.0	100.0

Cramer's V was calculated at 0.127 which indicates a very weak statistical relationship between these two variables. The wall was the most frequently cited purpose for each age group. The middle age group (those with children?) were the least likely to cite alternatives.

Activity 3

Using Pearson's again the correlation is given as:

r = 0.877

This indicates that there is a strong statistical association between money spent on advertising and the total visitor numbers.

Activity 4

SPSS computes the regression equation:

y = 6.16 + 0.93x

1. The first constant (6.16) indicates the total visitor numbers (6160) which would be achieved with no advertising expenditure. The second coefficient (0.93) indicates that for every £1000 spend on advertising an extra 930 visitors will be secured.

2. The model was highly successful as indicated by the strength of the correlation coefficient squared – the r^2 value of 0.77. This indicates that 77% of the variance in visitor numbers have (statistically) been accounted for by the model.

3. There are no outliers as such but there are two years which stand out with relatively high standardised residuals – years 1 and 7. A closer analysis of these years would suggest ways of improving the model.

4. If this amount was spent then the total expected visitors would be 71,260.

Activity 5

1. This can be done either as a straightforward regression or more correctly using the Autoregression option in the Time Series section of SPSS. In Time Series the equation is:

    y = −70858 + 35.9T   where T is the year.

2. The forecast for 1991 would be 619,000 using this model which is significantly higher than the straightforward regression suggests.

3. The exponential rate of growth in arrivals in the late 1980s is unlikely to be sustained and model is likely to be over optimistic.

Chapter 11: Inferential Statistics

Activity 1

1. This involves a considerable number of crosstabulations using those variables contained within questions 9 and 10 on the questionnaire against the variable *Origin*. Chi-square was used to test for differences at the 5% level and the following were noted as statistically significant:

- the scenery – $\chi^2 = 9.52$ df = 4 p = 0.049
- the wildlife – $\chi^2 = 10.6$ df = 4 p = 0.032
- unspoilt/tourist trap – $\chi^2 = 10.4$ df = 4 p = 0.034
- information on the Borders – $\chi^2 = 11.8$ df = 4 p = 0.038

In all the above cases UK visitors had stronger expectations than overseas visitors. This suggests that UK visitors had a stronger image of the area than those from overseas who were more uncertain as to what to expect. In other words the image of the tourist area is weaker amongst overseas markets.

2. This was tested using an independent samples t-test. Origin was used as the grouping variable. There were no statistically significant differences between the two categories of visitor.

3. This was tested as in (2) above. There were no statistically significant differences in overall levels of satisfaction between the two categories of visitor.

Activity 2

The null hypothesis: *There is no statistically significant difference between the performance of the two groups.*

The research hypothesis: *There are statistically significant differences between the two groups.*

Rejection level is p < 0.05.

The calculated value of Student's t is statistically insignificant, therefore the null hypothesis is accepted.

Index